Diversity Matters

Diversity Matters

Understanding Diversity in Schools

Lynn Kell Spradlin
West Chester University of Pennsylvania

Richard D. Parsons
West Chester University of Pennsylvania

THOMSON ™

WADSWORTH

Australia • Brazil • Canada • Mexico • Singapore • Spain
United Kingdom • United States

THOMSON

WADSWORTH

Diversity Matters: Understanding Diversity in Schools
Lynn Kell Spradlin, Richard D. Parsons

Education Editor: Dan Alpert
Development Editor: Tangelique Williams
Assistant Editor: Ann Lee Richards
Editorial Assistant: Stephanie Rue
Technology Project Manager: Julie Aguilar
Marketing Manager: Terra Schultz
Marketing Communications Manager: Tami Strang
Project Manager, Editorial Production: Tanya Nigh
Creative Director: Rob Hugel

Art Director: Vernon Boes
Print Buyer: Linda Hsu
Permissions Editor: Tim Sisler
Production Service: Sara Dovre Wudali, Buuji, Inc.
Copy Editor: Kristina Rose McComas
Cover Designer: Gia Giasullo
Cover Printer: West Group
Compositor: ICC Macmillan Inc.
Printer: West Group

Thomson Higher Education
10 Davis Drive
Belmont, CA 94002-3098
USA

For more information about our products, contact us at:
Thomson Learning Academic Resource Center
1-800-423-0563
For permission to use material from this text or product,
submit a request online at
http://www.thomsonrights.com.
Any additional questions about permissions can be
submitted by e-mail to
thomsonrights@thomson.com.

We dedicate this book to five special people, our children, who serve as our constant reminders that every person has a tremendous contribution to make to the world and it is up to each of us to open our eyes and minds to see that reality clearly for what it is—diversity at its finest. For it is the differences in thought and form in each of us that permit the development of our extraordinary strengths and creativity. We have learned from our children to use our lives in ways that count and represent who we mean to be.

Jordan Taylor Spradlin,

Dylan Alexander Spradlin,

M. Kristian Parsons,

Drew Michael Parsons, and

Jonathan F. Parsons

Brief Contents

Contents

CHAPTER 6   Learning from Asian American Stories   94

Preface

Typically, the Preface is seen as the part of the book you skip in order to get to the "meat" of the book. While that is certainly one way to proceed, let us suggest that you try a new strategy this time. Understand that while this book is a book about diversity, it is *not* like others you will find. Certainly, core concepts are presented and discussed, theories are addressed, and illustrations are provided. But more than simply providing you with information in an attempt to expand your understanding of diversity, *Diversity Matters: Understanding Diversity in Schools* challenges you on personal and emotional levels as well. So be prepared to be enlivened, enriched, and engaged.

A Book on Diversity?

For educators, diversity is anything but a new issue. Today's educators experience diversity challenges within their classrooms, curricula, schools, and school systems on a daily basis. Even though diversity is neither a new topic nor a new experience, most of today's educators lack the understanding and specific ways and means to utilize the rich resources that accompany diversity in ways that maximize learning and help all students feel a part of, as opposed to apart from, themselves, their classmates, and their schools.

It is not uncommon to encounter instances of student harm that stem from unintentional ignorance of societal barriers and cultural values and to encounter practices that negatively affect student adjustment and achievement.

For example, consider the supposedly "benign or neutral" hidden barrier that is created when teachers ask students to construct their family trees. Such an activity might require students to interact with immediate and extended family members to help them to identify and gain an understanding of their own rich family histories. But what is this assignment like for the student living in a shelter, the student in foster care, the student whose culture would see the family tree assignment in a totally different format, using circular rather than tree imagery, as might be the case for some Native American students, or the student whose culture encourages family privacy and limited personal disclosure? For these students, such a supposedly "benign" assignment could create emotional upset, embarrassment, family conflict, self-consciousness, alienation, feelings of inadequacy, and perhaps ultimately task failure. These frequent and less noticeable yet insidious occurrences of unethical practice actually do great harm in our schools because they draw clear lines for students that indicate who is included and who is not, whose family operates according to "proper" standards and whose does not, who will be accepted and who will not. Whether it is an educator acting without a clear conceptual theoretical framework for understanding diversity or one who lacks the knowledge and skills that develop with intercultural competence, these types of errors mitigate effective intercultural communication and reduce student adjustment and achievement. These educators, while not intending harm, hurt students in ways that cannot be fully measured. In so doing, they turn off students from learning, thus prohibiting them from accessing and utilizing the educational system to the fullest extent.

More than a Text—An Encounter

There is no effective "cookbook approach" to working with a diverse classroom population. What is needed instead and is offered within this book is a research-based, engaging approach for preparing readers to meet the unique demands of their intercultural interactions armed with knowledge and personal exploration that assures responsive and ethical intercultural communication. With a basis in current research and enriched by the individual voices of those with diverse worldviews, *Diversity Matters: Understanding Diversity in Schools* provides abundant practical and theoretically sound approaches for addressing the needs of students who are marginalized in today's schools.

But as noted at the beginning of this preface, this is *not* your typical book on diversity. It has been designed to actively engage you—intellectually and emotionally. It will move you from the realm of understanding (head), through personal valuing (heart), and finally to applying (voice) the information provided.

In order to move from the head to the heart to the voice, this text employs a number of unique elements. One predominant feature in this text is the extensive use of autobiographical case narratives (stories) to enrich your exposure to various cultural groups. They are used throughout this text to help you experience circumstances, issues, worldviews, and concerns of various persons from different cultural groups in their own voices rather than simply read about them in the third person. It is our hope that through using this particular learning strategy you will (1) increase your awareness of traditions and value systems of culturally diverse individuals; (2) explore your own cultural background and related value systems; (3) employ the specific reflection, field experience, and classroom application activities accompanying the narratives to further develop your understanding of diversity in the United States and how it affects student outcomes; and (4) find ways to integrate diverse worldviews in your personal and professional endeavors by creating and employing strategies for improving intercultural interactions and equitable learning communities. *Please read the About the Author pages before reading this text. These pages provide you with background information on the authors that creates a context for the text as well as the pedagogical approaches of the authors to assist in your synthesis of strategies and content contained within the text.*

Diversity Matters: Understanding Diversity in Schools is a text that will not permit you to be a passive reviewer or reader of material. The activities provided will invite you to actively identify the cultural imprints that have affected your cultural self. Further, you will be guided to explore your academic, racial, sexual-orientation, ethnic, gender, ability, and social-class roots. This enhanced self-awareness will provide you with comparison points to use as you begin to discover differences and similarities between yourself and members of other cultural groups. It is this knowledge, this heightened awareness of self and others, that will help you create an openness to considering information that conflicts with your own worldviews. As noted by others (for example, Covey, 1992[1]), being more self-aware allows us to more fully understand the way we approach life and the people we encounter. As we become more aware of how we see ourselves and perhaps how others see us, we will become more able to understand how others may see and feel about themselves and their world. Without such self-awareness, we are likely to "project our intentions on their behavior and call ourselves objective" (Covey, 1992, p. 67).

In addition to increasing your awareness and understanding, the text has been created in a way that will prepare you to create a personal activism plan that will produce an equitable and enriched learning environment. You will find that when you design ways for you and your students to productively acknowledge yourselves to one another and make clear your individual values and dispositions, your learning environment will produce fewer misconceptions and hidden agendas that would otherwise damage effective communication. As such, a network of specific community, school, and classroom interventions are suggested in this book.

Text Structure and Organization

Realizing that teacher and student identities are formed and often entrenched in many layers of experience, a significant focus for improving intercultural communication needs to address the influence of significant others, culture,

---

[1]Covey, S. (1992). The seven habits of highly effective people: Powerful lessons in personal change. *Emergency Librarian, 20*(1).

environment, and social context on interaction patterns and learning. *Diversity Matters: Understanding Diversity in Schools* provides information on the following six cultural factors as they relate to each cultural group presented in this text:

1. The group's historical and current treatment in the United States
2. The initial terms of incorporation of the group into U.S. society
3. Shared values and traditions of the group
4. The group's view of spirituality, including humans' orientation to nature
5. The group's acculturation issues, including experience with exclusion and alienation
6. The group's potential language differences, strengths, and challenges

In addition, each group's strategies for coping with oppression and potential barriers in learning relationships between group members and dominant-culture teachers are also discussed. These factors are explored throughout Chapters 5–12. They are also reflected in the many autobiographical narrative stories and suggested reflection, field experience, and classroom application activities. Throughout the text, you will find numerous illustrations and recommendations for application of specific theoretical constructs and models to use within classroom settings and schools. Further, you will find detailed presentation of the lived experience of those from diverse cultures–experiences told in their own voices. These engaging stories are used to give you an inside view of what it is like to be different. You become privy to the worries, struggles, and triumphs of various people as they engage in the sometimes treacherous waters of intercultural interaction in schools. You will hear from students, parents, and teachers alike as they navigate the U.S. school system, with all its problems and opportunities for growth and development. You can expect to feel very present in the process of this exploration.

To make the most of this text, we suggest that you keep track of your thoughts and feelings in a reflection journal in which you identify, compare, and contrast ways each chapter's set of autobiographical case narratives illustrates the six cultural factors and how those circumstances may differ from your own knowledge and experiences. In addition to our integration of narratives and illustrations, the chapters also include some or all of the following elements:

Chapter Objectives

Chapter Summary

Point of Reflection Exercises

Classroom Application Activities

Field Experience Activities

Important Terms

Enrichment (suggested autobiographies and readings)

Connections on the Web

ACKNOWLEDGMENTS

Throughout the text, numerous researchers and theorists are given credit for their contributions to this book. Others, cited within the text, have generously shared their stories and in so doing, have turned theory and research into personal, lived experience. We applaud and thank all of these individuals.

In addition to those cited, so many others have contributed to this text. If it were not for the care and wisdom of Karolyn Kell, the importance of this project would never have been recognized. And without the mentoring and guidance of Drs. Steve Miller and Eleanor Love, the seeds for this project would not have been planted. In addition, if it were not for the expert counsel of Dr. Latonya Thames Leonard and Professor Eric Rofes; the dedication of our graduate assistants, Jessica Keiser, Shelley Levine, and Tammi Schulman; and the ever-present support of our family members—Shannon Spradlin, Karolyn Kell, Leah Kell, Jason Kell, Lisa Moore, LaShon Kell-Moss, and Virginia Morton, the seeds for this project, once planted, would never have been given the nurturance, space, and time needed to mature.

We thank the following reviewers for their insightful comments: Janet Ahler, University of North Dakota; Jennifer Eddy, Queens College; Grace Essex, Ohio University; Gloria Graves Holmes, Quinnipiac University; Wanda Hutchinson, Athens State University; Renee Martin, University of Toledo; LeeAnn McNerney, Eastern Oregon University; Heather Merrill, Glendale Community College; Mary Ni, Salem State University; Susan Peters, Michigan State University; Heraldo Richards, Austin Peay State University; and Rudy Rodriguez, University of North Texas.

Finally, we want to acknowledge the expert guidance and continuous encouragement and support we received from our editor, Dan Alpert, at Thompson/Wadsworth and the superb work performed by Tanya Nigh, production manager; Kristina Rose McComas, copy editor; Sara Dovre Wudali, production editor; and Virginia Aretz, proofreader.

About the Authors

Andrea Daniels

Lynn Kell Spradlin, Ed.D.   As a professor in the Counseling and Educational Psychology Department at West Chester University of Pennsylvania, I have taught *diversity* to undergraduate and graduate students and university faculty members. In addition, my research explores many facets of diversity and social justice education, including race, gender, and social-class stratification effects on academic achievement. Over the past 11 years, I have come to understand effective strategies that engage students while integrating diversity in curriculum.

A common need expressed in educational institutions is the recruitment and retention of diverse faculty members and students. Educators' missions almost always include the following goal: *To provide the best educational opportunities possible to enable students to successfully address the concerns of a diverse society. To meet these objectives, we emphasize a deep knowledge of and respect for diversity and effective intercultural communication.*

However, as an African American female educator, I did not at first experience the warm and welcoming reception I had expected from my first section of predominantly White undergraduate and graduate college students when I taught diversity content. I was steeped in knowledge in the field and skilled as a counselor who specializes in group process, I thoroughly understood group dynamics and interaction skills. I had recently served as a high school theatre, speech, and English teacher and as a school and community counselor in culturally diverse settings. As such, I had accrued a great deal of successful experience with intercultural communication; effectively applied a vast knowledge of diversity in interactions with diverse populations, and cultivated a passion for teaching diversity principles and facilitating social justice education.

What I had overlooked was what Griffin (1997) called "common student reactions to social justice education."[2] Griffin's work reminded me that "when we raise social justice issues in a classroom we unsettle both unconscious and deeply held beliefs about society, self, and social relations. This disequilibrium can create resistance, as familiar ground shifts and students encounter uncertainty, doubt, and self-questioning as they attempt to regain their balance" (p. 292). She pointed out several different forms of student resistance that had become very familiar to me. Griffin identified that students may claim that the status quo is the natural order, invalidate minorities' experiences with oppression, assert the need to have their own pain and hurt recognized, invalidate the course, and even invalidate the instructor. "Sometimes students will claim that the teacher is biased, especially if she is a member of a target (minority) group . . . for being too personally involved to be objective. On the other hand, facilitators who are members of the agent (dominant culture) group are sometimes invalidated by both agent and target group participants because students do not understand how an agent can understand oppression without personal experience" (p. 293).

While dominant-culture teachers may choose to share their feelings experienced as they navigate processes involved in learning about oppression and accompanying White privilege, minority teachers do not have those options for joining with dominant-culture students as they explore threatening facets of oppression theory. Dominant-culture teachers are able to model their employment of coping mechanisms that facilitate acceptance and integration of the emotionally challenging subject matter, all the while aligning with dominant-culture students throughout the process—not only reminding their students that the journey of social justice education works to create opportunities for minorities but explaining how they as members of dominant culture have benefited from social justice education. On the other hand, minority educators must find alternate ways to create comfortable learning environments for dominant-culture and minority students—finding novel ways to join with predominantly White, middle-class, nondisabled, heterosexual students and minority students around an issue that can be divisive. I allowed this insight and information to challenge me to design diversity curricula that would be inviting and yet historically accurate, comprehensive, relevant, inclusive, progressive, and significant in its ability to affect positive change for a diverse group of students. This challenge led to the approach presented in this text.

I employ experiential, student-centered strategies that are mostly constructivist in approach. I provide my students with abundant opportunities to learn firsthand (if possible) or from reading the experiences (stories) of diverse peoples as they are told by the diverse peoples themselves; involve students in critical analysis of information and information sources, including theories, practices, and historical accounts; and then ask students to question previously assimilated concepts (their knowledge) and utilize self-reflection and

---

[2]Griffin, P. (1997). Facilitating social justice education courses. In M. Adams, L. A. Bell, & P. Griffin (Eds.), *Teaching for diversity and social justice: A sourcebook.* New York: Routledge.

communication skills to take actions that help them further understand and apply what they have learned. I have found that when students hear minority voices and perspectives; critically analyze diversity content and constructs; share their feelings, thoughts, and perspectives with others; and then create products that apply and extend their knowledge of oppression theory, they become advocates who want to share what they have learned about minority-group members and minority treatment in society. Along with the understandings they communicate, students often express outrage they feel toward institutional discrimination—a learning outcome that prepares them to maintain their resolve to act on the knowledge they have acquired as teachers, counselors, administrators, family members, and citizens. I provide students with opportunities to reflect on and express their feelings and beliefs that are triggered as they integrate information that is often different from their previous understandings about relations, power, society, schools, family, and self. Accompanying their exploration of oppression theory and principles are lived experiences and evidenced oppression outcomes that my students find compelling and useful.

As an educator of color, I realize the many assets I bring to this endeavor as well as maintain an awareness of students' potential reactions to me and my course content, and I know that my support, enthusiasm, knowledge, and skills are all significant. This text supplies ingredients that have been successful and enriching for me. I am excited to share them with you and to hear how you experience this approach. Please email me to share your views at LSpradlin@wcupa.edu.

Richard Parsons, Ph.D. In the past, when I have written an "About the Author Page," I may note that I am a professor of Counseling and Educational Psychology. I typically state that I have written 25 books and that in addition to being a professor at West Chester University, I also work as a licensed psychologist and consultant. While such information may be helpful in assisting the reader to place my writing within a particular frame of reference, it is really not so much "About the Author" as it is "About What This Author Does."

Coauthoring this text and working closely with my coauthor, Lynn Kell Spradlin, has challenged me to become more in touch with my "person" and not simply my "products." Researching and coauthoring this text have invited me to look within. I have been challenged to identify my own perspectives and operative values. I have been afforded the opportunity to share these with my coauthor, and as a result, I have become more aware of the uniqueness that each of us has brought to this project. Through this process of reflection, I have grown in my appreciation of the gift of diversity and personal uniqueness.

So what have I learned that may help you not just to know "About this Author" but may help you more fully appreciate what you are about to read? I have learned that as a teacher and counselor educator, my own teaching has been informed by three values.

First, it is clear to me that content specialization and competence are not sufficient if one is to be an effective educator. In addition to knowing our subject matter, it is essential we understand and employ the latest research to guide our pedagogy. Throughout the text, you will be introduced to just such theory and research.

Second, I have realized that as an educator I may serve as a resource of new information, information I am expected to share with my students. But this is only part of my role as educator. I have come to appreciate that real growth, real development, does not come simply through the accumulation of additional facts and figures. Fostering student development demands that I challenge their perspectives, their beliefs, their views of self and others. Coauthoring this text has been just such a challenge for me. Each chapter with its new information and new perspectives challenged my own worldview and as a result, my view of self. I hope that I have and will continue to respond to this challenge, with the result being my continued personal and professional growth. I note this as both an invitation and a warning. As you read the life stories presented throughout the text, you, too, will be enriched by facts and figures and challenged with the tension of a new perspective. I hope you embrace the challenge and respond with growth.

Finally, coauthoring this text reminded me of the fundamental truth that teaching and learning are *not* about "subject"; they are about "persons." Teaching and learning must involve the "person" of the student. While this may seem like an obvious and oversimplified statement, the truth is that the unique characteristics, motivations, learning styles, and life experience that each student brings to the classroom must be understood and incorporated into our pedagogy if we are to be successful educators.

Coauthoring this book has been a challenge for me. It has been a challenge that has invited me to question the old and most often untested beliefs that I have held. It has been a challenge to step away from my worldview in an attempt to become aware and sensitive to the worldview of others. And through this challenge, I have experienced the gift of personal and professional growth. I hope you experience the same!

Rick Parsons
2006
Lynn Spradlin
2006

Social Context of U.S. Schooling

Minority Experience

There never was in the world two opinions alike, no more than two hairs or two grains; the most universal quality is diversity.

Michel Eyquem de Montaigne (1553–1592)
French essayist and courtier

1 CHAPTER | Understanding What It Means to Have a Marginalized Status in the United States

Defining Marginalization

Simply open the door to any classroom and an important truth will become obvious. The most universal quality you encounter is diversity! Classrooms, like all aspects of society are marked by individual variations. Students vary in learning style, language, gender, socioeconomic status, sexual orientation, ability status, ethnicity, and culture. Students are unique in many ways—ways that must be understood, appreciated, and carefully considered during the learning process. Too often, the diversity found among students serves not as a cause for celebration nor as a rich resource within classrooms but rather as the basis, whether conscious or not, for frustration, bias, exclusion, devaluation, and marginalization.

The full extent to which diversity will shape the lives of teachers and students in schools remains to be seen. However, if U.S. Census data projections are correct, we are and will continue to become an increasingly diverse nation. According to census projections, the number of Latinos in the United States will grow to 98 million in the year 2050, African Americans will number 59 million, and the number of Asians and Pacific Islanders will increase to approximately 38 million (Henderson, 2000; U.S. Department of Education, 2004). Given these projections, we can expect that teachers will undoubtedly teach students from a wide range of language, social class, gender, ethnic, ability status, sexual orientation, and cultural backgrounds. Yes, a culturally diverse classroom is most likely the rule, not the exception, and such diversity has important implications for educators (Alba, Rumbaut, & Marotz, 2005; Alba, 2000).

Teachers will need to acquire new knowledge and keen awareness in order to meet the needs of diverse classrooms. They will need to increase their knowledge of diversity, their cultural sensitivity, and their intercultural communication skills and competence in order to meet the needs of a culturally diverse student population. In addition, teachers, as professional educators and advocates for all children, will need to develop the skills necessary to become allies and to work for changes in institutional policies, practices, and legislation in order to address discrimination that targets marginalized groups in the United States.

This book is intended to facilitate the professional development of educators who meet these standards. As the first step, this chapter will introduce you to the fundamental concepts of culture, **race**, ethnicity, social class, gender, sexual orientation, ability status, and marginalization.

CHAPTER OBJECTIVES

1. Define *race, ethnicity, social class, gender, sexual orientation*, and *disability*.
2. Define *privilege* and how individuals may experience privilege in one aspect of their life and marginalization in another.
3. Describe three types of racism.
4. Explain the terms *dominant culture, minority, assimilation, acculturation*, and *marginalization*.
5. Define *racism, sexism, classism, heterosexism*, and *ableism*.

CULTURE

A 5th-grade teacher shared with a colleague his concern about one of his students, Jim. The student, a recent transfer, was clearly motivated and achieving within the classroom but behaved in ways that concerned the teacher. The teacher was concerned that whenever an assignment involved formal oral presentations or simple oral responses to questions in the classroom, Jim would sit quietly and wait for others to begin speaking first. It seemed he never ventured an opinion without first observing everyone else to determine what they thought and how they felt. It became apparent that he never took a stand. The teacher was afraid that Jim's behavior might be an indication that he lacked maturity and the ability to make decisions, or perhaps he lacked confidence in himself. In either case, the teacher was certain that a referral to the school counselor was in order.

While Jim certainly may have lacked maturity, confidence, or decision-making skills and he may have benefited from a visit to the counselor, it is equally plausible that his behavior reflected not a skill deficit or a psychological problem but rather a different set of values and beliefs about what constitutes appropriate communication exchanges within the classroom. While the teacher's own values and expectations about the proper communication patterns may have resulted in his anticipating students to not only be assertive, decisive, and independent but also to be proud of those abilities. It is true that these values, while important among dominant-culture individuals in the United States, are not the values, experience, or expectations of all peoples, or of all students within his classroom. The teacher failed to realize that such standards are culturally relative and need not be viewed as the only "normal" and valued standards of ideal academic performance and social demeanor.

It would be better if this teacher realized that characteristics such as independence, decisiveness, and assertiveness—even commanding a distinct social presence—are clear reflections of socially constructed ideas of a particular **culture**. From this broader perspective, he may have posited that Jim *was* employing an appropriate form of communication and social exchange—a different form, one reflecting his own cultural background and associated value system. Case Illustration 1-1 further develops this point.

Our cultural heritage and background influence our lives in many ways. No aspect of human life is *not* touched and altered by culture. Our personalities, the way we think, and the ways we solve problems, as well as methods we use to organize ourselves, are all given shape, in large part, by cultural experiences. However, we frequently take the great influence of culture on our lives for granted and fail to identify the significant and sometimes subtle ways culture affects our behavior.

If teachers are to be effective, they must understand cultural diversity in its many forms and be skilled intercultural communicators. They will need to understand and appreciate the power of cultural values reflected in their students' behavior (Sleeter & Grant, 2002). Because "students who feel their culture is valued and understood by the school and the larger community tend to do better in school than those who feel it is rejected," it is important that educators understand and respect diverse cultural perspectives and ways of being in the world (Ashworth, 1992, p. 14).

Defining Culture

Culture and **subculture** are defined in various ways. Culture may be broadly described as encompassing a group's common beliefs, including shared traditions, language, styles, values, and agreement about norms for living. Culture, however, always intersects individuals' race, social class, gender, age, ability status, sexual orientation, and family traditions (Laird, 2000). *Culture*, as the term is used in this text, includes values, beliefs, notions about acceptable and unacceptable behavior, and other socially constructed ideas that members of the culture are taught (Garcia, 1994, p. 51).

Culture, in effect, defines one's thinking and behavior. If, for you, proper student behavior includes not only making decisions independent of others, speaking up about them, and feeling proud about such an accomplishment, you are not alone among your colleagues in the United States. Consider how most teachers would initially react to a student who, when called upon, leaped from

| **Case Illustration 1-1** | **Meet Jim: A Navajo Descendant** |

Jim is a 10-year-old boy who loves to play sports, especially soccer, and typically can't wait to master the next video game that comes on the market. Jim is not wild about school but all in all reports being happy with how things are going. In many ways, Jim is just like the other boys in his class. But in addition to being a bright, handsome, and energetic fifth grader, Jim is a descendent of Navajo Native Americans and at times finds himself functioning in two different cultures.

Some cultural differences are obvious, such as foods he eats, music he enjoys, occasions his family celebrates, and even the fact that, unlike many of the other students in his school, Jim lives not only with his parents and brother but with his grandparents and aunt as well. But beyond these are differences in the ways he has been taught to relate to adults, employ certain courtesies and conventions of language, and even approach new tasks.

As Jim explains it, it can be very confusing at times. "I mean, at school I'm supposed to act one way, but if I do that at home, my parents are disappointed." When asked if he can give an example, Jim continues: "Everybody at school likes to show off. The most important thing to them is their rep [reputation]. They call out in class and wave their hands around to get attention and then when they get the right answer, they act real superior—like they are the best students in the class. I mean, I like to compete with my brother when we play soccer or do a video game together, and I sometimes think I'm really good too, but I don't brag or show off in front of everybody. It's not

important." As Jim continues to share his experiences in school, he notes how difficult it is for him sometimes to participate in class. "In our class, the teacher will ask a question, and everybody immediately starts to call out answers—everybody trying to yell louder than the person next to them. It feels weird to me to do that. At home we don't yell out like that—we don't talk on top of each other. It's a lot more quiet at home. When my parents speak, I think about whether what I want to say contributes something important. I listen; I think. I spend a lot of time listening when I'm with my family. When you listen, after a while you know when it's important to speak. Sometimes, speaking is not needed at all. It's cool 'cause you know when you have something to add or not. And I don't understand why we always have to have these math competitions where you get on teams and try to answer more questions that the other team, so your team can get candy or something. It just seems silly. Why don't we just work together on our problems, rather than trying to see who is better than somebody else? I don't get it."

For Jim, the culture found within the classroom that supports individual competition, getting good grades at the expense of others, and raising hands and voices to be recognized is not congruent with values taught at home. As a result, he finds himself having to live in two cultures, often feeling torn at times by differing expectations and rules, pressured at school, and sometimes even looked down upon by those he is asked to respect, all simply for being himself.

his desk, stood straight, and in a somewhat monotone and very formal cadence responded to the teacher's question. Perhaps such behavior would be judged by a teacher to be inappropriate, just as Jim's behavior was judged. However, if the teacher encountering this student-response pattern taught at a military academy, such behavior might be considered quite appropriate and desirable, not at all weird, strange, or inappropriate. In this case, this student also was manifesting behavior that reflected the values and beliefs of his cultural group—in this case, values of his military background.

Exercise 1-1 | Point of Reflection: Identifying Aspects of Culture

Directions: Below you will find a description of values and beliefs held by a specific culture. A belief may be a part of your own cultural belief system or perhaps part of quite a different cultural value system from that to which you have been socialized. Identify those values/beliefs that are similar to ones you hold and those that are different. Then describe how each value/belief might be manifested within the classroom. Afterward, please share your reflection with a small group of your classmates or with your instructor and discuss beliefs you hold that may create intercultural communication barriers.

Cultural Value/Belief	The Value/Belief Listed in the First Column Reflects My Own Family Values—Yes or No?	How the Value/Belief Listed in the First Column May Be Manifested within the Classroom
Example: Respect shown to adults does not allow disagreement.	Yes. In my family, children are not allowed to challenge adults or to question their authority. This is not stated outright, but it is understood. My brothers, sisters, and I were always punished as children for talking back to our parents.	Students who were raised with this belief might not participate in classroom discussions, share differences of opinion, or offer alternative approaches to problem solving in the classroom, even if asked.
Individual competition and demonstration of achievement in front of group are respected.		
Adult/child relationships are formal and hierarchical. Adults hold all the power in the relationship.		
Ways of knowing can include subjective and intuitive (feeling-oriented) approaches.		

While it is extremely important for teachers to begin to understand the cultural values of others, at the same time it is equally important for them to increase their awareness of the values, beliefs, and cultural experience that shape their own lives. Exercise 1-1 will help you become more aware of the characteristics of your own culture—and the way these characteristics may play out in your own teaching behaviors.

Cultural Value/Belief	The Value/Belief Listed in the First Column Reflects My Own Family Values—Yes or No?	How the Value/Belief Listed in the First Column May Be Manifested within the Classroom
Holistic, rather than analytic, styles of thinking are encouraged. Effects on one's larger community are considered in individual decision making.		
Sharing personal and family information outside of the family is discouraged.		
Reflection and contemplation are respected.		
Collaboration is seen as essential for productivity and success.		
Children's relationships with adults are informal and close. Childhood is seen as a time when children learn to take responsibility, and they are eventually given power to make decisions that go with responsibility.		
Having a steady work pace accompanied by quick decision making is favored over prolonged periods of reflection for problem solving.		

Variation within Culture: Subculture

It is not uncommon to find references to "the" African American experience or Latino culture or to "the" culture of the Europeans. While those within a culture by definition share much in terms of values and behavior, such broad categorization fails to do justice to wide variation within each culture. Thus, a more functional approach to defining culture is one that recognizes intergroup and intragroup differences in culture as well as the plethora of subcultures that exist.

It is extremely important to note that not all people from one cultural group can be grouped together and assumed to be alike. You can assume that members of a group may share certain cultural characteristics, but you must also recognize subcultural, intracultural, and individual differences. Within a culture, sub-groupings around a more specific shared history of experience, social values, and role expectations exist. These subcultures can be formed along racial, ethnic, regional, economic, or social community lines. A subculture provides its members with values and expectations that may not be demonstrated by the larger cultural group or found elsewhere. In addition, these subcultural differences found between groups within a culture may result in the development of communication barriers, both for members within the same culture and for individuals across many different cultures.

To further complicate matters and to more accurately enrich this idea, we must also remember that within a culture or subculture, a person can be different from others of the same reference grouping as a function of her or his specific educational background, socioeconomic status, and regional particulars. These intracultural differences clearly depict the reality that while we are all *a part* of a culture, our uniqueness will always keep us somewhat *apart* from any one culture.

RACE

Probably no one term elicits more visceral, emotive reactions than the term *race*. For many, the mere mention of this term results in huge discomfort. And while the issue of race has sociopolitical and even moral ramifications, it is another element of microcultural diversity that needs to be thoroughly understood and enthusiastically respected and addressed by classroom teachers. Race is, in actuality, an anthropological concept used to classify people according to physical characteristics, such as skin and eye pigmentation, facial features, shape of head, and texture of body hair (Hernandez, 1989).

Race Is Not Ethnicity

Because *ethnicity*, when used in its broadest form, includes references to physical characteristics of a group of people, it is sometimes equated with and used interchangeably with *race* (Glazer, 1971). However, a more narrow and fruitful definition of *ethnicity* is taken from the Greek root word *ethos*, meaning nation (Feagin, 1989). Using this ideology, ethnicity distinguishes groups based on nationality and cultural, rather than physical, characteristics. As such, an ethnic group is defined as a group in which the members share a unique social, cultural, and sometimes language heritage that is passed down from one generation to the next (Schaefer, 1988).

Race: Not a Physically but a Socially Defined Construct

While the definition of *race* is historically founded on unique physical characteristics of a people, the ever-increasing mobility and migration of peoples from one geographic region to another, and the resulting interracial pairings, make valid and reliable identification of individuals along racial lines impossible. Yet even with this reality, the concept of race continues to play a role in distinguishing people. This is, in large part, because race has become a social rather than a physical construct. As a social construct, race is often used as an unjust, invalid standard upon which to generalize and draw conclusions about any one person or group of people. Because such racial bias has been identified and recognized as a damaging process, many educators ignore racial differences for fear of being perceived as racist.

Teachers are, frankly, pretty unsure about how to approach the issue of racial differences within their classrooms. Valli (1995), for example, noted that educators vacillate from believing that "teachers should be colorblind" to being color sensitive, from saying "I treat all students the same and pay no attention to the color of their skin" to claiming "If you don't see the color, you don't see the whole child—and her/his unique contributions" (p. 121). Understandably, many teachers wish to treat all students equally. But equitable treatment does not mean approaching and working with all students in the same way. Equitable treatment of students does not require homogenization and a flattening of all individual differences, including racial differences, even though, based on their actions, many educators still believe this is the case. In fact, Ladson-Billing (1994) noted: "The notion of equity as sameness only makes sense when *all* students are exactly the same" (p. 33). Failing to recognize and adequately address real differences may be one way to ensure inequity. Differences in achievement between racial groups, and potential reasons for such differences, need to be understood if they are to be corrected. And this will not and cannot happen as long as teachers attempt to wear "color-blinders."

Even with the limitations of classification by race, it is important not to dismiss the concept of race when recognizing and describing differences. Considered as a single identity, racial identification does not provide much information about a person. However, race as a construct is highly significant when used to identify cultural characteristics that subordinate and elevate groups based on societal laws, policies, and practices. In this sense, racial classifications can provide great insight into subordinated individuals' worldviews, dispositions, and behaviors. To put it simply, **racism** is first and foremost a system of advantage for dominant culture based on race (Tatum, 1992). It is important to note that despite the fact that most people can identify individuals who are disadvantaged in U.S. society (based on gender, sexual orientation, ability status, social class, or other group membership), other individuals are advantaged by the same system that systematically disadvantages **minority** group members. The net effect of prejudice (experienced by oppressed groups) places the object of prejudice at some disadvantage not merited by her or his misconduct (Allport, 1954). So, discontinuing the use of the concept of race when describing groups may sufficiently ignore the treatment differences various groups receive in society (Johnson, 1990). Such ignorance also would deny any exposure of racism, a process essential to affecting societal change and social justice for all minority groups.

Racial Identity Development of Minority Group Members

Helms (1990) defined *racial identity development* as "a sense of group or collective identity based on one's perception that she or he shares a common racial heritage with a particular racial group" (p. 3) (see Table 1-1). Cross (1971) identified five stages in African American racial identity development that were later used to describe the racial identity development of all minority group members (see Table 1-2).

Although the stages of racial identity development do not necessarily occur chronologically in a linear process, they are believed to include most racial interaction patterns involving minority group members and dominant culture

Table 1-1
Helms' (1990) White Racial Identity Development Model

1. **Contact Stage:** In this stage, a person lacks an awareness of racism and one's own White privilege. The person internalizes negative stereotypes about persons of color.

2. **Disintegration Stage:** During this stage, the person's lack of awareness of racism is replaced by discomfort, shame, and/or guilt. The person may at first deny that racism exists and near the end of this stage try to help other Whites see that racism does exist.

3. **Reintegration Stage:** In this stage, a person's desire to be accepted by her/his own group leads to a reshaping of his/her belief system that has become more accepting of racism. People may become stuck at this stage if they can avoid direct contact with people of color.

4. **Pseudo-Independent Stage:** In this stage, a person abandons beliefs of White superiority but may unintentionally perpetuate the status quo. The person may feel alienated from Whites (as a group) and rejected by people of color (as a group). During this stage, a person begins to seek out White antiracist allies and models and may attempt to disavow his/her own Whiteness through active affiliation with persons of color.

5. **Immersion/Emersion Stage:** During this stage, a person searches for a new, more comfortable way to be White. The person seeks to replace racially related myths and stereotypes with accurate information about what it means and has meant to be White in the United States. An important part of racial identity development at this point is learning about Whites who have been antiracist allies to people of color.

6. **Autonomy Stage:** In this stage, a newly defined sense of oneself as White energizes one's efforts to confront racism in one's daily life. A person in this stage is continually open to new information and ways of thinking about race. Alliances with people of color are more easily forged because antiracist attitudes and behaviors are more consistently expressed.

Source: Helms, J. E. (1990). *Black and white racial identity: Theory, research and practice*. Westport, CT: Greenwood.

Table 1-2
Cross's (1971) Minority Group Member Racial Identity Development Model

1. **Pre-Encounter Stage:** At this stage, the person internalizes negative racial stereotypes. A person in this stage may not be aware of racism.

2. **Encounter Stage:** This stage of racial identity development is typically precipitated by an event. The person in this stage is forced to acknowledge racism. At this point, the person begins to identify with his/her own race.

3. **Immersion/Emersion Stage:** During this stage, the person may avoid symbols of Whiteness. A person in this stage tends to surround herself/himself with visible symbols of his/her own race.

4. **Internalization Stage:** During this stage, a person is secure with her/his own sense of self as a racial being. There is less need during this stage to assert extreme pro–same-race attitudes and actions. A person in this stage is more open to joining with other racial groups.

5. **Internalization/Commitment Stage:** A person in this stage has found ways to translate his/her personal sense of self as a racial being into a plan of action or general sense of commitment to the concerns of people of color and to the concerns of social justice in general.

Source: Cross, W. E. (1971). The Negro to black conversion experience: Toward a psychology of black liberation. *Black World, 20,* 13–27.

in the United States (Cross, 1991). It is, therefore, another factor that affects differences in students' choices to cross racial boundaries in schools and that identifies social dynamics within minority community social structures, which also understandably influence the sometimes oppositional nature of individual students toward dominant-culture institutions and their teachers.

SOCIAL CLASS

A number of successful television shows take viewers behind the scenes and into the lived experiences of the rich in the United States—people who have money, power, and social status. MTV and other media show viewers the lifestyles (reality shows), homes (cribs), parties (Sweet 16), and cars (rides) of musicians, actors, sports stars, and other entertainers. It seems that to some degree many people in the United States dream of living lifestyles of the rich and famous, in hopes of someday becoming members of the upper social class.

Social class or *socioeconomic status* (SES) is the term used to distinguish a person's position in society relative to others within that society. Parental occupation, education level, political power, and income serve as the bases for a student's social class or socioeconomic status. But for educators, several questions arise: Other than perhaps the obvious material benefits, are there other important benefits or effects of socioeconomic status (SES)? Is student SES associated with academic achievement? Is a student's social class something a teacher should be sensitive to and plan for in teaching? The answer to all of these questions, as you will discover, is "yes"!

Social class differences do exist in the United States, and social class affects our lives in many significant ways. As with other ways of categorizing individuals, it is a serious mistake to stereotype people based solely on their socioeconomic status because intragroup social class differences in attitude, values, and beliefs may be sharply pronounced. But given this caveat, it is still vital for educators to be aware of the impact of socioeconomic status on students and the effects of social class on schooling and society.

Class distinctions determine the quality of the schooling we receive, the homes in which we live, the health and safety of our loved ones, the worldviews we hold, and how we relate to others in society. Social class differences, however, may be difficult to recognize and identify on a day-to-day basis.

In the United States, a great deal of effort is is put into to mystifying and hiding social class differences. Students and adults alike routinely wear clothes and buy cars, homes, and other visible possessions that are more expensive than they can afford in order to be perceived as being wealthier than they are. The media presents the illusion that the United States is an egalitarian society in which everyone has an equal chance to succeed and attempts to either downplay the existence of the poor by failing to present stories that depict the needs and issues of the poor (Manstios, 1995b) or by portraying the poor as undeserving and as having only themselves to blame for their position in life. When it comes to SES, myths abound. For example, many believe that the United States is mostly a middle-class country, with the wealth distributed mainly in the middle class. Contrary to this belief, U.S. Census Bureau reports reveal that less than 20 percent of the population in the United States own more than 80 percent of the wealth. But, while myths abound, there are "truths" about social class, truths that are crucial for teachers to understand.

The lack of opportunities for working class and poor students can be one of the most oppressive forces encountered. People do not choose to be working class or poor. Instead, they are confined by opportunities afforded or denied them by society. The lower one's class standing, the more difficult it is to secure safe housing, the more time is spent on everyday routine tasks in life, the greater the percentage of income that goes to pay for basic necessities, and the less likelihood one has to participate in enrichment and growth-related activities (Manstios, 1995a). Class standing, therefore, has a significant impact on educational attainment.

It is clear that the incremental lack of power and privilege associated with poverty negatively affects students' achievement in school. **Classism**, the institutionalized system in society that operates to disadvantage working-class and poor people, greatly influences students' motivation to achieve in school, as well as their levels of career ambition (Dodge, Pettit, & Bates, 1994). SES has been shown to affect students' performance in school (Reed & Sautter, 1990), discipline problems (Dodge et al., 1994), feelings of low self-esteem, and learned helplessness (Rice, 1993).

Schools are part of the societal social-class stratification system because they operate as social microcosms that embody and implement the prejudice, **oppression**, and discrimination evident in larger society. Specifically, according

Exercise 1-2	Classroom Applications: True or False SES Myths

Part I

Directions: Identify which of the following statements are true and which are false.

Statement	True	False
1. The largest number of poor people live in urban settings.		
2. The majority of poor children in the United States are African American.		
3. Families are impoverished because the household heads are unemployed.		
4. Almost 80 percent of all poor children who attend school live in single-parent households.		
5. There is little real difference in self-esteem levels and achievement-test scores across SES.		

Part II

Directions: Each of the previous statements is
false. With a classmate or your instructor, discuss
the potential impact that belief in these statements
may have on a teacher's interactions with students
in her/his classroom.

to Greer (1972), schools do the job today that they have always done. Schools
select individuals for opportunities according to a hierarchical schema that runs
closely parallel to existing social-class patterns. The resultant social structure
disadvantages working-class students, weakening their academic achievement
levels (Gans, 1995; Sennett & Cobb, 1972). Educational researchers have
documented a statistically significant relationship between working-class student
status and academic achievement. According to Wolf (1977), a poor child is
roughly twice as likely to be a low academic achiever as a child who is not poor.

While teachers cannot remedy all social inequities and problems of the
world, they can take steps to ensure that they do not negatively affect the
achievement of working class and poor students within their classrooms. It is
important that we examine our beliefs about social class and identify the subtle
yet profound effects these beliefs may have on our curriculum choices and
classroom interactions. Excercise 1-2 provides a structure for investigating

your beliefs about SES and considering the potential impact these beliefs may have on your teaching and your students.

SEX AND GENDER DISTINCTIONS

A first-grade teacher takes her students on a nature walk. After coming upon a large insect, the teacher exclaims, "Ooh, everybody leave that where it is. Don't touch it. You can look at it, but keep your distance." A male student pokes the bug, picks it up, and looks closely at it. This teacher could react in a number of ways. She could say, "Yuck, put that down. It's dirty." She could say, "Let me see what you have there, Bob," taking the bug from him and holding it out for the other students to examine. She could have picked up the bug in the first case and held it out for all of the children to see. The point is that this is a teachable moment. But it presents at least two questions: What might the teacher be teaching her young, impressionable first-grade male and female students? What might she be teaching about nature and about gender values, behaviors, and expectations?

Classrooms, curricula, and teachers' behaviors and comments within the classroom can teach much more than is identified in course objectives. Phrases such as "Okay, guys, settle down," "Joe, could you come up here and help me move this table?" and "Brittney, would you mind straightening up these art materials?" can be heard in almost any classroom on any given day. Each of these phrases, in and of itself, appears innocuous enough. However, if the phrases reflect an oversimplification of gender-based characteristics and expectations, there is a problem. Gender typing and bias can and have pigeonholed students into curriculum paths and career options (for example, entry into science and math careers for boys and into the helping professions and language and arts careers for girls), restricted social and recreational choices (for example, boys on the debate team, girls in sewing classes), and even affected the quality and quantity of teacher–student interactions experienced within classrooms (Merret & Wheldall, 1992). Gender and gender typing are constructs that each teacher must recognize and understand so as to avoid the subtle and sometimes not-so-subtle biasing effects that all too often occur.

Are There Differences between Boys and Girls?

Boys and girls are different. This we know to be true. The question is not whether boys and girls are different, but rather: In what ways are boys and girls different? Why do these differences occur? How do these differences affect learning in the classroom?

Gender schema theory suggests that genetic predispositions may account for some behaviors, personality traits, and interests. This same theory, however, notes that differential treatment remains the major source of differences in attitude, behavior, and achievement found between males and females (Bem, 1981). Differential treatment is pervasive in our society and clearly evident within our schools. Society's gender-based norms and expectations create role definitions for men and women that lead to the systematic marginalization of women as a group (Gilbert, 1992). This condition, which disadvantages women while advantaging men, is **sexism.**

Sex versus Gender

Sex refers to biological conditions of maleness or femaleness: the possession of the XY chromosomal configuration for males and the possession of the XX pattern for females, along with corresponding anatomical, hormonal, and physiological structures. As such, sex is ascribed or assigned at birth (Richardson, 1981). *Gender* is a learned psychological, social, and cultural aspect of a person that describes expected and sanctioned male and female behavior that results from socialization in the United States.

Recent attempts to describe brain-based differences in types of intelligence, psychological disorders, classroom behavior, and academic performance identify ways male and female students are disadvantaged in U.S. schools. Gurian and Henley (2001) described ways in which brain structures, hormonal differences, and functional and processing differences influence male and female student behavior. Nonetheless, most differences assumed to exist between the sexes are gender-related rather than sex-related—that is, learned rather than innate. Men are typically seen as masculine and are rewarded when they act in culturally approved, "gender-appropriate" ways, and likewise, women are applauded for acting in ways that are labeled feminine and are considered appropriate for women in this culture. Many of the so-called "gender-appropriate" feminine characteristics and behaviors are devalued in the United States. As such, women *and* men who adhere to them (exhibiting emotionality, nurturance, and delicacy) are devalued and systematically disadvantaged in society (Schaffer, 1981).

The American Association of University Women (1992) conducted a comprehensive examination of gender studies in education and found that U.S. schools shortchange girls. According to this report, "Girls and boys enter school roughly equal in mental ability. Twelve years later, girls have fallen behind their male classmates in key areas such as higher-level mathematics and measures of self-esteem" (p. 1). Sadker, Sadker, and Long (1993) also found that male students in elementary and middle school called out answers eight times more often than female students did and that when males called out, teachers listened. But when females called out, they were told to raise their hands if they wanted to speak. In addition, the researchers concluded that school authorities choose classroom activities that appeal to male students' interests and in formats in which males generally excel. Moreover, teaching methods that foster competition are standard, even though a preponderance of research has demonstrated that female students learn better when they undertake projects and activities cooperatively rather than competitively (Belenky, Clinchy, Goldberger, & Tarule, 1986; Brown, 1991; Gilligan, 1982; Radil, 1992).

According to Ostling and Urquhart (1992), girls face pervasive barriers to academic achievement and are systematically discouraged from pursuing studies that would enhance their prospects for well-paying jobs, even though the U.S. school classroom is in many ways technically a feminine domain. More than three-quarters of teachers are women. However, these mostly female teachers routinely hold male students in higher esteem, believing they are intellectually superior to female students and implementing curricula and instructional strategies that advantage boys. Although during childhood both sexes do equally well in math and science, girls outperform boys overall in the early grades. In verbal skills, girls move into the lead around 5th or 6th grade and thereafter do better than boys in writing and, by most measures, reading. Females constitute less than a third of students identified as emotionally disturbed or learning disabled. Despite teen pregnancy, girls are less likely to drop out of high school and are more likely to attend college (Ostling, 1992, p. 62).

However, according to Sadker, Sadker, and Long (1993), "males outperform females substantially on all subsections of the Scholastic Aptitude Test (SAT) and girls attain only 36 percent of the more than 6,000 National Merit Scholarships awarded each year. These awards are based on the higher Preliminary Scholastic Aptitude Tests (PSAT) scores attained by boys" (p. 119). Moreover, while women dominate the teaching profession and young female students generally succeed in the early grades and even outperform male students in some academic areas, the culture of the school is in fact masculine because schools are controlled by a male-dominated society (Noddings, 1992). And even successful female students have less confidence in their abilities, higher expectations of failure, habits of dependency, negative attribution styles, weakened leadership skills, and more modest occupational aspirations than boys do. Girls are less likely, therefore, to reach their potential than boys (Keating, 1990).

It is important to understand the social construction of gender and the often subtle ways in which schools, and specifically teachers, support, maintain, and even encourage differential treatment based on gender and thus disadvantage individual students in their classrooms. Exercise 1-3 will help you begin to identify the ways gender typing and gender bias manifest within the classroom.

Sexual Identity

Human sexuality is complex. *Sexual identity* is the degree to which we identify with the social and biological aspects of being a man or a woman. Some perceive sexual orientation and sexual identity to be simple, straightforward products of biology. Such a position, often termed "an Essentialist position," argues that sexual orientation is part of an individual's core being. This stance often leads to the conclusion that heterosexuality is the "right and correct" form of sexuality and thus homosexuality is "improper." It is important to note that not all people who exhibit so-called gender "nonconformity" are gay or lesbian; people who have various sexual identities and orientations actually engage in a whole range of sexual behaviors. Sexual orientation is an integral

| Exercise 1-3 | Field Experience: Strong Boy, Nice Girl |

Directions: The following exercise involves a classroom observation. As you observe the class, look for obvious and subtle forms of gender typing.

1. Seating: Are there discernable seating arrangements for boys and girls? If so, what is one potential impact of this arrangement?
2. Interaction: In a five-minute period, record how many times the teacher calls upon or verbally responds to boys and girls. Place a check mark in the box for each interaction.

	Boys	**Girls**
1. Calls upon a student who is raising hand.		
2. Selects a student to perform a task.		
3. Praises a student.		
4. Reprimands a student.		
5. A student volunteers to participate.		
6. A student is removed from participation.		

3. Language and References: Record any use of stereotypical language (for example, "Okay, guys . . ." or "Ladies!") or gender-based illustrations (for example, "Alice bought three dresses. . . .").
4. Activities: If during the observation the teacher directs students to engage in an activity, list the activity and the gender and age of the student(s) performing it. In addition, identify whether students *actively* participate in the activities assigned.

Examples:

Competitive activities	_____ girls	_____ boys
Individual tasks	_____ girls	_____ boys
Group work	_____ girls	_____ boys
Notetaking during group work	_____ girls	_____ boys
Leading during group work	_____ girls	_____ boys
Speaking for the group when reporting	_____ girls	_____ boys
Helping other students understand the assignment	_____ girls	_____ boys

Remember: Research predicts you will find that elementary and middle-school girls will reveal characteristics that might be defined as "gender-appropriate" for males. That is to say, they may exhibit the qualities of independence, assertiveness, and outspokenness. However, during high school, female students are said to display more "gender-appropriate" female behaviors.

Share your observations with your classmates, your colleagues, or your instructor, and discuss the implications of your observations.

part of sexual identity and is defined by who we are emotionally and/or to whom we are physically attracted. One's sexual orientation may be lesbian, gay, bisexual, transgender, or heterosexual.

Sexual Orientation

An aspect of humanness that serves as another basis for discrimination and various forms of differential treatment within society and within school classrooms is **sexual orientation**. For most people in dominant culture, attraction (physical and emotional) to a person of the opposite sex (heterosexual orientation) is assumed to be the norm. Often, heterosexuality is presented as the only acceptable sexual orientation. From this *heterosexist* position, those who partner with members of the same sex (homosexual orientation) are depicted as sexually deviant and pathologic. While the term *homosexual* is often applied to individuals whose partners are persons of the same sex, the use of term is seen as limiting because it places primary emphasis on an individual's sexual orientation, which is only one aspect of members of this cultural group. As with other marginalized groups, the nomenclature used for referring to gay people reveals evidence of their oppressed status in the United States. Clark (1977) explained that the term *gay* is a preferred label assigned by members of the group "as a way of reminding ourselves and others that awareness of our sexuality facilitates a capacity rather than creating a restriction. It means that we are capable of fully loving a person of the same gender by involving ourselves emotionally, sexually, spiritually, and intellectually" (p. 73). This terminology affirms gay culture (Rofes, 1989). While the terminology is becoming more widely used, members of this cultural group face widespread discrimination in society. **Heterosexism** is a system of advantage based on sexual orientation in which gay, lesbian, bisexual, and transsexual individuals are denied rights and opportunities enjoyed by those who identify themselves as heterosexual.

Kinsey, Pomeroy, and Martin's (1948) report on sexual behavior in the human male is credited with bringing homosexuality and bisexuality into U.S. consciousness. In it, Kinsey and fellow researchers found wide variations in sex concepts and behavior. They explained that the hetero/homo division of sexuality could not be divided neatly into two polar categories and said, "Only the human mind invents categories and tries to force facts into separate pigeonholes. The living world is a continuum" (Kinsey et al., 1948, p. 637). This report raised questions about what is considered "normal" and "abnormal" sexual behavior in males and females (Kinsey, 1941; Kinsey, Pomeroy, & Martin, 1953). However, the medical model that described homosexuality as a sickness prevailed until the late 1960s. At that time, New York City police conducted one of many raids of gay bars in Greenwich Village that touched off three days of rioting as gay men and lesbians forged a more unified public fight for their rights and survival. This incident, dubbed the Stonewall Riots, marked the birth of the modern gay and lesbian rights movement (Griffin, 1997). Still today, heterosexism is seen as the only "normal" and acceptable sexual orientation by members of dominant culture, leaving gay and lesbian individuals to face pervasive physical, psychological, legal, political, social, and economic threats, dangers, hardships, and losses. Statistics indicate that lesbian, gay, and bisexual people are among the most frequent targets of hate crimes (Miracek, Finn, & Cardell, 1992). And educators have been overwhelmingly resistant to acknowledging and addressing heterosexism in schools (Sears, 2005).

DEFINING DISABILITY

Just as institutional discrimination targets lesbian, gay, bisexual, transgender, and persons in the process of questioning their sexual identities (LGBTQ) students, and students with disabilities also experience pervasive marginalization in schooling and society. *Disability* has been defined as an observable, measurable characteristic of an individual that interferes with the individual's functioning—a functional limitation within the individual caused by physical, mental, or sensory impairment. While defining *disability* continues to be a matter of social debate and construction, recently the term has come to refer to a restriction or lack of ability to perform an activity in the manner or within the range considered "normal" for humans. *Impairment*, on the other hand, is defined as the loss or abnormality of psychological, physiological, or anatomical structure or functioning, and *handicaps* involve the loss or limitation of opportunities to take part in the "normal" life of the community on an equal level with others due to physical or social barriers. As such, handicaps may be considered barriers, demands, and environmental presses placed on persons by various aspects of their environments, including other people.

The medical model of disability focuses on individuals' functional limitations (impairments) and identifies impairments as the cause of disadvantages experienced by persons with disabilities. The social model, in contrast, shifts the focus from impairment to disability. In this case, *disability* refers to the disabling social, environmental, and attitudinal barriers rather than solely to individuals' "lack of ability." Thus, the only way to rectify disabling conditions using the medical model is through treatments and cures of individuals, while social change and the removal of disabling barriers are solutions for those who support the social model.

Even if the definition of *disability* was restricted to those having health problems or disabilities that prevent them from working or that limit the kind or amount of work one can do, in 2004 there would still have been an estimated 7.9 percent (plus or minus 0.2 percentage points) of civilian, noninstitutionalized men and women aged 18–64 in the United States categorized as disabled. This would amount to 14,152,000 of 179,133,000 Americans, or about 1 in 13 (Houtenville, 2005).

But even with advances in medicine, education, and laws attempting to remove barriers that exclude persons with disabilities, individuals with disabilities continually encounter discrimination ranging from outright intentional exclusion to a lack of access to substandard services, programs, activities, benefits, jobs, or other opportunities.

MARGINALIZATION: WHAT IT IS
AND HOW IT OPERATES

Historically, the United States has prided itself on being a cultural melting pot in which all cultures are blended or melted into one common culture. Immigrant groups, to this day, understand that living in the United States requires them to acculturate—to become "Americanized."

Acculturation refers to the acquisition of the cultural patterns of **dominant culture** while simultaneously relinquishing traditions and customs associated with one's own culture of origin. *Dominant culture* refers to groups in society that benefit from the power and prestige of their membership in the race, social-class, gender, ability status, and sexual-orientation groups that control society through policies, legislation, and practices that advantage them over marginalized groups. These groups experience *privilege*, or "unearned assets" that create and provide a constant stream of opportunities denied others in society (Lucal, 1996, p. 247). This system for relegating power to dominant culture is so entrenched that it perpetuates itself, while seeming to be so natural that it goes largely unrecognized by dominant-culture members (Vera, Feagin, & Gordon, 1995).

In her seminal work, McIntosh (1988) described White privilege as "an invisible package of unearned assets" that members of dominant culture can cash in on a daily basis (p. 76). As a White person, she notes: "If she has low credibility as a leader, she can be sure that her race is not the problem; she can choose public service accommodations (like hotel stays, apartment rentals, and so on) without fearing that people of her race cannot get in or will be mistreated in the places she has chosen; she can easily find academic courses and institutions that give attention only to people of her race; she can, if she wishes, arrange to be in the company of people of her race most of the time; she can turn on the television or open the front page of the newspaper and see people of her race widely and positively represented; she can arrange to protect her young children in school and society most of the time from those who might not like them based on their race; and she did not have to educate her children to be aware of systemic racism for their own daily physical protection" (pp. 79–81). Many U.S. citizens conversely are members of groups that are marginalized (for example, women or persons with disabilities) and also are members of groups who experience privilege (for example, middle-class or White individuals). Privilege in this sense confers dominance and permission to control by virtue of one's race, social class, ability, sex, ability status, and sexual orientation. The privilege of dominant culture allows dominant-culture individuals to decide which groups are accepted and therefore permitted by them to acculturate. Therefore, even the hope that minority group members will someday be acculturated and, hence, more able to reap rewards as fully recognized members of society is to a large extent dependent upon the wishes of dominant culture and is within their power to determine.

While acculturation may be a desired goal for some minorities, many find the idea of acculturation objectionable because it calls for relinquishing their traditional cultural values and norms in favor of those of dominant culture. Consider holidays that are set aside so that citizens are able to celebrate without missing work. Consider clothing, foods, and other goods that are readily available in stores so that citizens may conveniently purchase them, and languages that are respected and approved for use in businesses and schools. Do these traditions, characteristics, and cultural artifacts represent dominant or various different minority cultures and values? And, even though some minorities and their descendants may desire to become acculturated and may make every effort to adopt the culture of dominant society, total **assimilation** into dominant culture may actually be unattainable for most minorities because assimilation requires that they be fully accepted as equals by dominant-culture members of society. Under these conditions, many minority-group members often live, in a sense, on the fringe of societal opportunity, contributing to the resources and productivity of dominant culture while not completely assimilated or accepted and suffering the experience of **marginalization** through the processes of ethnocentrism, racism, classism, sexism, heterosexism, and ableism.

Because many teachers in today's classroom enjoy unearned privilege in one form or another (that is, race, social class, sexual orientation, gender, and/ or ability status), it is extremely important that they become self-reflective in seeking to identify their stereotypes and biases. The development of self-criticism and reflection skills along with a willingness and an openness to hear feedback that may reveal prejudices requires courage and fortitude. In fact, these practices are among the most challenging aspects of social justice education. Having the ability to take in, digest, analyze, and address feedback on one's shortcomings and then monitor one's behavior to ensure that lessons learned are performed in everyday life is the ultimate demonstration of learning (Adams, 1997). Teachers must work to model these qualities to facilitate their own development and encourage their students to learn from their example.

ETHNOCENTRISM

Listen! Listen to the language of those speaking about peoples who are different from themselves. Phrases such as "Why can't they be like us?" "They've been in this country long enough—why do they have to dress like that?" "Speak like that?" "Act that way?" reflect ethnocentrism. Individuals or societies who expect different cultural groups to acculturate are in essence saying that the existing dominant culture is superior to any other culture. Such sentiments are ethnocentric.

Ethnocentrism is the view that one's own group is the center of everything, and all others are scaled and rated with reference to it (Sumner, 1960). Ethnocentrism results in *prejudice,* which includes all negative attitudes, thoughts, and beliefs toward an entire category of people (Schaefer, 1988). People prejudge a person or group based on whatever information they have encountered about the person or group. Prejudice frequently goes overlooked because it is not always evident in one's behavior. It may manifest in any number of subtle and covert teacher attitudes and beliefs and in ways they may unconsciously treat students differently based on their racial, ethnic, gender, SES backgrounds, ability status, and sexual orientation.

RACISM, CLASSISM, SEXISM, HETEROSEXISM, AND ABLEISM

According to Jones (1972), there are three types of *racism*: individual, institutional, and cultural. Individual racism involves the personal attitudes, beliefs, and behaviors that assert the superiority of one's own race. Institutional racism is the pervasive social policies and laws that purposefully maintain the economic and social advantage of the dominant racial group in society. Finally, cultural racism involves societal customs and beliefs that promote the assumption that products are designed to address the needs and wishes of members of dominant culture and are superior to those of all other cultures. This last form of racism, cultural racism, determines the race of dolls manufactured and sold in stores, the racial tone of flesh-colored bandages that line the shelves of pharmacies, and so on.

Racism in the United States references attitudes and behaviors that denote the superiority of the dominant, White racial group. However, racism is not the only form in which superiority is assigned to one group over another. *Classism,* for example, is the beliefs and actions that decry the superiority of middle and capitalist social-class status; *sexism* involves all attitudes and actions that support the belief that males are superior to females; *heterosexism* denotes the belief system that heterosexuality is superior to homosexuality and other forms of sexuality; and *ableism* refers to the notion that persons with no identified physical or mental disabilities are superior to persons labeled disabled. These institutional "isms" result in a host of discriminatory policies, legislation, and practices that systematically oppress groups whose status is marginalized in the United States.

OPPRESSION AND MINORITY STATUS

Oppression is the state of being deprived of human rights and dignity while lacking the power to do anything about it (Goldenberg, 1978). Several terms are used in the fields of diversity and multicultural education to refer to oppressed groups in society. Each has drawbacks: The use of the term *disadvantaged,* for example, calls forth the idea of so-called "cultural deficiency" that members of minority groups are said to have. The term *minority* is often too narrowly equated with populations whose numbers make up less than 50 percent of the population.

In this text, we will refer to oppressed groups as "marginalized" or "minority" groups. In this sense, we mean these groups have marginalized status in society. The groups themselves are not marginal. The use of the term *minority group* may seem misleading because many scholars mean it to refer only to the numerical size and proportion of a group in relation to others in society. Wirth (1945), however, described minority status based on the concept of oppression. It is in this sense of minority as oppressed that we will use the term *minority* in this text. In this case, the term *minority* refers to those who, because of their cultural characteristics, are singled out from others in the society in which they live for differential and unequal treatment, and who therefore are objects of systematic collective discrimination.

FROM CONCEPTS TO LIVED EXPERIENCE

Too often texts on diversity get lost in abstract definitions, research, theories, and statistics, at the expense of lived experiences behind those definitions, theories, and statistics. Throughout this text, we will present theory and research, but we do not want to lose sight of the fact that lives are behind these data.

Students in classrooms care little if the discrimination they encounter is a form of racism, sexism, or any "ism" or whether they are considered members of minority or marginalized groups; what they know is what they have experienced. They know the constraints, the harm, the humiliation, and other elements of their oppression that impair their ability to thrive and grow in the directions they desire. It matters little to them what these ideas are called, and it matters greatly to all members of a society that these ills cease to continue.

So while it is important that we as educators understand the concepts presented within this chapter so that we may talk effectively with each other and think critically about these issues, remember that the facts, findings, and definitions do not tell the whole story. We must not diffuse our awareness and valuing of the human condition reflected in that information. As such, we end this chapter with a student's reflection of a school experience shaped by "isms," and an exercise designed to provoke thought about the injustices of a racist classroom (see Exercise 1-4).

ANNIE'S STORY

When I walked into the school in first grade holding my mother's hand, I knew I was going to have to prove something. They looked at us like we were so inadequate and foreign to them. I assume that because I'm Black, they promptly placed me in the lowest (remedial) reading group. Never mind that my mother told them I had been reading since I was 4 years old. She was a single parent who cleaned houses, so what did she know? I was eventually moved to the highest reading group by the end of the school year. But I boiled and churned through the whole process of proving to them that I was somebody, that I knew something, that I was even a better student than most of the White students in the school. This reality was so far from what they imagined could possibly be true that they could never see it—even with all the evidence I provided. When I graduated from that school with high honors, they were sure that they had "made me who I am." I knew who really made me: my mom—in every way, my mom.

Exercise 1-4	**Point of Reflection: Designing a Racist Classroom**

Directions: After reading Annie's story, think about the injustices she endured. So that you can get a good sense of what it takes to maintain such an oppressive school environment, this exercise asks you to work with a small group of your classmates to design a racist school.

1. Think about a group of students that will be oppressed in the make-believe school you will construct with your group members, then design specific policies, rules, attitudes, beliefs, strategies, and structures that oppress the group you have chosen and will keep them oppressed for generations to come. For example, you may want to create school rules and practices that let that group of students and all others in the school know that the group is inferior. Find specific ways to curtail their opportunities and squelch their hopes and beliefs in their abilities. Imagine all that you can add to the environment to ensure that the group is and stays oppressed.

PLEASE DO *NOT* READ BENEATH THE LINE UNTIL YOU HAVE CREATED (IN WRITING) YOUR RACIST SCHOOL WITH YOUR CLASSMATES. IT IS VERY IMPORTANT THAT YOU STOP READING BEFORE THE LINE UNTIL AFTER YOU HAVE FINISHED THIS PART OF THE ASSIGNMENT.

2. After you and your group members create your racist school, share your design with other groups of students in your class and discuss ways your newly created school is like schools that actually exist today. Explain what this means in terms of the experience of minority students in U.S. schools today.

Modifed from an activity by Katz, J. H. (1989). *White awareness: Handbook for anti-racism training.* Norman: University of Oklahoma Press.

SUMMARY

Culture Culture in a broad sense can be defined as characteristic[s] of [an] individual's society, or some subgroups within that society ... [it] includes values, beliefs, notions about acceptable and unacceptable behavior, and other socially constructed ideas that members of the culture are taught are "true" (Garcia, 1994, p. 51). It is important to remember that even within the same cultures, intergroup and intragroup differences exist.

Race *Race* is an anthropological concept used to classify people according to physical characteristics, such as skin and eye pigmentation, facial features, shape of head, and texture of body hair (Hernandez, 1989). However, race is most importantly a socially constructed construct with social relevance that is used to elevate a dominant group while oppressing others.

Ethnicity *Ethnicity* is defined as one's membership in a group that shares a unique social and cultural heritage that is passed down from one generation to the next (Schaefer, 1988).

Social Class *Social class* or *socioeconomic status* (SES) is the term used to distinguish people's relative position to others in society. Research has shown a relationship between SES and achievement.

Sex, Gender, Sexual Identity, and Sexual Orientation *Sex* refers to the biological condition of maleness or femaleness and is ascribed or assigned at birth, whereas *gender* is a learned psychological, social, and cultural aspect of a person that describes expected and sanctioned male and female behavior as a result of socialization. Gender schema theory suggests that differential treatment remains the major source of gender differences in attitude, behavior, and achievement.

Sexual identity is the degree to which we identify with the social and biological aspects of being a man or a woman. *Sexual orientation* determines the sex of the person to whom persons are attracted.

Disability A *disability* is an observable, measurable characteristic of an individual that interferes with the individual's functioning—a functional limitation within the individual caused by physical, mental, or sensory impairment.

Marginalization and Minority Status *Marginalization* and *minority status* result when groups in society are oppressed based on cultural characteristics that are deemed unacceptable by dominant culture.

Racism, Classism, Sexism, Heterosexism, and Ableism *Racism* is a system of advantage based on race that denotes the superiority of the White racial group in the United States; *classism* is beliefs and actions that provide privileges for and decry the superiority of middle and capitalist social-class status; *sexism* involves all attitudes and actions that support the belief that males are superior to females; and *sexual orientation bias* denotes the belief system that heterosexuality is superior to homosexuality and other forms of sexuality. *Ableism* refers to the notion that persons with no identified physical or mental disabilities are superior to persons labeled disabled.

Important Terms

ableism	dominant culture	marginalization	sexual identity
acculturation	ethnicity	minority	sexual orientation
assimilation	gender	oppression	social class
classism	handicap	race	socioeconomic status (SES)
culture	heterosexism	racism	subculture
disability	impairment	sexism	

Activities

As noted throughout the early portion of this chapter, it is our intent to add human experience to the sometimes sterile world of theory and research. As such, we have included a number of exercises and activities within the text. The following are a series of field experience questions related to the topics covered within this chapter. Use them to guide a classroom observation. Share your experiences with your instructor, your colleagues, or your classmates.

1. To begin to identify a school's culture, enter a school as a cultural anthropologist or archeologist might. View the artifacts on display, listen to the sounds, and observe the behaviors of those walking the halls or engaged in teaching and learning. Note specific language used by people in the schools (terms, phrases, acronyms, and so on) and identify terms that have special meaning or significance for members within the school community. Choose a particular phenomenon or issue in the school that you believe, based on your observations, is a cause of concern for any group of people in the school community. Develop a list of cultural characteristics evidenced through your observations (that is, include values and beliefs, and notions about acceptable and unacceptable behavior that are present). Then ask yourself the

following questions: (1) Is what I observed consistent with my own beliefs about the concern identified? (2) How might I feel if I spent many hours in this school community? (3) Would I receive different treatment in this school if I were a member of a racial, gender, sexual-orientation, ability-status or social-class minority group?

2. As you continue your observations, attempt to identify any "isms" that may be oppressive to some of the school community members (students, teachers, parents, and so on). Remember these may manifest in any number of subtle and covert teacher attitudes and beliefs and in ways they may unconsciously treat students differently based on their racial and ethnic backgrounds, socioeconomic class, or gender.

3. Research the phenomenon or issue of concern that you identified in Step 1. See what published authors and researchers have to say about what you observed. Summarize your findings.

4. Share your observations with your classmates, colleagues, or your instructor.

Enrichment

Apple, M. W. (2004). *Ideology and curriculum* (3rd ed.). New York: Routledge Falmer.

Ballantine, J. H. (Ed.). (1989). *Schools and society: A unified reader* (2nd ed.). Mountain View, CA: Mayfield.

Goodlad, J. I., & Keating, P. (Eds.). (1990). *Access to knowledge: An agenda for our nation's schools.* New York: College Entrance Examination Board.

Ladson-Billings, G. (2004). New directions in multicultural education: Complexities, boundaries, and critical race theory. In J. A. Banks, & C. A. M. Banks (Eds.), *Handbook of research on multicultural education* (2nd edition, pp. 50–65). San Francisco: Jossey Bass.

Rothenberg, P. S. (Ed.). (1997). *Race, class, and gender in the United States: An integrated study* (4th ed.). New York: St. Martin's Press.

Rumbaut, R. G., & Portes, A. (2001). *Ethnicities: Children of immigrants in America.* Berkeley: University of California Press.

Connections on the Web

http://www.msanetwork.org/

The Minority Student Achievement Network is an unprecedented national coalition of 21 multiracial, urban–suburban school districts across the United States. The Network's mission is to discover, develop, and implement the means to ensure high academic achievement for students of color, specifically African American and Latino students.

http://www.minedu.govt.nz/web/downloadable/dl8646_v1/quality-teaching-for-diverse-students-in-schooling.doc

This link provides a synthesis of evidence on quality teaching for diverse students.

http://bcol02.ed.gov/Programs/EROD/queries/word_specific_results.cfm?

This U.S. Department of Education website is an excellent education resource and organization directory with search capabilities.

REFERENCES

Adams, M. (1997). Pedagogical frameworks for social justice education. In M. Adams, L. A. Bell, & P. Griffin (Eds.), *Teaching for diversity and social justice: A sourcebook*. New York: Routledge.

Alba, R. (2000). Beyond the melting pot: 35 years later. *International Migration Review, 34*(1), 123.

Alba, R., & Nee, V. (2003). *Remaking the American mainstream: Assimilation and contemporary immigration.* Cambridge, MA: Harvard University Press.

Alba, R., Rumbaut, R. G., & Marotz, K. (2005). A distorted nation: Perceptions of racial/ethnic group sizes and attitudes towards immigrants and other minorities. *Social Forces, 84*(2), 901–909.

Allport, G. W. (1954). *The nature of prejudice.* Cambridge, MA: Addison Wesley.

American Association of University Women. (1992). *Shortchanging girls: Shortchanging America.* Washington, DC: Author.

Ashworth, M. (1992). *The first step on the longer path: Becoming an ESL teacher.* Markham, ON: Pippin Publishing Limited.

Belenky, M. F., Clinchy, B. M., Goldberger, N. R., & Tarule, J. M. (1986). *Women's ways of knowing.* New York: Basic Books.

Bem, S. (1981). Gender schematic theory: A cognitive account of sex typing. *Psychological Review, 88,* 354–364.

Brown, L. M. (1991). Telling a girl's life. Self-authorization as a form of resistance. In C. Gilligan, A. G. Rogers, & D. C. Tolman (Eds.), *Women, girls, and psychotherapy: Reframing resistance* (pp. 71–86). New York: Harrington Park.

Clark, D. (1977). *Loving someone gay.* Millbrae, CA: Celestial Arts.

Cross, W. E. (1971). The Negro to black conversion experience: Toward a psychology of black liberation. *Black World, 20,* 13–27.

Cross, W. E. (1991). *Shades of black: Diversity in African American identity.* Philadelphia: Temple University.

Dodge, K. A., Pettit, G. S., & Bates, J. E. (1994). Socialization mediators of the relation between socio-economic status and child conduct problems. *Child Development, 65,* 649–665.

Feagin, J. R. (1989). *Racial & ethnic relations.* Englewood Cliffs, NJ: Prentice Hall.

Gans, H. (1995). Deconstructing the underclass. In P. S. Rothenberg (Ed.), *Race, class, and gender in the United States: An integrated study* (pp. 51–56). New York: St. Martin's.

Garcia, E. (1994). *Understanding and meeting the challenge of student cultural diversity.* Boston: Houghton Mifflin.

Gilbert, L. A. (1992). Gender and counseling psychology: Current knowledge and directions for research and social action. In S. D. Brown, & R. W. Lent (Eds.), *Handbook of counseling psychology* (2nd ed., pp. 383–416). New York: Wiley.

Gilligan, C. (1982). *In a different voice: Psychological theory and women's development.* Cambridge, MA: Harvard University.

Glazer, N. (1971). Blacks and ethnic groups: The difference, and the political difference it makes. *Social Problems, 18,* 447.

Goldenberg, I. I. (1978). *Oppression and social intervention.* Chicago: Nelson Hall.

Greer, C. (1972). *The great school legend: A revisionist interpretation of American public education.* New York: Basic Books.

Griffin, P. (1997). Facilitating social justice education courses. In M. Adams, L. A. Bell, & P. Griffin (Eds.), *Teaching for diversity: A sourcebook* (pp. 279–298). New York: Routledge.

Gurian, M., & Henley, P. (2001). *Boys and girls learn differently: A guide for teachers and parents.* San Francisco: Jossey Bass.

Helms, J. E. (1990). *Black and white racial identity: Theory, research and practice.* Westport, CT: Greenwood.

Helms, J. E. (1995). An update of Helms' white and people of color racial identity development. In J. G. Ponterotto, J. M. Casas, L. A. Suzuki, & C. M. Alexander (Eds.), *Handbook of multicultural counseling* (pp. 181–198). Thousand Oaks, CA: Sage.

Henderson, G. (2000). Race in America. *National Forum, 80*(2), 12–15.

Hernandez, H. (1989). *Multicultural education: A teacher's guide to content and practice.* Upper Saddle River, NJ: Merrill/Prentice Hall.

Houtenville, A. J. (2005). *Disability statistics in the United States.* Ithaca, NY: Cornell University Rehabilitation Research and Training Center on Disability.

Johnson, S. D., Jr. (1990). Toward clarifying culture, race, and ethnicity in the context of multicultural counseling. *Journal of Multicultural Counseling and Development, 18,* 41–50.

Jones, J. M. (1972). *Prejudice and racism.* Reading, MA: Addison Wesley.

Keating, P. (1990). Striving for sex equity in schools. In J. I. Goodlad & P. Keating (Eds.), *Access to knowledge* (pp. 91–106). New York: College Board Publications.

Kinsey, A. C. (1941). Homosexuality: Criteria for a hormonal explanation of the homosexual. *Journal of Clinical Endocrinology, 1,* 424–428.

Kinsey, A. C., Pomeroy, W. B., & Martin, C. E. (1948). *Sexual behavior in the human male.* Oxford, UK: Saunders.

Kinsey, A. C., Pomeroy, W. B., & Martin, C. E. (1953). *Sexual behavior in the human female.* Oxford, UK: Saunders.

Ladson-Billings, G. (1994). *The dreamkeepers: Successful teachers of African American children.* San Francisco: Jossey Bass.

Ladson-Billings, G. (1995). Multicultural teacher education: Research, practice, and policy. In J. Banks, & C. A. McGee Banks (Eds.), *Handbook of research on multicultural education* (pp.747–759). New York: Macmillan.

Laird, J. (2000). Gender in lesbian relationships: Cultural, feminist, and constructionist reflections. *Journal of Marital and Family Therapy, 26*(4), 455–467.

Lucal, B. (1996). Oppression and privilege: Toward a relational conceptualization of race. *Teaching Sociology, 24,* 245–255.

Manstios, G. (1995a). Class in America: Myths and realities. In P. Rothenberg (Ed.), *Race, class, and gender in the United States: An integrated study* (3rd edition, pp. 131–143). New York: St. Martin's Press.

Manstios, G. (1995b). Media magic: Making class invisible. In P. Rothenberg (Ed.), *Race, class, and gender in the United States: An integrated study* (3rd ed., pp. 409–417). New York: St. Martin's Press.

McIntosh, P. (1988). White privilege and male privilege: A personal account of coming to see correspondences through work in women's studies.

Merrett, F., & Wheldall, K. (1992). Teachers' use of praise and reprimands to boys and girls. *Educational Review, 44*(1), 73–79.

Mirecek, J., Finn, S., & Cardell, M. (1982). *Gender roles in the relationships of lesbians and gay men, 8*(2), 45–49. (AN 11783047)

Noddings, N. (1992). The gender issue. *Education Leadership,* 65–70.

Ostling, R. N., & Urquhart, S. (1992). Is school unfair to girls? *Time, 139*(8), 62.

Radil, A. (1992). Can single-sex schools make a difference for girls? *Kids, Kids, Kids, 4,* 9–10.

Reed, S., & Sautter, C. S. (1990). Children of poverty: The status of 12 million young Americans. *Phi Delta Kappan, 71*(10), K1–K12.

Rice, P. F. (1993). *The adolescent: Development, relationships, and culture.* Boston: Allyn & Bacon.

Richardson, L. W. (1981). *The dynamics of sex and gender: A sociological perspective* (2nd ed.). Boston: Houghton Mifflin.

Rofes, E. (1989). Opening up the classroom closet: Responding to the educational needs of gay and lesbian youth. *Harvard Educational Review, 59*(4), 444–453.

Sadker, M., Sadker, D., & Long, L. (1993). Gender and educational equality. In J. A. Banks, & C. A. Banks (Eds.), *Multicultural education* (pp. 111–126). Needham Heights, MA: Allyn & Bacon.

Schaefer, R. T. (1988). *Racial and ethnic groups* (3rd ed.). Glenview, IL: Scott, Foresman.

Schaffer, K. F. (1981). *Sex roles and human behavior.* Cambridge, MA: Winthrop.

Sears, J. T. (1992). *Sexuality and the curriculum. The policies and practices of secondary education: Critical crisis in the curriculum.* New York: Teachers College.

Sears, J. T. (2005). Sexual minorities: Discrimination, challenges, and development in America. *Journal of Gay and Lesbian Issues in education, 3*(1), 107. (AN 19565589)

Sennett, R., & Cobb, J. (1972). *The hidden injuries of class.* New York: Vintage.

Sleeter, C. E., & Grant, C. A. (2002). *Making choices in multicultural education: Five approaches to race , class, and gender* (4th ed.). New York: John Wiley & Sons.

Sumner, W. G. (1960). *Folkways.* New York: Mentor.

Tatum, B. D. (1992). Talking about race, learning about racism: The application of racial identity development theory in the classroom. *Harvard Educational Review, 62,* 1–24.

U.S. Department of Education, National Center for Education Statistics. (2004). *The condition of education 2004.* Washington, DC: U.S. Government Printing Office.

Valli, L. (1995). The dilemma of race: Learning to be colorblind and color conscious. *Journal of Teacher Education, 46*(2), 120–129.

Vera, H., Feagin, J. R., & Gordon, A. (1995). Superior intellect? Sincere fictions of the White self. *Journal of Negro Education, 64*(3), 295–306.

Wirth, L. (1945). The problem of minority groups. In R. Linton (Ed.), *The science of man in the world crisis.* New York: Columbia University.

Wolf, A. (1977). *Poverty and achievement* (1991, No. 3). Washington, DC: National Institute of Education.

I came to the meeting kind of afraid ... but also excited. Maybe this time we could figure out what to do with Raul. I love him ... and he does so struggle in school ... always has. But like other times ... I've tried ... this time was just the same. I feel worse now than before I went. They say they want to meet with me and work on helping Raul, but when I try to say something, the principal and the teachers just keep talking over me. When I bring up something that I think might work or try to tell them how I feel about their suggestions, they say we'll talk about it at the next meeting ... but they never do. It's the same old thing ... I'm his mom ... but I have no say. We only meet or talk when they feel it is important ... not when I think it is. I guess ... what I feel is left out—like I'm nothing.

Words of Mrs. Esposito, mother of Raul

Often-Clashing Expectations

CHAPTER 2

Minority Family Attitudes, Academic Expectations, and Treatment in Schools

Much of the research on minority family interaction with schools focuses on parent involvement. Many school officials hold the view that minority parents with low educational attainment attach little value to or interest in their children's schooling. This is often cited as the reason for low levels of minority-parent involvement. These school administrators and teachers suggest that minority parents are irresponsible and disinterested. Some even believe parents of minority students are too lazy to come to the school to participate. Upon closer inspection, we find instead that many parents of minority students, like Raul's mother, are anything but lazy, irresponsible, and disinterested. They are more likely beaten down and out by years (perhaps even generations) of frustrations and experiences of being devalued in their interactions in schools.

Clearly the ways parents perceive their role in their children's schooling is, in part, a function of how school officials treat them. On the surface, invitations from school administrators to parents may appear to be a search for collaboration—working together as coequals in the education of their children. The reality, however, is more often than not outreach from those who see themselves as providers, overseers, and experts in their fields to parents who they perceive to be unknowing, uncaring, and uneducated. The goal implied in this type of correspondence (which is more of an insult than an invitation) is to transmit the "absolute knowledge and expertise" from school personnel about what is best for students to their families so they will fulfill their role in the so-called "partnership," which, as school personnel see it, is to simply agree with school officials and do whatever is being asked of them. This approach is a one-way model of provider–receiver service that actually decreases communication between families and schools, even when the goal is to increase parent involvement. Such patterns of communication place parents in a subordinate consumer/responder role as merely receptors of information and not in genuine participant roles in the schooling of their children (Smrekar & Cohen-Vogel, 2001).

For many minority parents who seek and anticipate a collaborative relationship with the school in which they are encouraged to offer ideas that will have an effect on school practices, policies, and curricula, the reality of being relegated to the role of passive recipient is disheartening. This is clearly evident in the words of Mrs. Esposito, Raul's mom, which began this chapter.

Further, when this experience is repeated and widespread, the impact is parent alienation and the loss of valuable allies and resources in the mission of educating students. The current chapter explores some minority family attitudes and expectations and communication barriers in schools, along with the impact these variables have on minority student achievement.

CHAPTER OBJECTIVES

1. Describe common school-related attitudes and expectations found among minority families.
2. Describe ways in which schools may alienate minority families and restrict their involvement.
3. Identify reasons for minority family confusion and ambiguity about the intentions of schools and teachers.
4. Identify barriers that separate families of minority students from schools.

DESIRE WITHOUT OPPORTUNITY: OPPOSITION AND ALIENATION

In contrast to the perception that minority parents do not care about their children's education, the truth is that all too often minority parents are not provided avenues or the opportunities to participate meaningfully in schools. Smrekar and Cohen-Vogel (2001) examined sources of minority parent participation in school-based activities and found that despite high verbal support for parent involvement among educators, school norms that reflect hierarchy over reciprocity, limited resources, and a lack of knowledge about how to involve parents in schools were key barriers. The researchers found that

---

Case Illustration 2-1 | **An Invitation to Parents**

The following is a copy of the "invitation" to parents to take part in a New York Learns Parent Night Program on PBS (February 28, 2002), entitled *Real Parents—Real Schools.*

Dear Parents and Families:
All parents want their children to do well in school and grow up to lead healthy, productive lives. When parents and families help children learn, students of all ages achieve more. Throughout New York State, we have many good examples of partnerships created by parents and schools working together on behalf of children. But gaps exist. Too many students do not have the knowledge and skills they need to be successful in school. We need to do better, and together, we can.

The education of our children is a shared responsibility. Schools need to be partners with parents, families and the community to help students achieve high academic standards. Our New York Learns Parent Night Program, *Real Parents— Real Schools*, broadcast on PBS February 28, 2002, provided an invitation to all parents to take a journey with us, and help us all to work together for our children. This guide, created for that program, is a starting point to help us all understand how we can help our children succeed in school. Thank you for joining us to make parent and family involvement a reality in all of our New York State schools.

Sincerely,

Richard P. Mills
Commissioner of Education

---

elements coming from both inside and outside schools hinder the quality of minority family–school interactions. Factors such as time, distance, and childcare restraints also served to lessen minority family involvement in schools. But sometimes the barriers exceed the obvious. Consider Case Illustration 2-1. This invitation "to all parents to take a journey with us and help us all to work together for our children" appears to be a useful way to involve parents, or is it?

While the invitation appears "inviting," a more insightful examination of the subtleties connoted reveals the existence of barriers that could exclude many parents from enthusiastically responding. Does the invitation provide the welcome, space, and opportunity for parents to help shape the strategies involved and the focus of the planned activities? Consider the parent who works late—are there provisions made for providing the information at another time, in other formats? Do all families have access to PBS and other needed resources? Can all parents read and understand the language of the letter? If you believe these to be good questions that you had not considered, you are not alone. Schools, classroom teachers, and entire school districts routinely send out "invitations" such as these to families. If schools want full parental participation, they must be sensitive to and capable of removing communication barriers that interfere with that participation.

BARRIERS TO FULL PARTICIPATION

The illustration of the invitation to participate in the afterschool focus group discussion presented in this chapter makes it clear that frequently (whether consciously or not) parents are kept at a distance when it comes to the education of their children. And while this may not be the intent, such distancing is magnified when it comes to minority parents, who are even further estranged due to the powerful barriers of difference (communication, customs, language, values) that restrict and inhibit their school involvement.

School Barriers

Minority students may encounter a number of school-related roadblocks as they embark on their journeys toward academic achievement. For example, it is common to find minority students attending schools with limited educational resources, deteriorating buildings, **restricted curricula**, **lowered expectations**, and uninviting **school climates**. These are but a few of the **school barriers** to their academic success.

U.S. educators often talk about the democratic right of all students to an education (Tyack, 2003). Sadly, when applied to many minority students, this "right" has been interpreted to mean the democratic right of all students to have access to *some* education. Ask any educator for her or his wish list for improve her or his school, and you are likely to hear the same list: more resources, more training, more funding. Clearly, schools operate on tight budgets and limited resources.

When limits exist, decisions must be made to determine the best use of these resources. Because dominant-culture students have strong political representation at the local, state, and national levels, as compared to low-income and minority students, the choice has consistently been to place resources where they are said to be able to do the most good—among students coming from dominant–culture, middle-class families. Federal school funding formulas continue to advantage these students. Research shows that gaps between opportunities to learn and students' appropriation of those opportunities are quite often produced and maintained by the amount of resources and quality of instruction students receive. This same research demonstrates that all too often, working-class and poor students are denied meaningful access to needed resources and quality instruction and thus knowledge in schools (Bourdieu, 1977; Gayle-Evans, 1993; Rose, 2000; Yair, 2000).

> Schools transmit dominant culture's socio-cultural values while excluding cultural features coming from other groups … and educational practices maintain and legitimize social inequities for some by not recognizing and valuing their cultural practices. Hence, many students are denied the possibility of achieving the same educational results as their peers from the majority culture. (Aguado, Ballesteros & Malik, 2003, p. 50)

Inner city, rural, low-income, and minority students are all too often short-changed.

In the midst of our flourishing economy, we are recreating a dual school system, separate and unequal, almost half a century after this was declared unconstitutional. We face a widening and unacceptable chasm between good schools and bad, between those youngsters who get an adequate education

| **Exercise 2-1** | **Field Experience: A Visit to the Schools That Have and Those That Have Not** |

Directions: Pencils, papers, and eyes wide open—it's time to practice observing and recording. The intent of this exercise is to give you a "sensory" experience to accompany the thoughts you are developing as a result of reading this chapter.

Your task is to visit two schools. Select a school that in your estimation has a new, modern, and well-equipped facility. Next, identify a school, perhaps in a poorer school district, that appears to be not only an older structure but one with evidence of being poorly maintained. As you visit the schools, observe the following:

1. How inviting is the exterior? Does the school appear to be "alive" and vibrant? Does it feel safe inside?
2. As you walk through the halls, what do you see? Evidence of student life and excitement? Bright and cheery decorations? Well-maintained walls, floors, and ceilings?
3. If possible, observe the desks, the labs, the lockers, text books, and so on. Do they reflect materials that are dated? Do they support or hinder the teaching–learning process?
4. How about noncurricular facilities, such as the cafeteria, gymnasium, lobby, auditorium, music classroom, or library? Do they appear inviting, comfortable, and/or well-equipped?
5. Finally, as you leave each school, first record your observations (take pictures, if it is permitted) and then imagine yourself a student in that school. What are your feelings and thoughts about being a student in that school? Are your reflections different for each school environment?

and those who emerge from school barely able to read and write. The Thomas B. Fordham Foundation's *A Nation Still at Risk* (1999) points out that the fortunate among us continue to thrive within and around the existing education system, but millions of Americans—mainly the children of the poor and minorities—do not enjoy these options. As noted by the report, the poor are "stuck with what 'the system' dishes out to them, and all too often they are stuck with the least qualified teachers, the most rigid bureaucratic structures, the fewest choices and the shoddiest quality." Perhaps a field trip would help to place a human face on these observations (see Exercise 2-1).

Restricted Curriculum and Tracking   Restricted Curriculum, tracking, and other ability-grouping practices have a negative influence on schools' intergroup relations because these practices tend to isolate students along cultural, racial, and economic lines and thereby perpetuate in-school segregation and unequal educational benefits. Schools determine how many advanced classes are offered, what is taught in advanced courses of study, how students' abilities are measured, and how students are placed into classes that offer specific curricula. These determinations work together to influence students' access to knowledge.

Such ability grouping, when viewed at the system level, dictates what classes are available to which students, and viewed from the level of the classroom, these practices define what knowledge and learning experiences are deemed suitable for particular students. The resulting differences in learning opportunities present significant schooling inequities. Depending on the class "level," students have access to significantly different types of knowledge and skills. Students in "high-ability" (advanced) classes are more likely to be exposed to topics and skills that assist them in preparing for college, while students in "low-ability" (average and low-level) classes are taught basic reading skills, using mostly workbooks and tasks that require memorization rather than critical thinking (Oakes & Lipton, 1990).

Ability grouping has the effect of segregating low-income and minority students into vocational and low-ability academic tracks within the school that alienates them, deny them access to the rich resources that are provided for "average" and "above average" ability students, and, therefore, doom them to academic failure (Garcia, 1994). Such curricula often lack relevance and fail to provide significant empowering relationships with qualified school personnel and the right to an effective education that equals that of other students. Sometimes this effect occurs unintentionally as teachers or other school officials track students into basic, average, or advanced reading groups and math curricula in elementary schools. But because this process of assignment is based on the use of inadequate placement measures and methods implemented within a biased educational system, what at first may look like an effort to facilitate the students' learning is in fact one that restricts learning and alienates those very students we are trying to help, therefore restricting their job and career options and ultimately their earning power and future socioeconomic success. Further, for many students, the placement in such ability groupings results in the development of a self-perception as less than adequate, thus producing an insidious cycle of lowered expectations, leading to less effort and motivation and resulting in poor performance, which in turn reinforces initial low expectations. Under these conditions, minority students receive differential and weakened forms of instruction in which they are academically socialized to be passive consumers of purportedly static knowledge that works to hinder rather than benefit their achievement.

School Climate   It is not only access to curriculum and education resources that can inhibit the development of minority students; quite often the very psychosocial climate of the school—of the classroom itself—can act to hinder student achievement. Often, minority students and their families are confronted by subtle and sometimes not-so-subtle messages that they are neither valued nor welcomed as full participants in the educational system. Consider the feelings of Raul's mother, expressed in the opening vignette of this chapter. While on the surface it appeared she was invited to participate in the education of her son, her experience seemed to suggest something different. The issue of school climate effects on student achievement is discussed further in Chapter 3; Exercise 2-2 serves as an introduction to the topic.

Barriers Stemming from Minority Communities

It is not unusual to find that minority students' academic motivation, levels of involvement in school, and eventual achievement are inhibited, not only by the

| Exercise 2-2 | **Point of Reflection: School Climate Survey** |

Directions: Think about the elementary, middle, or high school in which you were previously enrolled. (If you were homeschooled, interview someone who attended school in order to answer the following questions.)

1. Forget the grades you received in this school. How good do you think your own work in school was?

   Excellent   1

   Good   2

   Same as most other students   3

   Below most other students   4

   Poor   5

2. How good a student did the teacher you liked the best expect you to be in school?

   One of the best   1

   Better than most other students   2

   Same as most other students   3

   Not as good as most other students 4

   One of the worst students   5

3. How many students did not do as well as they could do in school because they were afraid other students would not like them as much if they did well?

   Almost all of the students   1

   Most of the students   2

   About half of the students   3

   Some of the students   4

   None of the students   5

4. When you attended the school, did you believe that people like you did not do well in school?

   Strongly agree   1

   Agree   2

   Not sure   3

   Disagree   4

   Strongly disagree   5

5. How many teachers in the school tried to help students get better grades when they were struggling?

   Almost all of the teachers   1

   Most of the teachers   2

   About half of the teachers   3

   Some of the teachers   4

   Almost none of the teachers   5

6. How good a student did your family members expect you to be in that school?

   One of the best   1

   Better than most other students   2

   Same as most other students   3

   Not as good as most other students 4

   One of the worst students   5

7. How did you feel when you were in the school?

   Very comfortable   1

   Pretty comfortable   2

   Somewhat comfortable   3

   Uncomfortable   4

   Very uncomfortable   5

8. How did teachers and school staff treat you?

   Very warmly with lots of respect   1

   Respectfully   2

   With some kindness and respect   3

   With little respect and kindness   4

   Very coldly with no respect   5

9. How involved were you with extracurricular activities in the school?

   Very involved in lots of clubs/teams   1

   Pretty involved in some clubs/teams   2

   Involved in a couple of clubs/teams   3

   Not very involved   4

   Not at all involved   5

continued

10 Would you recommend the school to a member of your family?	Go back and look at your responses to the questionnaire items. What do they tell you about the school's psychological climate? Write a reflection discussing the elements of school climate that you feel are the most important for creating a positive learning environment.
I would strongly recommend it 1	
I would not recommend it 2	

conditions experienced in schools but also as an outgrowth of forces working from within minority communities.

Cultural Inversion   Ogbu (1990) found that a frequent response of minority students and their families to the discrimination they face in schools is **cultural inversion**. *Cultural inversion* is the process of regarding certain forms of behavior, symbols, and meanings as inappropriate for a minority-group member to exhibit because they are seen as characteristic of White America. There is an interesting scene in the movie *Stand and Deliver* (Warner Brothers, 1988), the true-life story of Jaime Escalante, a successful teacher working with students in a poor Los Angeles high school. In the scene, a student in Mr. Escalante's class asks him for two copies of the textbook so that he can keep one at home to study and one in his desk. The student explained, "I can't let my 'homies' see me hauling books around." Mr. Escalante gave the student three books in that scene from the movie—one for his desk, one for home, and one for his locker. Such behavior on the part of the student is reflective of cultural inversion. In order to save face and to fit in with his cultural group, he must not be seen as compliant and conforming to school rules (therefore aligning with the oppressor). Sometimes seemingly oppositional behavior and resistance to participation in schools are actually examples of cultural inversion, and as with the case of Jaime Escalante as he was portrayed in *Stand and Deliver*, a sensitivity and the willingness to adapt on the part of the teacher or other school official could help to keep a student who is trying to decide whether or not to cross cultural boundaries on track to achieving his or her goals.

Cultural inversion may serve as a foundation for a minority group's collective opposition to discrimination faced in school and society. The students described in Case Illustration 2-2 were neither limited by their abilities nor their aspirations. Rather, like many minority students, they chose to express their strengths in other ways.

The forms of opposition displayed by students can be subtle or, in this case, not-so-subtle ways to express their displeasure and opposition to a social structure that limits their attainment of highly valued social goals, including education and economic viability (Fordham, 1982). For these students, academic success is weakened when the outdated texts used are missing reflections of their lives and culture (relevance), the supplies are old and often unusable, the teachers are inexperienced and lack expertise in their fields (relationships), and the chances of continuing in their development and being employed to use these skills are restricted (rights). It is important to note that

Case Illustration 2-2	We Don't Need School

The teacher, new to the school, began her first day and her first math class by greeting the 22 energetic eighth graders sitting before her. She was nervous because this was her first "real" teaching job, and it was in fact the first time she had ever been in an inner-city school. The students appeared enthusiastic, alive, and willing to share as she moved through the initial exchange of pleasantries and introductions. However, the atmosphere in the classroom soon changed.

As the teacher transitioned from the welcoming activities to a discussion of the course and course material, the tone, the classroom climate, the attitude and behavior of the students, changed. Students began to grumble and make comments ("This is boring—why do we have to?") as she directed them to take out their books. Two boys sitting in the back of the room (who previously had been quite active in their participation during the initial "ice breakers" and introductions) slouched down in their seats and folded their arms somewhat defiantly across their chests.

The teacher, feeling uncomfortable and not knowing what to do, repeated her direction that they open their books. "Okay, this is math . . . ," but before she could finish, one of the boys yelled out, "We don't need no stinkin' math!" and the other children laughed and shouted in agreement. Soon the second boy echoed the sentiment by saying, "Yep . . . the only math I need is to know how much change I get back after I buy a pack of cigarettes." By now the other students were yelling out in support of the two, and the teacher felt as if she had lost all control. The class initially appeared engaged and eager to begin—even these two boys. The instigators initially appeared to be bright leader types, each with peer respect and a good sense of humor. What happened?

this type of opposition among minority group members allows for the display of opposition without crossing the lines of "bad" behavior for which they can be formally sanctioned. The boys in our illustration were certainly a disruption, but not so much so that they would be removed or severely punished. As such, this type of opposition is an ingenious response and coping strategy utilized to maintain cultural integrity and discrimination in the learning process. Coping skills such as these help group members fight for their group's pride within a system that denies them and their cultural group.

Quiet–Private Aspirations   A mistake many educators make is to assume that minority students and their families do not care about education. The truth is that while minority students generally voice high educational and occupational aspirations for themselves, these expressions are not often heard by members of the dominant culture, especially when the forces of cultural inversion and minority group stereotyping are at work. Further, even when the minority students aspire to high occupational goals tied to educational attainment, they often fail to translate their expectations into successful school behaviors. As noted by Valentine and Loyd (1989), too often minority students, in an attempt to cope with the dominant cultural values found within the school, develop strategies that are generally incompatible with academic achievement. Thus, while their actions may suggest an attitude of "We are too cool for school" or "We don't need to learn this stuff," underlying that behavior is the belief that "we don't trust you or your system. We can learn, but we won't learn from you."

Struggles between Dominant and Minority Cultures Tatum (1987) explained that for some African American students to succeed, a renunciation of their Black cultural frame of reference is required. Forced to relinquish their own culture or reject the dominant White culture, many African American students consciously or unconsciously tailor their academic performance to the scaled-down expectations of school officials. And those who attempt to achieve by crossing cultural boundaries often become alienated from their own community (Smith & Andrews, 1988). Fordham (1996) explained that minority students who are perceived by their peers to be aligned with school authorities, as evidenced by their compliance with school rules and efforts to study, may be labeled "sell-outs," meaning, at least in the eyes of some minority students, that "to achieve is to be White."

Barriers Stemming from Past Generations

Minority parents—as do their counterparts in the dominant culture—view schooling as a vehicle for financial success; the acquisition of social skills, including respect and discipline; and the obtainment of technological and academic knowledge. Parents with such beliefs will most likely attempt to encourage and support their children in their educational endeavors. For some, however, the hope that schooling is the door through which their children will begin to experience the "American Dream" is questioned, given their own personal experiences in school.

Some minority parents express a belief in the value of formal education for success in life, while they may still be plagued by their personal experiences and knowledge of oppression and discrimination in schools—a situation that results in their distrust of educational institutions and resistance to support the school when conflict between their children and the school arises. These feelings of distrust often lead to ambiguity on the part of minority parents. When that ambiguity is communicated (consciously or not) to their children, minority students respond through cultural inversion and other forms of resistance that embody their parents' lack of confidence that they will be treated fairly in schools. These resistance behaviors, while understandable, jeopardize academic outcomes and lead to weakened minority student achievement.

FROM CONCEPTS TO LIVED EXPERIENCE

The ringing of the school bell on the first day of school is one that stimulates many feelings, especially if you are new to the school process. Children entering schools for the first time may be torn between the anxiety of leaving home and the excitement of growing up. Parents have mixed feelings as well—joy for all that the day may bring and yet anxiety about whether it will go as well as they hope, wondering if their children will find the support, encouragement, and stimulation they need to maximize their growth and development.

But first-day expectations, aspirations, hopes, dreams, and experiences vary dramatically, given the opportunities afforded students, school climates, cultures in which they spend many years of learning, and the subtle and not-so-subtle messages conveyed to them by administrators, teachers, and even their own families and peers.

And while we can speak of dominant culture, oppressed minorities, lowered expectations, barriers within and beyond, and uninviting cultures, the reality may be, instead, the death of hope, the squelching of dreams, and the fear and rejection that is the school experience for some minority students. Consider the following excerpt from a story by Dana Williams (2005), entitled "Caroline is a Boy."

JOHN S.

John S. left behind more than most students when he graduated from high school last year. Aside from saying goodbye to friends and familiar surroundings, he left behind his birth name of Caroline and many of the daily indignities he faced as a transgendered student at a high school in upstate New York.

The stares and jokes in the locker room. The sneaking into bathrooms when no one else was around—the teachers who either refused or forgot to call him John instead of Caroline. And a school administration he says not only misunderstood his needs but also failed to try.

John was more than ready to leave all that behind. He skipped a grade and completed the mandatory graduation requirements early, earning his high school diploma a full year ahead of schedule. (p. 1)

SUMMARY

School Barriers Individual achievement is limited when minority students attend schools with limited educational resources, deteriorating buildings, **restricted curriculum**, lowered expectations, and uninviting school climates.

Restricted Resources and Funding Research demonstrates that, all too often, working-class and poor students are denied meaningful access to needed resources, quality instruction, and thus knowledge in schools.

Restricted Curriculum Often, students are "tracked" according to "ability" level. Such grouping dictates what classes are available to which students and what knowledge and learning experiences are deemed suitable for particular students. The resulting differences in learning opportunities present significant schooling inequities. When this process of assignment is based on the use of inadequate placement measures and methods implemented within a biased system, what at first

may look like an effort to facilitate the students' learning is in fact one that restricts learning and alienates those very students we are trying to help.

School Climate Quite often, minority students and their families are confronted by subtle and not-so-subtle messages that they are neither valued nor welcomed as full participants in the system. Insensitive timing of meetings, the use of written and oral communications that do not reflect respect for family input or minority cultural values, and programs that are simply inaccessible to minority families are but a few ways schools create an unwelcoming climate for minority families.

Barriers stemming from the Minority Community It is not unusual to find that minority students' academic motivation, levels of involvement, and eventual achievement are inhibited, not just by the conditions experienced in school but also as an outgrowth of forces working from within minority communities. Cultural inversion is the process of regarding certain forms of behavior, symbols, and meanings as inappropriate for a minority to exhibit because they are seen as characteristic of White America. Under this pressure, minority students may develop strategies that are generally incompatible with their academic achievement in the academy.

Important Terms

ability grouping	lowered expectations	school barriers	tracking
cultural inversion	restricted curriculum	school climate	

Activities

A quick search through the literature will reveal numerous articles, position papers, and books describing the "separate but unequal" treatment that many minority students experience within U.S. schools. This literature highlights statistics on money allocated to various school districts, standardized test scores, and even student activities (existent or not). What is often missing from these reports is the experience—the frustration of the deadening experience that can result from attending a school that alienates rather than facilitates.

Here are a series of field experience questions related to the topics covered within this chapter. Use them to guide a classroom observation. Share your experiences with your classmates, your colleagues, or your instructor.

1. Visit two different schools (one located in an upper-middle or upper SES community and one in a lower-middle to lower SES setting) and spend a day shadowing a single student in each, or follow two students in the same setting but in different curriculum tracks. Then answer the following questions:
   a. Were the same or similar teaching techniques employed? If not, what differences did you note and what impact did the different teaching approaches have on the students' attitudes and achievement?
   b. Were texts, supplemental teaching materials, and even the decorations in the classrooms of the same quality and effectiveness?
   c. How would you evaluate the classroom climates? Supportive? Encouraging? Open? Welcoming? Or were they combative, tense, or flat?

If you noted a difference in the teaching style, quality of materials, and/or climate of the school and classroom in these two observations, come up with some hypotheses about the potential impact on the students who experience these two different sets of conditions.

2. Schedule an appointment with a school, an administrator, or perhaps a school counselor and ask about the following:
   a. The manner in which parents are invited to participate in the education of their children (for example, open houses, parent nights, parent/teacher meetings, Internet homework support, e-mail)
   b. The steps that the school administration, staff, and teachers take to provide alternative means for parental involvement when specific parents or groups of parents cannot access the mainstream methods (that is, work in the evening or have no one to watch the younger child, no home computer, difficulty with speaking/reading English, and so on)

Share your observations with your instructor and your classmates in small groups to develop a list of strategies geared to increase the level of responsiveness to all parents as well as increase the active engagement of all parents in the education of their children.

Enrichment

Delpit, L. (1995). *Other people's children: Cultural conflict in the classroom.* New York: W. W. Norton & Co.

Fordham, S. (1996). *Blacked out: Dilemmas of race, identity, and success at Capital High.* Chicago: University of Chicago.

Tatum, B. D. (1987). *Assimilation blues: Black families in a White community.* Northampton, MA: Greenwood Press.

Connections on the Web

www.education-world.com/a_special/parent_involvement

This website for Education World focuses on practical ways in which schools do and can involve parents.

www.pta.org

This site provides information on a national standard for parent involvement, along with information and resources for implementing programs to involve parents.

www.ericdigests.org/pre-9218/risk.htm

This article contains suggestions for involving at-risk families in their children's education.

REFERENCES

Aguado, T., Ballesteros, B., & Malik, B. (2003). Cultural diversity and school equity: A model to evaluate and develop educational practices in multicultural education contexts. *Equity and Excellence in Education, 36*(1), 50–63.

Andersen, M. L., & Collins, P. H. (2004). *Race, class, and gender: An anthology* (5th ed.). Belmont, CA: Wadsworth/Thomson.

Bourdieu, P. (1977). Cultural reproduction and social reproduction. In J. Karabel & A. H. Halsey (Eds.), *Power and ideology in education* (pp. 487–510). New York: Oxford University.

Carter, R. T., & Goodwin, A. L. (1994). Racial identity and education. In L. Darling-Hammond (Ed.), *Review of research in education: Vol. 20* (pp. 291–336). Washington, DC: American Educational Research Association.

Fordham, S. (1982, December). *Cultural inversion and black children's school performance.* Paper presented at the annual meeting of the American Anthropological Association, Washington, DC.

Fordham, S. (1996). *Blacked out: Dilemmas of race, identity, and success at Capital High.* Chicago: University of Chicago.

Garcia, E. (1994). Understanding and meeting the challenge of student cultural diversity. Boston: Houghton Mifflin.

Gayle-Evans, G. (1993). *Making cultural connections for African American children under six: Affirming culture through literature and the arts.* Paper presented at the Annual Conference of the Southern Association on Children under Six, Biloxi, MS, March 25–27.

Merton, R. K. (1968). *Social theory and social structure.* New York: The Free Press.

Oakes, J., & Lipton, M. (1990). Tracking and ability grouping: A structural barrier to access and achievement. In J. I. Goodlad & P. Keating (Eds.), *Access to knowledge: An agenda for our nation's schools.* New York: College Entrance Examination Board.

Ogbu, J. U. (1990). Minority education in comparative perspective. *Journal of Negro Education, 59,* 45–55.

Ogbu, J. U. (1992). Understanding cultural diversity and learning. *Educational Researcher, 21,* 5–24.

Rose, S. J. (2000). *Social stratification in the United States.* New York: New Press.

Smith, K. L., & Andrews, L. D. (1988, April). *An explanation of the beliefs, values, and attitudes of black students in Fairfax County.* Paper presented at the annual meeting of the American Educational Research Association, New Orleans.

Smrekar, C., & Cohen-Vogel, L. (2001). The voices of parents: Rethinking the intersection of family and school. *Peabody Journal of Education*, *76*(2), 75–101.

Tatum, B. D. (1987). *Assimilation blues: Black families in a White community*. Northampton, MA: Greenwood.

Thomas B. Fordham Foundation. (1999). *A nation still at risk*. College Park, MD: ERIC Clearinghouse on Assessment and Evaluation. (ERIC Document Reproduction Service No. ED429988)

Tyack, D. (2003). *Seeking common ground: Public schools in a diverse society*. Cambridge, MA: Harvard University.

Valentine, P., & Lloyd, A. (1989, March). *Living in Franklin Square: An exploration of black culture*. Paper presented at the annual meeting of the American Educational Research Association, San Francisco.

Williams, D. (2005). Caroline is a boy. *Teaching Tolerance*, *27*, 1.

Yair, G. (2000). Educational battlefields in America: The tug-of-war over students' engagement with instruction. *Sociology of Education*, *73*(4), 247–269.

This is the first time I felt welcome—truly welcome in a school. When I walk down the halls, I feel connected. I feel like the teachers and principals like me. They know who I am and they like who I am. We have these classes called Affective Skills that the school counselors teach. They are fun, and they help me learn to express my feelings—get things off my chest. We have assignments where we have to interview a family member to find out ways the school could do better. It's neat that they listen to my grandma like this— she's really smart.

Katherine, 10th-grade Cuban student attending a private school

School Climate

CHAPTER 3

Effects on Minority Student Achievement and Socio-emotional Adjustment

Walking down the hall and feeling connected, liked, and valued is what all students, and their families, should feel as they enter schools. Feeling unwelcome, unsafe, and alone in schools is not what students and their families expect. Students feeling detached and alienated from the environments in which they are to learn is anything but welcoming, supportive, and facilitative of academic achievement. And while the mission for most schools is to provide structures and processes necessary to facilitate students' educational development, many are failing minority students (Aguado, Ballesteros, & Malik, 2003; Rubin, 2006). It is clear that more than a traditional delivery of academic curricula is required to fulfill this mission. Fostering student academic achievement and development necessitates the establishment and maintenance of a school climate that meets the needs of a diverse population of students and their families, who have highly diverse values, languages, and social norms (Sugai & Horner, 2002)

At a minimum, students must feel safe in school. Students and their families must be able to trust that they will be acknowledged, valued, attended, respected, and included. Students need to be able to focus on learning and not worry about whether or not they will be the objects of neglect, prejudice, and rejection in their schools. Yet, for many minority students, the school day is a day of total immersion in a hostile environment. It is a day where survival, not growth, takes center stage. Students in such settings experience a school climate that fails to nurture the academic, social, and emotional growth that every student deserves.

What type of climate is needed? How is such a school climate created and maintained? While the first question may be answered easily, addressing the second question will take some proactive advocacy to even approximate. Further, it must be understood that the weight of producing a school climate that meets the needs of all the school's constituents can be overwhelming for all concerned. And, while it is the responsibility of the building principal and administrative staff to shape the school climate, each school official, including each teacher, school counselor, and staff member, also must take responsibility for providing and promoting the most favorable learning conditions for all students. However, members of the school community are likely to have differing ideas about how a school should function. Gathering a team representing all members of the school community in order to define schoolwide behavioral *expectations* (not just for students but for all members of the school community) is a good first step toward defining a positive school climate (Lewis & Sugai, 1999). Including all constituents in this process is essential. It is easy to forget that students are connected to families and broader communities of potential school partners who are significant in the lives of each student. But it is important to remember that if a school's actions alienate and otherwise turn off the families of students, in many ways they alienate and turn off the very people schools seek to include, empower, and educate. Schools must respect and embrace all of their partners in order to effectively educate students.

This chapter will describe school climate variables and the impact these elements have on student achievement. Further, the chapter will explore some minority family attitudes, expectations, and communication barriers that are experienced in schools.

CHAPTER OBJECTIVES

1. Identify significant dimensions of school climate.
2. Describe the effects of school climate on the academic success of students.
3. Describe various elements of positive school climate.
4. Explain possible areas of conflict between minority family attitudes and expectations and some elements of school climate.
5. Identify barriers to effective, facilitative home–school communication.

THE SCHOOL AS A SOCIAL SETTING

Schools are more than buildings made of steel and stone. They are more than curricula. Schools are active, living compilations of individuals interacting around a common purpose—education. As such, schools are truly settings that embody **human ecology.**

Schools are settings with unique interactions, relationships, and interdependencies among all those operating within the environment. They also are environments shaped by and reflective of many societal forces and pressures, including institutional racism, sexism, classism, ableism, and heterosexism.

| **Case Illustration 3-1** | **Two Schools: Focusing on Product or Person?** |

J. R. Anderson Elementary School

Established in 1950, J. R. Anderson Elementary School is in pretty good shape for its 50-plus years in existence. Clearly, some fresh paint and a few new windows here and there would certainly help. But for all outward appearances, it is much like any other elementary school.

Entering the lobby, you immediately become aware that, contrary to your initial impression, this school is *not* like any other elementary school. It is deadly quiet—in the middle of the day! As you walk through the lobby toward the main office, you realize that not only are the lobby and the building clean but they are almost septic—sterile. The walls are bare; no student work is displayed and there is no evidence of class projects, activities, or coming events. As you look up and down the halls, signs of life are hard to find. Classroom doors are closed; all students are at their desks (which are nice and straight and orderly); and teachers, in almost lockstep fashion, stand at the front of the classroom lecturing. The "business" of the class—the lesson plan—appears to be being delivered, but the sense of excitement, the joy of learning, and the energy of childhood seem to have taken leave.

J. L. Allen Elementary School

Cloaked in the yellowish brick of its day, J. L. Allen Elementary School is a school that attests to its years of service. The doors to the school are huge, old metal doors that, while clean, could certainly use some paint. Allen Elementary was also built in the early 1950s and clearly begs for a new life, but only on the outside.

On entering the lobby, you are struck by the color and the vibrancy of the building. Children's work fills the hallways. A banner congratulating the chess club for a victory and a poster announcing the Halloween dance are posted outside the main office. Through open doors, you can hear teachers providing instruction and children engaging in activities that take them all over their classrooms. It is clear that there is life at Allen Elementary. Although the bones are old, the spirit of the school is alive and well.

The degree to which the school setting supports healthy, stimulating, and growth-oriented interactions and relationships strongly influences the degree to which academic achievement occurs.

As is true with any other institution, to be effective, schools must have common goals and articulated roles that are embraced and enacted by its members. They must also establish social norms, values, and operational assumptions that support the performance of these roles and the achievement of goals formed. It is these social norms, values, and operating assumptions that give form to the culture and climate of schools—a culture and climate that can either facilitate or hinder student development. Consider the case of the two schools described in Case Illustration 3-1. Think about how you would feel working and learning in each of these schools.

SCHOOL CLIMATE VARIABLES

A school's climate consists of all attitudes and behaviors of individuals within the school system. **School climate** involves at least four key relationships: (1) the relationships of students to themselves; (2) the relationships between students and their peers; (3) the relationships between students and their families and communities; and (4) the relationships between students and their school personnel, including teachers, administrators, and staff (Dorsey, 2000). In addition to these factors, the participants' **beliefs**, **values**, and attitudes that serve as the foundation for the styles of interaction found to exist within schools also contribute to school climates (Welsh, 2000). A school's climate helps to establish and communicate the parameters of acceptable behavior and therefore is an essential factor that affects the achievement of the mission of any one school (Welsh, 2000; Lockwood, 1997).

Warmth and Inclusion

School climate is enhanced by effective communication, clear role definitions, and the existence of **warmth** and **inclusion** of all school-community members. Typically, low teacher morale and high student disorder result when schools have administrative staffs who lack effective communication with faculty, students, and their families or who do not work together with the entire school community to solve problems (Anderson 1998; Jenkins, 1997; Sherman et al., 1997). Further, students inhabiting schools in which they do not believe they belong and in which they feel uncared for by school personnel experience higher levels of dysfunction (Gottfredson, 1989). Conversely, high **expectations** among school staff and students; respectful treatment of students; active engagement of students and their families; and cooperative social relationships among students, faculty, administration, and the school community positively affect school climate and performance (Stockard & Mayberry, 1992).

Norms and Beliefs

Another less obvious set of factors that influences school climate is the unspoken **norms** and beliefs about how school personnel (including teachers, administrators, and staff) feel about and treat each other and students, and how students feel about and treat school personnel. These norms and beliefs appear in school rules and policies that regulate school curriculum and interaction patterns (Hernandez, 2004). However, the policies and practices that govern those within the school often neglect the input of all school constituents. As such, they indirectly send the message that the perspectives of students, their families, and sometimes their teachers and other staff members are devalued. Such messages often lead to distrust, disorder, dissatisfaction, and dysfunction. Consider the "message" conveyed by the practices of the school described in Case Illustration 3-2. If the teacher was feeling undervalued to the degree exhibited in the case, imagine how the students in that school might have felt!

ASSESSING SCHOOL CLIMATE

Common to most definitions of school climate are the identification of elements and characteristics that affect students' feelings of **safety** and security, levels of acceptance, expectations for success, and actual achievement outcomes within

| **Case Illustration 3-2** | **Warehouse or Schoolhouse?** |

It is my first day teaching and, needless to say, I was both excited and apprehensive. I literally received my assignment the night before school opened. As prepared as I could be with less than a 24-hour notice, I marched in the school only to find the building principal had no clue who I was or why I was there.

After a couple of calls to the personnel office, things were cleared up, and I was identified as "Oh, the new guy . . . in science!" Quite an introduction—one adding to my anxiety! But the fun didn't stop there.

I was given my room number and handed my roster without any explanation. I entered the room where I was to teach science and found that it was shared with the social studies teacher during my planning and lunch periods and had no materials, space, instruments—or anything that may suggest this was a science class. When I informed the administration of the apparent "mistake," I was told that it wasn't a mistake, that the district didn't provide science equipment to the school, and I could "just teach science using simulated experiments and other materials . . . you know, kids like videos and stuff!"

It was 90 minutes into my first day of teaching. I felt overwhelmed and hopeless. To beat it all, it seemed I was the only one who cared!

the learning environment. Ross and Lowther (2003) suggested that school climate encompasses seven dimensions: (1) **effective leadership**; (2) **order**; (3) **comfort**; (4) **parent involvement**; (5) **community involvement**; (6) **instructional programs**; and (7) the **degree of student, faculty, staff, and community cooperation and participation**. Table 3-1 provides a set of critical elements needed for the creation and maintenance of a positive school environment. These can be used both as criteria for assessment of and guideposts for improving school climates.

EFFECTS OF SCHOOL CLIMATE ON STUDENTS

When assessing school climate as a factor that affects student performance, teachers must initially consider the degree to which the environment affords students' physical and psychological safety. Research shows that schools that

Table 3-1
Critical Elements of a Positive School Environment

The following are elements that help create positive school climates:

1. Schools led by visionary leaders who can communicate and collaborate

2. Orderly schools in which students, faculty, administrators, staff, and families understand behavioral expectations established by all parties concerned

3. Schools in which all constituents feel comfortable, accepted, respected, and valued

4. Schools that genuinely and effectively involve parents and the community

5. Schools that provide instructional programs that result in academic achievement and high levels of student academic self-concept and social identity

6. Schools that boast high levels of community participation and cooperation in which all constituents regularly take part in working to identify strengths and weaknesses and improve school functioning

7. Schools that communicate high expectations for students and provide instruction that helps students meet such standards of achievement

| Case Illustration 3-3 | **Why the Snickering?** |

Jerome was a small, fair-haired sixth grader. While not very active in sports, he showed a gift for art and creative hobbies. Jerome was considered a bright student who never caused any problems. He tended to have few friends and enjoyed talking to girls about fashion, Hollywood, and television soap operas.

Jerome's previous teachers described him as a funny, energetic, and insightful student who loved to "add his own 2 cents" to every classroom discussion. This enthusiasm and high level of participation began to diminish rapidly as he moved from elementary to middle school.

Eight weeks into the school year, Jerome's teachers expressed concern over his failure to participate in class, his unwillingness to volunteer, and his frequent complaints of headaches and stomachaches accompanied by frequent requests to go see the nurse. The school counselor was invited to observe Jerome and see if perhaps there was something she could do.

What she observed was shocking. Not only did she see Jerome's peers making comments about Jerome's voice and mannerisms—implying he was a "girl" and calling him gay—but, more shocking, she saw a couple of occasions where after Jerome was "forced" to respond in class, the teachers were seen rolling their eyes and nonverbally conveying a message that displayed disapproval of Jerome's communication style. It is no wonder that Jerome, a bright and previously achieving student, was finding it easier to withdraw than to persevere.

provide safety (including safety from public ridicule and excessive criticism) facilitate student learning (Alexander & Murphy, 1998; Murphy, Weil, & McGreal, 1986), whereas students who are educated in climates in which they encounter ridicule and devaluation, especially when students attempt to participate and share their own perspectives, are unlikely to continue to take risks that decrease their involvement and result in the loss of necessary opportunities to achieve. Consider the example in Case Illustration 3-3. Clearly, ridicule, even if experienced indirectly, is damaging.

As is exhibited in the case of Jerome, the climate of a school sets the stage for encouraging or discouraging student motivation and achievement (Raviv, Raviv, & Reisel, 1993). But the impact of a school's climate affects much more than a student's level of motivation and achievement; school climate also directly affects students' self-concepts, life chances, and opportunities.

What happens when students encounter a school climate that is psychologically unsafe, rejecting, and/or alienating? What happens to the student who experiences a school climate that offers low expectations and limited opportunities for academic success? Such circumstances have an impact that engulfs one's entire educational experience and spreads well beyond the walls of the classroom and the hours of a school day.

Research (for example, Brookover, Beady, Flood, Schweitzer, & Wisenbaker, 1979) demonstrates that students' views of the importance of schooling, their academic self-concept, the presence or absence of feeling academic futility in their school environments, and the extent to which students feel alienated and/or oppositional toward school curricula and officials affect their academic achievement and social-emotional adjustment. Further, minority students who experience environments that fail to support and reinforce their diverse worldviews, experiences, and values may end up believing that in order to achieve they must reject aspects of their culture—that is, they must act more like members of dominant culture in order to be perceived as good students and be provided with opportunities to achieve in school. As Ogbu (1990) pointed out that in reference to African American students, achievement for some requires them to become more like Whites. The result of denying one's culture, in essence what is often seen as "selling out," can be devastating in terms of the students' loss of cultural identity, psychosocial wellbeing, and community connections (Fordham, 1996; Smith & Andrew, 1988; Spradlin, Welsh, & Hinson, 1999; Valentine & Lloyd, 1989).

INVOLVING MINORITY FAMILIES AND COMMUNITIES

A crucial feature for creating a positive school climate that empowers minority students and their families is the presence of effective parent and community involvement. As was noted in Chapter 2, minority students often feel alienated from schools when their families are not involved in the school's mission and execution of that mission to educate their children.

Despite the expected verbal support for parent involvement among educators and parents alike, "parents continue to be kept at a distance in most schools" (Swap, 1993, p. 13). And when communication does occur, it is typically formal and one-way, that is, from the school to home and most often as a result of a problem or crisis described by the school (Henderson, Marburger, & Ooms, 1986).

Instituting and maintaining parental involvement are not easy. Multiple barriers restrict the formation of collaborative relationships between students' homes and the school. Factors such as changing demographics that restrict the time and availability of teachers and parents alike, school norms that reflect hierarchy over reciprocity, limited resources, and a lack of knowledge about how to effectively involve and motivate parents must be addressed if parental involvement is to be actualized. Exercise 3-1 invites you to identify ways a

---

| Exercise 3-1 | Field Experience: Communicating and Inviting |

Directions: Contact the principal from a respected high school or other nearby school. Explain to the principal that you understand that schools are interested in communicating with families and inviting input into the education of their children. Explain also that you understand that being able to connect and work with families may be difficult.

1. Ask the principal to identify the primary barriers to including families and community in the process of educating students.

2. Ask the principal to describe steps he or she has found helpful in overcoming these barriers and increasing family involvement.

3. Share your findings with your instructor, your colleagues, or your classmates in small-group discussion. Then, identify common barriers and effective strategies.

school may overcome barriers to include parents and communities in the education of children.

In order to reach out and engage parents and communities, school personnel must most certainly learn to listen. It is essential that school personnel ask the question: "What can students' families tell us that will help us understand their needs and wishes so that we will know which actions increase and decrease their genuine involvement in the school's mission?" Asking this question and truly listening to the responses may help identify and address factors that currently alienate parents from schools (Goodson 1991; Swartz, 2003). Further, such a step may begin the process needed to empower students' families and include them as essential partners in the creation of a positive learning environment. Table 3-2 provides a few guidelines for facilitating this process of empowering and including families.

SOCIAL CLASS AND SCHOOL CLIMATE

Only about 1 in 10 low-income parents belong to parent–teacher organizations nationwide (Educational Testing Service, 1992). Statistics like this may mislead educators to believe that working-class, poor, and minority parents do not care about their children's education. Although class-related childrearing practices and occupational socialization (see Bronfenbrenner, 1966; Heath, 1982; Kohn, 1969, 1971; Wright & Wright, 1976) may negatively affect some families' involvement, schools are often unaware of reasons working-class and poor families may have attitudes and utilize childrearing and communication strategies that negatively affect their children's achievement. With increased understanding of low-income families' educational values and the relation of these values, ideas, and attitudes to their school participation, schools will be better able to determine ways to improve school climates.

Quite often, working-class lifestyles and values are not represented in school curricula. For many working-class families, practical and applicable skills and knowledge are highly valued. School curricula primarily reflect theoretical constructs and instructional activities that may not seem relevant to actual life and work circumstances. In addition, due to family income limitations, enrichment programs, college preparation courses, and afterschool activities may be inaccessible to poor and working-class students. Further, if school meetings and parent services offered by the school can only be accessed at times during which parents are working in jobs from which they cannot get release time or by means that may not be readily available to working-class and poor students and their families (for example, e-mail, websites), a clear, disenfranchising message is conveyed. Finally, biased testing and school accountability standards that ignore the advantage enjoyed by middle- and upper-class students have been found to further contribute to the disaffection of marginalized students and their families (Rustique-Forrester & Riley, 2001).

Schools must be charged with helping to create human capital in schools that include working-class and poor students by working collaboratively with them

Table 3-2
Empowering and
Including Parents

1. Provide for multiple levels of family participation, making sure all contact with students' families is positive, warm, respectful, and genuine. A good rule of thumb is never to ask a question of families to which you think you already know the answer. Go into communications with families with openness to learning from them and hearing new information that will be helpful to you.

2. Implement different modes of warm, inviting contact. It is helpful to develop a relationship *before* beginning any problem solving. Use various modes of communication with the families of students (for example, home visits, phone calls, e-mails, written letters) to convey your sincere interest in and positive feelings about their children.

3. Create networks that make it easy for families to be involved with the school (for example, involving families in the writing of school and classroom newsletters, asking for family input directly by phone or note before decisions are made that parents will be asked to support). When working in committee formats, be sure to share names and contact information.

4. Communicate appreciation and respect for diverse cultural values, language differences, and resources presented by students' families.

5. Be flexible and responsive to families' needs and wishes when scheduling times and locations for meetings.

6. Create ways to involve parents as equals in social arenas in which friendship and trust can form (for example, arrange bowling nights, movie weekends, school picnics).

and their communities to construct and reinforce the presentation of their perspectives in programming, curricula, policies, and practices (Coleman, 1991).

FROM CONCEPTS TO LIVED EXPERIENCE

As noted in the Preface of this book, too often texts on diversity get bogged down by an overabundance of definitions, research, theories, and statistics—at the expense of lived experience behind those definitions, theories, and statistics. The experience of a hostile, nonsupportive, devaluing school environment cannot be understated. The impact of such an environment on a student's sense of self, level of aspiration, and actual achievement can be devastating. The following personal narrative is that of a Mexican American preservice teacher who experienced firsthand and recounts what it was like to attempt to thrive in an unwelcoming educational setting. His story displays his determination to be the type of teacher that he needed most: one who truly cared.

FROM STUDENT TO TEACHER

My name is Richard, but I went through most of my school years being called names like "Bean Eater," "Wet Back," "Pedro," or something else. You see, I'm Mexican—well, more like 75 percent Mexican and 25 percent who knows what. My mother (who is 100 percent Mexican) and I moved to this town when I was 8 years old, and it has been all downhill since.

I have forgotten much of what the students I went to school with did to me. But I still remember the daily name-calling. I remember having to fight a lot: ambushes from behind, sucker punches, being held back while others pounded me. I remember being spit on. I remember a gang of laughing punks taking my books and throwing them in the toilet, and I can remember teachers, I will never forget how the teachers added to the whole problem—pointing me out as a Mexican, using me as a part of their lesson—you know, "This is what Puerto Ricans eat . . . right, Richard?" It was a joke. They had to know that kids didn't like Mexicans and made fun of me all the time. I know the teachers heard them calling me names in class. But still, they just turned their heads and acted like everything was fine with them. It killed me. If even one of them had showed that they were on my side—that they respected me—it would have saved me.

The students' relentless attacks on me began on the first day I went to school and continued until I dropped out (at 16). I never understood why they wanted to waste their time pickin' with me. I was pretty big for my age . . . and I remember I really liked math class . . . I could have played football if they didn't think I was a troublemaker. The teachers hated me because they thought I didn't care about school. Actually, I loved school at first—I loved learning new stuff—but when I tried to participate, I could hear the comments being made. I didn't know how to act, how to be, how to take it all. No one at school could see me.

When I started high school, I made myself fight back. If they gave me a dirty look, I would pop [them]. They backed off. But that's not what I really wanted. By the middle of tenth grade, I had no one to talk to at all. Not even teachers would look at me in the face anymore. They didn't see me—it was like I was invisible. I didn't exist.

That's when I said enough is enough—they don't want me, they don't want my family, they don't want to be fair, they don't want to see.

Well, you got the picture. I'm 23 years old now. I got my GED, in spite of those idiots, and I'm going to school to become a teacher. I'll listen to the kids that no one else sees. I'll be a real teacher who helps rather than harms students.

SUMMARY

The School as a Social Setting Schools are settings in which there are unique interactions, relationships, and interdependencies among all persons operating within the environment. The degree to which the school setting supports healthy, stimulating, and growth-oriented interactions and relationships strongly influences the degree to which academic achievement will occur.

School Climate Variables School climate has been described as involving four key relationships: (1) the relationship of a student to him- or herself; (2) the relationship of a student to his or her peers; (3) the relationship of a student to his or her parents and community; and (4) the relationship of a student to his or her school workers, including teachers, administrators, and staff. School climate also reflects beliefs, values, attitudes, and styles of interaction found to exist within schools.

Factors such as high expectations among school staff and students; positive treatment of students; active engagement of students and their families; and positive social relationships among students, faculty, administration, and the school community positively affect school climate.

School Climate: Impacting Students Students' views of the importance of schooling, their academic self-concept, the presence or absence of academic futility in their school environments, and the extent to which students feel alienated and/or oppositional toward school officials affect their academic achievement and social-emotional adjustment.

Involving Family and Community A crucial feature in creating a positive school climate for minority students and their families is the presence of effective, collaborative family and community involvement. Teacher attitudes toward parents and their skill in developing parent-involvement strategies are significant in creating a positive school climate.

Quite often, working-class lifestyles and values are not represented in school curricula, which contribute to the fact that only about 1 in 10 low-income parents belong to parent–teacher organizations nationwide.

Important Terms

beliefs	effective leadership	instructional programs	safety
comfort	expectations	norms	school climate
community involvement	human ecology	order	values
degree of participation	inclusion	parent involvement	warmth

Classroom Application Activities

The following are a series of field experience questions related to the topics addressed in this chapter. Share your experiences with your instructor and classmates in small-group discussion.

A. ACTIVITY 1: IDENTIFYING THE IMPACT OF SCHOOL CLIMATE

Interview four people in your life by asking them to respond to the following questions. As your review their answers, what conclusions can you draw about the effect of school climate on student learning?

1. Remember a time when you felt humiliated in a class or when participating in a school activity. How did it affect your ability to function that day? How did it affect your view of the class (or activity or school)?
2. Describe a classroom, teacher, or particular experience you had in school where you felt extremely safe and able to risk sharing your opinion, your perspectives, and your answers. What made that environment feel safe?

3. If you were to suggest to school administrators one thing they could do to make a school warm, supportive, and facilitative, what would you suggest?

After reviewing the responses, share your observations and conclusions with your instructor, your colleagues, or your classmates. Identify the degree to which the shared lived experiences reflect the concepts and research presented within this chapter.

B. ACTIVITY 2: A PARENT'S PERSPECTIVE ON SCHOOL CLIMATE

Interview three parents and ask them the following questions.

1. To what degree do you feel heard by your children's school administration, staff, and teachers?
2. What things can you identify as factors that reduce your active participation in school affairs?

3. If you were asked by faculty and administration how they might improve parental involvement in their school, what recommendations would you make?

Share your observations with your instructor, your colleagues, or your classmates, and identify

the degree to which the shared lived experiences reflect the concepts and research presented within this chapter.

Enrichment

Alvine, L., & Cullum, L. (Eds.). (1999). *Breaking the cycle: Gender, literacy, and learning, 7–12.* Peterborough, NH: Heineman Boynton-Cook.

Brookover, W.R., Beady, C., Flood, P., Schweitzer, J., & Wisenbaker, J. (1979). *School social systems*

and student achievement: Schools can make a difference. Brooklyn, NY: Praeger.

Nieto, S. (1996). *Affirming diversity: The sociopolitical context of multicultural education* (2nd ed.). White Plains, NY: Longman Publishers.

Connections on the Web

http://www.pta.org

This site offers strategies for making schools welcoming to all parents.

http://www.projectappleseed.org/

The website for Project Appleseed, the national campaign for improving public education, is an

excellent resource on improving school–community and school–parent relationships.

http://www.eyeoneducation.com/

This site is an excellent resource for books and materials on improving school and community relationships, creating positive school climates, and involving parents within the school.

REFERENCES

Aguado, T., Ballesteros, B., & Malik, B. (2003). Cultural diversity and school equity. A model to evaluate and develop educational practices in multicultural education contexts. *Equity and Excellence in Education,* 36(1), 50–63.

Alexander, P., & Murphy, P. (1998). The research base for APA's learner-centered psychological principles. In N. Lambert & B. McCombs (Eds.), *How students learn: Reforming schools through learner-centered education* (pp. 25–60). Washington, DC: American Psychological Association.

Anderson, D. C. (1998). Curriculum, culture, and community: The challenge of school violence. In M. Tonry & M. Moore (Eds.), *Youth violence* (pp. 317–363). Chicago: University of Chicago.

Banks, J. A. (1995). Multicultural education: Its effects on students' racial and gender attitudes. In J. Banks & C. A. McGeeBanks (Eds.), *Handbook of research on multicultural education* (pp. 617–627). New York: Macmillan.

Bronfenbrenner, U. (1966). Socialization and social class through time and space. In R. Bendix & S. M. Lipset (Eds.), *Class, status, and power* (pp. 239–270). New York: Free Press.

Brookover, W. R., Beady, C., Flood, P., Schweitzer, J., & Wisenbaker, J. (1979). *School social systems and student achievement: Schools can make a difference.* Brooklyn, NY: Praeger.

Coleman, J. (1991). *Parental involvement in education.* Washington, DC: U.S. Department of Education, Office of Educational Research and Improvement. (ERIC Document Reproduction Service No. ED334028)

Comer, J. (1980). *School power.* New York: Free Press.

Comer, J. (1988). *Educating poor minority children. Scientific American,* 259(5), 42–48.

Dorsey, J. (2000). Institute to end violence [Online version]. In *End School Violence.* Retrieved May 2002, from http://www.endschoolviolence.com/strategy/

Educational Testing Service. (1992). *America's smallest school: The family*. Princeton, NJ: Author.

Epstein, J. L. (1985). Parents' reactions to teacher practices of parent involvement. *Elementary School Journal, 86,* 277–294.

Epstein, J. L. (1995). School/family/community partnerships: Caring for the children we share. *Phi Delta Kappan, 76,* 701–712.

Epstein, J. L., & Becker, H. (1982). Teachers' reported practices of parent involvement: Problems and possibilities. *Elementary School Journal, 83,* 103–114.

Epstein, J. L., & Dauber, S. L. (1991). School programs and teacher practices of parent involvement in inner-city elementary and middle schools. *Elementary School Journal, 91,* 291–305.

Fordham, S. (1996). *Blacked out: Dilemmas of race, identity, and success at Capital High*. Chicago: University of Chicago.

Goodson, I. (1991). Sponsoring the teacher's voice: Teachers lives and teachers. *Cambridge Journal of Education, 21*(1), 35–46.

Gottfredson, D. (1989). Developing effective organizations to reduce school disorder. In O. Moles (Ed.), *Strategies to reduce student misbehavior* (pp. 87–104). Washington, DC: Office of Educational Research and Improvement. (ERIC Document Reproduction Service No. ED311608)

Heath, S. B. (1982). Questioning at home and at school: A comparative study. In G. Spindler (Ed.), *Doing the ethnography of schooling* (pp. 102–131). New York: Holt, Rinehart, & Winston.

Henderson, A., Marburger, C., & Ooms, T. (1986). *Beyond the bake sale: An educator's guide to working with parents*. Columbia, MD: National Committee for Citizens in Education. (ERIC Document Reproduction Service No. ED270508)

Hernandez, T. J. (2004). A safe school climate: A systemic approach and the school counselor. *Professional School Counselor, 7*(4), 256–263.

Jenkins, P. (1997). School delinquency and the school social bond. *Journal of Research in Crime and Delinquency, 34,* 31–35.

Kohn, M. (1969). *Class and conformity*. Homewood, IL: Dorsey.

Kohn, M. (1971). Social class and parent–child relationships. In M. Anderson (Ed.), *Sociology of the family* (pp. 323–338). Middlesex, UK: Penguin.

Ladson-Billings, G. (1989, May). *A tale of two teachers: Exemplars of successful pedagogy for black students*. Paper presented at the Educational Equality Project Colloquium, New York, NY.

Lewis, T., & Sugai, G. (1999). Effective behavior support: A systems approach to proactive school-wide management. *Focus on Exceptional Children, 31*(6), 1–24.

Lockwood, D. (1997). *Violence among middle school and high school students: Analysis and implications for prevention*. National Institute of Justice Research in Brief, pp. 1–9.

Murphy, J., Weil, M., & McGreal, T. (1986). The basic practice model of instruction. *Elementary School Journal, 87,* 83–95.

Nietlo, S. (1996). *Affirming diversity* (2nd ed.). White Plains, NY: Longman.

Ogbu, J. U. (1974). *The next generation: An ethnography of education in an urban neighborhood*. New York: Academic.

Ogbu, J. U. (1990). Minority education in comparative perspective. *Journal of Negro Education, 59,* 45–55.

Ogbu, J. U. (1992). Understanding cultural diversity and learning. *Educational Researcher, 21,* 5–24.

Raviv, A., Raviv, A, & Reisel, E. (1993). Environmental approach used for evaluating and educational innovation. *Journal of Educational Research, 86*(6), 317–325.

Ross, S. M., & Lowther, D. L. (2003). Impacts of the co-net school reform design on classroom instruction, school climate, and student achievement in inner-city schools. *Journal of Education for Students Placed at Risk, 8*(2), 215–246.

Rubin, B. (2006). Tracking and detracking: Debates, evidence, and best practices for a heterogeneous world. *Theory into Practice, 45*(1), 6–14.

Rustique-Forrester, E., & Riley, K. (2001) *Bringing disenfranchised young Black people back into the frame: A UK perspective on disaffection from school and the curriculum*. Paper presented at the Annual meeting of the American Educational Research Association, Seattle, WA, April 10–14.

Sherman, L. W., Gottfredson, D., MacKenzie, D., Eck, J., Reuter, P., & Bushway, S. (Eds.). (1997). *Preventing crime: What works, what doesn't, what's promising*. Washington, DC: U.S. Department of Justice, Office of Justice Programs.

Shields, P. M. (1989). Federal mandates for citizen participation: The case of parents and compensatory education. *Dissertation Abstracts International, 50*(6), 1490A.

Shields, P. M., & McLaughlin, M. W. (1986, May). *Parent involvement in compensatory education programs* (Center for Educational Research at Stanford Report No. 87-CERAS-6). Stanford, CA: Stanford University.

Smith, K. L., & Andrew, L. D. (1988, April). *An explanation of the beliefs, values, and attitudes of black students in Fairfax County.* Paper presented at the annual meeting of the American Educational Research Association, New Orleans.

Spradlin, L. K., Welsh, L. A., & Hinson, S. L. (1999). Exploring African American Academic Achievement: Ogbu and Brookover Perspectives. *Journal of African American Men, 12,* 17–32.

Spradlin, L. K. (1999). Taking black girls seriously: Addressing discrimination's double bind. In L. Alvine & L.Cullum (Eds.), *Breaking the cycle: Gender, literacy, and learning, 7–12.* Peterborough, NH: Heineman Boynton-Cook.

Stockard, J., & Mayberry, M. (1992). *Effective educational environments.* Newbury Park, CA: Corwin.

Sugai, G., & Horner, R. (2002). Introduction to the special services support in schools on positive behavior. *Journal of Emotional and Behavioral Disorders 10*(3), 130–136.

Swap, S. M. (1993). *Developing home-school partnerships: From concepts to practice.* New York: Teachers College.

Swartz, E. (2003). Teaching white preservice teachers: Pedagogy for change. *Urban Educaton 38*(3), 255–278.

Tatum, B. D. (1997). *"Why are all the black kids sitting together in the cafeteria?" and other conversations about race: A psychologist explains the development of racial identity.* New York: Basic Books.

Thompson, A. (1998). Not the color purple: Black feminist lessons for educational caring. *Harvard Educational Review, 68,* 522–554.

Valentine, P., & Lloyd, A. (1989, March). *Living in Franklin Square: An exploration of black culture.* Paper presented at the annual meeting of the American Educational Research Association, San Francisco.

Welsh, W. (2000). The effects of school climate on school disorder. *Annals of the American Academy of Political and Social Science, 567,* 88–107.

Wright, J. D., & Wright, S. R. (1976, June). Social class and parental values for children: A partial replication and extension of the Kohn thesis. *American Sociological Review, 41,* 527–537.

The true aim of everyone who aspires to be a teacher should be not to impart his own opinions, but to kindle minds.

Frederick William Robertson

The Classroom Teacher

CHAPTER **4**

A Powerful Influence

Most of us agree that kindling minds is a noble goal for educators, yet education does not always result in empowered students with liberated minds. Teachers' knowledge, skill, and personal qualities can serve as inspirations—as models for all students in their classes—or they can serve as major causes for the death of spirit, the loss of inquiry, and students' questioning of self.

While each teacher in training has been taught the necessity of instructional expertise and content knowledge, it is important to remember that teachers are more than transmitters of information (Cochran-Smith, 2004; Delpit, 1995). They provide the stimuli for developing student interest; implement strategies that enliven concepts; and supply counsel for those with concerns, guidance for those seeking direction, and support for all students during the process of their education.

The expectation that teachers be available to students for intellectual and emotional guidance can be daunting when one realizes that all messages conveyed through teachers' language, actions, and even lack of action prove to be powerful influences on their students. Teaching is an awesome experience, and being a teacher is an awesome responsibility—one that demands more than simply depositing information. "Real learning does not happen until students are brought into relationship with the teacher, with each other, and with the subject" (Palmer, 1993, p. xvi).

This chapter explores teacher qualities and behaviors that affect student achievement and social adjustment in the classroom.

CHAPTER OBJECTIVES

1. Describe teacher qualities that affect student achievement.
2. Describe teacher qualities that encourage student psychosocial adjustment.

3. Define self-efficacy.
4. Describe the ways a teacher can demonstrate value for students.
5. Describe qualities needed to effectively facilitate the learning and development of minority students.

MORE THAN CONTENT KNOWLEDGE OR PEDAGOGICAL SKILLS

Expert teachers most certainly have a command of their subject area, but, in addition to being a storehouse of knowledge, expert teachers have effective systems for understanding the process of and problems encountered in teaching and learning. For example, effective teachers are adaptable and flexible in their approaches. They can adjust lesson plans, knowing they are but one road map to desired learning outcomes. The expert teacher understands there is more than one way to approach a topic, develop a test, and engage students in the learning process.

In addition to having pedagogical and **content expertise,** expert teachers have specific personal qualities and interpersonal skills that contribute to their effectiveness (see Entwistle & Tait, 1990; Lowman & Mathie, 1993; Ramsden, 1992; Swartz, White, & Stuck, 1990). Successful teachers are able to establish **interpersonal rapport,** exhibit enthusiasm, and demonstrate respect for their students. Along with comprehensive knowledge of learner development, teachers must acquire knowledge of diversity and intercultural competence in order to meet the educational needs of students.

VALUING SELF-AWARENESS AND REFLECTION

It is obvious that effective teachers must have knowledge of cultural diversity. They will most likely employ diverse curricula that include and recognize diverse perspectives, histories, and contributions coming from members of marginalized groups. However, to truly be effective, more than a comprehensive knowledge of diversity topics and subject matter is required.

Teachers' self-reflection and development of **cultural consciousness** are imperative for improving the educational opportunities and outcomes for minority students (Gay & Kirkland, 2003). To be effective in multicultural classrooms, teachers must be committed to becoming more aware of who they are as people and what they believe, including being willing to identify and question their cultural assumptions (Gay, 2002; Ladson-Billings, 2001). Without reflecting on one's own perspectives, biases, and relative position in society, little more than good intentions to value diversity can be delivered. Case Illustration 4-1 provides a clear example of a young, White, male teacher coming to grips with the impact of his biases, assumptions, and insulated consciousness.

While Louis's experience is certainly unique to him and his specific background, it is important to realize that all teachers have preconceived ideas about issues of race, disability, sexual orientation, ethnicity, gender, and class.

Case Illustration 4-1 | Louis: One Teacher's Reflections on Personal Assumptions and Attitudes

I remember the day. It was my first teaching job— just out of college and eager to make a major impact on my students. During my senior year, I had toyed with the idea of joining the peace corps or perhaps teaching in a poor rural area. It was my social justice sensibility, my responsibility—or at least that's what I kept telling myself. Well, as things turned out, I took a job in an upper-middle-class, suburban district.

I really thought I was a person that was culturally sensitive who valued diversity, and as such I decorated my room to reflect the various cultures I knew about. While the school had been almost exclusively White for many years, a recent redistricting resulted in the inclusion of African American and Asian American students. On my first day of class, I noticed that Cassie was the only Asian student in my homeroom. Cassie was an attractive student, dressed in jeans and a tee shirt, physically perhaps a bit less mature-looking than the other girls in class. Cassie was polite in homeroom but tended to keep to herself. When the homeroom had a lively discussion about a possible nickname and logo (a tradition at this school), I noticed that Cassie barely participated.

Concerned, I went out of my way to alert the school counselor about Cassie's apparent social exclusion. I also decided to try to intervene myself, and given Cassie's studious nature, I contacted the yearbook advisor to see if perhaps he could reach out to Cassie, thinking that writing for the yearbook staff would provide her with an entry into some social contact with others in the school. Finally, I contacted Cassie's mother to set up a meeting to share my concern, and that's when the reality—of my bias—hit me square in the face.

In conversation with Cassie's mother, I shared my concern about [Cassie's] apparent inability to fit in with her peers in homeroom. I invited her [mother]

to come in and talk with me so that I could better understand what life was like for Cassie. Cassie's mother was almost saintly in her restraint. She listened to me, she thanked me for my concern, and then she asked me if I also wanted her husband to come to the meeting. I know it's a silly thing, but I didn't even think about a two-parent family. I presumed Cassie lived in a poor area that had recently started busing students to the school. When I said certainly, she stated that her husband's schedule was pretty open because he owned his own business but that she would have to check with her secretary to see what her court docket looked like before committing to a date. Owned a business? Court docket? I just assumed Cassie was one of the children from the redistricted area. But my wake-up call came when she informed me that Cassie was, in fact, very involved in school and had always been— her activities had become excessive during the last two years. She was a member of the chess club, sang in the chorus, ran cross-country, played volleyball and soccer, and in the spring, she was almost always in the school play. She stated that last year Cassie had a lot of friends at school and was elected homeroom representative. She shared that Cassie's idea this year was to lay low in homeroom because she didn't want to be elected again, and she didn't want to have to say "no" and disappoint people.

Sensing my embarrassment, she asked whether I still wanted to see her and her husband. I told her that I looked forward to meeting the two of them but felt that it could wait until the first scheduled parent– teacher conference. I was finally coming to terms with what I didn't know about diversity and how stupid I must have looked to her. I have used this experience to keep me from making judgments about any of my students. Now, I talk directly to students for whom I have concern to find out what they're thinking. I'm a better teacher for it.

Like any other prejudices, these beliefs and attitudes will be exhibited in their actions and practices. In this case, Louis's actions, well-intended as they might have been, were neither appreciated nor would they prove helpful in that they were based solely on his biased assumption that a quiet, Asian American student in a classroom of White students must be intimidated, socially isolated, poor, and in need of "rescue."

Pohan (1996) noted, "[D]ifferential **expectations** lead to differential treatment, which results in differential student outcomes" (p. 5). Teacher beliefs influence the type of activities in which students are engaged, the feedback students receive, and the degree of interaction that takes place between teachers and students. It is, therefore, important to examine teachers' beliefs and the effects of these beliefs on classroom practices and most importantly, the academic achievement of their students (Jones, 2004).

A number of researchers have suggested the importance of personal reflection and self-assessment for working effectively with culturally diverse students. Gorski (1997), for example, called for teachers to reflect on their experiences and assess their attitudes, prejudices, and values as they relate to dealing with people from different ethnic groups. Banks and colleagues (2001) noted that in order for teachers to respond sensitively to the cultural diversity in their classrooms, they must look first at their own cultural backgrounds and understand how their biases affect their interactions with students. It is clear that to be effective, teachers need to develop a personal and professional code of ethics and **critical consciousness** related to race, gender, social class, sexual orientation, and ethnic diversity. Only through the development of such a code of ethics and heightened consciousness will they be able to develop intercultural competence and culturally responsive teaching (Exposito & Favela, 2003; Gay & Kirkland, 2003).

An excellent example of this type of reflection has been offered by Frank (2002), a White, middle-class female in U.S. society. Frank noted that her attitudes, behaviors, and words needed to reflect and embody humanity, not just those who "looked" like her. Frank described how she opened herself to the challenges offered by others who were not like her. Challenges not only to her thinking and her assumptions but also to her behavior were addressed to provide her with cultural insight. She highlighted the importance of under-standing who she is, not just in terms of labels but also in terms of her relative place in society and the privileges it affords. Exercise 4-1 will help you begin this process of self-reflection.

RACIAL IDENTITY DEVELOPMENT

Frank's (2002) reflections are poignant. They also are prescriptive in that they remind us that teachers must reflect on their own racial identities and how they are affected by racism in society (see Chapter 1, Tables 1-1 & 1-2). And, while the stages of racial identity development do not necessarily occur chronologically or in a strict linear fashion, as noted in Chapter 1, they are believed to include most racial interaction patterns involving minority group members and

Exercise 4-1	**Classroom Applications: Roundtable Feedback**

Directions: In groups of eight students or less, sit in a circle with your group members. Review the following guidelines before you begin the discussion.

Discussion Guidelines:

1. A group member volunteers to share an issue of concern for her/him related to diversity (for example, "I don't know much about people from different groups. I fear I will not be an effective teacher of diverse students because of this," or "I am not patient when I hear accents that are different from my own. I find myself tuning out and even thinking negatively about people who speak with an accent.").

2. That same group member shares his/her concern and then asks the group for specific feedback related to the concern (for example, "I would like to know what you would think of a teacher who does not have much experience with diversity," or "Please give me suggestions to help me change this behavior.").

3. Before other members of the group provide the feedback requested, they may each ask one question to clarify the request and make sure they will provide the feedback requested. During this go-round at which members seek clarification about the request for feedback, the group member with the concern answers the questions posed as succinctly as possible and does not add additional information that is not queried.

4. After the clarification round is complete, each group member provides the feedback requested

in as honest and yet constructive manner as possible. It is helpful to begin by saying, "If I were experiencing this concern, I would . . ." or "If I encountered this behavior, I'd feel distanced from that person because . . .," and so on.

5. *It is very important that the person who is seeking the feedback NOT be allowed to comment as each group member provides her/his feedback.* No questions may be asked at this point, and no responses to the feedback may be given. The only activity that should go on at this point is each member sharing honestly and sensitively while the person who is seeking feedback silently listens and writes down what is communicated.

6. After all group members have provided feedback, the person seeking feedback should respond to all the feedback provided. Using the notes he or she took as each group member provided feedback, the person seeking feedback should first thank the group for taking time and energy to think about and respond honestly to her/his concern and then tell each member how he or she intends to use the feedback provided.

This activity will take at least 40 minutes to complete. In order for each person in the group to have an opportunity to experience this wonderful opportunity to gain self-reflection and feedback utilization skills, this activity should be repeated enough times throughout the semester that every group member has an opportunity to share a concern.

dominant culture in the United States. It is, therefore, another factor that affects differences in teachers' comfort levels and abilities to interact effectively with students from different racial groups (Adams, 1997). As such, it is recommended that teachers reflect on their own evolution through the racial identity development models (be they members of dominant or minority groups) as they seek to discover their own intercultural strengths and limitations. The value of reflection on racial attitudes and one's racial consciousness is immense. It provides teachers increasingly more awareness of what they feel and believe in relation to student diversity, where these thoughts and feelings might come from, what realities of humanity are not seen, and what privileges are given to some individuals yet denied to others (Frank, 2002). This value of self-reflection is reinforced in Exercise 4-2.

| Exercise 4-2 | Classroom Application: The Value of Reflection |

Directions: As noted, it is important to understand who you are, not just in terms of labels but in terms of your relative position in U.S. society and the privileges and advantages that you experience based on that position. The goal of this exercise is not to create guilt or embarrass you but to help you become more aware and sensitive to what is given freely to you and denied to others who are different from you.

1. In the chart you will find a listing of identity categories. Identify how you fit within each category and then identify one of the social benefits that may accompany each characteristic. Share your reflections with someone who is culturally different from you.

Category	Your Personal Identification	What Benefits Are Afforded?	What Challenges or Disadvantages Are Encountered?
Gender			
Social class			
Profession			
Cultural background			
Physical stature (height/weight)			
Skin color			
Ethnicity			
Educational background			
Couple status			

Exercise 4-2	Continued

Category	Your Personal Identification	What Benefits Are Afforded?	What Challenges or Disadvantages Are Encountered?
Sexual orientation			
Age			
Disability status			
Language(s) spoken			

2. After completing the first two columns, go back and identify challenges or disadvantages that you experience and feelings you have that are associated with these disadvantages. Consider what you would want teachers to know and do to address the disadvantages you have identified.

MEANS OF INFLUENCE

Modeling High Self-Efficacy and Enthusiasm

Having a belief in one's competence as a teacher also can positively affect teacher effectiveness and student achievement (Bruning, Schraw, & Ronning, 1995). This sense of personal competence within the field of education has been termed *self-efficacy* (Bandura, 1977). According to Bandura (1977), high self-efficacy is a function of a person's belief (1) that he/she can successfully perform behavior required to produce desired goals and (2) that one's behaviors will lead to desired outcomes.

Teachers with high levels of teaching efficacy increase student achievement. Teachers with high self-efficacy model a belief in their abilities and success. In so doing, they take responsibility for the learning process and outcomes and invest in continuous reflection, problem-solving, and improvement strategies as they strive for teaching excellence. These teachers demonstrate the ability to review their performance, not only believing "I can do better" but also implementing plans for improvement. When teachers systematically evaluate the success of their strategies and then create new strategies to improve their outcomes that are continually monitored and assessed, they are conducting *action research* (Sagor, 1992; Stringer, 1999). This is a powerful tool and aspect of effective reflection and teacher self-efficacy that can be modeled for students.

Teachers with high self-efficacy hold positive expectations for their students. They generally offer abundant praise rather than criticism, do not lose hope or reduce their expectations for low-achieving students, and are generally student centered—effectively engaging learners in the active construction of their own knowledge (Kagan, 1992). Further, high self-efficacy teachers tend to be flexible and adaptable in employing curriculum materials and developing lesson strategies (Poole, Okeafor, & Sloan, 1989). Not only do these strategies promote greater student achievement, but the modeling of self-efficacy also serves to facilitate students' development of their own levels of self-efficacy within classrooms in which it is exhibited (Schunk, 1990, 1991), whereas teachers expressing low self-efficacy and expectations for students can inadvertently confirm students' predictions of their own limited abilities and thus lend to students' lack of motivation and limited success (Weinstein, 1998). Another potential outgrowth of self-efficacy is the development of intercultural competence. If teachers assess their outcomes and find that they are unprepared to understand and proactively address diversity in their classrooms, they will seek knowledge of and experience with diversity, which will lead to their intercultural competence over time.

In addition, a natural outgrowth of high self-efficacy is **enthusiasm** for the subject matter one teaches. Self-efficacious teachers are enthusiastic about their lessons—and expect their students to learn. Brophy and Evertson (1976) found that successful teachers see teaching as an interesting and worthwhile challenge. They embrace problems as they arise and believe solutions can be found, whereas teachers with low self-efficacy see teaching as a chore to be endured—a dull and often unpleasant job requiring patience (waiting for students to finally catch on) rather than enthusiastically seeking new ways to reach students. When confronted with difficulties, these teachers often give up, shedding the responsibility for student learning and blaming their students for not learning. These teachers do not believe they can make a difference, have generally low expectations (particularly for low-achieving students), and as a result exhibit little enthusiasm for engaging in the process of teaching and reaching students.

The idea that enthusiasm can be "catching" certainly applies to classroom dynamics. Research suggests that teachers who are enthusiastic about their subjects not only increase student achievement but also facilitate their students' enthusiasm in the learning process, sense of self-confidence, and self-efficacy (Perry, 1985; Perry, Magnusson, Parsonson, & Dickens, 1986).

The value of teacher self-efficacy and enthusiasm as it relates to student motivation and academic self-concept is highlighted in Case Illustration 4-2, the story of Annesah, an Indian writer working in northern California.

CARE AND CONCERN

As highlighted in the previous chapter, research has demonstrated that students tend to be motivated and to achieve at higher levels when they are educated in safe, trustworthy, and supportive environments, with teachers who exhibit care

Case Illustration 4-2 | # Annesah: Enthusiasm and Efficacy

I was never really a star student. I did okay. I was one of the kids that went through school doing the minimum, never a problem or a concern . . . just not investing much of myself in the process of learning. School wasn't my thing.

Well, at least not for the first eight years! Now with my master's in English and working for a large newspaper on the West Coast as a freelance writer, I guess writing and education *is* my thing, and I owe it all to Mr. Peter Duncan, my ninth-grade English teacher.

Mr. Duncan was hard—real hard. He gave us lots of vocabulary words to master every evening, he made us produce essays weekly, and each marking period he assigned extensive research papers. Mr. Duncan was very hard, and he would accept nothing but our best. Hand in something that was done at the last minute? He would smile, thank you for the "draft," and assign a new deadline for the finished product. We all became familiar with the "draft," and while we moaned and groaned, I would bet there is not one of his students who doesn't think he was the greatest.

Mr. Duncan had excellent credentials. He also had 15 years of teaching experience when I first met him. But, truthfully, it wasn't his knowledge or his competence in presenting lessons that opened my heart and mind to the joy of writing. It was his enthusiasm.

Mr. Duncan would light up whenever he read a well-written passage. He would become really excited when a student would incorporate word play or skillfully employ a fitting metaphor. It was impossible not to be excited in his class. It wasn't an act. He was so genuine and into it. It was a privilege to attend his classes, although I didn't realize that then. You could tell that he loved literature; he loved poetry and well-written prose. But, most importantly, he loved to watch us grow! He loved to challenge us to greater achievement and would encourage and support us along the way, using a myriad of creative projects, including field trips, plays, and music.

Mr. Duncan's enthusiasm inspired us. He would celebrate our rewrites, he would extol our accomplishments, and he would publicly affirm our efforts. But for me, the most important thing he did was to simply believe in me. He saw in me the ability to express myself and my view of the world in words well before I knew who I was or what my worldview entailed. He saw me before I saw myself, and his excitement in my discoveries made me want to discover that much more.

Mr. Duncan was more than a competent teacher—he was a man who loved his profession, loved his subject area, and loved sharing it. I benefited, to say the very least!

and concern for them individually (McCombs, 1998; Brown & Atkins, 1993). Effective teachers realize and value the fact that they do not teach mathematics or literature or social studies; instead, they teach *students*. These teachers value the uniqueness of each student and are committed to their students' growth and development. They are teachers who (1) show respect, (2) value individuality, (3) understand students' learning styles and barriers, (4) extend themselves to find ways to engage students in learning, and (5) go the extra mile to let students know they want to authentically join with them as partners in their own education (Bosworth, 1995). Effective teachers maintain and continually develop these personal characteristics in efforts to help their students connect with them, other students, and the subject matter taught (Black & Howard-Jones, 2000). Exercise 4-3 operationalizes these qualities and invites you to reflect on your own experience with caring teachers.

| Exercise 4-3 | **Point of Reflection: A Caring Teacher** |

Directions: The purpose of this brief exercise is to help you connect your personal experience to the concept and value of caring as a teacher trait. The exercise is best performed with a partner/classmate.

1. As quickly as possible, attempt to identify, by name and grade, five teachers you had in your K–12 education.
2. Using a scale of 1 to 10, with 1 indicating "least effective" and 10 indicating "most effective," assess each of the teachers listed on a scale of teacher effectiveness.
3. For each of the following, identify a teacher who best represents the statement.
   a. This teacher would spend time outside of class getting to know students.
   b. This teacher would make time to ask how students were.
   c. This teacher would praise students for their efforts.
   d. This teacher would make sure students knew that their contributions were valuable, even when their responses to academic questions were incorrect.
   e. This teacher would use soft reprimands (private) rather than publicly reprimanding students for misbehavior.
   f. This teacher seemed to know what students were saying even when they struggled to "get it out" when they participated in class.
   g. In class discussion, this teacher tried to encourage all ideas and perspectives on issues discussed.
   h. This teacher showed little favoritism based on gender, class, race, disability, sexual orientation, or ethnicity.
   i. Even when correcting students, this teacher made them feel that it was their behavior, not the students as people, that was being corrected.
4. Did you notice that one or two teachers' names kept appearing on your list? Were the names that appeared most often also teachers with higher effectiveness scores? The items listed in #3 are characteristics of a caring teacher. Share your observations with your instructor and classmates in small-group discussion and see if their "caring teachers" were also those identified as most effective. Then list qualities you have already that will lead to your becoming a caring teacher.

For Further Reflection

Obtain and view the movie *Stand and Deliver*. Write a reflection about what you learned regarding caring and effective teacher attitudes and actions from Jaime Escalante as his true-life story is depicted in the movie.

RESPECT FOR AND VALUE OF STUDENTS

Research (for example, Entwistle & Tait, 1990; Evans, 2002; Patrick & Smart, 1998) suggests that effective teachers are not only highly organized and challenging but also genuinely respect their students and treat them as partners. While recognizing a clear distinction in terms of roles, responsibilities, knowledge, and skills, effective teachers are able to value students as co-equal human beings sharing in the process of their academic and social development.

Such valuing requires that teachers demonstrate a deep **nonevaluative respect** for the thoughts, feelings, and potential of each student. Certainly a teacher who uses sarcasm and/or in any other way makes fun of or makes a "lesson" of students at students' social and emotional expense does not value the humanity of students. When classroom correction is necessary, the focus and process of these activities should be shaped by caring and respect for students. Every way a teacher reprimands students should have as its goal the fostering of growth and learning within students. These behaviors should never be used to punish but rather should be used to teach self-control, human compassion, and respect for others. Exercise 4-4 will provide you with an opportunity to observe valuing in action.

McDermott and Rothenberg (2000), in studying the characteristics of exemplary teachers in low-income urban schools, found effective urban teachers to be those who construct respectful and trusting relationships with students and their families. In their study, effective teachers valued students' ideas. This valuing was demonstrated in the way they accommodated students' input in the teaching process.

In order to build a trusting, respectful relationship, teachers must understand the individuality of each student and vital teacher–learner relationship dynamics (McDiarmid, 1991). One interesting approach to developing this understanding was described by Giroux (1993). Giroux suggested that teachers must listen critically to the voices of their students. He noted that "teachers become **border-crossers** through their ability to not only make different narratives available to themselves and other students but also by legitimating difference as a basic condition for understanding the limits of one's own voice" (p. 170). Both teachers and students benefit from this process of "border-crossing" by encountering different perspectives and therefore expanding their knowledge of others and their worldviews.

FROM CONCEPTS TO LIVED EXPERIENCE

With knowledge and skill, the classroom teacher can influence, should influence, the lives of those in his or her charge. But sometimes, perhaps most of the time, it is not the knowledge or the skill that most affects students. It is the very person of the teacher and the values he or she embodies that reaches students. We may never be sure of the impact teachers have, but if you are committed to developing your self-efficacy, you may experience something similar to that shared by the following White, male college professor.

A PROFESSOR'S REFLECTION

In 1968, I graduated from college and found myself teaching U.S. history in an urban high school. I'm embarrassed to say that I was always only one chapter ahead of the students I was teaching. Like many novice teachers, I simply wasn't prepared to effectively teach my subject matter on a daily basis. Later I obtained a job teaching high school psychology that also required me to develop a psychology program for this school—and so began my career as a psychology teacher.

Fast forward to 2004! No longer teaching in high school, I have for many years been privileged to work in a university setting. I have been able to teach, research, and write. But as most professors will report, I never really knew day to day if I was having an impact on my students.

| Exercise 4-4 | Valuing in Action |

Directions: The following exercise will require classroom observations. In the table listing teacher behaviors, Column A has a listing of behaviors that reflect a valuing and respectful approach to teacher–student relationships. Observe a teacher in class for approximately 30 minutes. As you observe the teacher interacting with his/her students, keep a tally of the frequency with which the teacher exhibits each of the behaviors listed in Column A. Keep your tally (check marks) in Column B to record the frequency with which you observe such behaviors.

In addition to keeping a frequency count of these behaviors, write down your observations of the general atmosphere and climate of the classroom, as well as the level of student participation (for example, Are all children engaged, active, interactive? Is the energy level high? Low?).

Compare in small-group discussion your observations with those of a classmate who observed another class and teacher. In reviewing your data, does there appear to be any connection between the degree to which a teacher exhibits signs of respect and valuing and the level of engagement of her/his students? Describe (in writing) why you feel that may be the case.

Column A: Teacher Behaviors and Reactions	Column B: Frequency with which the Behaviors Were Observed
Invites students to share ideas	
Takes time to listen to students' questions and responses and checks to see that he/she (the teacher) accurately understands what is being conveyed	
Corrects behavior and responses in a nonjudgmental way	
Provides evidence of respecting student feelings (list an example that you observed)	
Provides evidence of respecting different perspectives and orientations (list an example that you observed)	
Reminds students within the class to be respectful to other students (for example, to listen, to not make sarcastic or evaluative comments about other students)	

One day, returning to my office after class, I opened an e-mail from a professor at a major university in the Midwest. The professor introduced himself and went on to ask me about some research I had done a number of years back. I wrote him back explaining my research and giving him permission to use it. Well, I thought that was nice, affirming, supportive, kind of made my day. But the best was yet to come!

This professor, now occupying an endowed chair and quite recognized in his field, sent me a little thank-you e-mail and added the following P.S.:

"This may sound a bit strange, but if you are the same person who taught me psychology in high school back in 1970, I have to tell you that you changed my life!"

Changed his life? Wow! Pick me up off the floor!

He went on to say that it wasn't so much the brilliance of my lesson plans but the fact that I made him feel as if I cared for him and believed in him. He said [that] prior to having me as a teacher, his experiences in school always made him feel dumb. He began to believe he would never amount to anything, doomed to be a failure, but as he explained, "You always gave me encouragement . . . never gave up on me . . . made me feel like my answers, my work, even my effort were important contributions to the class. As I sat in your class, I began to think about doing the same thing someday. I knew there were other kids feeling as I did, and I knew that a teacher who really cared and valued each student could make a difference. I wanted to do that for some other student, and that's why I went on to college and my doctoral program. It was amazing. You let me know I was important and had something to offer, and I believed you."

He ended by saying, "Well, I really have no way of saying thanks, other than I hope to 'pay it forward' and will continue to work to make a difference in my students' lives like you did for me."

SUMMARY

More than Content Knowledge or Pedagogical Skills In addition to exhibiting content and pedagogical expertise, expert teachers are described as having specific personal qualities and interpersonal skills that contribute to their effectiveness. Successful teachers are able to establish interpersonal rapport with their students, exhibit enthusiasm, and demonstrate respect for their students. These qualities, along with an awareness of personal values and assumptions about different cultural backgrounds, are essential for those teaching in diverse classrooms.

Valuing Self-Awareness and Reflection To be effective, teachers must know and be interested in becoming more aware of who they are as people and what they believe, including the identification and questioning of their biases and assumptions. Otherwise, their differential expectations for students will lead to differential treatment, which results in differential student outcomes. In order for teachers to respond sensitively to the cultural diversity in their classrooms, they must first look at their own cultural backgrounds and understand how their biases affect their interactions with students.

Modeling High Self-Efficacy and Enthusiasm Having a belief in one's competence as a teacher (that is, self-efficacy) helps teachers positively affect student attitudes and achievement. Teachers with high self-efficacy hold positive expectations for their students. They generally utilize praise rather than criticism, do not lose hope or reduce expectations for low-achieving students, and are generally student-centered—effectively engaging students in the construction of their own knowledge. Not only does this promote greater student achievement but also teachers are able to model self-efficacy, which serves to facilitate the students' development of their own levels of self-efficacy as learners.

Teacher Care and Concern Research has demonstrated that students tend to be more motivated and as a result more achieving when they are educated in safe, trustworthy, and supportive environments, with teachers who exhibit care and concern for them as individual students.

Respect and Value for Students Effective teachers value students as co-equal human beings sharing in the process of education. Such valuing requires a teacher to demonstrate a deep nonjudgmental respect for the thoughts, feelings, and potentials that each student brings to the classroom.

Important Terms

border-crossers	cultural consciousness	interpersonal rapport	self-awareness
content expertise	differential expectations	nonevaluative respect	self-efficacy
critical consciousness	enthusiasm	pedagogical expertise	

Classroom Application Activity

The teacher is certainly a powerful force in a student's academic development and the formation of a child's sense of personal efficacy and worth. Quite often, the teacher selects and employs strategies and behaviors to give shape to students' academic achievement and sense of self. Sometimes, these influences are less clear and intentional to the teacher who manifests them. The following are a series of field-experience questions related to the topics addressed in this chapter. Use them to guide a classroom observation. Share your experience with your instructor and classmates in small-group discussion.

1. In observing a classroom, imagine yourself in the place of various children within that class. How do you feel as the smart student? The student failing to know the answers to questions? The talkative student? The minority student?
2. How are warmth and caring demonstrated or not demonstrated in the classroom? Are teacher warmth and caring dependent on performance or given freely to all students?
3. How does the teacher respond to challenges coming from students? How does the teacher handle difference of opinions in the classroom?
4. How is teacher enthusiasm expressed or not? Is enthusiasm tied to material? Content? Teaching activity? What effect does the teacher's level of enthusiasm have on the students? Is it "catching"?
5. How does the teacher model self-efficacy? How does the teacher reinforce signs of student self-efficacy?

Enrichment

Bucher, R. D. (2000). *Diversity consciousness: Opening our minds to people, cultures, and opportunities*. Upper Saddle River, NJ: Prentice Hall.

Howard, G. R. (1999). *We can't teach what we don't know: White teachers, multiracial schools*. New York: Teachers College.

Tatum, B. D. (1997). *"Why are all the black kids sitting together in the cafeteria?" and other conversations about race. A psychologist explains the development of racial identity*. New York: Basic Books.

Connections on the Web

http://ncee.education.ucsb.edu/discussionareas.htm

> The National Coalition for Equity in Education provides information on classroom practice, curricula, and climate as they impact equity in education.

http://www.nwrel.org/request/oct00/textonly.html

> This booklet from the Northwest Regional Educational Laboratory provides insight into the role of

teacher and factors in teaching that influence achievement.

http://web.syr.edu/~jlbirkla/kb/s_webres.html

> This site contains an annotated bibliography on social learning theory and self-efficacy.

REFERENCES

Adams, M. (1997). Pedagogical frameworks for social justice education. In M. Adams, L. A. Bell, & P. Griffin (Eds.), *Teaching for diversity and social justice: A sourcebook*. New York: Routledge.

Bandura, A. (1977). Self-Efficacy: Toward a unifying theory of behavioral change. *Psychological Review, 84,* 191–215.

Banks, J. A., Cookson, P., Gay, G., Hawley, W. D., Irvine, J. J., Nieto, S., et al. (2001). Diversity within unity: Essential principles for teaching and learning in a multicultural society. *Phi Delta Kappan, 83*(3), 196–203.

Black, R. S., & Howard-Jones, A. (2000). Reflections on best and worst teachers: An experiential perspective of teaching. *Journal of Research and Development in Education, 34*(1), 1–13.

Bosworth, K. (1995). Caring for others and being cared for: Students talk about caring in school. *Phi Delta Kappan, 76,* 686–693.

Brophy, J., & Evertson, C. (1976). *Learning from teaching: A developmental perspective.* Boston: Allyn & Bacon.

Brown, G., & Atkins, M. (1993). *Effective teaching in higher education.* London: Routledge.

Bruning, R., Schraw, G., & Ronning, R. (1995). *Cognitive psychology and instruction* (2nd ed.). Upper Saddle River, NJ: Prentice Hall.

Cochran-Smith, M. (2004). *Walking the road: Race, diversity, and social justice in teacher education.* New York: Teachers College.

Delpit, L. (1995). *Other people's children: Cultural conflict in the classroom.* New York: New Press.

Entwistle, N. J., & Tait, H. (1990). Approaches to learning, evaluations of teaching, and preferences for contrasting academic environments. *Higher Education, 19,* 169–194.

Evans, J. F. (2002). Effective teachers: An investigation from the perspectives of elementary school students. *Action in Teacher Education, 24*(3), 51–62.

Exposito, S., & Favela, A. (2003). Reflective voices: Valuing immigrant students and teaching with ideological clarity. *Urban Review, 35*(1), 73–91.

Frank, J. L. H. (2002). My voice is changing. *Multicultural Perspectives, 4*(1), 41–44.

Gay, G. (2002). Preparing for culturally responsive teaching. *Journal of Teacher Education, 53*(2), 106–116.

Gay, G., & Kirkland, K. (2003). Developing cultural critical consciousness and self-reflection in preservice teacher education. *Theory into Practice, 42*(3), 109–135.

Giroux, H. (1993). *Border crossings.* New York: Routledge.

Giroux, H. (1999). Rewriting the discourse of racial identity: Toward a pedagogy and politics of whiteness. In C. Clark & J. O'Donnell (Eds.), Becoming and unbecoming white (pp. 224–252). Westport, CT: Bergin & Garvey.

Gorski, P. (1997). *Initial thoughts on multicultural education-multicultural pavilion.* New York: Macmillan.

Helms, J. E. (1995). An update of Helm's White and people of color racial identity development. In J. G. Ponterotto, J. M. Casas, L. A. Suzuki, & C. M. Alexander (Eds.), *Handbook of multicultural counseling* (pp. 181–198). Thousand Oaks, CA: Sage.

Jones, H. (2004, March). A research-based approach to teaching to diversity. *Instructional Psychology, 31*(1), 18–25.

Kagan, D. (1992). Professional growth among preservice and beginning teachers. *Review of Educational Research, 62,* 129–169.

Ladson-Billings, G. (2001). *Crossing over to Canaan: The journey of new teachers in diverse classrooms.* San Francisco: Jossey Bass.

Lowman, J., & Mathie, V. A. (1993). What should graduate teaching assistants know about teaching? *Teaching of Psychology, 20,* 84–88.

McAvin, M. W., & Gordon, L. V. (1981, October). Attributions of interpersonal values and teaching effectiveness. *Psychological Reports, 49*(2), 539–542.

McCombs, R. (1998). Integrating metacognition, affect, and motivation in improving teacher education. In N. Lambert & B. McCombs (Eds.), *How students learn: Reforming school through learner-centered education* (pp. 379–408). Washington, DC: American Psychological Association.

McDermott, P., & Rothenberg, J. (2000). *The characteristics of effective teachers in high poverty schools—triangulating our data.* (ERIC Document Reproduction Service No. ED442887)

McDiarmid, G. W. (1991). What teachers need to know about cultural diversity: Restoring subject matter to the picture. In M. M. Kennedy (Ed.), *Teaching academic subjects to diverse learners* (pp. 257–269). New York: Teachers College.

McIntosh, P. (1998). White privilege: Unpacking the invisible knapsack. In P. S. Rothenberg (Ed.), *Race, class, and gender in the United States: An integrated study* (4th ed., pp. 87–143). New York: St. Martin's.

Palmer, P. J. (1993). *To know as we are known: Education as a spiritual journey.* San Francisco: Harper & Row.

Patrick, J., & Smart, R. M. (1998). An empirical evaluation of teacher effectiveness: The emergence of three critical factors. *Assessment & Evaluation in Higher Education, 23*(2), 165–179.

Perry, R. (1985). Instructor expressive: Implications for improving teaching. In J. Donald & A. Sullivan (Eds.), *Using research to improve teaching* (pp. 35–49). San Francisco: Jossey Bass.

Perry, R., Magnusson, J., Parsonson, K., & Dickens, W. (1986). Perceived control in college classroom: Limitations in instructor expressiveness due to noncontingent feedback and lecture content. *Journal of Educational Psychology, 78,* 96–107.

Pohan, C. A. (1996). Preservice teachers' beliefs about diversity. Uncovering factors leading to multicultural responsiveness. *Equity and Excellence in Education, 29*(3), 62–69.

Poole, M., Okeafor, K., & Sloan, E. (1989, April). *Teachers' interactions, personal efficacy and change implementation.* Paper presented at the Annual Meeting of the American Educational Research Association, San Francisco.

Ramsden, P. (1992). *Learning to teach in higher education.* London: Routledge.

Sagor, R. (1992). *How to conduct collaborative action research.* Alexandria, VA: Association for Supervision and Curriculum Development.

Sarason, S. (1990). *The predictable failure of educational reform: Can we change course before it's too late?* San Francisco: Jossey Bass.

Schunk, D. (1990, April). *Perception of efficacy and classroom motivation.* Paper presented at the annual meeting of the American Educational Research Association, Boston.

Schunk, D. H. (1995). Self-efficacy and education and instruction. In J. E. Maddus (Ed.), *Self-efficacy, adaptation and adjustment* (pp. 213–278). New York: Plenum.

Sheets, R. H. (2000). Advancing the field or taking centre stage: The White movement in multicultural education. *Educational Researcher, 29,* 15–21.

Singham, M. (1998). The canary in the mine: The achievement gap between black and white students. *Phi Delta Kappan, 80,* 9–15.

Stringer, E. T. (1999). *Action research.* Thousand Oaks, CA: Sage Publications.

Swartz, C. W., White, K. P., & Stuck, G. B. (1990). The factorial structure of the North Carolina Teacher Performance Appraisal Instrument. *Educational and Psychological Measurement, 50,* 175–185.

Tabachnick, B. C., & Fidell, L. S. (1989). *Using multivariate statistics,* (2nd ed). New York: Harper Collins.

Wentzel, K. R. (2002). Are effective teachers like good parents? Teaching styles and student adjustment in early adolescence. *Child Development, 73*(1), 287–302.

Weinstein, R. S. (1998). Promoting positive expectations in schooling. In N. M Lambert & B. L. McComb (Eds.), *How students learn: Reforming schools through learner-centered education* (pp. 81–111). Washington, DC: American Psychological Association.

Young, B. N., Whitley, M. E., & Helton, C. (1998). Students' perceptions of characteristics of effective teachers. (ERIC Document Reproduction Service No. ED426962)

Minority Voices

Windows for Gaining Cultural Insight

We view this place [North America] as being given to us by the Creator to take care of and to pass on to our future generations. We believe all other people are visitors, and when they leave, we'll still be here to pick up the pieces, no matter what shape it's in.

B. Mulhern (1988, p. 1)
"Wisconsin's Indians: Their Progress, Their Plight"

5 CHAPTER | Learning from Native American Stories

Even though U.S. society and its schools emphasize individualism, competition, and consumption, the words expressed by the Chippewa Native bring into awareness the value of the human role of steward—caretaker but not owner of the land. Consider how your own life decisions and behaviors may be changed if you held this view of humans' relationship to nature and the importance of watching over the land for all to come.

The values underlying this statement and the impact such values have on the decisions and behaviors of people who hold them is a focus of this chapter. In this chapter, you will encounter the lives, perspectives, and lived experience of Native Americans who share their stories. It highlights values, traditions, and experiences of Native peoples as they come to bear on their relationship with U.S. schools and society.

As noted in the Preface of this book, this chapter and the seven chapters that follow are organized around six cultural factors that identify different aspects of culture and that structure categories of information about each of the marginalized groups presented in this text. These factors include (1) the historical and current treatment of the cultural group in the United States, (2) initial terms of incorporation of the group into the United States, (3) shared values and traditions of the cultural group, (4) the group's view of spirituality (including the group's view of humans' relation to nature and the temporal focus of life), (5) group acculturation patterns and experiences with exclusion and alienation, and (6) language differences, strengths, and challenges of the group. In the narratives that present the voices of members of this group, you will be able to identify barriers in learning–teaching relationships that group members experience in their interactions with dominant-culture teachers and schools and identify their coping strategies for addressing oppression.

CHAPTER OBJECTIVES

1. Describe the early experience of Native Americans in North America.
2. Describe salient values held by traditional Native Americans.
3. Identify ways the people profiled in the case narratives experienced and addressed the six cultural factors explored in this text.
4. Explain academic and intercultural interaction implications related to the six cultural factors for members in this ethnic group.
5. Describe coping strategies utilized by members of this group.
6. Identify classroom strategies for cultivating the resources provided when traditional Native American worldviews are integrated into the curriculum.

CULTURAL FACTOR 1: HISTORICAL AND CURRENT TREATMENT IN THE UNITED STATES

Historically, dominant culture in the United States, including federal laws, policies, and institutions (schools, churches, agencies), has deliberately attempted to destroy Native American culture and cultural institutions (Lame Deer & Erodes, 1972; Metcalf, 1979). Prior to 1492, it is estimated that 3 to 5 million indigenous people lived in North America. Precipitated by deadly contact with Europeans, the indigenous population in America was reduced to 250,000 by 1850 (U.S. Bureau of the Census, 2003).

Ford (1983) recounted five stages of U.S. government policy toward Native Americans. The first stage involved the **removal** of Native Americans. Because Native Americans did not make "good" slaves and were from the onset at odds with European individualistic and capitalist orientations, White settlers in North America from the 17th century to the 1840s sought to remove Native Americans from North America. They began to acquire Native-controlled lands by killing Native Americans in large numbers (Tatum, 1997). The next stage **relocated** Native Americans to **reservations.** From 1860 to the late 1920s, Native Americans were driven from their expansive lands in North America and forced to live on small plots of land defined by the U.S. government. Forced to leave their homes, they were denied their ways of living in harmony with nature and their environment. In addition, the U.S. government attempted to "civilize" Native Americans in order to save the person beneath the "savage." In concert with the establishment of reservations, the creation of off-reservation boarding schools was one of the major strategies used to facilitate the acculturation of Native Americans. For over 50 years, schools like the Carlisle Indian School in Carlisle, Pennsylvania, established in 1879, housed thousands of Native American children who were forcibly removed from their families. With their families too far away to protect and nurture them, Native American children were physically and sexually abused, and were not only forced into hard labor but also forced to deny their cultural heritage. It was not until the 1930s that the U.S. practice of removing Native American children from their families was reversed (Tatum, 1997). The third stage was that of **reorganization.** From the 1930s to the

1950s, when the U. S. government permitted schools on reservations, systematic cultural repression was the focus. The fourth stage, **termination,** occurred during the 1950s and 1960s. During this period, the U.S. government sought to terminate relations with Native American nations, to end Native American so-called "dependence" on the federal government, and to integrate acculturated Native Americans into mainstream dominant culture. Many Native Americans were forced to work and live in urban areas in order to make money to survive. Traditional Native American cultural values could not be practiced under these conditions. The upheaval, cultural conflict, language barriers, and discrimination they encountered (for which they were vastly unprepared) led to widespread alcoholism, suicide, and death for many (Tatum, 1997). In addition, at this time large tracts of Native American lands were illegally sold, which further increased their poverty. From the mid 1970s up until the present, the U.S. government has emphasized Native American **self-determination.** As such, after the U.S. government denied Native Americans the right to act independently throughout their relations with them, they are now encouraging Native Americans fend for themselves after oppressing them throughout history and depleting all their resources. When Native Americans resisted the termination policy that ended in the 1960s, the pan-Indian movement that forced the federal government to condemn its legalized destructive policies toward Native Americans was born, and in the 1980s and 1990s, legislation that promoted Native American–controlled schools, protected Native American religious freedom, and preserved traditional Native American languages was passed (Tatum, 1997).

While this phase of self-determination is welcomed by many traditional Native Americans, overwhelming struggles created by their oppression and marginalization remain. Throughout history, the successes and innovations of Native American culture have been denigrated and denied (Vogel, 1987; Deloria, 2003) to such an extent that even today, the greatest struggles Native Americans face are those of survival and identity. Pulitzer prize-winning author N. Scott Momaday, speaking at a 1992 celebration of the 500th anniversary of Columbus's arrival in the Western Hemisphere, described what life is like for him living in the United States:

> ... how to live in the modern world ... how to remain Indian, how to assimilate without ceasing to be Indian ... with our languages being lost, at a tremendous rate, poverty is rampant, as is alcoholism ... It's a matter of identity. It's thinking about who I am. I grew up on Indian reservations, and then I went away from the Indian world and entered a different context.

> But I continue to think of myself as Indian. I write out of that conviction. I think this is what most Indian people are doing today. They go off the Reservation, but they keep an idea of themselves as Indians. That's the trick. (quoted in Tatum, 1997, pp. 148–149)

Attempting to keep alive a sense of one's culture is an enormous task for minority groups who are oppressed and alienated in the United States. And while many works highlight this struggle and evidence the destruction of Native cultures, it must also be noted that there is a tremendous cost to society of lost knowledge and resources when oppression reins. Not only do Native Americans suffer incredibly but opportunities for dominant culture to benefit from Native American cultural values are also lost. Because Native American tradition encompasses a broad "culture that offers valuable lessons for the contemporary industrial generation in danger of being crushed by the sheer weight of 'civilization,' and [that] therefore often sacrifices the deepest and most meaningful values of life by identifying with an endless series of distracting and often destructive gadgets" (Brown, 1964, p. 9), dominant culture could greatly benefit from its teachings.

Over 2 million Native Americans and Alaska Natives currently live in North America (U.S. Bureau of the Census, 1993). There are 505 federally recognized tribal entities and an additional 365 state-recognized tribes and bands. Native Americans represent more than 500 different cultural communities defined as *sovereign entities* by the U.S. government. It is conservatively estimated that there are 250 Native groups not recognized by the U.S. government. More than half of Native Americans live in urban areas, and most large cities have at least 10,000 Native American residents. However, approximately 50 percent of the Native American population live west of the Mississippi River. According to U.S. Census reports, more than half of all Native Americans in the United States live in Oklahoma, California, Arizona, New Mexico, Alaska, or Washington State. Only 22 percent of Native Americans currently live on reservations (U.S. Bureau of the Census, 1993).

Many Native Americans continue to face enormous economic, social, and psychological challenges. Native American unemployment rates ranging from 18 percent to 66 percent soar above the rates of 5.8 percent to 7.4 percent for the U.S. population at large (Office for Governmental Affairs and the Rural Condition, 1985). The Native American median income is only 50 percent of that for Whites (U.S. Department of Health and Human Services, 1977). High-school dropout rates reach 60 percent for Native American schoolchildren (Gade, Hurlburt, & Fuqua, 1986), and Native American adolescent suicides have increased 1,000 percent over the past 20 years (Berlin, 1984); Native Americans also show high rates of drug use (Beauvais, 1980) and an alcoholism rate that is double the national average (Bock et al., 1972).

CULTURAL FACTOR 2: INITIAL TERMS OF INCORPORATION INTO U.S. SOCIETY

The initial terms of minority group members' incorporation into U.S. society (be it voluntary or involuntary) and the patterns of adaptive responses minority group members exhibit in response to the discriminatory treatment they receive may account for many of the differences in their social adjustment and academic success (Ogbu, 1992). **Voluntary minorities** are those groups of people whose ancestors came to the United States in search of greater economic opportunities. Voluntary minority group members are said to believe that they will succeed in mainstream society through hard work and compliance with

Intercultural Communication Strategies for Teachers 5-1

Classroom Applications: Informing and Inviting

A review of the history of Native Americans highlights their struggle for personal and cultural survival. Their shared cultural history would lead to mistrust of the dominant culture and the anticipated pressure to acculturate at the cost of losing cultural identity. Knowing this can help you create effective learning communities for these students. Specifically, you should do the following:

- Keep in mind that these students and their families bring with them a history of experience with discrimination in schools and in larger society. With these experiences often come caution and mistrust.
- Do not assume that your policies, procedures, and instructional strategies are understood and valued opportunities. Send frequent commu-

nications home that invite questions, reactions, and suggestions.

- From the beginning of the school year and throughout the year, remind the students about the importance of bringing their perspective and worldviews into the classroom. Invite them to share their perspectives on the topics discussed and the approaches taken within the classroom.
- Reread the quote that opens this chapter. With it as a filter, how do you envision altering lesson plans you create? Classroom rules and procedures? Style of interacting? Through ongoing reflection such as this, you may find an increased awareness and with it an increased sensitivity to the diversity of your students.

authority. These individuals' parents, grandparents, and great-grandparents chose to enter the United States, often favorably comparing the treatment received in the United States to that in their countries of origin. In contrast, **involuntary minorities** are groups whose ancestors suffered slavery or colonization in the United States and who historically have been denied true **assimilation** into U.S. society. Involuntary minorities are keenly aware of the intergenerational oppression received.

When Europeans arrived in North America in the 1400s, they attempted to make Native Americans slaves. However, Native Americans' knowledge of the terrain and defiant refusals to be held in bondage resulted in frequent attempted and successful escapes, making Native Americans difficult slaves for Europeans to own (Kolchin, 1993).

The extreme oppression and colonization experienced at the hands of dominant culture in North America led Ogbu (1990) to categorize Native Americans as involuntary minorities. Going a step further, it is not hard to understand that students who are members of **involuntary minority** groups are more likely than students who are members of voluntary minority groups to reject dominant-culture paths to success and equate compliant behaviors with denying their cultures, in essence, "selling-out" their families, culture, and cultural values (Ogbu, 1990). For insight into this phenomenon, consider the experience of Mary Crow Dog. As you read her story, identify the impact school officials' treatment of her had on her academic achievement.

MARY CROW DOG

And that priest they sent here from Holy Rosary in Pine Ridge because he molested a little girl. You [dominant culture] couldn't think of anything better than dump him on us. All he does is watch young women and girls with that funny smile on his face. Why don't you point him out for an example?

Charlene and I worked on the school newspaper. After all, we had some practice. Every day we went down to Publications. One of the priests acted as the photographer, doing the enlarging and developing. He smelled of chemicals, which has strained his hands yellow. One day he invited Charlene into the darkroom. He was going to teach her developing. She was developed already. She was a big girl compared to him, taller too. Charlene was nicely built, not fat, just rounded. No sharp edges anywhere. All of [a] sudden she rushed out of the darkroom, yelling to me, "Let's get out of here! He's trying to feel me up. That priest is nasty." So there was this too to contend with—sexual harassment. We complained to the student body. The nuns said we just had a dirty mind.

We got a new priest in English. During one of his first classes, he asked one of the boys a certain question. The boy was shy. He spoke poor English, but he had the right answer. The priest told him, "You did not say it right. Correct yourself. Say it over again." The boy got flustered and stammered. He could hardly get out a word. But the priest kept after him: "Didn't you hear? I told you to do the whole thing over. Get it right this time." He kept on and on.

I stood up and said, "Father, don't be doing that. If you go into an Indian's home and try to talk Indian, they might laugh at you and say, 'Do it over correctly. Get it right this time!'" He shouted at me, "Mary, you stay after class. Sit down right now!" I stayed after class, until after the bell. He told me, "Get over here!" He grabbed me by the arm, pushing me against the blackboard, shouting, "Why are you always mocking us? You have no reason to do this." I said, "Sure I do. You were making fun of him. You embarrassed him. He needs strengthening, not weakening. You hurt him. I did not hurt you." He twisted my arm and pushed real hard. I turned around and hit him in the face, giving him a bloody nose. After that, I ran out of the room, slamming the door behind me. He and I went to Sister Bernard's office. I told her, "Today, I quit school. I'm not taking this anymore. None of this treatment. Better give me my diploma. I can't waste any more time on you people."

Sister Bernard looked at me for a long, long time. She said, "All right, Mary Ellen, go home today. Come back in a few days and get your diploma." And that was that. Oddly enough, that priest turned out okay. He taught a class in grammar, orthography, composition, things like that. I think he wanted more respect in class. He was still young and unsure of himself. But I was there too long. I didn't feel like hearing it. Later he became a good friend to the Indians, a personal friend of myself and my husband. He stood up for us during Wounded Knee and after. He stood up to his superiors, stuck his neck way out, became a real people's priest. He even learned our language. He died prematurely of cancer. It is not only the good Indians who die young, but the good [W]hites, too. It is the timid ones who know how to take care of themselves who grow old. I am still grateful to that priest for what he did for us later and for the quarrel he picked with me—or did I pick it with him?—because it ended a situation which had become unendurable for me. The day of my fight with him was my last day in school. (Crow Dog & Erodes, 1990, pp. 39–41)

| Exercise 5-1 | **Point of Reflection: A Young Student's Diary Entry** |

Directions: The following will require you to use your imagination and to let go of your current sense of who and where you are at the present time.

1. Imagine that you are a young Native American between the ages of 8 and 11, and you have just been placed, against your parents' wishes, in a boarding school.

2. Picture a school that has only White teachers, administrators, and staff and mostly White children from Anglo-Saxon, Protestant backgrounds. The school requires a strict dress code requiring the wearing of uniforms and Oxford shoes, along with specified hair lengths and styles and prohibition of makeup or jewelry. Meals are provided on a rigid schedule and consist primarily of dishes and styles of cooking that are unfamiliar to you. Families are permitted to write and call regularly, but visitations are allowed only on designated parent–family days.

3. As you finish your first day in this school, you come to your room and begin to write in your journal. Write a diary entry that describes what it feels like to be a young Native American student living in these conditions who has been taken from family (isolated far from home), had hair and clothes dramatically altered, and been forced to speak only English (a language you don't know). Imagine the extreme living circumstances you encounter and, as you write, describe the feelings you believe might be present in the absence of care and support from your family while coping within a hostile environment.

4. Generate a list of words describing the feelings you, or anyone who is an involuntary minority, might have toward dominant-culture teachers in U.S. schools. How might these feelings affect your achievement?

Exercise 5-1 will provide you with the opportunity to imagine yourself in the place of a young Native American student.

CULTURAL FACTOR 3: SHARED VALUES AND TRADITIONS

Because of the large number of tribes and languages spoken, it is important to realize the tremendous diversity among Native Americans (Attneave, 1982; Manson, 1986). Even with this caveat, it is possible to identify similarities in values that exist across tribes and regions (Blanchard & Mackey, 1971; Lazarus, 1982; National Indian Child Abuse and Neglect Resource Center, 1980; Richardson, 1981: Trimble, 1981).

The values of traditional Native American culture arose primarily (but not exclusively) within the context of a nomadic hunting and gathering economy that has been almost completely destroyed. As with African Americans, Asian Americans, and Latinos, extended-family and kinship obligations are considered very important for Native Americans. Therefore, group needs are commonly seen as more significant than individual needs. Communal sharing with those who have less is generally expected and rewarded in Native American culture (Sutton & Broken Nose, 1996). But it must be noted that while tribes may share these values with traditional Native American culture, individuals within this group may vary in the degree to which they hold and manifest these values.

As is true for all minority peoples, the degree to which the Native American cultural values are embodied is determined by the degree to which individuals embrace traditionalism in contrast to the degree of acculturation in mainstream society that they have experienced (Attneave, 1982).

Native American women are typically seen as equal to Native American men, but that does not mean they assume the same roles and functions. Gender roles among different tribes and ancestry are specific to tribes. For example, among Pueblo Indians, men worked in cornfields controlled by female members of their tribe yet dominated religion and politics. Pueblo women built and owned the family home, and it is through women that many Native American peoples trace descent (Deloria, 2000).

Native American gender roles prescribe male bravery and strength. Males are expected to protect and be loyal to the tribe. Typically, hunting and survival skills were passed down from one generation to the next, with the bravest and strongest but also wisest becoming leaders of the tribes. Tribal leaders played significant roles in maintaining cultural continuity, and Native American women were equally important to the survival of the tribe and were treated accordingly. Besides childrearing, women were responsible for direct care of the elderly and the daily operations of the tribe. Cooking, tailoring, and washing were also traditional tasks assigned to women in Native American culture.

As you reflect on what you have read, it is quite possible that the history of your family, your incorporation into dominant U.S. culture, the values you hold, and the gender roles you assume may be quite different from or in some ways like those described here for Native Americans. Before proceeding, stop and reflect on what has been presented, especially as it relates to conflicts in values, traditions, and expectations found in a typical dominant-culture classroom (see Exercise 5-2).

CULTURAL FACTOR 4: VIEW OF SPIRITUALITY AND HUMANS' RELATION TO NATURE

Traditional Native American values include an orientation that reveres harmony with nature versus dominant culture's view of nature as subjugated to man. Native Americans believe that all creation is equal—that all living things are interdependent and that humans must value the sanctity of the wholeness of the universe in its purity. These beliefs contradict dominant-culture beliefs of human superiority over nature and the need for humans to own, control, change, and otherwise dominate all aspects of it.

Mind, body, spirit, and nature are perceived as one process, with little separation existing between religion, medicine, and all activities of daily life (Kaplan & Johnson, 1964; Richardson, 1981), just as there is no separation of

Exercise 5-2 | Classroom Applications: The Confluence of Values

Directions: In the first column of the table are descriptions of characteristics that have been associated with Native American peoples. In the middle column are descriptions of typical processes or procedures found within dominant-culture schools. Your task is to describe the effect experienced when these two value systems meet. Describe how you think students placed in this situation, in which both are important, may react. Share your hypotheses with your instructor and classmates in small-group discussion in order to develop strategies geared to reduce any negative impact.

Native American Characteristic	School Orientation, Process, or Procedure	Anticipated Impact
Value community before the individual	• Spelling bees • Voting for most-popular or most-talented students • Awards assemblies	
Emphasize cooperation and sharing	• Homework assignments • Seatwork assignments • Working at the board • Participating in debates	
Respect for nature	• History class discussions based on content from standardized textbooks • Ecology projects • Discussions of U.S. capitalism in social studies classes	
Reverence for all that is living	• Dissection assignments • Insect collection assignments • Classroom pets	
Spirituality over materialism	• Use of extrinsic motivation (prizes, stickers, awards) • Homecoming queen contests • Providing incentives for students to sell booster ads for band	
A present focus rather than a future focus	• Curriculum mapping for future college and career • Essay assignment titled "What I Want to Be When I Grow Up" • Use of portfolio as a means of assessing student progress	
Valuing of fate and destiny versus self-determination	• Goal-setting in the process of problem solving	

life in nature. In Native American culture, reverence for nature and for all forms of life is central. Qualities of the Creator are said to be reflected in all forms of nature, so each aspect of nature is seen as a link to the Creator (Brown, 1964).

A key concept of Native American philosophy is holism, and one of the most important symbols is the circle, or hoop of life. Consider the importance of the circle as evidenced in the words of Black Elk, a Sioux medicine man:

> Everything an Indian does is in a circle, and that is because the Power of the World always works in circles, and everything tries to be round. In the old days when we were a strong and happy people, all our power came to us from the sacred hoop of the nation, and so long as the hoop was unbroken, the people flourished. (Brown, 1964, pp. 13–24)

When traditional Native Americans come together as a group, they meet in a circle formation depicting the importance of all present, the equality distributed among all, and the belief in loyalty to the group that keeps the circle whole.

Traditional Native Americans see themselves as extensions of the tribe. The individual is a part of a whole, and the wholeness of the tribe provides strength and gives meaning to life. For example, one petal of a flower has little beauty by itself, but together the petals make up the experience, beauty, and wholeness of the flower. Similarly, in traditional Native American culture one is judged primarily in terms of whether his or her behavior contributes to the harmonious functioning of the tribe. Native American philosophy does not oppose individual accomplishment but sees the individual as an extension of the tribe. Therefore, artistry and sport accomplishment reflect positively on the group, its teachings, and the wholeness of Native American culture.

The strong valuing of spirituality can be seen in the practice of the Native American transforming rituals of the vision quest and sweat lodge, which still serve as rites of passage or processes for religious renewal. These ceremonies often include fasting to allow one's mental capacities to be more attentive to the natural world. The vision quest, in which a youth is taken to a remote and isolated area for four days and nights without food and water, offers time for reflection and prayer and examination of one's goals and plans. This ritual directs individuals toward a focus on their relationship with the universe and the role they are to play in it. Individuals marshal their abilities, skills, fears, experiences, goals, and hopes to further their quest for spiritual knowledge.

Similarly symbolic of important cultural tenets, the circular shape of the sweat lodge (tepee) represents the Universe itself, and the pit at the lodge's center is the navel of the Universe wherein dwells the Great Spirit, with the fire representing the power of the Creator. The willow branches that form the frame of the lodge represent all growing things, whose annual cycles of defoliation and refoliation symbolize the death and rebirth of the spirit. The rocks in the firepit represent the earth and the indestructible nature of the Creator. The water sprinkled on the rocks is the Creator's ever-flowing life-giving spirit. The steam is both the holy breath of the Universe and the visible prayers of the people. The opening of the flap of the sweat lodge that lets cool air and light in symbolizes liberation from the darkness of ignorance and entering the world of light and truth and goodness (Brown, 1964; Halifax, 1979).

Traditional Native American rituals and values like these are oriented to help group members fully experience the present and to follow old ways versus a dominant–culture orientation to the future and toward progress and change at the expense of attending to needs and life goals in the present. Native Americans are sometimes mistakenly judged as lazy or undependable if they do not arrive on time for scheduled commitments. Such behavior reflects not a lack of commitment or irresponsibility but instead a respect for and focus on the here and now. A traditional Native American might ask, "Why would someone miss or hurry something solely for the sake of finishing at a certain point in time?"

In addition, Native American culture emphasizes a belief in destiny in contrast to dominant-culture attitudes that espouse the idea that if one wants something to happen, it is up to the individual to make it happen. One consequence of this cultural belief is that Native Americans place less emphasis on planning and scheduling. As a culture, Native Americans place more emphasis on seeing how situations develop and on valuing the present and what it brings as it unfolds, and less value on planning for the future.

CULTURAL FACTOR 5: ACCULTURATION AND EXPERIENCE WITH EXCLUSION AND ALIENATION

More than 75 percent of the total Native American population lives off-reservation (U.S. Bureau of the Census, 1981). Many leave the reservation in search of work in order to care for their families. The transition is difficult, especially when Native Americans move to high-density urban areas. It is not uncommon for transitioning Native Americans to feel lonely, insecure, and alienated (Carlson, 1975).

The dominant culture has exerted enormous force and pressure on Native Americans to adopt its values. As a result, a great deal of cultural heritage was lost as generations of Native American children were raised in the boarding schools and foster homes of dominant culture—environments that had shaping the Native children to become more "White" as their mission. The degree to which **acculturation** has occurred, along with the decline of interest in traditional Native American culture, varies considerably among Native Americans (Heinrich, Corbine, & Thomas, 1990). Some fight to hold on to their Native American traditions while functioning within the dominant culture. These individuals may dream of making enough money in U.S. cities to move back to reservations when they retire. They may make long commutes to the reservation for feasts, powwows, religious ceremonies, and visits with relatives. They may fear that the traditions will be lost because of the exodus of so many Native Americans to cities (Mulhern, 1988).

Such a response to acculturation has been described as **traditionalism** (Valle, 1986). **Biculturalism** is another response to the pressures of acculturation. Bicultural individuals are said to have a dual perspective. They are a part of two systems: the larger system of the dominant society and the smaller system of the individual's immediate cultural environment. To survive in both systems, individuals consciously perceive, understand, and compare simultaneously the values, attitudes, and behavior of the larger societal system with those of individuals' immediate family and community systems, often finding conflict that leads them to choose to express themselves most freely in whichever environment feels most comfortable and beneficial to them in various situations, including schools (Hanson & Eisenbise, 1981). A third position on the continuum of acculturation would be **total cultural assimilation.** While the complete loss of one's native culture and the total cultural assimilation into that of the dominant culture may not be a problem for some Native Americans, for others it is viewed as cultural genocide (Ford, 1983).

Responding to the pressure to assimilate can take its toll. Consider the concerns of a Native American parent of a 14-year-old boy who is struggling with his own identity as a Native American living as a minority within dominant culture:

> I am so worried. He doesn't spend time with his father or me anymore. He is always going out with his [W]hite friends or going to his room. When we ask why he never sees his other friends who lived on the reservation with us, he says it is because he doesn't want to. He says we're all too "weird"—the way we dress, the things we eat, the things we do. It's too strange for him. It is as if he is ashamed of us, his family—ashamed of who he is.

Intercultural Communication Strategies for Teachers 5-2

Classroom Applications: Pressure and Pressured

As noted in the text, the loss of one's native culture and total cultural assimilation into that of the dominant culture may not be a problem for some Native Americans, but for others it is viewed as cultural genocide. Where any one Native American student may exist along the continuum of acculturation is hard to know, but all require teacher support in addressing discrimination and other psychosocial concerns experienced in schools. The following will help you to provide that support.

- Provide students with the freedom to make choices in the classroom. Allow for choices between written and oral and between group and individual assignments when possible. In addition, provide various and diverse resources from which students can learn.

- Ask families and other community members of your students to help you create book lists, field-trip destinations, and guest-speaker possibilities.

- Use journal-writing assignments frequently to give your students outlets for expression and the opportunity for regular individualized communication with you.

- Be sensitive to the fact that not all Native American students are at the same point along the acculturation continuum. While some may want to give voice to their traditions, rituals, and values, others may be attempting to more closely fulfill dominant-culture expectations.

CULTURAL FACTOR 6: LANGUAGE DIFFERENCES, STRENGTHS, AND CHALLENGES

There are 304 federal Native American reservations, and over 150 tribal languages are still spoken today (Bureau of Indian Affairs, 1988). Even so, the elimination of Native American language is almost complete.

Native Americans have been forced to replace Native languages with English in order to survive in dominant culture–controlled boarding schools, reservations, and institutional policies and practices. As such, Native American languages have been systematically discounted and erased.

Traditional Native American speech patterns are often slower and softer than dominant-culture speech, with few interjections into the conversation of others. Intense eye contact is avoided, as it may be considered a sign of rudeness. Native Americans may exhibit limited facial expression and may appear guarded, aloof, or cold. In addition, Native American responses may seem delayed, if they occur at all. Silence is seen as a sign of equilibrium. The fruits of silence are self-control, courage, patience, dignity, and reverence. Nonverbal communication through rituals, signing, drumming, and dancing are highly prized, as they are perceived to be more in concert with nature and others than are solitary verbal monologues. Traditional Native Americans emphasize learning through observation, listening, and practice. As such, children are taught through demonstration rather than verbal communication. While these descriptors of Native American communication styles seem benign, consider the effect when this style encounters the expectations, demands, and models of communication reinforced within dominant culture schools, as seen in the following exchange between a Native American student, Lydia, and a White sixth-grade teacher, Mr. Wright, during her first day at Pennington Middle School.

Mr. Wright:	"What's wrong?"
Lydia (Looking down):	[silence]
Mr. Wright:	"Lydia … I'm speaking to you."
Lydia (softly):	"Nothing is wrong, Mr. Wright."
Mr. Wright:	"Lydia, would you look at me? You seem like something is wrong. Are you upset? Is someone bothering you or teasing you?"
Lydia (averting eyes):	[long hesitation]
Mr. Wright:	"Well?"
Lydia:	"I am sorry, Mr. Wright, but I don't know what you want me to say. School is fine … very nice."
Mr. Wright:	"I don't get it … I just can't reach you."
Lydia (looking dispassionate):	[silence]

One can assume that Mr. Wright is concerned for his student—concerned that the way she looks and responds to him is a "sign" that something is wrong. It may be that the only thing "wrong" is Mr. Wright. Mr. Wright clearly does not understand that Lydia is thinking about each question posed and is responding with honesty, respect, and cultural dignity.

POTENTIAL BARRIERS IN LEARNING–TEACHING RELATIONSHIPS WITH DOMINANT-CULTURE TEACHERS AND SCHOOLS

In addition to conflicts in values, communication patterns, and learning-style preferences discussed in this chapter, Native Americans go largely unrecognized in U.S. schools. Because many Native Americans in the United States today have last names that originated in Europe and there are wide variations in the physical appearance of Native Americans, it is quite possible that students with Native American backgrounds may provide teachers with no visible signs of their ancestry. Due to the high proportion of mixed-heritage individuals, it may be difficult for teachers to determine whether there are Native Americans students in their classrooms (Little Soldier, 1997). This potential for invisibility in the dominant culture can prove to be a major obstacle for Native Americans as they seek to retain their cultural heritage and identity and to have their perspectives included in U.S. schools.

AN UNRECOGNIZED HISTORY

Not only is it difficult for members of this group to be recognized as Native Americans, but they also face a major lack of recognition of their existence in North American, in particular U.S. history. Native American writings, worldviews, and contributions typically are not included in texts and curricula, and Native American leaders and philosophies are not embraced in the media or dominant-culture consciousness. In many ways, it is as if Native Americans do not exist in U.S. schools and culture.

The absence of contemporary images of Native Americans in popular culture is widespread. Even in places with a large and visible Native American population, they are presented as people of the past rather than people of the present. Consider the messages conveyed in the profiles of Native Americans depicted in the artifacts that dominant culture has reinforced (see Exercise 5-3).

WHEN VALUES AND DEMANDS CLASH

As previously noted, traditional Native American values embrace cooperation and conscious submission of the self for the welfare of the group versus the dominant-culture value that stresses competition, with each individual maximizing her/his own welfare in order to succeed in life, often at the expense of others. This may not seem, at first glance, to be an obstacle for Native Americans within dominant-culture schools. However, consider a simple and typical situation in which an individual student is asked to answer a

| Exercise 5-3 | **Point of Reflection: Redskins, Tomahawk Chants, and Other Cultural Icons** |

Directions: Gather data from the following sources in order to develop a profile of Native Americans as they are currently depicted in dominant culture.

Source of Data	Image Projected
Identify two sports teams that use a logo or symbol associated with Native Americans (for example, Atlanta Braves, Washington Redskins).	
Review the art of Frederic Remington or Charles Russell.	
Use a U.S. history textbook and identify: 1. The context (or circumstances) in which Native Americans are discussed 2. The image employed to depict Native Americans	
Locate advertisements and commercials with a Native American theme (for example, "It's Barbie as an American Indian caring for her cousin, Baby Blue Feather™. This Collector Edition Barbie wears a tan buckskin-like dress with matching boots. The tiny papoose she carries has a 'buckskin' headband and diaper and comes with a matching backpack. Children will love the magical story Barbie tells. From the American Stories Series™, this very special Barbie doll comes with her own historical storybook, so she's educational as well as fun").	

1. Reflect on what you have read about Native American culture in this chapter. Describe how the information you have learned from your research for this exercise would affect the lives of Native Americans living in the United States. Do the characterizations accurately reflect their values and help them feel connected to dominant culture? Discuss your views in writing or with classmates.

2. Consider the significant cultural principles presented in this chapter and determine if there is evidence that Native American values and culture are understood in dominant culture.

question in class, a process repeated throughout every classroom in the United States on any given day. For a traditional Native American student who answers the question correctly it is an act of individual superiority, while answering it incorrectly or standing mute would bring humiliation to the individual and the group. This is a classic no-win situation brought on by cultural value differences and conflicts. In another example, consider the practice of a spelling bee, honors

Intercultural Communication Strategies for Teachers 5-3

Classroom Applications: Making Classrooms and Curricula Reflective of Student Experience

- Teachers need to become more aware of Native American cultural values. Classroom activities need to be shaped to reinforce values and strategies employed in the home.
- Use demonstration, modeling, and coaching during "hands-on" instructional activities. Native American students may prefer global/holistic approaches that offer visual and tactile stimuli.
- Move beyond commercial curriculum materials; tailor readings, activities, and illustrations to students' experiential backgrounds.

- Become aware of alternative curriculum material appropriate to your students' backgrounds (for example, oral and written Native American literature suitable for classroom use and integration of Native American history and governance into the social studies curriculum).
- Employ more cooperative group work as opposed to heavy reliance on individual classroom activities or competition within the classroom.

ceremony, or any activity that attempts to highlight the superiority of one student over another. In isolation these seem like typical and normal educational strategies. However, contrast these with traditional Native American values, which are grounded in a holistic approach to life and living where all aspects of life are seen as connected and cherished for the roles they play in the cycle of life. Is there conflict? Would a traditional Native American student experience turmoil and confusion when confronted by a culture that emphasizes individual achievement even, and sometimes especially, at the expense of another?

FROM CONCEPTS TO LIVED EXPERIENCE

In the following narrative from Mary Crow Dog, she describes Native American history in her own voice. As you read, look for the values manifested as they reflect that which was presented in this chapter.

WOUNDED KNEE

When I heard the words "Wounded Knee," I became very, very serious. Wounded Knee—*Cankpe Opi* in our language—has a special meaning for our people. There is the long ditch into which the frozen bodies of almost 300 of our people, mostly women and children, were thrown like so much cordwood. And the bodies are still there in their mass grave, unmarked except for a cement border. Next to the ditch, on a hill, stands the white-painted Catholic church, gleaming in the sunlight, the monument of an alien faith imposed upon the landscape. And below it flows *Cankpe Opi Wakpala*, the creek along which the women and children were hunted down like animals by Custer's old Seventh, out to avenge themselves for their defeat by butchering the helpless ones. That happened long ago, but no Sioux ever forgot it.

Wounded Knee is a part of our family's history. Leonard's great-grandfather, the first Crow Dog, had been one of the leaders of the Ghost Dancers. He and his group had held out in the icy ravines of the Badlands all winter, but when the soldiers came in force to kill all the Ghost Dancers, he had surrendered his band to avoid having his people killed. Old accounts describe how Crow Dog simply sat down between the rows of soldiers on one side, and the Indians on the other, all ready and eager to start shooting. He had covered himself with a blanket and was just sitting there. Nobody knew what to make of it. The leaders on both sides were so puzzled that they just did not get around to opening fire. They went to Crow Dog, lifted the blanket, and asked him what he meant to do. He told them that sitting there with the blanket over him was the only thing he could think of to make all the hotheads, white and red, curious enough to forget fighting. Then he persuaded his people to lay down their arms. Thus he saved his people just a few miles away from where Big Foot and his band were massacred. (Crow Dog & Erodes, 1990, pp. 124–125)

SUMMARY

Cultural Factor 1: Historical and Current Treatment in the United States   Historically, dominant culture in the United States, including federal laws, policies, and institutions (schools, churches, agencies), has deliberately attempted to destroy Native American culture and cultural institutions, through five stages:

- Stage One: Removal (killing Native Americans)
- Stage Two: Reservations (isolation)
- Stage Three: Reorganization (systematic cultural repression)
- Stage Four: Termination (integration of acculturated Native Americans)
- Stage Five: Self-determination (encouragement to make their own way)

Cultural Factor 2: Initial Terms of Incorporation into U.S. Society   Native Americans are an involuntary minority group, having been colonized and denied assimilation into U.S. society.

Cultural Factor 3: Shared Values and Traditions   Because of the large number of tribes and languages spoken, it is important to realize the tremendous diversity among Native Americans. The values of traditional Native American culture arose primarily (but not exclusively) within the context of a nomadic hunting and gathering economy that has been almost completely destroyed. Extended-family and kinship obligations are considered very important for Native Americans. As such, group needs are more significant than individual needs.

Cultural Factor 4: View of Spirituality and Humans' Relation to Nature   Traditional Native American values include an orientation of harmony with nature versus dominant culture's view of nature as subjugated to man. A key concept of Native American philosophy is holism, and one of the most important symbols is the circle, or hoop of life. Mind, body, spirit, and nature are perceived as one process, and little separation exists between religion, medicine, and the activities of daily life. Traditional Native Americans see themselves as extensions of the tribe. The individual is a part of a whole, and that wholeness of the tribe gives meaning to life.

Traditional Native American values are oriented to the present and to following old ways versus a dominant-culture orientation to the future and toward progress and change. Native American culture emphasizes a belief in destiny in contrast to dominant-culture attitudes that if you want something to happen, it is up to you to make it happen. Native American women are seen as equal to Native American men. Gender roles among different tribes and ancestry, however, are group specific.

Cultural Factor 5: Acculturation and Experience with Exclusion and Alienation Some Native Americans fight to hold on to their traditions while functioning within the dominant culture; this is a traditional response to acculturation. A bicultural response is one in which the person attempts to be part of two systems: the larger system of the dominant society and the smaller system of the individual's immediate social environment. The final position on the continuum of acculturation would be total cultural assimilation.

Cultural Factor 6: Language Differences, Strengths, and Challenges Through dominant culture–controlled boarding schools, reservations, and institutional policies and practices, Native American languages have been systematically discounted and erased. Native American speech patterns are often slower and softer than dominant-culture speech. Native Americans may exhibit limited facial expression and may appear guarded, aloof, or cold.

Silence is seen as a sign of equilibrium. The fruits of silence are self-control, courage, patience, dignity, and reverence. Nonverbal communication, however, through rituals, signing, drumming, and dancing, is highly prized as it is perceived to be more in concert with nature and others than are solitary verbal monologues.

Potential Barriers in Learning–Teaching Relationships with Dominant-Culture Teachers and Schools Native Americans go largely unrecognized in U.S. schools. There is a lack of recognition of their existence in North American history. Native American writings and contributions typically are not included in curricula, and Native American leaders and philosophies are not embraced in the media or dominant-culture consciousness. In many ways, it is as if Native Americans do not exist in U.S. schools and culture.

Important Terms

acculturation	relocation	self-determination	traditionalism
assimilation	removal	termination	traditional Native American values
biculturalism	reorganization	total cultural assimilation	
involuntary minority	reservation		voluntary minority

Enrichment

Crow Dog, M., & Erodes, R. (1990). *Lakota woman.* New York: Harper Perennial.

Gilliland, H. (1995). *Teaching the Native American* (3rd ed.). Dubuque, IA: Kendall/Hunt.

Lame Deer, J., & Erodes, R. (1972). *Lame Deer: Seeker of visions.* New York: Simon & Schuster.

Nabokov, P. (Ed.). (1991). *Native American testimony: A chronicle of Indian–White relations from prophecy to the present, 1492–1992.* New York: Viking.

Connections on the Web

http://www.ableza.org/

Ableza is a Native American Arts and Media Institute in San Jose, CA. The Institute is dedicated to promoting, preserving, and protecting traditional and contemporary arts by Native American peoples.

The website provides resources for those working with and teaching Native American students.

http://falcon.jmu.edu/~ramseyil/natauth.htm

This teacher resource for Native American authors provides biographies, bibliographies, lesson plans, online e-texts, and critical reviews of selected authors whose works are taught in the public schools or at the university level. Literature includes both adult and juvenile.

http://edtech.kennesaw.edu/web/natam.html

This resource and research site offers multiple links. Of special interest is "Appropriate Methods when Teaching about Native Americans—Do's and Don'ts."

REFERENCES

Attneave, C. L. (1982). American Indians and Alaska native families: Emigrants in their own homeland. In M. McGoldrick, J. Pearce, & J. Giorando (Eds.), *Ethnicity & family therapy* (pp. 55–83). NewYork: Guilford.

Beauvais, F. (1980). *Preventing drug abuse among American Indian young people.* Ft Collins, CO: Colorado State University. (ERIC Document Reproduction Service No. ED196630)

Berlin, I. N. (1984). *Suicide among American Indian adolescents.* National Indian Court Judges Association. (ERIC Document Reproduction Service No. ED245847)

Blanchard, E., & Mackey, J. (1971). *The American Indian.* (SRS Training Grant 755 770). Washington, DC: National Rehabilitation Association.

Bock, G., Fortuine, R., Bergman, R., Bopp, J., Exendine, J., Lafromboise, R., et al. (1972). *Alcoholism—A high priority health problem.* Rockville, MD: Indian Health Service Task Force on Alcoholism. (ERIC Document Reproduction Service No. ED148536)

Brown, J. (1964). *The spiritual legacy of the American Indian.* Wallingford, PA: Pendle Hill.

Bureau of Indian Affairs. (1988). *American Indians today.* Washington, DC: Author.

Carlson, E. (1975). Counseling in native context. *Canada's Mental Health, 23,* 7–9.

Crow Dog, M., & Erodes, R. (1990). *Lakota woman.* New York: Harper Perennial.

Deloria, P. J. (2003). American Indians, American studies, and the ASA. *American Quarterly, 55*(4), 669–680.

Deloria, Jr., V. (2000). The "vanishing" Americans. *Indian Life, 21*(1), 12–14.

Ford, R. (1983). *Counseling strategies for ethnic minority students.* Tacoma, WA: University of Puget Sound. (ERIC Document Reproduction Service No. ED247504)

Gade, E., Hurlburt, G., & Fuqua, D. (1986). Study habits and attitudes of American Indians: Implications for counselors. *School Counselor, 34,* 135–139.

Halifax, J. (1979). *Shamanic voices: A survey of visionary narratives.* New York: Dutton.

Hanson, W. D., & Eisenbise, M. D. (1981). *Human behavior and American Indians.* San Francisco: San Francisco State University. (ERIC Document Reproduction Service No. ED231589).

Heinrich, R. K., Corbine, J. L., & Thomas, K. R. (1990). Counseling Native Americans. *Journal of Counseling & Development, 69,* 128–133.

Kaplan, B., & Johnson, D. (1964). The social meaning of Navaho psychopathology and psychotherapy. In A. Kiev (Ed.), *Magic, faith, and healing* (pp. 203–229). New York: MacMillan.

Kolchin, P. (1993). *American slavery, 1619–1877.* New York: Hill & Wang.

Lame Deer, J., & Erodes, R. (1972). *Lame Deer: Seeker of visions.* New York: Simon & Schuster.

Lazarus, P. (1982). Counseling the Native American child: A question of values. *Elementary School Guidance and Counseling, 17,* 83–88.

Little Soldier, L. (1997, April). Is there an Indian in your classroom? Working successfully with urban Native American students. *Phi Delta Kappan, 650–653.*

Manson, S. M. (1986). Recent advances in American Indian mental health research: Implications for clinical research and training. In M. R. Miranda, & H. H. L. Kitano (Eds.), *Mental health research and practice in minority communities: Development of culturally sensitive training programs* (pp. 51–89). Rockville, MD: National Institute of Mental Health. (ERIC Document Reproduction Service No. ED278754)

Metcalf, A. (1979). Family reunion: Networks and treatment in a Native American community. *Group Psychotherapy, Psychodrama & Sociometry, 32,* 179–189.

Momaday, N. S. (1991). Confronting Columbus again. In P. Nabokov (Ed.), *Native American testimony: A chronicle of Indian–White relations from prophecy to the present, 1492–1992* (p. 438). New York: Viking.

Mulhern, B. (1988). Wisconsin's Indians: Their progress, their plight. *The Capital Times,* p. 1.

National Indian Child Abuse and Neglect Resource Center. (1980). *The social worker and the Indian client.* Tulsa, OK: Anton.

Office for Governmental Affairs and the Rural Condition. (1985). *American Indian unemployment: Confronting a distressing reality.* Washington, DC: Full Employment Action Council. (ERIC Document Reproduction Service No. ED275472).

Ogbu, J. U. (1990). Minority education in comparative perspective. *Journal of Negro Education, 59,* 45–55.

Ogbu, J. U. (1992). Understanding cultural diversity and learning. *Educational Researcher, 21*(8), 5–24.

Richardson, E. H. (1981). Cultural and historical perspectives in counseling American Indians. In D. N. Sue (Ed.), *Counseling the culturally different.* New York: Wiley.

Sutton, C. T., & Broken Nose, M. A. (1996). American Indian families: An overview. In M. McGoldrick, J. Pearce, & J. Giorando (Eds.), *Ethnicity and family therapy* (pp. 31–44). New York: Guilford.

Tatum, B. D. (1997). *"Why are all the Black kids sitting together in the cafeteria?" and other conversations about race.* New York: Basic Books.

Trimble, J. E. (1981). Value differentials and their importance in counseling American Indians. In P. Pedersen, J. Draguns, W. Lonner, & J. Trimble (Eds.), *Counseling across cultures* (pp. 203–226). Honolulu: University Press of Hawaii.

U.S. Bureau of the Census. (1981). *Census of the population: 1980.* Washington, DC: U.S. Government Printing Office.

U.S. Bureau of the Census. (1993). *We, the first Americans.* Washington, DC: U.S. Government Printing Office.

U.S. Bureau of the Census. (2003). *Statistical Abstract of the United States: 2003* (123rd ed.). Washington, DC: U.S. Government Printing Office.

U.S. Department of Health and Human Services. (1977). *Health of the disadvantaged chart book.* Washington, DC: U.S. Government Printing Office.

Valle, R. (1986). Cross-cultural competence in minority communities: A curriculum implementation strategy. In M. R. Miranda, & H. H. L. Kitano (Eds.), *Mental health research and practice in minority communities: Development of culturally sensitive training programs* (pp. 51–89). Rockville, MD: National Institute of Mental Health. (ERIC Document Reproduction Service No. ED278754)

Vogel, V. J. (1987). The blackout of native American cultural achievements. *American Indian Quarterly, 11,* 11–35.

In one of my first freshman classes at the university, I found myself sitting next to a white student I had known slightly at high school. I sat silent and tense, not even turning to look at her because I didn't want to speak first and be rebuffed. Eventually, she turned to me and said, "Yoshi, aren't you going to speak to me?"

Yoshiko Uchida (1982, p. 41)
Desert Exile: The Uprooting of a Japanese-American Family

6 CHAPTER | Learning from Asian American Stories

While this is certainly not an unusual question or circumstance, the question is laden with emotionally charged cultural considerations. At first glance, you might think that Yoshi is shy or perhaps disinterested in this classmate. But when you place this exchange within the cultural context in which it exists, you become aware that Yoshi's perspective, as a Japanese American in this situation, brings to consciousness a myriad of intercultural communication barriers. Her silence, restraint, and deference were not signs of shyness, rudeness, disinterest, or social ineptitude but rather a way of coping in an environment that she knew from experience was fraught with uncertainty, potential rejection, and various forms of discrimination.

The term Asian Americans is a collective reference to Asian and Pacific Islander populations who live in the United States. Tatum (1997) identified various cultural groups included among the collective, including people from East Asia (for example, persons with Chinese, Japanese, and Korean cultural backgrounds), from Southeast Asia (for example, persons with Vietnamese, Laotian, and Burmese cultural backgrounds), from the Pacific Islands (for example, persons with Samoan, Guamanian, and Fijian cultural backgrounds), from South Asia (for example, persons with Indian, Pakistani, and Nepali cultural backgrounds), from West Asia (for example, persons with Iranian, Afghani, and Turkish cultural backgrounds), and from the Middle East (for example, persons with Iraqi, Jordanian, and Palestinian cultural backgrounds). Asian Americans encompass at least 43 ethnic groups from the Pacific Islands and the continent of Asia. Religious beliefs vary greatly among these groups and include Buddhism, Islam, Christianity, Hinduism, Shintoism, and animism (Lee, 1996; Yashima & Tanaka, 2001).

Yoshiko's story is one of two that are the focus of this chapter, which explores ethnic group values, traditions, conflicts, and coping strategies common to many Asian Americans.

CHAPTER OBJECTIVES

1. Describe common values and worldviews of persons in Asian American ethnic groups.
2. Identify ways persons profiled in the case narratives experienced and addressed the six cultural factors explored in this text.
3. Explain academic and intercultural interaction implications related to the six cultural factors for members in this ethnic group.
4. Describe coping strategies utilized by members of this group.
5. Identify classroom strategies for cultivating the resources provided when traditional Asian American worldviews are integrated into your curriculum.

CULTURAL FACTOR 1: HISTORICAL AND CURRENT TREATMENT IN U.S. SOCIETY

The first cultural factor illuminates the historical and current treatment of Asian people in U.S. society. Like other immigrant groups, Asian Americans have experienced a history of discrimination at the hands of dominant culture in the United States (Daniels, 1971; Jones, 1972; Nishi, 1982; Sue & Sue, 1993). Knowledge of this often unspoken and barely visible part of U.S. history is important for understanding current perspectives, values, and interaction patterns of members of this cultural group.

Because it is important to understand your own culture if you are to move beyond simply knowing about other cultures to understanding the feelings and experiences of others, take some time to reflect and critically examine your own values and beliefs about communication before identifying the interaction behaviors that are common to members of this group. Exercise 6-1 is provided to help you with this reflection.

Background

The first Chinese immigrants came to the United States in response to the social and economic instability occurring in China in the mid 1840s (DeVos & Abbot, 1966). At that time, Chinese men were often hired as cheap labor to help build the transcontinental railroad (Daniels, 1971). This required them to leave their families behind in China. However, White American hostilities toward the Chinese grew when labor jobs in the United States became scarce in the late 1870s. At that time, numerous laws (denying citizenship, home ownership, and the right to marry) were passed. For example, the **Page Law** prohibiting the immigration of Chinese contract laborers was passed in 1875. Such laws culminated in the **Federal Chinese Exclusion Act of 1882**, which was not

Exercise 6-1 | Point of Reflection: A Reflection and an Awareness

Directions: Respond to this series of questions with the first thoughts that come to mind. Write these down and share your responses with a classmate, a colleague, and/or your instructor in small-group discussion. Take note of the differences you observe when you compare your responses to the responses of others.

By examining your own preferences, you may better appreciate the idea that some traditional Asian American cultural beliefs that may have previously seemed exotic or alien to you are actually in some ways quite similar to your own values and preferences. All are values, behaviors, and attitudes learned in context that serve as ways to navigate life and function within the context of one's unique cultural experiences.

After reading the chapter, return to your responses and compare your responses to the questions with what you imagine may be the responses of traditional Asian American students to these same questions.

1. Imagine that you have an important question and the teacher is currently explaining a point to the class. What do you do?

2. Assume you are sitting at the table during a family dinner. Perhaps you have a grandparent or an elderly aunt or uncle in attendance. If the discussion around the table focuses on something about which you feel strongly or that makes you feel uncomfortable, what do you do?

3. You are currently in a meeting in which all of the members are sharing their ideas about an important policy or procedure. Do you initiate conversation and share your ideas, wait to be asked, wait for silence, or hold your thoughts to yourself? Explain your responses.

repealed until 1943 when the United States sought to form an alliance with China during World War II.

The Japanese experienced similar severe discrimination when they began immigrating to the United States. While many Japanese people initially served as cheap agricultural laborers, the more the Japanese experienced success in the fishing and farming industries, the more Americans responded with prohibitive legislation, much like the Chinese experienced (Kitano, 1969). Certainly, the low point of American responses to Japanese immigrants came in 1942 when more than 111,000 Japanese were "relocated" into **internment camps** in several different locations in the United States. In so doing, the government interned its own citizens, thus violating the fifth and fourteenth amendments to the Constitution providing for "due process" and "equal protection under the law for all citizens." This forced eviction and complete disruption of the lives, homes, relationships, jobs, belongings, and privacy of Japanese American men, women, and children was allowed under the guise of "military necessity" after the bombs fell on Pearl Harbor in 1941. It is interesting to note that although the United States was also at war with Germany and Italy, Americans with ancestors from those countries were not placed in internment camps (Uchida, 1982).

More than 250,000 Southeast Asian refugees were admitted to the United States between 1975 and 1979 (U.S. Department of Health and Welfare, 1979). During the evacuation of Saigon in 1975, many of the first immigrants were educated Vietnamese government employees and their families (Chan, 1981). Between 1980 and 1984, an additional 450,000 refugees arrived in the United

States from the same area (U.S. Bureau of the Census, 1985, 1986). Some from Cambodia and Laos among this group were also educated and spoke some English. However, subsequently, many immigrant refugees from these areas came from rural and farming communities and were less well-prepared to cope with the rigors of acculturation. Many of these immigrants suffered long stays in refugee camps in Thailand and Malaysia. They were often separated from their families and experienced great uncertainty about their futures. Family reunification legislation currently permits an ongoing stream of refugee immigrants into the United States (U.S. Committee for Refugees, 1987). Not surprisingly, Southeast Asian immigrants face similar discrimination confronted by Chinese and Japanese Americans in the United States. However, many may be much less prepared to acculturate (Nicassio, 1985).

Current Conditions

In 1980, more than 2.5 million Asian immigrants entered the United States, up from under 500,000 in 1960. The Immigration Act of 1990 increased the numbers of Asians coming to the United States by raising the total quota and reorganizing the system of preferences to favor certain professional groups. This allowed Asians with training in medicine, high technology, and other specialties to enter more easily. In 1990, nearly 5 million Asian immigrants were reported, second only to those coming from Latin America. According to the U.S. Census, an estimated 12.5 million people currently living in the United States identify themselves as Asian or Asian in combination with one or more races. This group comprises 4.4 percent of the total population. Pacific Islanders or Native Hawaiian citizens number 935,600, comprising 0.3 percent of the total United States population. The annual income of Asian and Pacific Islander households is $53,635—the highest of any racial group in the United States. The poverty rate for Asians and Pacific Islanders remains at an all-time low of 10.2 percent. In addition, at 47 percent, Asian and Pacific Islanders currently have the highest proportion of college graduates of any racial or ethnic group (U.S. Bureau of the Census, 2003). Such statistics, on first review, might appear to suggest that Asian Americans are the "**model minority**." Yet, while supported by this reporting of these census data, the concept of a "model minority" is truly a myth.

These references to higher median income do not take into account a higher percentage of more than one wage-earner in families and immigration policies' targeting of Asian professionals for entry into the United States. And while there are high numbers of well-educated Asian Americans, a large number remain uneducated. In addition, there is little recognition that while Chinatowns and Japantowns are popular tourist attractions, they are, in fact, low-income areas in which the population is very dense and poor. Unemployment, health problems, poverty, and violence pervade these communities.

A "Model Minority" Group

The fact that Asian Americans are largely perceived to be a model minority group limits financial and social support for this group. Asian American students are routinely depicted in the media as star students (especially in the math and science fields) who are supported by their industrious parents dedicated to their education and upward mobility. And while such a stereotype might appear to be beneficial and certainly is helpful in many ways to Asian Americans, it also disguises institutional racism and systematic discrimination that Asian Americans receive in the United States. In terms of intergroup relations, such overly favorable depictions of Asian Americans pits them against other minority groups who have not received such good press from the media and who are often accused of being lazy or stupid and incapable of accomplishing the perceived academic success of Asian Americans in the United States. A closer examination of educational attainment statistics reveals wide variations among Asian Americans. For example, high school completion rates are 35 percent for Cambodians, 36 percent for Laotians, and 58 percent for Vietnamese students, well below the 82 percent average for Asian Americans as a group (Tatum, 1997).

Therefore, the view that Asian Americans are all successful and functioning well is a popular and widespread belief that does not tell the whole story of this marginalized group who have in the past experienced and continue to experience insidious institutionalized acts of discrimination. The model minority myth discounts and even dismisses the disadvantage and discrimination Asian Americans still face. A report by the 1986 Commission on Civil Rights highlights the prevalent discrimination current Asian Americans encounter. This report noted that anti-Asian activities, including violence and intimidation, continue to occur.

CULTURAL FACTOR 2: INITIAL TERMS OF INCORPORATION INTO U.S. SOCIETY

Many Chinese and Japanese immigrants fit into the category of **voluntary minorities** in that their ancestors came to the United States voluntarily in search of greater economic opportunities. Those who came to the United States with this hope and orientation generally believed that they would succeed in mainstream society through hard work and compliance with authority. There were, however, members of this cultural group, such as the Southeast Asian refugees, who experienced little or no choice in their immigration. These **involuntary minorities** may display opposition to society and its institutions due to the oppression received from being forcibly incorporated into U.S. society. As such, they are less likely to adopt the same compliant behaviors that may be used by voluntary minorities in efforts to achieve (Ogbu, 1990). Their lack of trust that dominant culture and its systems will treat them fairly and their acute awareness that the "deck" is stacked against them may keep them from aligning with dominant culture in any of its institutions, including schools.

Therefore, it is important not to lump all minority group members who share a common ethnic background together in one category. The terms of their incorporation into society alone may account for extreme differences in attitude and adjustment.

Sensitivity to History, Current Treatment, and Initial Terms of Incorporation

Knowledge of the histories, current treatment, and initial terms of incorporation into society of Asian American students will help you prepare to create effective learning communities for them. Specifically, you should do the following:

- Keep in mind that these students and their families bring with them a history of experiences with discrimination brought about in schools and in larger society. With these experiences come caution and mistrust.

- Address trust issues proactively through the utilization of cohesion-building activities in the classroom and such activities that spread to the families of students through newsletters, telephone calls, and interactions in students' homes and communities. For example, you can spend time at the beginning of the year and throughout the learning process facilitating structured activities to help learners feel connected to you and their classmates.

- Begin the school year by sending information home on a regular basis that informs individual student's families about the student's strengths, successes, and school interactions. Such strategies seek to actively form relationships with students and their families around positive aspects of the student. Gradually, as trust builds, you will be able to use the strong relationship bonds you have built with students and their families to effectively address challenges and difficulties if these students encounter them throughout the learning process.

CULTURAL FACTOR 3: SHARED VALUES AND TRADITIONS

Much of the information contained in this chapter is based on generalizations that may or may not account for cultural differences you may encounter with Asian American students and their families. Like all bodies of knowledge, what we know about different ethnic and cultural group values must be considered information that must be further refined through one's specific knowledge of specific circumstances for individuals in the group. That is to say, no tenet or principle may be applied absolutely to all members of this group or any other.

This is especially important to remember given that the term *Asian American* refers to at least 30 distinct subgroups that differ from each other in language, religion, and cultural values (Yoshika et al., 1981). Within the broader ethnic group of Asian Americans, many differing and often conflict-filled worldviews exist. For instance, among Chinese Americans, cultural differences exist between persons who have immigrated from Hong Kong, Taiwan, and mainland China.

However, even with the great variability within the Asian American population, some values, traditions, and beliefs are commonly shared among members of this group. Having a basic knowledge of cultural elements that are exhibited as shared values, traditions, and characteristics is an important foundation on which to begin one's understanding of issues and conflicts experienced.

Sensitivity to Variations and Uniqueness

Given levels of acculturation, minority racial identity development, diverse ethnic backgrounds, and individual experiences, Asian American students vary greatly in terms of identity.

- Because one's identity is very important for self-confidence and direction, categorizing members of this group as "Asian" or "Asian American" denies significant aspects of each individual student and may negatively affect their academic work. Create times in the school day for individual conferences with your students to offer each student an opportunity to share information with you about his/her family heritage.
- Some Asian American families have immigrated to the United States in hopes of finding opportunities, while others have been forced from their homeland. It is important to be sensitive to differences in initial incorporation into society that may dramatically affect the ways students and their families feel about school. Work to create a climate in your classroom that does not force students to regurgitate what you teach them. Instead, strive to create an environment in which all of your students discover and construct their own knowledge using engaging activities that you facilitate.
- Students of Asian descent are not spokespeople for their ethnic groups or examples of

Asian culture. First, educate yourself (through reading and listening to others) about members of ethnic groups enrolled in your classes. Second, do not put minority students on the spot by placing them in the position of educating their peers and you about their culture unless you ask each student (dominant-culture and minority students alike) to share cultural values and traditions with the class.

- In forming work groups, do not assume that students of Asian descent prefer and can work well together. Remember—there is no one "Asian" culture—and concerns can stem from differences within and between their histories, languages, religions, and so on.
- Not all students share similar learning style preferences; this is true for those of Asian descent as well. Therefore, employing a variety of instructional approaches is best.
- With the value and respect many Asian American's afford to those who are older and in positions of prestige (for example, teachers), Asian American students may find it difficult to approach you outside of class, even if they require help. Be sensitive to the subtle signs that a student may wish to talk with you and be proactive in requesting to speak individually with your students about topics that go beyond their academic performance to include their social and emotional adjustment in school.

One of the most important shared values of traditional Asian culture is the strongly held belief in **filial piety** (a supreme respect and devotion to one's family). This value takes formal root in the form of Confucianism, which holds filial piety as a major principle and defines specific rules of conduct in family relationships. Several key concepts follow from the principle of filial piety:

- Family roles are highly structured, hierarchical, male-dominated, and paternally oriented.
- The welfare and integrity of the family are of great importance. The individual is expected to repress emotions, desires, behaviors, and

individual goals to further the family welfare and to maintain its reputation. The individual is obligated to achieve so as to not bring shame on the family. There is pressure, therefore, to keep problems within the family.

- Interdependency is highly valued in traditional Asian culture and stems from the strong sense of obligation to the family. This concept influences relationships among and beyond nuclear family members. The family provides support and assistance for each individual member; in turn, individual members provide support and assistance for the entire family. Further, modesty, discipline, and restraint are qualities that are generally valued among many Asian Americans. Such qualities, relationships, interactions, and obligations are important standards of behavior and are considered lifelong commitments. Goals for members of the group include the development of community and support for other members as opposed to the dominant-culture values emphasizing autonomy and independence. These concepts are critical for understanding Asian American students and their families. Therefore, teachers and school officials should avoid seeing members of this group as incapable of assertiveness, codependent, or enmeshed when they observe behaviors consistent with traditional Asian cultural values and beliefs.

Intercultural Communication Strategies for Teachers 6–3

Infusing Curriculum

Knowledge of commonly shared Asian values, beliefs, and traditions provides teachers with a resource bank of information and ideas to infuse their curricula with diverse worldviews.

- Seek out and include lost and intentionally omitted information from Asian history as curricular content essential to your field.
- Examine your procedures and routines to see if they reflect a dominant-culture bias. That is to say, ask yourself, "Do I value impulsivity (getting one's hand up as quickly as possible to answer a question in the classroom) versus reflection (taking one's time to think deeply about the connections between variables presented in the classroom and then thoughtfully formulate a thorough response)?"

- After using knowledge of the commonly shared values of Asian culture to examine your own practices in the classroom, design ways to make use of cultural elements from Asian culture that would improve the learning environment for all students. For example, an emphasis on cooperation and cooperative learning could be implemented in the classroom to reinforce the interdependence stressed in Asian culture. Specifically, you could utilize base groups (small, cooperative peer-learning communities in the classroom) that are formed at the beginning of the year and to which students return frequently throughout the school year in order to work together in analysis, problem-solving, and task-oriented activities and assignments.

Traditional Asian relations and family structures are patriarchal. Fathers are often aloof and remote and tend to be authoritarian. Communication flows from the top down, and family conflicts are minimized. Mothers are primarily charged with caring for and guiding the education and development of their children. Traditionally, male children may be favored over female children and provided with more benefits and educational opportunities. Asian girls are expected to obey their fathers, carry out domestic duties, marry, and become obedient helpers to their husbands. When children achieve in school, it is a source of pride and accomplishment for their mothers as well as for the students themselves. Similarly, dishonor brought to the family by any one member reflects on all family members. The power of one's name and the maintenance of the family's reputation is clearly noted in the words of Pang-Mei from Chang's *Bound Feet and Western Feet: A Memoir* (1966):

> Now, as you know, we Changs are very proud people. We believe firmly in the Chinese saying, "Your reputation is your second life." This means that to lose your good reputation, your family name, is almost as bad as it is to lose life itself. We Changs lost everything when we were young, but we never lost the Chang name, and this is important. We stayed together as a family and held on to our dignity, our *zhiqi*. Watch people when they win, and you will learn something. But watch people when they lose, and you will learn even more. Our misfortune made us strong, helped us become who we are today. Understand that and you will understand your bloodline.

CULTURAL FACTOR 4: VIEW OF SPIRITUALITY AND HUMANS' RELATION TO NATURE

Traditional Asian values also place great emphasis on understanding and respecting nature. In poetry, art, and all aspects of life, symbols from nature and legend that provide meaning and can be interpreted for guidance are abundant. Adherence to a framework of disciplined reflection and purposeful action are all hallmarks in this belief system.

While Asian Americans embrace varying theologies and institutional religious practices, three have often been most associated with Asian culture: Buddhism, Confucianism, and Taoism. For those that embrace the spiritual concept of reincarnation (for example, Buddhism), pain and suffering in this life may be accepted as one's fate. A major principle of Confucianism is filial piety; and from a Taoist perspective, maintaining harmony and balance with nature is important for one's spiritual well-being. The concept of maintaining harmony extends to social relationships, and as such Asian family members may seek to avoid conflict and confrontation with others; may appear passive, indifferent, or indecisive; and may be overtly compliant and agreeable when, in fact, they may disagree with others.

In general, Asian Americans as a group tend to be more formal, structured, cautious, reserved, and conservative than members of dominant culture. There is a concerted emphasis on learning from the past in Asian culture that provides a temporal focus of life on the past. In addition, Asian Americans tend to maintain a focus on the future in their attempts to strive for better lives for themselves and their children.

For Asians who embrace Buddhism as a spiritual structure, time is viewed as circular rather than linear. Many Asians believe in the concepts of reincarnation and karma. Simply stated, karma refers to the notion that what happens to you in this life is due to your behaviors and actions in your past life, and your behaviors and actions in this life will influence what will happen to you in the next.

CULTURAL FACTOR 5: ACCULTURATION AND EXPERIENCE WITH EXCLUSION AND ALIENATION

Acculturation, the process of adopting dominant culture attitudes, values, and behavior, is quite often a double-edged sword for Asian and Asian American students. You will see in Yoshiko Uchida's story how her cultural values emphasizing restraint and modesty become components of her protective coping strategies to address discrimination she faces as she attempts to acculturate (Burleson & Mortenson, 2003). She exhibits the tendency of stifling her own feelings and wishes in efforts to escape from the intercultural interaction without rejection. However, to fully acculturate, stifling behaviors proved insufficient. In her story, Yoshiko explained how she was forced to relinquish her value of restraint and modesty in favor of dominant-culture values endorsing assertiveness, directness, and a kind of marketing of oneself that is often interpreted in dominant culture as confidence.

YOSHIKO'S STORY: JAPANESE IN THE UNITED STATES

I think the first time I became acutely aware of the duality of my person and the fact that a choice in loyalties might be made was when I went with my cousins in Los Angeles to an event at the Olympic Games. Dressed in my red, white, and blue outfit, I was cheering enthusiastically for the American team when I became aware that my cousins were cheering for the men from Japan. It wasn't that they were any less loyal to America than I, but simply that their upbringing in the tightly knit Japanese American community of Los Angeles and their attendance at Japanese Language School has caused them to identify with the men who resembled them in appearance. But I was startled and puzzled by their action. As Japanese as I was in many ways, my feelings were those of an American and my loyalty was definitely to the United States.

As I approached adolescence, I wanted more than anything to be accepted as any other white American. Imbued with the melting-pot mentality, I saw integration into white American society as the only way to overcome the sense of rejection I had experienced in so many areas of my life. The insolence of a clerk or a waiter, the petty arrogance of a bureaucrat, discrimination and denial at many establishments, exclusion from the social activities of my white classmates—all of these affected my sense of personal worth. They reinforced my feelings of inferiority and self-effacement I had absorbed from the Japanese ways of my parents and made me reticent and cautious.

For many years I never spoke to a white person unless he or she spoke to me first. At one of my freshman classes at the university, I found myself sitting next to a white student I had known slightly at high school. I sat silent and tense, not even turning to look at her because I didn't want to speak first and be rebuffed. Finally, she turned to me and said, "Yoshi, aren't you going to speak to me?"

Only then did I dare smile, acknowledge her presence, and become the friendly self I wanted to be. Now, my closest friend for the past 20 years has been a white person, but if I had met him in college, I might never have spoken to him, and probably would not have gone out with him.

When I was in junior high school, I was the only Japanese American to join the Girl Reserve Unit at our school and was accepted within the group as equal. On one occasion, however, we were to be photographed by the local newspaper, and I was among the girls to be included. The photographer casually tried to ease me out of the picture, but one of my white friends just as stubbornly insisted on keeping me in. I think I was finally included, but the realization of what the photographer was trying to do hurt me more than I ever admitted to anyone.

In high school, being different was an even greater hardship than in my younger years. In elementary school one of my teachers had singled out the Japanese American children in class to point to our uniformly high scholastic achievement. (I always worked hard to get A's.) But in high school, we were singled out by our white peers, not for praise, but for total exclusion from their social functions. There was nothing I could do about being left out, but I could take precautions to prevent being hurt in other ways. When I had outgrown my father's home haircuts and wanted to go to a beauty parlor, I telephoned first to ask if they would take me.

"Do you cut Japanese hair?" "Can we come swim in the pool? We're Japanese." "Will you rent us a house? Will the neighbors object?" These were the kinds of questions we asked in order to avoid embarrassment and humiliation. We avoided the better shops and restaurants where we knew we would not be welcome. Once during my college years, when friends from Los Angeles came to visit, we decided to go dancing, as we occasionally did at the Los Angeles Palladium. But when we went to a ballroom in Oakland, we were turned away by a woman at the box office who simply said, "We don't think you people would like the kind of dancing we do here." That put enough of a damper on our spirits to make us head straight for home, too humiliated to go anywhere else to try to salvage the evening.

Society caused us to feel ashamed of something that should have made us feel proud. Instead of directing anger at society that excluded and diminished us, such was the climate of the times and so low our self-esteem that many of us *Nisei* tried to reject our own Japaneseness and the Japanese ways of our parents. We were sometimes ashamed of the *Issei* in their shabby clothes, their rundown trucks and cars, the skin darkened from years of laboring in sun-parched fields, their inability to speak English, their habits, and the food they ate.

I would be embarrassed when my mother behaved in what seemed to me a non-American way. I would cringe when I was with her as she met a Japanese friend on the street and began a series of bows, speaking all the while in Japanese.

"Come on, Mama," I would interrupt, tugging at her sleeve. "Let's go," I would urge, trying to terminate the long exchange of amenities. I felt disgraced in public.

Once a friend from Livingston sent my parents some pickled *daikon*. It had arrived at the post office on Sunday, but the odor it exuded was so pungent and

| Exercise 6-2 | **Point of Reflection: Reflecting on Yoshiko** |

Directions: Review Yoshiko's story. Write down the feelings and attitudes/opinions you feel toward her. Identify which of these feelings, attitudes, and opinions could influence your relationship with her as her teacher. For example, if you find that you are feeling sorry for Yoshiko, might you be overprotective of her in class or less than constructively critical of her work? How might these teacher responses affect her achievement and her peer interactions?

1. Write a reflection that describes what you would like to remember from this story for your work with members of Asian minority groups. Consider how you might be perceived by Asian students, what you do that may be helpful or harmful as you interact, and what you would want your students to experience in their interactions with you.

2. Share your reflections with a classmate, colleague, and/or teacher in small-group discussion.

repugnant to the postal workers that they called us to come immediately to pick it up. When the clerk handed the package to me at arm's length with a look of disgust, I was mortified beyond words. (Uchida, 1982, pp. 40–42)

The narrative shared by Yoshiko calls attention to the cultural conflicts encountered in the process of her acculturation. It is clear that her acquisition of dominant-cultural standards of behavior required a true loss of self that was not easily or perhaps even willingly sought and acknowledged (Adkinson, Morten, & Sue, 1992). Use Exercise 6-2 to connect Yoshiko's story with associated feelings.

We know that minority groups respond in numerous and distinct ways to cultural conflict they experience when dominant-culture norms violate their cultural standards of behavior and ways of thinking. Their responses can vary from the rejection of their own cultural backgrounds entirely to a retrenchment and adherence to traditional cultural values in an attempt to resist acculturation. Still others' behaviors and attitudes fall somewhere in between these two patterns of coping. According to Park (1950), the **marginal man** (a person caught between two cultures) lives in "a permanent state of crisis due to an internalized cultural conflict—manifesting in intensified self-consciousness, restlessness, and malaise" (p. 356). The acculturation process that occurs as minority-group members interact in and seek to incorporate into U.S. society is linked directly or indirectly to several psychological problems, including feelings of inferiority and depression (DeVos, 1980; Kitano, 1969, 1989; Nidorf, 1985). Further, the requirements associated with acculturation for students in U.S. schools may negatively affect relationships, effective communication, and ultimately academic achievement.

Yoshiko Uchida's account is a story of the gradual loss of cultural identity that may occur during the acculturation process and what is often referred to as "self-hatred," or hatred of one's own culture. While such behavior is typically perceived by theorists and school officials, including teachers and counselors, as being unhealthy, deprived, uninformed, irreverent, and just plain wrong-headed, few members of acculturated groups in U.S. society cannot identify with the conflicted feelings Yoshiko expressed—people whose own stories echo these fears, insecurities, and seemingly disloyal sentiments as well. The complexity of these feelings makes them difficult to understand and communicate to others who have not experienced them, thus further complicating and impairing intercultural relations.

As described, Yoshiko is one who is seeking entrance into society while operating with less power. From this powerless position, she is required to defer to the wishes and standards of the dominant system while disguising and suppressing her own thoughts, needs, feelings, and wishes out of necessity for survival. The questions Yoshiko learned to ask to spare additional hurt and humiliation (for example, "Do you cut Japanese hair?" "Can we come swim in the pool? We're Japanese." "Will you rent us a house? Will the neighbors object?") are further examples of not only the extent to which she must go to attempt to reduce the discrimination and exclusion that she battles in the process of acculturation but also the psychological toll and resulting cultural alienation that is clearly understood in the asking of these questions.

How gracious a hair stylist must be to be willing to cut the hair of a marginalized person in society! How generous the pool operators who are willing to let a minority group member "contaminate" their pools! When considered in this light, it is no wonder members of this group may be hesitant to initiate conversations (as was seen in the story presented at the beginning of this chapter), due to the risks entailed. It is also no wonder that many feel torn apart by their yearning to be a part of, while at the same time apart from, the dominant culture. This process of aligning with one's oppressor, while objectionable to the oppressed, is often seen as the only available means of survival and will enable eventual progress within the context of a stratified society. This aspect of acculturation—feeling torn between remaining apart from while needing, desiring to be a part of the dominant culture—is commonly experienced by minority students and their families. It is a point highlighted at the end of this chapter in the story of Pang-Mei.

CULTURAL FACTOR 6: LANGUAGE DIFFERENCES, STRENGTHS, AND CHALLENGES

Languages used by members of this cultural group provide great richness and means of personal expression that cannot be accomplished using the English language. However, language challenges and interpersonal communication with dominant-culture individuals are of particular concern for Asian Americans. English language and grammar are extraordinarily different from Chinese, Japanese, Korean, and other Asian languages. The English language is incredibly difficult to learn and use effectively for Asian Americans. To greatly compound the problem, the English as a Second Language (ESL) programs in schools, which are charged with the insurmountable task of teaching all students whose first language is not English to speak fluent English, are underfunded and ill-equipped with persons who speak the huge variety of world languages to effectively teach minority ESL students the language of dominant culture in the United States.

POTENTIAL BARRIERS IN LEARNING–TEACHING RELATIONSHIPS WITH DOMINANT-CULTURE TEACHERS AND SCHOOLS

Cultural emphasis on restraint, respect for authority, and discretion may lead Asian American students to refrain from asking questions during class when needed. They may also be unlikely to challenge viewpoints or openly disagree with peers in group discussion. Displaying respect for others and keeping the peace are cherished qualities for traditional members of this ethnic group. Depending on students' levels of acculturation, their orientations to dominant culture (be they voluntary or involuntary), and their stages of racial identity development (see Chapter 1 for information on racial identity development), Asian American students may or may not appear compliant and deferential in the classroom. In addition, it may appear that Asian American students agree with adults when they nod their heads out of respect for authority. Teachers need to be careful to identify the actual thoughts and feelings of Asian American students that may not be consistent with their nonverbal behavior and facial expressions. In addition to working to understand how these students actually feel in the classroom, teachers must also work to improve the climate and their individual relationships with each of their students and their families in efforts to create positive collaborative learning environments.

Language is a huge hurdle for many schools. Asian students may miss out on a considerable part of each school day when their English language deficits are ignored or dealt with ineffectively due to the lack of expertise, training, and resources to help them translate content material into their languages of origin or learn English well enough to understand and communicate in each of the subjects taught.

FROM CONCEPTS TO LIVED EXPERIENCE

Similar to Yoshiko Uchida's story, in Pang-Mei's story we find that not only must adaptation be a prime consideration for Asian and Asian American students but also issues of personal and psychological survival must be faced. The impact of discrimination and rejection on those who attempt to retain their cultural identities while functioning within the dominant society is great.

Pang-Mei gives voice to suspicions borne from her experience of discrimination in U.S. society. As you read her story, you will see how this discrimination and the resulting suspicions chafe at the very core of her identity and, therefore, her relationships with members of dominant culture as well as with her own cultural group.

PANG-MEI'S STORY: AN IDENTITY IN FLUX

How exotic, quixotic Hsu Chih-mo must have seemed to his Western friends: an intelligent, extravagantly romantic Chinese discovering kindred spirits and traditions in the West. Hsu Chih-mo had the best of both worlds, I thought. I envied his being able to mix in the western world so well—better than I, and I was brought up here. How did he do it, become friends with Westerners and not have them call him "Chink," not have them call him names? It seemed that he had everything: the admiration of the Chinese and the admiration of the westerners. Or was it that he accepted Englishmen, treated them with a blindness he did not have toward his fellow countrymen? Toward his own wife? Most of my friends were non-Chinese also. Did that mean that I was like Hsu Chih-mo, a sucker for white faces?

When I was in college I envied those Chinese who associated primarily among themselves, speaking Chinese to one another and hanging around in a large group. They always looked so comfortable. Whereas, whenever I was with other Chinese, I could not help but feel self-conscious, concerned as we walked around campus that others might think we were foreigners, outsiders.

At the same time I could not be with my Western friends and walk by a group of Chinese without wondering what they thought of me. Did they think I had disdain for my own heritage? I had trouble with everyone. For example, if I walked into a Chinese restaurant and the waiter began speaking in Chinese to me immediately, I felt put upon. But, if he did not speak Chinese with me, I was equally disturbed.

I wanted to go out with Chinese men. However, I also wanted to go out with Western men, but only on the condition that they knew something about China. Yet, Western men who dated mainly Chinese women aroused my suspicion. Did such men consider us Chinese women more subservient or exotic than our American counterparts? To my even greater distaste were those Westerners who claimed so great an affinity with China that they thought they knew the Chinese better than we knew ourselves. And most of all, I hated anyone, man or woman, who dared attempt to explain me to myself. (Chang, 1996, pp. 110–111)

SUMMARY

Cultural Factor 1: Historical and Current Treatment in the United States The first Chinese immigrants came to the United States in response to the social and economic instability occurring in China in the mid-1840s. At that time, numerous laws (denying citizenship, home ownership, and the right to marry) were passed to discriminate against Chinese people. While initially serving as cheap agricultural laborers, the more the Japanese experienced success in the fishing and farming industries, the more Americans responded with prohibitive legislation

Many of the first Vietnamese, Cambodian, and Laos immigrants were educated government employees and their families. Subsequently, many immigrant refugees from this area came from rural and farming communities and were less well-prepared to cope with the rigors of acculturation in the United States.

Cultural Factor 2: Initial Terms of Incorporation into U.S. Society Many Chinese and Japanese immigrants fit into the category of "voluntary minorities." There, were, however, other individuals in the cultural group, such as Southeast Asian refugees, who experienced little or no choice in their immigration. These "involuntary minorities" are more likely to experience greater discord with and discomfort in their interactions with the dominant culture.

Cultural Factor 3: Shared Values and Traditions One of the important shared elements of traditional Asian culture is the strongly held beliefs in filial piety (a supreme respect and devotion to one's family). Interdependence, respecting nature, and adhering to a framework of disciplined reflection and purposeful action are also valued among traditional members of the group.

Cultural Factor 4: View of Spirituality and Human's Relation to Nature While Asians embrace varying theologies and institutional religious practices, three have often been most associated with Asian culture: Buddhism, Confucianism, and Taoism. For those that embrace the spiritual concept of reincarnation (for example, Buddhism), pain and suffering in this life may be accepted as one's fate. A major principle of Confucianism is filial piety; and from a Taoist perspective, maintaining harmony and balance with nature is important to one's spiritual well-being.

Cultural Factor 5: Acculturation and Experience with Exclusion and Alienation Responses to acculturation can vary, from the rejection of one's own cultural background entirely to a retrenchment and adherence to traditional cultural values in an attempt to resist assimilation. The acculturation process has been linked directly or indirectly to several psychological problems, including feelings of inferiority, depression, and weakened academic achievement.

Cultural Factor 6: Language Differences, Strengths, and Challenges Languages used by members of this cultural group provide great richness and means of expression that cannot be accomplished using the English language. However, language challenges and interpersonal communication with dominant culture are particular concerns for Asian Americans. English language and grammar are extraordinarily different from Chinese, Japanese, Korean, and other Asian languages. It is incredibly difficult for Asian Americans to learn and use it effectively. To greatly compound the problem, the English as a Second Language (ESL) programs in schools, which are charged with the insurmountable task of teaching all students whose first language is not English to speak fluent English, are underfunded and ill-equipped.

Potential Barriers in Learning/Teaching Relationships with Dominant-Culture Teachers and Schools Cultural emphasis on restraint, respect for authority, and discretion may lead Asian American students to refrain from asking questions during class when needed. They may also be unlikely to challenge viewpoints or openly disagree with peers in group discussion. Displaying respect for others and keeping the peace are cherished qualities for traditional members of this ethnic group.

Language is a huge hurdle for many schools. Asian students may miss out on a considerable part of each school day when their English language deficits are not adequately addressed.

Important Terms

Federal Chinese Exclusion Act of 1882
filial piety
internment camps
involuntary minorities
marginal man
model minority
Page Law
voluntary minorities

Enrichment

Chang, P. M. (1996). *Bound feet & western dress: A memoir.* New York: Doubleday.

Daniels, R. (1971). *Concentration camps USA: Japanese Americans and WWII.* New York: Holt, Rinehart, & Winston.

Houston, J. W., & Houston, J. (1973). *Farewell to Manzanar.* New York: Bantam Books.

Kitano, H. H. L. (1969). *Japanese Americans: The evolution of a subculture.* Englewood Cliffs, NJ: Prentice Hall.

Uchida, Y. (1982). *Desert exile: The uprooting of a Japanese-American family.* Seattle: University of Washington.

Connections on the Web

www.casanet.org/library/culture/communicate-asian.htm

Beyond Culture: Communicating with Asian American Children and Their Families is an excellent site with suggestions on how to connect with and facilitate collaboration with families of Asian American schoolchildren.

http://www-rcf.usc.edu/~cmmr/Asian.html

This website for multicultural and multilingual research is an excellent source of reference material on Asian and Pacific Island culture.

newton.uor.edu/Departments&Programs/AsianStudiesDept/asianam-acad

This site for Asian American studies offers resources for teaching and research.

REFERENCES

Adkinson, D. R., Morten, G., & Sue, D. W. (Eds.). (1992). *Counseling American minorities: A cross-cultural perspective* (4th ed.). Dubuque, IA: Brown & Benchmark.

Burleson, B. R., & Mortenson, S. R. (2003). Explaining cultural differences in the evaluation of emotional support behaviors: Exploring the mediating influences of value systems and interaction goals. *Communication Research, 30*(2), 113–146.

Chan, K. (1981). Education for Chinese and Indochinese. *Theory into Practice, 20*(1), 35–44.

Chang, P. M. (1996). *Bound feet & western dress: A memoir.* New York: Doubleday.

Daniels, R. (1971). *Concentration camps USA: Japanese Americans and WWII.* New York: Holt, Rinehart, & Winston.

DeVos, G. (1980). Acculturation: Psychological problems. In I. Rossi (Ed.), *People in culture.* New York: Praeger.

DeVos, G., & Abbot, K. (1966). *The Chinese family in San Francisco.* Unpublished master's thesis, University of California, Berkeley.

Ford, R. (1983). *Counseling strategies for ethnic minority students.* Tacoma, WA: University of Puget Sound. (ERIC Document Reproduction Service No. ED247504)

Jones, J. M. (1972). *Prejudice and racism.* City, MA: Addison Wesley.

Kitano, H. H. L. (1969). *Japanese Americans: The evolution of a subculture.* Englewood Cliffs, NJ: Prentice Hall.

Kitano, H. H. L. (1989). A model for counseling Asian Americans. In P. B. Pedersen, J. G. Draguns, W. J. Lonner, & J. E. Trimble (Eds.), *Counseling across cultures* (pp. 139–152). Honolulu: University of Hawaii.

Lee, E. (1996). Asian American families: An overview. In M. McGoldrick, J. G. Giordano, & J. K. Pearce (Eds.), *Ethnicity and family therapy* (2nd ed., pp. 227–248). New York: Guilford.

Nicassio, P. M. (1985). The psychological adjustment of the Southeast Asian refugee. *Journal of Cross-Cultural Psychology, 16*(2), 153–173.

Nidorf, J. F. (1985). Mental health and refugee youths: A model for diagnostic training. In T.C. Owan (Ed.), *Southeast Asian mental health* (pp. 391–430). Rockville, MD: National Institute of Mental Health.

Nishi, S. M. (1982). The educational disadvantage of Asian Pacific Americans. *P/AMHRC Research Review, 1,* 4–6.

Ogbu, J. U. (1990). Minority education in comparative perspective. *Journal of Negro Education, 59,* 45–55.

Park, R. E. (1950). *Race and culture.* Glencoe, IL: Free Press.

Sue, D., & Sue, D. (1993). *Counseling the culturally different: Theory and practice.* New York: Wiley.

Tatum, B. D. (1997). *"Why are all the Black kids sitting together in the cafeteria?" and other conversations about race.* New York: Basic Books.

Uchida, Y. (1982). *Desert exile: The uprooting of a Japanese-American family.* Seattle: University of Washington.

U.S. Bureau of the Census. (1985). *Statistical abstract of the United States.* Washington, DC: U.S. Department of Commerce.

U.S. Bureau of the Census (1986). *Statistical Abstract of the United States.* Washington, DC: U.S. Department of Commerce.

U.S. Bureau of the Census. (2003). *Statistical Abstract of the United States: 2003* (123rd ed.). Washington, DC: U.S. Government Printing Office.

U.S. Committee for Refugees. (1987). World refuge survey: 1986 in review. Washington, DC: American Council for Nationality Service.

U.S. Department of Health and Welfare. (1979). *The congress Indochinese refugee assistance program.* Washington, DC: Social Security Administration Office of Refugee Affairs.

Yashima, T., & Tanaka, T. (2001). Roles of social support and social skills in the intercultural adaptation of Japanese adolescents. *Psychological Reports Part 2, 88*(3), 1201–1211.

. . . you scale the seven flights to an oasis on the roof, high above the city noise, where you can think to the rhythms of your own band. Discordant notes rise with the traffic at five, mellow to a bolero at sundown. Keeping company with the pigeons, you watch the people below, flowing in currents on the street where you live, each one alone in a crowd, each one an island like you.

Judith Ortiz Cofer (1996, p. ix)
An Island Like You: Stories of the Barrio

7

CHAPTER

Learning from Latino/a Stories

Cofer describes her experience with acculturation through the images of her poetry. Her description is of a flight to a rooftop in an effort to find an oasis within a city, where she can reconnect with her culture.

The current chapter explores the stories of Latino/as. As with the two previous chapters, the focus of this chapter is on the rich traditions, shared values, experiences with conflict, and coping strategies of this cultural group. Autobiographical case narratives are presented to highlight the six major cultural factors presented in this text.

As you come to more fully understand the culture and lived experience of Latino/as, you will be more able to create learning environments that prove most effective for students who share this background.

CHAPTER OBJECTIVES

1. Describe common values and worldviews of Latino/as.
2. Identify ways in which the people profiled in the case narratives experienced and addressed the six cultural factors explored in this text.
3. Explain academic and intercultural interaction implications related to the six cultural factors for members in this ethnic group.
4. Describe coping strategies utilized by members of this group.
5. Identify classroom strategies for cultivating the resources provided when traditional Latino/as' worldviews are integrated in curricula.

CULTURAL FACTOR 1: HISTORICAL AND CURRENT TREATMENT IN THE UNITED STATES

The Latino population is an ethnically diverse group comprised of Mexican Americans, Puerto Ricans, Cubans, and Central and South Americans, each coming from a distinct land of origin, yet all are linked by a common language and cultural heritage. Some Latino groups have recently immigrated, while others have been in the United States since long before the arrival of the Pilgrims (Barrett et al., 2005). While the terms *Latino* and *Hispanic* have both been used to identify members of this minority group, *Hispanic* is a term used by the U.S. Bureau of the Census to include persons of Spanish origin or descent and those who designate themselves as Mexican, Mexican American, Chicano, Puerto Rican, or Cuban. It has been used by the government as an ethnic label to denote ethnically mixed combinations of White, Black, indigenous Indian, and Latin American ancestry. In contrast, *Latino*, a preferred term for many members of this minority group, emphasizes a Latin American background as opposed to being a label placed by dominant culture that unites a group of Spanish-speaking (Hispanic) people.

Latinos are the largest and fastest-growing minority group in the United States. More than 60 percent of Latinos in the United States have Mexican ancestry, a population that includes recent Mexican immigrants and U.S.-born Mexican Americans (also called Chicanos) whose ancestors lived in the Southwest generations before Europeans landed in North America.

The history of Chicanos reflects that of other involuntary minority groups in the United States. Following the U.S. conquest and annexation of Mexican territory in 1848 and with the resulting domination of these Mexican residents of the United States came their involuntary incorporation into dominant culture. And, as with other such minorities, the involuntary incorporation was incorporation only in name. These individuals were segregated into a few states (for example, Texas and California) that passed laws to oppress them, including outlawing the use of Spanish in schools.

Like the conquered Mexicans, Puerto Ricans did not choose to become U.S. citizens. Puerto Rico became an unincorporated territory of the United States in 1898, ceded by Spain at the conclusion of the Spanish-American War. Puerto Rico struggled to become independent from Spain while fighting subjugation by the United States. When U.S. policy attempted to replace Spanish with English as the dominant language for school instruction in Puerto Rico, the residents resisted, culminating in a student strike at Central High School in San Juan. The U.S. government responded by passing the Jones Act of 1917 that imposed citizenship on Puerto Ricans but simultaneously denied them the right to vote.

In 1951, Puerto Ricans were permitted to vote on whether to remain an independent territory or to become a commonwealth of the United States. Puerto Ricans chose to become a commonwealth, which gave them greater control of their schools, including the restoration of the Spanish language as the language of instruction. However, economic conditions in Puerto Rico have

| Exercise 7-1 | Field Experience: Not One But Many |

Directions:

1. Select any two of the previously mentioned Latino ethnic groups. Find articles that describe the cultural values and traditions of each of these two groups. Alternatively, interview two people from each of the selected groups, gathering information about their values and practices, including their perspectives on family, church, and community. What values and traditions do they uphold and pass on?

2. Compare and contrast the data reflecting the cultural values and traditions of each of the two groups you studied. What similarities and differences do you find among the groups you researched? With which values and traditions do you identify? Consider the advantages that stem from cultural values and traditions that Latino students may share. List these characteristics. Finally, identify ways in their classrooms that teachers may be able to build on the characteristics you have listed to positively affect the academic achievement of students who possess these qualities.

encouraged many of its residents to move to Northeastern cities in the United States, especially during the 1940s and 1950s. The difficulty of finding stable work in Puerto Rico and the United States forced many Puerto Ricans to move back and forth in order to earn a living. As a result, Puerto Ricans tend to be among the poorest of the Latino groups in the United States, with a poverty rate at near 60 percent (U.S. Bureau of the Census, 2000).

A third Latino group, Cuban Americans, is, in general, older and more affluent than other Latino groups in the United States. Cubans have lived in Florida and New York since the 1870s, but experienced their largest immigration to the United States in 1959, following the revolution led by Fidel Castro. The first wave of immigrants was considered for the most part upper-class individuals. During this early phase of immigration, many Cubans were able to leave Cuba with much of their personal wealth, and many quickly established businesses in the United States. The next immigrants to leave Castro's Cuba were middle-class professionals and skilled workers. Unlike their predecessors, they were unable to bring their possessions with them but received support from the U.S. government. The last major group of Cubans who immigrated to the United States arrived in 1980, having lived under a socialist government for much of their lives. These Cubans were, as a group, much poorer and less educated than earlier refugees from Cuba (Leslie & Leitch, 1989). Exercise 7-1 will help you explore diversity among Latino groups.

Latinos are one of the fastest-growing ethnic minority groups in the United States, growing five times as fast as any other group (U.S. Bureau of the Census, 2003). Not only are Latinos unique in terms of their high growth rate in the United States but as a group, they are also unique because they have tended to settle in fewer areas of the United States than other ethnic groups have. Nearly 90 percent of the Latino population is located in nine states: California, Texas,

New York, Florida, Illinois, New Jersey, Arizona, New Mexico, and Colorado. In addition, the vast majority of the population is concentrated in urban centers of U.S. cities. These two factors, close clustering and rapid growth, have provided both strengths and challenges for the group (Suarez-Orozco & Suarez-Orozco, 1995).

On the one hand, the densely populated Latino community has served to help preserve traditional culture by providing opportunities to hand down values, knowledge, beliefs, and customs from one generation to the next. Further, such demography has provided the group with a degree of political power in states heavily populated by Latino/as. On the other hand, their minority status (which contributes to low-paying jobs and high unemployment), a high growth rate, and close clustering of the Latino population in major urban centers in the United States have led to problems as well, such as poverty, enrollment in poor schools, underachievement in U.S. schools, overcrowded housing, and neighborhood violence. The poverty rate for Latino/as in the United States is astounding. According to the U.S. Bureau of the Census (2003), approximately 28 percent of Latino families live in poverty, compared to 9.2 percent of non-Latino families.

CULTURAL FACTOR 2: INITIAL TERMS OF INCORPORATION INTO U.S. SOCIETY

Many of the early Latino immigrants came to the United States from nonindustrial, agrarian-based countries. Most were monolingual, speaking only Spanish, and were unskilled for working industrial jobs in cities. As such, the majority of the Latino population was forced to join the millions of other minority groups in competition for low-paying jobs in the United States. One exception to these economic conditions was the immigration pattern of the initial group of Cuban immigrants. The first of the immigrants from Cuba were mostly highly educated, middle-class, skilled workers. Skilled or unskilled, incorporation was not easy for Cuban immigrants. Their traditions, customs, and language separated and, in many cases, isolated many Latinos from dominant culture. Further, the conditions under which they left their homelands and immigrated to the United States often hindered the process of their incorporation into U.S. society. For example, refugees arriving from El Salvador and Nicaragua faced and continue to face additional challenges stemming from the civil wars in which they and/or their families have been embattled. Whereas other politically exiled refugees like Cubans and many Chileans may have anticipated their immigration and made arrangements to establish support before coming to the United States, many displaced persons, like those coming from Central America, who had experienced a history of oppression and exploitation in their country of origin became members of the poor and working class in the United States. These individuals often left their countries without preparation or support and were suddenly relocated in the United States with few resources from a forced immigration (Leslie & Leitch, 1989).

Coming from such upheaval and violence, this group of Latinos, having lived life as refugees fearing deportation, is often reluctant to trust governmental institutions. In addition, parents of children in this cultural group may closely monitor and try to protect their children from institutional discrimination and harm out of anxiety learned in their pervasive exposure to war (Petuchowski, 1988). Keeping close to home, close to family, and closed to others understandably interfere with many Latinos' transition and establishment of intercultural relationships in the United States.

CULTURAL FACTOR 3: SHARED VALUES AND TRADITIONS

Many Latino/as are united by customs, language, religion, and values. There is, however, extensive diversity among members of this group. One characteristic of particular importance for most Latino/as is commitment to family, which involves loyalty, a strong support system, a belief that a child's behavior reflects the honor of the family, and a duty to care for immediate and extended family members.

Traditionally, Latino families are patriarchal. Fathers are authoritarian, and wives do not publicly question their husbands' decisions. However, the appearance of power distribution between Latinos can be deceiving. It is important to be aware that **Latinas** hold a special position of respect in the household. They are revered by their husbands and children for their strength and work.

Males are expected to have **machismo.** But machismo, which in dominant culture typically refers to male chauvinism, in Latino culture is actually a form of chivalry that includes gallantry, courtesy, charity, and courage (Baron, 1991). It is this machismo that requires Latinos to protect their wives and family and at the same time display sexual prowess, masculinity, and strength by remaining emotionally withdrawn and sometimes having extramarital affairs.

Latinos are expected to be rational, brave, independent, and virile, while Latinas are expected to be submissive, dependent, and pure (Semour, 1977). **Marianismo,** which is a traditional Latina's socialized code of behavior, dictates that Latinas remember their docile and subjugated place in society, put their own needs below those of their husbands and families, refrain from criticizing their husbands, keep personal problems to themselves, and remain faithful to the marriage and family at all costs (Gil & Vazquez, 1990).

The importance of fathers and family of origin can be seen in Spanish tradition, in which **patrilineal descent** is traced via naming through wives' second-to-last name. A mother's maiden name (her father's) also may become her child's last name.

In traditional Latino culture, extended family members are considered integral. **Familismo** (familism), which extends kinship beyond nuclear-family

| Exercise 7-2 | Point of Reflection: Uncovering Media Messages |

Directions:

1. Many of the values held as part of Latino/a culture are in direct contrast to dominant-culture values. As you view movies, watch television, and read magazines and newspapers, identify five different views of what makes a "good life." Record the images and essential messages and values you observe in viewing these media.

2. Describe the values implied or conveyed. Contrast these values endorsed by dominant culture with those promulgated within Latino

culture. For example, perhaps a movie plot involves disbelief that a grown man lives at home with his parents, as in *Failure to Launch* (Paramount Pictures, 2006). Would such a belief system conflict with Latino/as cultural values?

3. Review your data and discuss with a colleague, classmate, and/or instructor the possible impact these messages may have on young Latino/as and the resulting potential for family/community conflict.

---

boundaries, is also highly valued. Familism emphasizes interdependence over independence, affiliation over confrontation, and cooperation over competition (Bernal & Gutierrez, 1988; Falicov, 1982, 2005). Are the roles reflected here represented in dominant-culture schools? Consider Exercise 7-2 "Uncovering Media Messages."

As an extension of familism, Latinos tend to be a cohesive cultural group. Personal security is gained through a strong family bond rather than from solitary actions and self-reliance. One manifestation of familism that is unlike the dominant-culture view of school and work as tools for gaining independence from their families is the Latino tendency to value school and work, because success in both arenas creates possibilities for supporting and remaining in close contact with their families (Suarez-Orozco & Suarez-Orozco, 1995). In general, Latinos value a collective community and exhibit a willingness to sacrifice for the welfare of the group. Trust among group members and interdependence are emphasized.

Other values extending from this cultural group's value of interdependence are *simpatia*—the promotion of pleasant, nonconflicting social relationships—and displaying *respeto* (respect). For members of the group, *simpatia* and *respeto* are manifested in appropriate deferential behavior toward others on the basis of age, socioeconomic status, gender, and authority. In addition, members of the group may strongly believe that one's behavior outside the family reflects directly on the family. As such, each individual is responsible for the reputation of the entire family.

While history is valued and kept alive through family narratives, the primary orientation of traditional Latino/as is to the present. Unlike many in the dominant culture who find their days and their lives driven by appointment books, calendars, and to-do lists, Latino culture does not emphasize rigid

| Exercise 7-3 | **Classroom Applications: Discovering Cultural Insight** |

Directions:

1. Cut about 100 phrases or words and images from various magazines to develop a collage box of your clippings. Make sure you use magazines that reflect different gender, cultural, age, and social-class interests and preferences. As you cut out words and images, do not think too much about which phrases or words and pictures you clip. Instead, cut out anything that catches your eye and interest.

2. Using your collage box, find about 10 phrases, words, and/or pictures that depict significant values endorsed by Latinos. Construct a collage from these materials.

3. Construct a second collage that depicts dominant-culture values.

4. Review both collages with a colleague, class-mate, and/or teacher and identify the primary messages conveyed in each collage.

5. After reflection, develop three strategies for ensuring that the values endorsed by Latinos are present in the materials, resources, and curricula you intend to employ as a teacher.

6. Keep your collage box of clippings to use to enhance additional reflections suggested in this text. When you utilize images as well as words in your reflections, you engage additional creative energies that will sharpen your thinking and analysis.

keeping to scheduled time commitments. Whereas a person from the dominant culture may interpret a guest coming late to a dinner party as disrespectful, it would not necessarily be interpreted that way by a Latino. Instead, when a guest is 20 minutes late to arrive for a meal, Latinos may see it as a guest giving the host and/or hostess more time to prepare the meal so it can be enjoyed by all. Exercise 7-3 will help you develop more insight into Latino values and discover the challenges of attempting, in a culture with dominant values, to teach the values held by Latinos.

CULTURAL FACTOR 4: VIEW OF SPIRITUALITY AND HUMANS' RELATION TO NATURE

Latino/as also tend to extend their value of interdependence to include nature. However, nature is not conceptualized as something to be controlled or mastered. With a strong, agrarian background, Latino culture values nature, seeing in it a partner for life.

Richly colored by Catholicism, Latino spirituality reflects a strong belief in **cultural fatalism.** The belief often takes the form of a resolution to the way things are and as the way they are meant to be. The belief is simply one that reflects the position that things that happen are *meant* to happen and are beyond individuals' control; this belief is embodied in the phrase: "It was God's will."

Research has identified the importance of religion in Latino culture. In fact, Latino adolescents are more inclined than dominant-culture adolescents to adopt their parents' commitment to religion (Black, Paz, & DeBlassie, 1991).

Case Illustration 7-1	**Aria**

My story discloses the essential myth of childhood—inevitable pain. If I rehearse here the changes in my private life after my Americanization, it is finally to emphasize the public gain. The loss implies the gain: the house I returned to each afternoon was quiet. Intimate sounds no longer rushed to the door to greet me. There were other noises inside. The telephone rang. Neighborhood kids ran past the door of the bedroom where I was reading my schoolbooks—covered with shopping-bag paper.

Once I learned public language, it would never again be easy for me to hear intimate family voices. More and more of my days was spent hearing words. But that was only by a way of saying that the day I raised my hand in class and spoke loudly to an entire roomful of faces, my childhood started to end.

I grew up a victim to disabling confusion. As I grew fluent in English, I no longer could speak Spanish with confidence. I continued to understand spoken Spanish. And in high school, I learned how to read and write Spanish. But for many years I could not pronounce it. A powerful guilt blocked my spoken words; an essential glue was missing whenever I'd try to connect words to form sentences. I would be unable to break a barrier of sound, to speak freely. I would speak, or try to speak, Spanish, and I would manage to utter halting, hiccupping sounds that betrayed my unease.

When relatives and Spanish-speaking friends of my parents came to the house, my brother and sisters seemed reticent to use Spanish, but at least they managed to say a few necessary words before being excused. I never managed so gracefully. I was cursed with guilt. Each time I'd hear myself addressed in Spanish, I would be unable to respond with any success. I'd know the words that I wanted to say, but I couldn't manage to say them. I would try to speak, but everything I said seemed to me horribly anglicized. My mouth would not form the words right. My jaw would tremble. After a phrase or two, I'd cough up a warm, silvery sound. And stop.

Source: "Hunger of Memory." Richard Rodriquez. Copyright 1982. Reprinted by permission of David R. Godine, Publishers.

CULTURAL FACTOR 5: ACCULTURATION AND EXPERIENCE WITH EXCLUSION AND ALIENATION

Unique stresses created by the process of immigration to another country and discrimination faced in the new country can create severe psychological distress for many immigrants. The process of acculturation and adaptation can proceed through a series of stages. These stages, while not rigidly linear might include: (1) initial joy and relief, (2) disillusionment with the new country, and (3) acceptance of the good and the bad in the host country (Arrendondo-Dowd, 1981). Evidence of movement through stages of acculturation and adaptation can be seen in both internal processes and external conflicts, even about the process itself.

Consider the conflict experienced by a Latina confronted with dominant culture that empowers women to be free of gender-based stereotypes yet who attempts to be true to her culture and those behaviors associated with *marianismo* (see Case Illustration 7-1). Or consider a young Latino who enjoys activities that may be viewed as feminine, according to culturally defined gender-role definitions. Sanchez, Colon, and Esparza (2005) described a encounter in which a Latino father was perplexed and embarrassed by his 14-year-old son's love of crocheting and even more so by his son's apparent lack of shame in reaction to his father's disapproval.

Addressing the conflict between valuing one's family, history, and cultural legacy while finding a place within the dominant society can be particularly stressful. Adolescent Latinos are especially challenged as they try to balance their cultural values, including strong family loyalty, language differences, and their need to find a place among their school peers, whose dominant-cultural values of self-expression and individuality may conflict with their family values and beliefs.

CULTURAL FACTOR 6: LANGUAGE DIFFERENCES, STRENGTHS, AND CHALLENGES

Sociolinguistic studies in the Latino community have shown the important ways in which language usage relates to issues of identity, racial stigma, and social power relations (García, Morin, & Rivera, 2001; Torres, 1997). Language for traditional Latinos is inextricably linked to cultural identity. It is not only an instrumental tool for communication but also an expression of cultural values. Research suggests that feelings of racial, ethnolinguistic, and economic subordination play key roles in one's willingness to adopt dominant-culture language (see Zentella, 1997; Urciuoli, 1997). How Latino/as reflect and relate to their language and how it contributes to their ethnic identity will largely be affected by their degree of racial identity development and the degree of stigma experienced. The Spanish language continues to be devalued in U.S. society. Such discrimination facilitates a loss of cultural identity that weakens Latino connections with others in the Latino community once the English language is acquired. Consider the stifling of expression described in Case Illustration 7-1 and the experience of a young Puerto Rican girl who experienced discrimination in her interactions with dominant-culture school (see Case Illustration 7-2).

Even though proficiency in one's native language positively correlates with proficiency in a second language, English-as-a-Second-Language (ESL) programs, in which only the English language is taught, continue to be the main method for accommodating students' needs to acquire the language of dominant culture in U.S. schools. There is abundant research demonstrating the superiority of bicultural language programs for teaching non-English-speaking students to become fluent in the English language while retaining their native language. Still, English-only ESL programs are widely utilized because they do not require the utilization of Spanish-speaking teachers as bicultural language programs do. Latino students who do not speak English when they enter U.S. schools have little chance of being able to learn math, language arts, science, and social studies concepts in academic subjects when they are provided with three or less years of access to English-only ESL programs for English instruction dispersed in segments throughout their school day. The

| Case Illustration 7-2 | **The Importance of Language** |

The school building was not a welcoming sight for someone used to the bright colors and airiness of tropical architecture. The building looked functional. It could have been a prison, an asylum, or just what it was: an urban school for the children of immigrants built to withstand waves of change, generation by generation. Its red brick sides rose to four solid stories. The black steel fire escapes snaked up its back like an exposed vertebra. A chain-link fence surrounded its concrete playground. Members of the elite safety patrol, older kids, sixth graders mainly, stood at each of its entrances, wearing their fluorescent white belts that criss-crossed their chests and their metal badges. No one was allowed in the building until the bell rang, not even on rainy or bitter-cold days. Only the safety-patrol stayed warm.

My mother stood in front of the main entrance with me and a growing crowd of noisy children. She looked like one of us, being no taller than the sixth-grade girls. She held my hand so tightly that my fingers cramped. When the bell rang, she walked me into the building and kissed my cheek. Apparently my father had done all the paperwork for my enrollment, because the next thing I remember was being led to my third-grade classroom by a [B]lack girl who had emerged from the principal's office.

Though I had learned some English at home during my first years in Paterson, I had let it recede deep into my memory while learning Spanish in Puerto Rico. Once again I was the child in the cloud of silence, the one who had to be spoken to in sign language as if she were a deaf-mute. Some of the children even raised their voices when they spoke to me, as if I had trouble hearing. Since it was a large troublesome class composed mainly of [B]lack and Puerto Rican children, with a few working-class Italian children interspersed, the teacher paid little attention to me. I relearned the language quickly by the immersion method. I remember one day soon after I joined the rowdy class when our regular teacher was absent and Mrs. D., the sixth-grade teacher from across the hall, attempted to monitor both classes. She scribbled something on the chalkboard and went to her own room. I felt a pressing need to use the bathroom and asked Julio, the Puerto Rican boy who sat behind me, what I had to do to be excused. He said that Mrs. D. had written on the board that we could be excused by simply writing our names under the sign. I got up from my desk and started for the front of the room when I was struck on the head hard with a book. Startled and hurt, I turned around expecting to find one of the bad boys in my class, but it was Mrs. D I faced. I remember her angry face, her fingers on my arms pulling me back to my desk, and her voice saying incomprehensible things to me in a hissing tone. Someone finally explained to her that I was a new, that I did not speak English. I also remember how suddenly her face changed from anger to anxiety. But I did not forgive her for hitting me with that hard-cover spelling book. Yes, I would recognize that book even now. It was not until years later that I stopped hating that teacher for not understanding that I had been betrayed by a classmate, and by my inability to read her warning on the board. I instinctively understood then that language is the only weapon a child has against the absolute power of adults.

Source: Cofer, J. O. (1990). *Silent Dancing: A Partial Remembrance of a Puerto Rican Childhood* (pp. 65–66). Houston: Arte Publico.

truth is, these students have a slim chance of becoming fluent and proficient in English, and their achievement drops accordingly (Moran & Hakuta, 1995). In fact, special-education classrooms have become a dumping ground for students whose first language is not English—mistaking their lack of English-language

Intercultural Communication Strategies for Teachers 7.1

Classroom Applications: Learning to Include

Some Latinos students have little or no association with Latino culture. For others, being Latino is an all-encompassing aspect of their daily lives. Teachers should not assume that each student whose surname suggests a Latino background can present the Latino perspective or is fluent in Spanish. In order to facilitate positive interactions, teachers should do the following:

• Avoid generalizations about Latino/as. This will provide opportunities for all students to display their cultural characteristics within an open, nonjudgmental learning environment.

• Because of various levels of interest, family exposure, and competency, not all students share the same knowledge of Spanish language. Invite the students to use and make reference to words, metaphors, and stories from their culture, but do not assume they can or wish to do so.

• Acknowledge and celebrate cultural diversity through the use of varied learning curricula and resources, including Latino poetry, stories, and perspectives.

proficiency for learning disabilities. Such occurrences greatly stigmatize and disadvantage these students.

Teachers of Spanish-speaking students who are aware of Spanish-language devaluation in the United States can improve the learning environment in their classrooms by speaking in English and Spanish during class. If teachers do not speak Spanish, they may arrange to have Spanish-speaking members of the community act as interpreters in the classroom and arrange Spanish lessons for all students in the class. Teachers may also encourage their students to employ Spanish within the classroom setting and/or in their assignments. However, it is a mistake to assume that all Latinos are fluent in Spanish. Many Latino students lack fluency in Spanish or may only possess some spoken communication skills. It is clear that teachers should avoid forming generalizations and, instead, gain specific knowledge and understanding of each of their student's language strengths and challenges.

POTENTIAL BARRIERS IN LEARNING–TEACHING RELATIONSHIPS WITH DOMINANT-CULTURE TEACHERS AND SCHOOLS

As noted earlier in this chapter, a focus on interdependence and cooperation in the attainment of goals conflicts with dominant-culture emphasis on individualism (Vasquez, 1990). The result is Latino students' weakened achievement when conventional classroom teaching approaches are employed. Teaching styles and preferences that transmit information without engaging students in the learning process negatively affect Latino student achievement

Intercultural Communication Strategies for Teachers 7.2

Classroom Applications: Beyond Content to the Sensitizing Process

Teachers must review the content of their curricula to make sure that it adequately incorporates the values, beliefs, traditions, and language of diverse students. Beyond a focus on content, it is important for teachers to review the way they enact the processes they employ.

Research suggests that the most effective communication processes are those that emphasize learning-style strengths of one's students. This same research would suggest that Latino students prefer kinesthetic modes of instruction, sufficient instructional structuring of assignment and activities, variety as opposed to routines, and an emphasis on cooperation and collaborative learning. Use this information to review your current preferred methods for learning or teaching. Ask yourself the following questions and use them to guide both the what and the how of teaching:

1. Do I prefer telling rather than showing in instruction?
2. Do I prefer assignments that encourage individual achievement more than collaborative work and cooperation?
3. Do I prefer to have time in which students can practice what has just been learned so feedback can be provided, or is there little time in instruction for guided practice?
4. Do I prefer the use of routine activities and assignments over variety and a change in pace and activity type?
5. Do I prefer to model assignment expectations using demonstration, or do I clearly explain what students are required to do when completing assignments?

(Dunn, Griggs, & Price, 1993). For example, Yong and Ewing (1992) reported that Latino/as' strongest perceptual strength was kinesthetic. Thus, when placed in a classroom in which the teacher relies on lecture methods and/or the use of PowerPoint or overhead presentations, as opposed to an actively engaging and experiential (hands-on) approach, Latino students may find themselves at a disadvantage. Black, Paz, and DeBlassie (1991) found that Hispanic secondary school students exhibited lower levels of self-esteem than did their dominant-culture counterparts.

On October 12, 2001, President George W. Bush signed Executive Order 13230, charging a presidential advisory commission with developing an action plan to close the educational achievement gap for Hispanic Americans. Unfortunately, the commission found that Latino/a students continue to be disadvantaged in U.S. schools. The report concluded:

- One of every three Hispanic American students fails to complete high school.
- Only 10 percent of Hispanic Americans graduate from four-year colleges and universities, with fewer than 100,000 graduating each year.
- The federal government does not adequately monitor, measure, and coordinate programs and research to the benefit of Hispanic American children and their families, despite the rapidly growing Hispanic American population in the United States.

FROM CONCEPTS TO LIVED EXPERIENCE

Classroom barriers for Latino/as should be obvious but often are not. An example is contained in the following excerpt, which brings to life the experiences of being Latina in the United States. These are the reflections of Carla Garcia as she enters her new American school.

CARLA GARCIA

The day the Garcias were one American year old, they had a celebration at dinner. Mami had baked a nice flan and stuck a candle in the center. "Guess what day it is today?" She looked around the table at her daughters' baffled faces. "One year ago today," Papi began orating, "we came to the shores of this great country." When he was done misquoting the poem on the Statue of Liberty, the youngest, Fifi, asked if she could blow out the candle, and Mami said only after everyone had made a wish. "What do you wish for on the first celebration of the day you lost everything?" Carla wondered. Everyone else around the table had their eyes closed as if they had no trouble deciding. Carla closed her eyes too. She should make an effort and not wish for what she always wished for in her homesickness. But just this last time, she would let herself. "Dear God," she began. She could not get used to this American wish-making without bringing God into it. "Let us go back home, please," she half prayed and half wished. It seemed a less and less likely prospect. In fact, her parents were sinking roots here. Only a month ago, they had moved out of the city to a neighborhood on Long Island so that the girls could have a yard to play in, so Mami said. The little green squares around each look-alike house seemed more like carpeting that had to be kept clean than yards to play in. The trees were no taller than little Fifi. Carla thought yearningly of the lush grasses and thick-limbed, vine-laden trees around the compound back home. Under the amapola tree her best-friend cousin, Lucinda, and she had told each other what each knew about how babies were made. What is Lucinda doing right this moment? Carla wondered.

Down the block the neighborhood dead-ended in abandoned farmland that Mami read in the local paper the developers were negotiating to buy. Grasses and real trees and real bushes still grew beyond the barbed-wire fence posted with a big sign: PRIVATE, NO TRESPASSING. The sign has surprised Carla since "forgive us our trespasses" was the only other context in which she had heard the word. She pointed the sign out to Mami on one of their first walks to the bus stop. "Isn't that funny, Mami? A sign that you have to be good." Her mother did not understand at first until Carla explained about the Lord's Prayer. Mami laughed. Words sometimes meant two things in English too. This trespass meant that no one must go inside the property because it was not public like a park, but private. Carla nodded, disappointed. She would never get the hang of this new country.

Mami walked her to the bus stop for her first month at her new school over in the next parish. The first week, Mami even rode the bus with her, transferring, going and coming, twice a day, until Carla learned the way. Her sisters had all been enrolled at the neighborhood Catholic school only one block away from the house the Garcias had rented at the end of the summer. But by then, Carla's seventh grade was full. The nun who was the principal had suggested that Carla stay back a year in sixth grade, where they still had two spaces left. At 12, though,

Carla was at least a year older than most sixth graders, and she felt mortified at the thought of having to repeat yet another year. All four girls had been put back a year when they arrived in the country. Sure, Carla could use the practice with her English, but that also meant she would be in the same grade as her younger sister, Sandi. That she could not bear. "Please," she pleaded with her mother, "let me go to the other school!" The public school was a mere two blocks beyond the Catholic school, but Laura Garcia would not hear of it. Public schools, she had learned from other Catholic school parents, were where juvenile delinquents went and where teachers taught those new crazy ideas about how we all came from monkeys. No child of hers was going to forget her family name and think she was nothing but a kissing cousin to an orangutan. . . .

As the months went by, she neglected to complain about an even scarier development. Every day on the playground and in the halls of her new school, a gang of boys chased after her, calling her names, some of which she had heard before from the old lady neighbor in the apartment they had rented in the city. Out of the sight of the nuns, the boys pelted Carla with stones, aiming them at her feet so there would be no bruises. "Go back to where you came from, you dirty spic!" One of them, standing behind her in line, pulled her blouse out of her skirt where it was tucked in and lifted it high. "No titties," he snickered. Another yanked down her socks, displaying her legs, which had begun growing soft dark hairs. "Monkey legs!" he yelled to his pals.

"Stop!" Carla cried. "Please stop."

"Eh stop!" they mimicked her, "Plees eh-stop! "They were disclosing her secret shame: her body was changing. The girl she had been back home was being shed. In her place—almost as if the boys' ugly words and taunts had the power of spells—was a hairy, breast-budding grownup no one would ever love. (Alvarez, 1991)

SUMMARY

Cultural Factor 1: Historical and Current Treatment in the United States The term *Hispanic* was used by the U.S. Bureau of the Census as an ethnic label to denote ethnically mixed combinations of European White, African Black, indigenous Indian, and Latin American ancestry. *Latino* is preferred by many members of this minority group as a way of emphasizing their Latin American background as opposed to the label (Hispanic) placed on them by dominant culture.

Latinos are the second-largest and fastest-growing minority group in the United States. The Latino population is expected to surpass the African American population in number within this century and become the largest minority

group in the United States. The Latino population is an ethnically diverse group comprised of Mexican Americans, Puerto Ricans, Cubans, and Central and South Americans, each representing a distinct land of origin. Yet, all are linked by a common language and cultural heritage.

Cultural Factor 2: Initial Terms of Incorporation into U.S. Society Latino immigrants came to the United States from nonindustrial, agrarian-based countries. Many were monolingual, speaking only Spanish, and were unskilled for working in industrialized jobs in cities. This first wave of immigrants from Cuba were mostly highly educated, middle-class, skilled workers. Regardless of being skilled or unskilled, incorporation was not easy for Cuban immigrants because of the ways their traditions, customs, and language separated and, in some cases, isolated them from dominant culture.

Cultural Factor 3: Shared Values and Traditions   One characteristic of paramount importance in most Latino cultures is commitment to family. *Familismo* (familism), which extends kinship beyond nuclear family boundaries, is highly valued. It emphasizes interdependence over independence, affiliation over confrontation, and cooperation over competition. Other values extending from the emphasis on group and relationship include *simpatia*, the promotion of pleasant nonconflicting social relationships; and *respeto* (respect). Males are expected to have *machismo*, that is, show chivalry, gallantry, courtesy, charity, and courage. Latinas are expected to be submissive, dependent, and pure.

Marianismo, which is a traditional Latina's socialized code of behavior, dictates that Latinas remember their docile and subjugated place in society, put their own needs below those of their husbands and families, refrain from criticizing their husbands, keep personal problems to themselves, and remain faithful to the marriage and family at all costs. However, Latina mothers are revered and powerful family members.

Cultural Factor 4: View of Spirituality and Humans' Relation to Nature   Spirituality, including a deep respect for nature and cultural fatalism, is valued in Latino/a culture. Cultural fatalism (which is closely linked to Latin American spirituality and religious convictions) is the belief that things are meant to happen and are beyond individuals' control.

Cultural Factor 5: Acculturation and Experience with Exclusion and Alienation   Stages of acculturation may involve (1) initial joy and relief, (2) disillusionment with the new country, and (3) acceptance of the good and the bad in the host country. Evidence of movement through stages of acculturation and adaptation can be seen in both internal processes and external conflicts.

Cultural Factor 6: Language Differences, Strengths, and Challenges   Sociolinguistic studies in the Latino/a community have shown the important ways in which language usage relates to issues of identity, racial stigma, and social power relations. Language for traditional Latino/as is inextricably linked to cultural identity. It is not only an instrumental tool for communication but also an expression of cultural values. U.S. school and society devaluation of the Spanish language negatively affects Latino/a cultural integrity and academic achievement.

Potential Barriers in Learning–Teaching Relationships with Dominant-Culture Teachers and Schools   One of every three Latino/a students fails to complete high school. Only 10 percent of Latino/as graduate from four-year colleges and universities, with fewer than 100,000 graduating each year. The federal government does not adequately monitor, measure, and coordinate programs and research to benefit of Latino/a children and their families, despite the rapidly growing Latino population in the United States.

Important Terms

cultural fatalism	Latinas	marianismo	respeto
familismo	Latino	patrilineal descent	simpatia
Hispanic	machismo		

Enrichment

Alvarez, J. (1991). *How the Garcia girls lost their accents*. New York: Penguin Group.

Augenbraum, H., & Stavans, I. (Eds.). (1993). *Growing up Latino: Memoirs and stories*. New York: Houghton Mifflin.

Cofer, J. O. (1990). *Silent dancing: A partial remembrance of a Puerto Rican childhood*. Houston: Arte Publico.

Cofer, J. O. (1996). *An island like you: Stories of the barrio*. New York: Puffin.

Palacios, A. (1994). *Standing tall: The stories of ten Hispanic Americans*. New York: Scholastic.

Pang, V. O. (2001). *Multicultural education: A caring-centered, reflective approach*. Boston: McGraw Hill.

Connections on the Web

http://eire.census.gov/popest/estimates.php

This U.S. Census Bureau website provides useful data for advanced discussion around data analysis reports.

www.smithsonianeducation.org/educators/resource_library/hispanic_resources.html

This interactive, educational webzine for teachers and students features the Smithsonian American Art Museum's collection of art by Latino artists.

www.educationworld.com/a_sites/sites052. shtml

This site is an excellent resource site for teachers, with many useful links.

REFERENCES

Alvarez, J. (1991). *How the Garcia girls lost their accents*. New York: Penguin Group.

Arrendondo-Dowd, P. (1981) Personal loss and grief as a result of immigration. *Personnel and Guidance Journal*, 59, 376–378.

Baron, A., Jr. (1991). Counseling Chicano college students. In C. Lee & B. Richardson (Eds.), *Multicultural issues in counseling: New approaches to diversity* (pp. 171–184). Alexandria, VA: American Association for Counseling and Development.

Barrett, S. E., Lau Chin, J., Comas-Diaz, L., Espin, O., Greene, B., & McGoldrick, M. (2005). Multicultural feminist therapy: Theory in context. *Women & Therapy*, 28(3/4), 27–61.

Bernal, G., & Guiterrez, M. (1988). Cubans. In L. Comas-Diaz & E. E. H. Griffin (Eds.), *Clinical guidelines in cross-cultural mental health*. New York: Wiley & Sons.

Black, C., Paz, H., & DeBlassie, R. (1991). Counseling the Hispanic male adolescent. *Adolescence*, 6, 223–232.

Cofer, J. O. (1990). *Silent dancing: A partial remembrance of a Puerto Rican childhood*. Houston: Arte Publico.

Cofer, J. O. (1996). *An island like you: Stories of the barrio*. New York: Puffin.

Dunn, R., Griggs, S., & Price, G. (1993). Learning styles of Mexican-American and Anglo-American elementary-school students. *Journal of Multicultural Counseling and Development*, 21(4), 237–247.

Falicov, C. J. (1982). Mexican families. In M. McGoldrick, J. K. Pearce, & E. E. H. Griffin (Eds.), *Clinical guidelines in cross-cultural mental health*. New York: Wiley & Sons.

Falicov, C. J. (2005). Emotional transnationalism and family identities. *Family Process*, 44(4), 399–406.

García, O., Morin, J. L., & Rivera, K. M. (2001). How threatened is the Spanish of New York Puerto Ricans? Language shift with Vaivén. In J. A. Fishman, (Ed.), *Can threatened languages be saved? Reversing language shift, revisited: A 21st-century perspective* (pp. 44–73). Buffalo, NY: Multilingual Matters.

Gil, R. M., & Vazquez, C. I. (1990). *The Maria paradox: How Latinas can merge Old-World traditions with New-World self-esteem*. New York: Berkely.

Leslie, L. A., & Leitch, M. L. (1989). A demographic profile of recent Central American immigrants: Clinical and service implications. *Hispanic Journal of Behavioral Science, 11*(4), 315–329.

Moran, C. E., & Hakuta, K. (1995). Bilingual education: Broadening research perspectives. In J. Banks, & C. M. Banks (Eds.), *Handbook of research on multicultural education* (pp. 445–462). New York: Simon & Schuster.

Petuchowski, S. R. (1988). *Psychological adjustment problems of war refugees from El Salvador.* Unpublished doctoral dissertation, University of Maryland, College Park, MD.

Sanchez, B., Colon, Y., & Esparza, P. (2005). The roles of sense of school belonging and gender in the academic adjustment of Latino adolescents. *Journal of Youth & Adolescence, 34*(6), 619–628.

Semour, M. N. (1977). Psychology of the Chicana. In J. C. Martinez (Ed.), *Chicano psychology* (pp. 329–342). New York: Academic.

Suarez-Orozco, C., & Suarez-Orozco, M. (1995). *Transformations: Immigration, family life, and achievement motivation among Latino adolescents.* Stanford, CA: Stanford University.

Torres, L. (1997). *Puerto Rican discourse: A sociolinguistic study of a New York suburb.* Mahwah, NJ: Lawrence Erlbaum.

Urciuoli, B. (1997). *Exposing prejudice: Puerto Rican experiences of language, race and class.* Boulder, CO: Westview.

U.S. Bureau of the Census. (2000). *Resident population estimates of the U.S. by age and sex.* Retrieved September 3, 2004, from http://www.census.gov/population/estimates/nation/unitfile 2-1.txt

U.S. Bureau of the Census. (2003). *Statistical abstracts of the United States: 2003* (123rd ed.). Washington, DC: U.S. Government Printing Office.

Vasquez, J. (1990). Teaching to the distinctive traits of minority students. *The Clearing House, 63*(7), 299–304.

Yong, F., & Ewing, N. (1992). A comparative study of the learning-style preferences among gifted African-American, Mexican-American and American-born Chinese middle-grade students. *Roeper Review, 14*(3), 120–123.

Zentella, A. C. (1997). *Growing up bilingual: Puerto Rican children in New York.* New York: Blackwell.

My ma was cook, an' used to clean house. I liked dustin' part best 'cause I could git my hands on de books and pictures dat ole Marse has spread out all over his readin' room. Ole Missus used to watch me mos' times to see dat I didn't open no books. Sometimes she would close up all de books an' put 'em on de shelf so's I couldn't see 'em, but Marse never liked her messin' wid his things. Dere was one book dat I was crazy about . . . didn't know nothin' of what it was 'bout, but it had a lot of pictures, Injuns and Kings and Queens wid reefs on dere heads. Used to fly to dat book and hold it lookin' at de pictures whilst I dusted wid de other hand. One day while in de readin' room I heard a step comin' fum de kitchen. 'Fore I could move, de door opened an' someone came in. Thought sure it was Missus, but it was Marsa. He looked at me an' saw what I was doin', but he never said nothin'. I closed de book up an' put it back in place. Was scared fo' many a day dat I was gonna git a hidin', but guess he never tole Missus after all. Was a long time 'fore I teched any more books.

Negro in Virginia quoted in Perdue, Barden, and Phillips (1976, pp. 97–98)
Weevils in the Wheat: Interviews with Virginia Ex-Slaves

It's hard to tell small children about slavery, hard to explain that young Black men were lynched, and that police turned fire hoses on children while other men bombed churches, killing Black children at their prayers. This is a terrible legacy for all of us.

Elementary school teacher quoted in Tatum (1997, p. 41)
"Why are all the Black kids sitting together in the cafeteria?"

Learning from African American Stories

CHAPTER **8**

It is difficult to describe and discuss the experience of North American slavery—it is an experience of inhumanity that is almost impossible to fully grasp—so horrible that it would not be believed it if were not for the narratives (like the first one at the beginning of this chapter) of ex-slaves who found ways to learn to read and write to make their stories permanent. Slavery resulted in a legacy that continues to shape the social identities of African Americans *and* members of dominant culture. It shapes the current sociopolitical landscape and continues to affect all intercultural relationships in the United States.

This chapter explores stories of African Americans and cultural group values, struggles, and coping strategies. As with the previous chapters, case narratives are presented to highlight the six major cultural factors. Through understanding issues and cultural aspects that are relevant to African Americans, you will increase your ability to make your classroom an effective learning community for members of this cultural group.

CHAPTER OBJECTIVES

1. Describe common African American values and worldviews.
2. Identify ways the people profiled in the case narratives in this chapter experienced and addressed the six cultural factors explored in this text.
3. Explain academic and intercultural interaction implications related to the six cultural factors for members in this cultural group.
4. Describe coping strategies utilized by members of this group.
5. Identify classroom strategies for cultivating the resources provided when traditional African American worldviews are integrated into your curriculum.

CULTURAL FACTOR 1: HISTORICAL AND CURRENT TREATMENT IN THE UNITED STATES

Sumtimes I rocks my baby,
Sumtimes I sees him cry.
But we gon' have a good time
Way bye an' bye

Den I rocks my baby all the time
And keep the bad things 'way
So his little eyes will laugh at me
All the livelong day.

We gon' have a good time
Way bye an' bye

Alice McGill (2000, p. 4), *In the Hollow of Your Hand: Slave Lullabies*

Passed down from slaves in the oral tradition, slave songs contain the essence of African American survival in the United States. They help teach the history of African Americans and describe the horrors of slavery. The words contain overwhelming sorrow and hardship but also belief in a better time to come. Thus, "We gon' have a good time, way bye an' bye" communicates the message that current and future generations of African Americans will survive even in the midst of incredibly savage treatment at the hands of slaveholders.

Slaves were not allowed to learn to read and write, and they were punished if they were caught singing songs that did not meet with the approval of their masters. So they sang songs in secrecy or disguised their songs to sound harmless even when they were used to help show escaped slaves routes of the underground railroad or to describe their disparaging feelings as they struggled to endure slavery. When gathered together, slaves would sing songs to strengthen one another and to report news via the slave grapevine. These aspects of African American language and song still continue in part today as features of meaning systems that facilitate African American discourse. Such forms of communication help to create a collective identity that slaveholders and oppression following slavery attempted to but could not erase.

U.S. society was built on the backs of forced labor. Legal in all parts of the United States by the early 18th century, slavery was the dominant labor system of the Southern colonies. Colonists captured, imported, enslaved, battered, and killed hundreds of thousands of Africans in order to meet their economic needs. This inhumane treatment of a whole population of people was considered "highly successful" for Whites and so it continued for centuries. White slaveholders (masters) preferred African slaves to indentured European servants because, once purchased, they became their permanent property:

> Unlike the European indentured servants, slaves were held permanently rather than for a few years, and female slaves passed their status on to their children. Thus, although they cost more than indentured servants to purchase, African slaves turned out to be a better long-term investment for the colonists. So much so, that by the 18th century, slavery became entrenched as a pervasive—and in many colonies central—component of the social order, the dark underside of the American dream. (Kolchin, 1993, pp. 3–4)

Emancipation?

Slavery continued in the United States for more than 244 years. The process of freeing slaves, while mandated by President Lincoln's signing of the **Emancipation Proclamation** in 1863, continued until the passage of the Thirteenth Amendment to the Constitution in 1865, which barred slavery everywhere in the United States. However, the process of emancipation took a long time, leaving remnants that still exist today. Imagine yourself in the place of these individuals: being held in an unfamiliar hostile environment; bearing constant assaults both overt and covert, such that dread pervades every aspect of your existence; held in strange surroundings with no connections to your past and no hope for a future, knowing no one beyond the brutality you experience who could or would help extricate you, your children, your family, or your kind from the deplorable conditions you were forced to endure; knowing nothing but unending work and insults at the hands of your assailants; expecting nothing but ridicule and physical torture, day after day for generations. And when finally, inconceivably it would seem, the practice that held you as a slave is outlawed, it takes more than two years for you to actually experience your so-called "freedom." It is impossible to truly imagine the kind and amount of fortitude and coping mechanisms that were generated by African American slaves in order for their survival.

Additional amendments followed that were to help African American ex-slaves obtain their rights in U.S. society. The Fourteenth Amendment proclaimed freed slaves to be U.S. citizens, and the Fifteenth Amendment provided African Americans with the right to vote. Yet, to this day, descendants of slaves continue to experience a lack of basic freedoms guaranteed to all citizens of the United States (Giddings, 2001).

Freedom—Yet Not Free

While seminal legislation put a formal end to slavery, the reality of full inclusion in U.S. society continues to remain an unpaid debt to African Americans. Racism serves as the primary means for limiting the opportunities of African Americans for economic advancement (White, 1999).

Most African Americans in the antebellum South worked as agricultural laborers for Whites, just as they had worked as slaves. All the while, pervasive, racially inspired physical and psychological violence was inflicted on them— violence that especially targeted independent African Americans whose behavior seemed to the perpetrators to be insufficiently deferential. In the late 1800s, African American teachers, ministers, landowners, and politicians were special targets of abuse, burnings, whippings, and lynchings, which supported the existent widespread **institutional discrimination** against African Americans. Even though not all Whites supported the racist attacks, and some actively opposed them, the attacks set the tone for social relations in the Post-Reconstruction South. This set of circumstances let all "freed" slaves know that while they had been guaranteed "official freedom" via legislation, they were anything but "free" to live, work, or even move about in the environments in which they existed. Consider the experience of Booker T. Washington (during his travels in the 1800s):

> While I was in charge of the Indian boys at Hampton, I had one or two experiences which illustrate the curious workings of caste in America. One of the Indian boys was taken ill, and it became my duty to take him to Washington, deliver him over to the Secretary of Interior, and get a receipt for him, in order that he might be returned to his Western reservation.

> At that time I was rather ignorant of the ways of the world. During my journey to Washington, on a steamboat, when the bell rang for dinner, I was careful to wait and not enter the dining room until the greater part of the passengers had finished their meal. Then, with my charge, I went to the dining saloon. The man in charge politely informed me that the Indian could be served, but that I could not. I never could understand how he knew just where to draw the color line, since the Indian and I were about the same complexion. The steward, however, seemed to be an expert in the matter. An illustration of something of this same feeling came under my observation afterward. I happened to find myself in a town in which so much excitement and indignation were being expressed that it seemed likely for a time that there would be a lynching. The occasion of the trouble was that a dark-skinned man had stopped at a local hotel. Investigation, however, developed the fact that this individual was a citizen of Morocco, and that while traveling in this country he

| Exercise 8-1 | **Point of Reflection: What It Is Like** |

Directions: Your task is to go through your typical day more mindful of the number of public facilities, services, and arenas in which you engage. For example, did you take public transportation today? Did you eat in the university dining hall or local fast-food restaurant? Did you use a public facility (like a library, sports club, or entertainment venue)?

1. List all the services, facilities, or social activities you experienced and then imagine how you would have been affected if you were denied access? Where would you have eaten? What would you do if you were denied access to a restroom or other public facility? Describe the feelings of constraint and entrapment you might encounter.

2. Add to this reflection an awareness of your requirement to defer to all those in dominant culture that you may encounter in the day. Let yourself think about what it would feel like to be required to avert your eyes, so you do not appear too bold by making eye contact with others. Allow yourself to realize that your life is in danger at all times. At any moment, someone may want to entertain himself or herself by degrading you in front of others or causing you physical injury. As you allow yourself to experience feelings associated with these conditions, write about how these circumstances might affect your outlook on life, relationships, and achievement.

spoke the English language. As soon as it was learned that he was not an American Negro, all the signs of indignation disappeared. The man who was the innocent cause of the excitement, though, found it prudent after that not to speak English. (Washington, 1965, p. 83)

In this excerpt, Booker T. Washington described how he was "careful to wait and not enter the dining room until the greater part of the passengers had finished their meal." And even then, he was instructed that he could not sit or be served! Before continuing on, reread the words of Booker T. Washington and complete Exercise 8-1. The exercise is intended to help you move from an understanding of this historical experience to an appreciation of the lived experience of discrimination and prejudice.

Separate and Unequal

In the 1896 *Plessy v. Ferguson* court case, the Supreme Court upheld the **separate but equal doctrine** in educational facilities. This ruling resulted in more than 50 years of segregated schooling in the South and the migration of many African Americans to the North throughout the 1900s. At the height of this period, referred to as the **Jim Crow** era, African Americans were not allowed to eat in most dominant-culture restaurants, stay in White-only hotels, sit in most bus seats, or in any way assimilate in dominant culture.

In 1954, the ***Brown v. The Board of Education of Topeka Kansas*** court case declared racial discrimination in schools to be unconstitutional. African Americans were officially provided with access to all public facilities. As you may know from your studies of U.S. history, the process of desegregating U.S.

schools and public facilities did not occur without an enormous amount of civil rights demonstrations on the part of African Americans and their White allies. For example, only after Rosa Parks' refusal to surrender her seat to a White man on a bus led to her arrest and Dr. Martin Luther King and 50 leaders in the African American community organized the Montgomery, Alabama bus boycott were all seats on public buses finally opened to African Americans. The boycott had deprived the bus company of 65 percent of its income. Through this type of social justice advocacy, African Americans were able to affect dominant-culture economics in ways that were convincing and ultimately successful. Almost a year later, the Supreme Court decided bus segregation violated the Constitution. Similarly, two of the many courageous fights African Americans waged on a daily basis in order to gain the rights they had been legally promised by the Constitution were the eventual desegregation at Little Rock Central High School in 1957, in which nine young African American school children walked into an all-White school to be educated amid screaming White rioters who yelled obscenities at them each day they returned to school, enduring the degradation of constant bullying and exclusion when White parents took their children out of the school rather than have their children seated next to African American children; and the 1960 sit-in at the lunch counter of a Woolworth's in Greensboro, North Carolina, where teenagers fought for access to public facilities for all African Americans.

Affirming Rights and Freedoms

Beyond civil rights actions by African Americans and their allies to achieve access to public facilities, many battles for equal rights in U.S. society were waged and continue today. For example, the effects of **aversive racism** in past and current hiring and admissions procedures and decisions are still prevalent (Alba & Nee, 2003; Rumbaut & Portes, 2001). *Aversive racism* refers to the adapted attitudes that result when individuals have internalized racist beliefs about minorities and these strongly held beliefs (conscious or not) influence their judgments in decision making in all aspects of human life (Dovidio, Mann, & Gaertner, 1989).

The Civil Rights Act, passed barely more than 40 years ago in 1964, declared basic human rights to fair housing, job opportunities, and the like for African Americans that had been denied them for the more than 100 years after slavery ended. It was 14 years later still when the Supreme Court ruled that race could be a factor in making college admissions decisions. This was the start of **affirmative action** policy in the United States (Orfield & Kurlaender, 2001).

Affirmative Action

Tatum (1997) described the start of affirmative action in the United States: The term *affirmative action* was introduced in an Executive Order signed by President Lyndon Johnson in 1965. The order required federal contractors to take affirmative action to ensure that all applicants, without regard to their race, color, religion, sex, or national origin, were hired and treated fairly in their employment. Employers were required to use every effort necessary to implement strategies that would result in equal employment opportunities for historically disadvantaged groups. The order did not, however, specify *how* affirmative action programs would be designed. To this day, there is great debate and variety in the ways these programs have been developed and implemented throughout the United States. Nevertheless, affirmative action policies that outline institutions' attempts to make progress toward equality of opportunity for groups currently underrepresented in significant positions in society typically take either a process-oriented or a goal-oriented approach.

Process-oriented affirmative action programs seek to create a fair application process in hopes that such a process will result in fair outcomes. These types of programs are often preferred by dominant culture because this approach supports the ideology of the United States as a meritocracy in which anyone can succeed if his or her work merits it. Unfortunately, the process-oriented approach, along with the meritocracy myth, does not account for the aversive racism and discrimination that are sure to interfere with decisions made during application processes.

Goal-oriented affirmative action programs, on the other hand, attempt to employ open and fair processes as well, but they go a step further. With this approach, once a pool of qualified applicants has been identified, those among the pool of equally qualified applicants who move the organization closer to its diversity goals are then favored for hiring or admittance over other equally qualified applicants. So when all candidates are equally qualified, if a certain candidate provides the organization with something extra that is valued by the organization (in this case, diversity), that candidate is favored for acceptance. Acting in this manner is not dissimilar to the way decisions are made when diversity is not the consideration. In other words, if an organization were attempting to hire an employee and two White males applied for the same position, both applicants equally qualified, the organization would attempt to identify other qualities and characteristics of each candidate that would make one more desirable for employment. They would consider what each would bring to the position and what the organization most valued among employment criteria. Goal-oriented affirmative action seeks to place diversity high on the list of employers' and organizations' lists of values. Even with the continued assaults on affirmative action policies and practices, affirmative action is a necessary step in the journey toward equality for African Americans and other minority groups who continue to be systematically disadvantaged in the United States by racism, sexism, and the like (Beauchamp, 1998; Orfield & Kurlaender, 2001; Leach, 2004).

Current Conditions

It is estimated that 38.3 million U.S. residents self-identify as African American or African American in combination with one or more other races. This population makes up approximately 13.3 percent of the total population of the

Intercultural Communication Strategies for Teachers 8-1

Classroom Applications: Infusing Curriculum

For teaching to be effective, lessons need to be meaningful, incorporating the values, beliefs, traditions, and language of the students into curricula. Such strategies increase the personal relevance of the material presented and help provide for an expanded knowledge base and diverse worldviews. Consider the following:

• Examine the content of your curricula to determine if it adequately and accurately reflects

the rich history and contributions of African Americans.

• Review assignments to identify the degree to which they represent worldviews and perspectives of African Americans.

• Ask yourself if your assignments, examples, resources, materials, and so on are relevant to students' out-of-school interests and knowledge domains.

United States. In terms of educational, employment, and economic profiles, census data reveal the following:

• Among African Americans age 25 and over, 80 percent hold at least a high school diploma, 17 percent of African Americans age 25 or older have at least a Bachelor's degree, and 1 million African Americans age 25 or older hold an advanced degree (for example, Master's, Ph.D., M.D., or J.D.).
• There are a reported 2.6 million African American military veterans.
• The annual median income in 2003 of African American households was $29,177.
• About 24 percent of African Americans have incomes that fall below the poverty level in the United States.

These data reveal that African Americans continue to struggle for educational and economic opportunities in U.S. society (Katz & Baraly, 1933; Rumbaut & Portes, 2001). Some would argue that, based on the success Africans Americans have carved out of the pervasive discrimination they have faced, African Americans no longer experience institutional discrimination in the United States. After all, some have said, "They [African Americans] can vote, live where their money permits them, eat where their appetites dictate, work at jobs for which their skills qualify them. They have civil rights" (Raspberry, 1990, p. 96). While many would like to believe that the problem of race in the United States is solved, it is obvious that there is much work to do toward achieving social justice and cultural pluralism.

CULTURAL FACTOR 2: INITIAL TERMS OF INCORPORATION INTO U.S. SOCIETY

African Americans and their ancestors, who suffered slavery and who historically have been denied true assimilation into U.S. society, are considered "involuntary minorities" in the United States (Ogbu, 1990). As stated

Intercultural Communication Strategies for Teachers 8-2

Classroom Applications: Sensitivity to Involuntary-Minority Group Member History

Descendants of involuntary-minority groups are aware that when their ancestors were incorporated into the United States, it was not seen as a great escape into freedom, prosperity, and the pursuit of happiness. Instead, incorporation into U.S. society for African Americans meant imprisonment, enslavement, torture, degradation, and murder. Knowledge of the initial terms of incorporation into society of African Americans will help you prepare to create effective learning communities for these students. Specifically, you should do the following:

- Keep in mind that students and their families bring with them a history of experiences with discrimination brought about in schools and in larger society, and with these experiences may come caution, mistrust, and even anger.
- Understand that for some, to "make it" means turning their backs on their cultural heritage and identity. Recognize the history that undergirds the pressure to resist "selling out," and acknowledge the strengths and contributions of African American culture and heritage.
- When discussing the history of immigrants in the United States, help the students recognize the differential impact of voluntary and in-

voluntary minority experiences with and orientations to dominant culture.

- Provide invitations to parents to work as collaborators in their child's education. Respecting their valuing of education, eliciting their input, and incorporating their resources and contributions make *partnership* more than just a word.
- Learn to read between the lines. When a student presents as rebellious or resistant, ask yourself if it is possible the student is responding to biased treatment and cultural codes of behavior.
- Show flexibility and adaptability to make your classroom open and accessible for all students. Make sure students are provided with choices and opportunities to achieve that do not require them to merely regurgitate information you have transmitted to them.
- Listen intently to the concerns expressed by students and make sure students know they are heard by you, that you understand their concerns, and that you will work with them to find ways to help correct problems related to their performance in your classroom.

previously in this text, voluntary-minority group members are said to believe that they will succeed in mainstream society through hard work and compliance with authority. These individuals' ancestors have chosen to enter the United States, often favorably comparing the treatment received in the United States to that in their countries of origin.

Involuntary minorities, however, keenly aware of the intergenerational oppression received since their ancestors were forcibly incorporated into U.S. society centuries ago, are less likely to adopt the compliant behaviors that have led to academic and economic success for voluntary minorities and members of dominant culture. Instead, involuntary-minority students are more likely to reject dominant-culture paths to success and to equate compliant behaviors with **"passing"** as or **"acting"** White (Fordham, 1993; Ogbu, 1990).

CULTURAL FACTOR 3: SHARED VALUES AND TRADITIONS

African Americans typically value family (including extended family). As with Native American, Latino, and Asian American families, sometimes more than one generation in an African American family lives in one home. Grandparents, cousins, and other family members may live together in efforts to pool resources and combat the economic disadvantages they face. Many African Americans are raised to rely on and care for family members, no matter what the circumstances. Respect for elders and devotion to parents is central in the lives of many African Americans. Even when family members do not live together in the same dwelling, loyalty between children and parents is often strong. In addition, a fictive kinship often exists among African Americans that forms close and lasting "family" relationships between African Americans who are not biologically related. In this way, African Americans are able to pull together as a community to care for one another.

Sibling responsibility for each other and family-member support for all other family members are stressed. Many African Americans strongly believe the message that one helps another and shares one's resources for survival of the group. Elders are responsible for passing down the values, stories, and traditions of the group; as such, they play a key role in family and community systems. It is their job to teach African American children how to survive in dominant culture and how to respond to the racism they confront. Another system central to maintenance and promulgation of these values is the church. The significance of the church to African Americans will be discussed in detail later within this chapter (see the discussion under Cultural Factor 4).

In White's (1999) *Too Heavy a Load: Black Women in Defense of Themselves 1894–1994,* she described a speech delivered by South Carolina teacher, Mary Church Terrell, at the Mt. Zion AME Church in 1916. Terrell's speech illustrates characterizations, treatment, and values of African American women of that time that have endured to the present:

> "We have our lives to lead," she told them. "We are daughters, sisters, mothers, and wives. We must care for ourselves and rear our families, like all women." Going on, she spoke of the special mission of the educated black woman. "We have to do more than other women. Those of us fortunate enough to have education must share it with the less fortunate of the race. We must go into our communities and improve them, we must go out into the nation and change it. Above all, we must organize ourselves as Negro women and work together. . . ." Terrell went on to tell them about how representatives of different clubs had organized the National Association of Colored Women in 1896 when they met formally to protest an insulting letter by James Jacks, the white president of the Missouri Press Association. She told them how Jacks had attempted to silence the effective antilynching campaign of Ida B. Wells by labeling all black women prostitutes and thieves. She asked them to turn their numbers "to face that white man and call him a liar. . . ." She asked them, "And who were the Negro women who knew how to carry their burden in the heat of the day?" . . . By the time she finished heralding Harriet

Tubman, Sojourner Truth, and many other women who had worked for the race, all in the audience were ready to rise and follow in the footsteps of their great grandmothers. Before she ended, she asked, "WHO OF YOU KNOW HOW TO CARRY YOUR BURDEN IN THE HEAT OF THE DAY?" (pp. 22–23)

Dominant culture in the United States has throughout history held a fascination and at the same time a particular disdain for African American females (Young, 1986). In African villages, women are independent in many ways because they work and often have complete control of their daily tasks and earnings. "Even though African women may be subordinate in their roles as wives, as mothers and sisters, they wield considerable authority, power, and influence. Wives may kneel before their husbands, but sons prostrate before their mothers. And, seniority is determined by age, rather than by gender" (Sudarkasa, 1981, p. 43). However, in the United States, a whole history of oppression has shaped the way African American men and women are viewed by dominant culture.

The African slave trade and resulting concerted efforts to obliterate African culture, families, values, traditions, and institutions served to dehumanize African men *and* women in the eyes of dominant culture. Males were portrayed as oversexed beasts that would ravage White women if not controlled completely through force, using any means necessary. And whereas both African men and women were seen and generally treated as less-than-human savages throughout slavery, African women, perhaps for practical purposes, were ascribed some human qualities so as to exploit their usefulness as house servants and mammies. Males who worked as house servants were seen as "Uncle Toms" who had sold out other slaves in order to win the master's favor, so they could reap their own personal rewards of safety and comfort. As such, they were seen by Whites and African Americans alike as having no power or authority. African female slaves were often chosen for their beauty or skills (judged by White standards) to work and live in their masters' houses. This circumstance created opportunities for their masters to rape them on a regular basis. To this day, the stereotype of African American women as promiscuous, immoral "jezebels" remains (Fordham, 1993). DuBois (1969) wrote:

> I shall forgive the White South much in its final judgment day; I shall forgive its slavery, for slavery is a world-old habit . . . but one thing I shall never forgive, neither in this world or the world to come: its wanton and continued and persistent insulting of the Black womanhood which it sought and seeks to prostitute to its lust. (p. 169)

However, the utility of the African female extended beyond that of sexual surrogate. When needed for the fields, the African female was seen as an asexual field hand with strength equal to African men, as in the case of Sojourner Truth, and when needed for child care, they were viewed as neutered **"mammies,"** like the stereotyped Aunt Jemima.

It is significant to note that targeted discrimination and a highly publicized aspect of racism (the "absence of African American fathers") in U.S. society has had devastating effects on the African American family and the ability of

African Americans to develop economic resources sufficient to support their families. African American males are profiled by U.S. law enforcement to such an extent that they are arrested five times more often than dominant-culture males, even though the amount of illegal activity among both groups is similar. Yet, the fact that uncles, brothers, and grandfathers in the African American community often fill the role of protector and provider in families when needed is not featured in the media.

The depiction of the African American male as absent from the African American family does not take into account the legacy of slavery that prohibited African American males from protecting and providing for their families. This depiction exists despite the fact that 68 percent of African American households are headed by two parents (U.S. Bureau of Census, 2003).

Male slaves were so targeted for abuse and publicly attacked and slandered during slavery and thereafter that African American females have known for centuries that they must be able to provide for themselves and their children if they are to survive. These indelible marks on the African American family required African Americans to create a different and powerful sense of family (fictive kinship) among members in the African American community. Today, broad archetypes continue to exist for African American males and females: African American males are widely seen as Uncle Toms who sell out their own kind to do the White man's bidding or as shiftless, irresponsible fathers who are uncouth and uneducated and who do not provide for themselves or their families. African American females are seen as either promiscuous, dangerous temptations for White males who derive benefits they do not deserve or as nonthreatening, unattractive, and compliant work horses valued only for their work products. All four stereotypic roles stem from conditions of slavery in which African American male slaves had no ability to protect themselves and their families from the brutality they endured and in which African American female slaves were forced to endure the sexual attacks of White males and the mistreatment and disdain of White females for being the objects of White males' desire. Coping strategies for such treatment among African American male and female slaves involved acquiescing to Whites for their survival and the survival of their family members. The male and female slaves who served in White houses and benefited in part from such circumstances were largely perceived to be sellouts (Uncle Toms and Aunt Jemimas). To this day, colorism stemming from perceived approaches African Americans have used to address their oppression creates divisions among members of the African American community. *Colorism* refers to the differential treatment people of color receive from dominant culture and other people of color based on the lightness or darkness of their skin. Because standards of beauty in U.S. society are predominantly defined as valuing physical features that are most like features prized in dominant culture and because those whose physical features closely match those of dominant culture experience greater acceptance and related opportunities, individuals with dark skin who have features very different from members of dominant culture are further disadvantaged. As occurred during slavery, many African Americans who enjoy the unearned privileges bestowed upon them because of their lighter skin pigment are found objectionable and may therefore be alienated from other members of the ethnic group. The pervasive racism that shaped the lives of African Americans as slaves embraces the stereotypes of African Americans as drop-out dads, welfare mothers, prostitutes, cleaning ladies, criminals, and down-and-out laborers in U.S. society and reinforces the effects of colorism within the African American and other ethnic group communities. These conditions create extreme challenges for African Americans.

In particular, African American women face great barriers in attempting to advance in society (Spradlin, 1999). Throughout history and still today, African American women have not been able to benefit from the perceived virtuous characteristics of White womanhood (dependence, purity, and silence), nor can they gain acceptance for utilizing strategies that are effective for males in society (independence, dominance, and objectivity).

> At a time when their white peers were riding the wave of moral superiority that sanctioned their activism, Black women were seen as immoral scourges. Despite their achievements, they did not have benefit of discriminating judgment concerning their worth as women . . . Black women were seen as having all the inferior qualities of White women without any of their virtues. (Giddings, 2001, p. 81–82)

As such, networks and support systems for White women were not opened and to a great extent remain closed to African American women. At the same time, African American women are not often invited and welcomed to join country clubs, high teas, or sewing circles; they are not welcomed on the golf courses, on the basketball courts, or at the poker tables of White or African American men. African American women are not applauded for their decisiveness or abilities to command as men are, nor are they lauded for their demure and attractive demeanors as white women are. They seek to achieve in dominant culture without relying on the "softness" and likeability of White women (see Wade, 2001) and the power associated with being male. Successful African American women of today have carved out qualities stemming from their slave history and a history of discrimination that associates them with hard work, strength, creative problem-solving skills, and diligence. For many in dominant culture, African American women are those "loud Black voices" (Fordham, 1993) that may offend the ears of dominant culture while demanding acknowledgement of their value and worth—presenting their cases with great passion and confidence borne of their conviction to achieve despite their discriminatory treatment. However, the brilliance of their "loud voices" and all the strengths they bring to the U.S. classroom are often eclipsed by the negative images that have been painted of them in dominant culture.

Education is a highly prized value among African Americans as a way to achieve personal and family goals. However, the salience of education is often diluted by the realization that African American students experience systematic discrimination in U.S. schools—knowledge that the deck is stacked against them (Ogbu, 1992). For example, overrepresentation of African American males in special education programs is a pernicious problem that continues to

| **Case Illustration 8-1** | **Primary Support** |

I work three jobs to keep my son in his piano lessons. Sometimes he doesn't want to practice—all his friends are right outside our window playing ball. He practices on a keyboard because we can't afford a piano. I'm working on buying one though—his teacher says that he needs to be able to hear the distinct tone of a good piano in order to continue to improve. For now, he uses the piano at school sometimes, but he has to practice at least an hour a day and I can't always get him to school for that. He has a gift—you know—plus, they tell me playing the piano improves math skills and concentration. I know it's really good for him, even if he doesn't become a famous pianist. I've got to keep him in those lessons if he's to have the chances he deserves in life. Lord knows I have no business spending money on something like this. I can't even pay my bills half the time without juggling this and that and borrowing from family and friends when it gets really close. My mother wanted me to be a dancer—you know. I used to take lessons from a woman who had a school down the street from our house. She was a former prima ballerina who opened a school to give back to the community. But, after a while, my mother couldn't keep up with paying for the lessons and getting me there. I had to babysit a lot for my brothers and sisters. It just wasn't right to take food out of their mouths so I could dance around all afternoon. She couldn't keep taking from them to give to me. It did give me a lift—when I was dancing. I used to feel like I was somebody special. I did pretty well in school for awhile. But now I clean other people's houses. It's not too bad. My regular customers are pretty good to me. I also drive a school bus and wait tables. I did okay in school but I was nothing special. Now, my son, he's special. I'm going to give him what I couldn't have or I'll die trying.

plague public schools in the United States. Placements begin early and have longstanding negative ramifications for students (Patton, 1991). "Labels have damaged many children, particularly minority group children whose cultures and lifestyles differ sufficiently from the 'norm' to make any measurement of their abilities and aptitudes by norm-biased scales a certain disaster for them" (Gorham, Des Jardins, Page, Pettis, & Scherber, 1976, p. 155). Labeling negatively affects their perceptions of themselves and their behavior. These perceptions and behavior then serve as the basis for the formation of lowered expectations for their performance in school (Ysseldyke, Algozzine, & Thurlow, 2000). Case Illustration 8-1 serves as an example of these concerns.

CULTURAL FACTOR 4: VIEW OF SPIRITUALITY AND HUMANS' RELATION TO NATURE

Many African American Christians who were abolitionists, such as Frederick Douglass and those that followed his example, for example Martin Luther King Jr., worked with the community of African American churches as a foundation upon which to continue the march toward freedom.

Today, the African American church is often embraced by African Americans as a rock in a weary land—a shelter in the time of storm. As might be expected, the church is central to meeting the spiritual needs of many African Americans. But it has come to represent even more than a place of worship for its members. The church can serve as a vehicle for meeting many of the educational, political, economic, and social needs of African Americans. It

Exercise 8-2	Field Experience: A Community Church

Directions: It is suggested that you consider this exercise only if church attendance is something that you value and not simply engage in this activity as an educational assignment or experimental task.

1. Locate a clearly identified African American church (for example, African Methodist Episcopal Church). Call the church (Pastor, Minister)

and ask if it would be okay for you to attend services.

2. Following your attendance and participation in the church service, record your reflections on the experience, especially in light of how it was similar to and/or distinct from your previous church experiences. Share these reflections with a classmate, colleague, or your instructor.

serves as a meeting place for defense against discrimination and a launching pad for social and political reform.

For African Americans, the church remains a place where everybody is somebody. Social class is largely de-emphasized in the church community. It may be one of the only public spaces where African Americans feel accepted and affirmed in the United States. But far more than a base for political activism or social freedom, the church is a place of shared values that provide the nutrients of life for its members. Ann Smith, an African American mother of four, explains the role of church in her family's maintenance and development.

> Church is where we teach our children to understand who they are and what we expect them to be. It reminds us to stay focused and to stay together. I want my children to know that there is a place where they will always belong. Our church teaches us all to be leaders and to be proud. Church *is* our family. (personal communication)

Exercise 8-2 invites you to experience the encompassing sense of community that may be encountered at an African American church.

CULTURAL FACTOR 5: ACCULTURATION AND EXPERIENCE WITH EXCLUSION AND ALIENATION

Among involuntary-minority group members, instrumental adaptive responses are ways in which these individuals may try to cope with their limited access to jobs, wages, education, housing, and wealth in the United States in efforts to make a space for themselves in dominant culture. Of course, not all members of minority groups react to racial stratification in the same ways. There is a full range of ways members within the same minority group react to the derogatory treatment they receive. For example, civil rights activism and rioting are both examples of instrumental adaptive responses. Such variation in form may be influenced by differences in social class and individual coping and conflict-resolution styles (Ogbu, 1990).

Intercultural Communication Strategies for Teachers 8-3

Classroom Applications: Extending Curricula through Mentoring

A group mentoring approach can help you maximize community resources and decrease minority student resistance in schools. Organize mentoring meetings with three to five mentors from the African American community and five to seven students to discuss issues that pertain to school climate, community resources, African American history, and current treatment in U.S. society, gender differences, and expectations. Meetings should take place weekly for a period of at least six weeks. Students should be asked to come prepared with questions for the group of mentors each week. By taking on this responsibility, they understand that they may direct the focus of the discussion when they feel the need. However, because mentors take responsibility for presenting information on predetermined topics, students are provided with an outline of the topics for each session that supports their personal and academic growth. Teachers provide a comfortable, consistent space complete with refreshments and arrange for all participants to have a copy of two books that also are discussed by the participants each week. Students and their mentors each pick out a book they would like the group to read and discuss. As such, the group mentoring sessions take on the feel of a book club. Students and mentors take turns facilitating the book discussions. This is another way to let the students know they are a critical component in their own education and support. Teachers must show their enthusiasm for the venture by taking responsibility for providing the consistent meeting space and refreshments and by encouraging regular attendance from students. This way all three constituents of the mentoring program demonstrate a vested interest in the success of the endeavor. Success should be measured through evaluations conducted at the end of each set of meetings. Finally, strengths and weaknesses of the program and personal gains from having participated in the group mentoring program can be shared with the parents of the students and members of the school community.

Involuntary-minority group members also utilize **expressive adaptive responses** to respond to societal discrimination. For example, *cultural inversion*—seeing certain ways of being as linked to dominant–culture and therefore inappropriate for them is an expressive adaptive response many African American students employ at some point in their development. Members of this cultural group may create systems of meaning—ways of dressing, speaking, and acting that unify them as a collective while they subtly oppose dominant-culture expectations of them. Some African Americans may attempt, instead, to do the opposite. They may "pass," attempting to fit in with dominant culture by trying to be more like "them"—"acting White," in which case they play down their blackness and accentuate the dominant-culture values and behaviors they are able to exhibit. Passing, while not the only response to institutional discrimination, is certainly not rare. Ogbu (1991) noted that "some Blacks who benefited from the changes in opportunity structure since the 1960s chose to disaffiliate with the Black community and passed culturally into the White community" (p. 443).

While "passing" distances African Americans from other African Americans and African American culture, cultural inversion serves to unify

African Americans and separate the group from dominant culture for the purpose of maintaining cultural belonging and networks that were removed generations ago during slavery but that remain under attack today in broader society. As such, cultural inversion may be utilized by African American students to increase their feelings of personal and collective cultural integrity even though they conflict with behaviors that would lead to academic success in U.S. schools. Fordham (1982) has found:

> The subtle opposition of cultural inversion appears to be a frequent response to conquest and domination. Unable to overtly display their displeasure or opposition to the social structure which limits their obtainment of the most highly valued social goals, those social groups excluded from the cultural center of the social system frequently resort to methods which are considered inappropriate by the conquering group, but which at the same time enable the dominated group to retain some sense of self-respect and group identity. (p. 7)

CULTURAL FACTOR 6: LANGUAGE DIFFERENCES, STRENGTHS, AND CHALLENGES

In general, African Americans are more dramatic and expressive in their speech and language patterns than are members of dominant culture. During communication, African Americans tend to be more person oriented vs. object or topic oriented. African Americans tend to be more affectionate than dominant-culture members and more direct and assertive during argumentation. African Americans tend to enjoy interaction and integration in communication (Labov, 1973). As in African American churches, a rhythmic volleying back and forth is often preferred over a monolithic dialogue.

Because the African languages were taken from African slaves when they were brought to this country, a language system that has been referred to as African American Vernacular English, sometimes called **Ebonics**, permitted a common language linked to cultural identity for the group (Wolfram & Thomas, 2002, Rickford & Rickford, 2000). *Ebonics* became a household word in the United States and in the world in the 1990s, when the school board of the Oakland, California, Unified School District (OUSD) passed what is known as the "Ebonics Resolution." While the reactions of theoretical and applied linguists (for example, Linguistic Society of America, Board of Directors of Teachers of English to Speakers of Other Languages) were generally in favor of the Ebonics Resolution, public reaction to this resolution was, in a word, explosive.

It is often assumed that cultural language systems like Ebonics or African American Vernacular English (AAVE) represent incorrect pronunciations and grammar usage of the English language. Instead, such formats reflect a language system that incorporates patterns, symbols, and meanings that are elements in a specific linguistic system (Rickford & Rickford, 2000; Baugh, 2000; Green, 2002). The so-called grammar and pronunciation errors are

Classroom Applications: Responding to Language Differences

Inviting inclusion and participation of African American students within your classroom may be facilitated through the valuing and acknowledgement of different language systems. Specifically, you should do the following:

- Help students develop positive attitudes toward different language systems by teaching the history and components of cultural languages.
- Help students identify origins of variations in language used within the popular media (including music, poetry, and television).

- Assist students in learning to understand the importance of matching language type to settings and goals.
- Provide opportunities to learn, model, and practice different language systems within context (for example, in reading poetry and prose, in classroom presentations, with friends, during mock job interviews).

instead variances in grammar and speech patterns that are not mistakes made by speakers but rather specifc linguistic patterns repeated over and over in the use of the language system.

While the debate over the Ebonics Resolution has fallen silent, the issue remains one that needs to be addressed because many teachers continue to discriminate against students who employ cultural languages, and such treatment is another example and reflection of the devalued status of African Americans in the United States. Exercise 8-3 will help you reflect on ways to handle such challenges when they arise.

Ogbu (1990) has contended that utilization of various coping strategies by involuntary-minority group members over time has shaped African American community norms, values, and collective competencies. Because racial identity was and is jeopardized in the process of subordination experienced by involuntary-minority group members in the United States, he has hypothesized that a renegotiated collective cultural frame of reference emerged that often acts in opposition to dominant-culture behavioral expectations. The formulation of African American style to include the development of hip-hop and rap, hairstyles from afros to corn rows, and the wearing of specific clothing styles and brands serve to support racial identity, supply integrity, and create symbolic differences in communication preferences and interaction styles. Interestingly, of late many of these elements created in opposition to dominant culture have been co-opted by members of dominant culture (that is, the dominant-culture acquisition of African American clothing, hair, music, and communication preferences and styles).

In terms of school adaptation, Ogbu (1992) described five roles African American students may adopt to allow for achievement within the confines of racially antagonistic conditions often experienced in U.S. schools. These roles include: (1) the **assimilator role**, (2) the **emissary role**, (3) the **alternator role**, (4) the **regular role**, and (5) the **ambivalent role** (see Table 8-1).

| Exercise 8-3 | **Classroom Applications: A Professional Stance** |

Directions: Several approaches have been suggested to address concerns about minority students' use of familial language. Here you will find brief descriptions of other such proposals. Your task is to provide the descriptions to teachers in your school, at your field placement, or to a few professors in your field of study. Ask them to state their professional stance on these proposals. What do they see as the possible benefits (value) or detriments (costs) of these programs? What alternatives to the programs do they suggest? Finally, after reflecting on their comments, identify your position along with the rationale and research upon which it is based.

1. **The Oakland Ebonics Resolution:** (a) The language patterns of African American students are genetically based, do not constitute a dialect of English, and originated in West and Niger Congo African Language Systems; (b) these language patterns should be officially recognized as the primary language of African American students, who should have access to the same types of programs and funding that are available to other students whose primary language is not English; and (c) an academic program should be designed and implemented to instruct African American students in their primary language and facilitate the acquisition and mastery of SAE (Standard American English).

2. **Bridge:** This reading curriculum originally developed by Gary Simpkins, Grace Holt, and Charletta Simpkins in the 1970s is based on contrastive readings and exercises in the language and culture of AAVE (African American Vernacular English) and SAE.

3. **Bidialectal Communication:** This program employed in the Dekalb County, Georgia, school district program teaches 5th- and 6th-grade students to switch from their "home speech" to "school speech."

POTENTIAL BARRIERS IN LEARNING–TEACHING RELATIONSHIPS WITH DOMINANT-CULTURE TEACHERS AND SCHOOLS

Relating, as they may, from the perspective of those who have been marginalized, African American families and students may display suspicions related to the ways African American students are treated in schools. For example, parents may resist forcing their children to rigidly adhere to school rules and codes of conduct simply because they are school policies. Their mistrust of the system is formed by what has been called a "healthy paranoia" when it comes to their interactions with society's institutions—including schools. Ever mindful that they are the same institutions that disadvantaged them and generations of their family members, parents may be careful to look out for the psychological safety of their children even if that means refusing to require them to comply with school rules—rules that may be unintentionally biased, devaluing, or unfair. Yet, even with this suspicion and desire to protect their children, parents of minority students are also called to make the best of the school experience and thus are likely to be strong advocates for quality education for their children. Their ambiguity about whether or not to support school officials in their mandates—whether to, in fact, join with the school—is

Table 8-1 Adapting to Antagonistic Conditions of U.S. Schools		
The assimilator role	Adopted by academically successful African American students who opt to attempt to disassociate themselves from African American cultural elements in order to adopt dominant-culture cultural elements.
The emissary role	Adopted by African American students who play down racial identity and cultural elements in order to succeed but do not completely reject African American culture and identity.
The alternator role	Employed by African American students who opt to deliberately follow school rules of behavior and standard practices while attempting to participate in African American culture within their communities and at home.
The regular role	Utilized by African American students who have been accepted as members of African American culture but who do not abide by all African American cultural norms (for example, these students may maintain close family ties and camouflage academic abilities from their peers).
The ambivalent role	Endorsed by African American students said to be caught between the desire to fit in with African American peers and the desire to achieve in school. School success for these students is often erratic as they pivot back and forth between attempting to be perceived as good students by school officials and being seen as true members of African American teen subculture by their peers.

often interpreted by school authorities as a lack of care and concern for their children's education. If minority parents do not attend PTA meetings or enroll their children in afterschool activities, these actions may be perceived as a lack of interest or an unwillingness to do all that is recommended for school success. Instead, this refusal to be part of a system that marginalizes them may represent their lack of trust that their children will be treated fairly and that their children will, in fact, actually benefit from playing by the rules set for them in school.

FROM CONCEPTS TO LIVED EXPERIENCE

The story of Ms. A., while not presented here in its entirety, is one of struggle and triumph. It is a story of a journey of self-discovery, adaptation, and growth as this woman grows from a struggling student to a professor with a Ph.D. in curriculum and instruction attempting to make such growth easier for others. The brief portion of this story presented here highlights one form of adaptation in schooling.

MS. A

In 1976, I enrolled in a Nashville elementary school as a first grader. Nineteen seventy-six was a very eventful year. In addition to being our country's 200th birthday, 1976 marked the beginning of forced busing in my neighborhood schools. Forced busing meant that early each morning Black elementary school children would rise to board buses that would carry them to their newly racially desegregated white school while white high school students would board buses destined for the Black side of town.

The purpose of the busing mandate was to achieve racial balance in our southern community public schools. Racial balance meant that the student body population had to be at least 70 percent white and 30 percent Black.

I cannot recall the actual percentage of Black children who were bused to my elementary school in 1976. But, I can recall there were only three Black students in my first-grade classroom, and I was one of them. We had a Black teacher, Mrs. Enuf [pseudonym] whom I will never forget. Forever etched in my memory is how evil she was toward her African American students. As a schoolgirl, I remember thinking that Mrs. Enuf was mean to us because she did not like Black people. In my eyes, Mrs. Enuf's ill treatment toward us reflected white supremacist logic. Consequently, my Black classmates and I referred to Mrs. Enuf as an Oreo, black on the outside but white on the inside.

In class, Mrs. Enuf would constantly paddle her Black students on our hands and humiliate us before the class by sending us to the corner. Her actions toward my white classmates were totally different. These white students never seemed to do anything wrong and always ended their day with a candy treat.

I realized early that the white kid's way of responding and interacting with our teacher must have been the right way. Although I was clearly aware that there was nothing I could do to make Mrs. Enuf like me, I learned early that if I could read and do my class assignments then I would avoid some humiliation and, perhaps on occasion, receive some candy. I believe the possibility of the candy treat more than the avoidance of humiliation enticed my desire to do what was necessary to receive some of the pleasure afforded the white children. In spite of Mrs. Enuf's hateful ways, the sharing of candy was a signification of personal gratification. Although it was clear that she did not like me, at least with the exchange of candy, my taste buds would be satisfied. (Hollingsworth, Didelot, & Smith, 2003)

SUMMARY

Cultural Factor 1: Historical and Current Treatment in the United States Unlike the European indentured servant, African slaves were held permanently rather than for a few years, and African American female slaves passed their status on to their children. Slavery continued in the United States for at least 244 years. In the 1896 *Plessy v. Ferguson* court case, the Supreme Court upheld the separate but equal doctrine in educational facilities. A presidential order obligated federal contractors to take affirmative action to ensure that applicants are employed without regard to their race, color, religion, sex, or national origin. Process-oriented affirmative action programs work to create fair application processes in hopes that such pro-

cesses will result in fair admissions and hiring outcomes. Goal-oriented affirmative action programs attempt to ensure a fair application process and, if all things are equal in terms of job qualifications, to select a candidate that also furthers the organization's goals for increased diversity.

Cultural Factor 2: Initial Terms of Incorporation into U.S. Society African Americans are considered involuntary minorities. Voluntary-minority group members are descendents of those who were said to believe that they would succeed in mainstream society through hard work and compliance with authority. Involuntary minorities are less likely to adopt compliant behaviors that have led to academic and economic success for voluntary minorities and members of dominant culture because they are descendents of those who were involuntarily incorporated into U.S. society through conquest, slavery, or colonization. As such, they may have experienced generations of oppression that result in a knowledge that the deck is stacked against them.

Cultural Factor 3: Commonly Shared Values and Traditions Respect for elders and devotion to family is central in the lives of many African Americans. Sibling responsibility for siblings and family member support for all other family members are stressed.

Education is another value prized by African Americans as a way to achieve personal and family goals. In African villages, women are independent in many ways because they work and often have complete control of their daily tasks and earnings. Even though African women may be subordinate in their roles as wives, as mothers, and as sisters, they wield considerable authority, power, and influence. African male slaves were prohibited from protecting and providing for their families, and African female slaves were exploited in their slave roles. Negative images of African American males and females stem from injustices endured during slavery and racism that still exists today.

Cultural Factor 4: View of Spirituality and Humans' Relation to Nature Church is more than just a place of worship. Church has served and continues to serve as a vehicle for meeting many of the educational, political, economic, and social needs of African Americans.

Cultural Factor 5: Acculturation and Experience with Exclusion and Alienation Instrumental adaptive responses are ways in which African Americans may try to make a space for themselves in dominant culture. For example, civil rights activism and rioting are both examples of instrumental adaptive responses. Involuntary-minority group members also utilize expressive adaptive responses that are distinct, personal ways of responding to the societal discrimination they face. For example, involuntary-minority group members may attempt to utilize cultural inversion or attempt to fit in with dominant culture by trying to be more like Whites by "passing" or "acting White." Because racial identity is jeopardized in the process of subordination experienced by involuntary-minority group members, a renegotiated collective cultural frame of reference emerges that often acts in opposition to dominant-culture behavioral expectations. **Cultural inversion** is involuntary-minority group members' regard of certain forms of behavior, symbols, and meanings as inappropriate for them because they are seen as characteristic of White America.

Cultural Factor 6: Language Differences, Strengths, and Challenges Because the African languages were taken from African slaves when they were brought to this country, a language system that is commonly referred to as Ebonics has permitted a common language linked to cultural identity for the group. Such formats reflect a legitimate language system.

Ogbu (1992) described five roles African American students may adopt to allow for achievement within the confines of racially antagonistic conditions often experienced in U.S. schools. These roles include: (1) the assimilator role, (2) the emissary role, (3) the alternator role, (4) the regular role, and (5) the ambivalent role.

Potential Barriers in Learning/Teaching Relationships with Dominant-Culture Teachers and Schools Relating, as they may, from the perspective of those who have been marginalized, African American families and students may display suspicions related to the ways they are treated within schools. In cases where parental involvement seems limited, this refusal to be a part of a system that marginalizes them may represent their lack of trust that they will be treated fairly and that their children will, in fact, actually benefit from playing by the rules set for them in schools.

Important Terms

acting White

affirmative action

alternator role

ambivalent role

assimilator role

aversive racism

Brown v. the Board of Education of Topeka, Kansas

cultural inversion strategies

Ebonics

Emancipation Proclamation

emissary role

expressive adaptive responses

goal-oriented affirmative action

institutional discrimination

involuntary minorities

Jim Crow

mammies

passing

process-oriented affirmative action

regular role

separate but equal doctrine

Enrichment

Baugh, J. (2000). *Beyond Ebonics: Linguistic pride and racial prejudice.* Oxford, UK: Oxford University.

Cole, J. B. (2003). *Gender talk: The struggle for women's equality in African American communities.* New York: Ballantine.

Franklin, J. H. (Ed.). (1965). *Three Negro classics.* New York: Avon.

Giddings, P. (2001). *When and where I enter. The impact of Black women on race and sex in America.* New York: Perennial.

Grant, J. (Ed.). (1968). *Black protest: History, documents, and analyses. 1619 to the present.* New York: Fawcett Premier.

Green, L. (2002). *African American English: A linguistic introduction.* Cambridge, UK: Cambridge University.

Guinier, L., & Sturm, S. (2001). *Who's qualified?* Boston: Beacon.

Hacker, A. (1992). *Two nations: Black and white, separate, hostile, unequal.* New York: Charles Scribner's Sons.

Harris, F. R., & Wilkins, R. W. (Eds.). (1988). *Quiet riots: Race and poverty in the United States.* New York: Pantheon.

Hayre, R. W., & Moore, A. (1997). *Tell them we are rising: A memoir of faith in education.* New York: John Wiley & Sons.

Perdue, C. L., Barden, T. E., & Phillips, R. K. (Eds.). (1976). *Weevils in the wheat: Interviews with Virginia ex-slaves.* Charlottesville: University of Virginia.

Williams, L. (2000). *It's the little things: Everyday interactions that anger, annoy, and divide the races.* New York: Harcourt.

Connections on the Web

http://usinfo.state.gov/usa/blackhis/resource.htm

The site provides narratives and personal stories recounting the experience of being African American in the United States. It also provides excellent links.

www.kn.pacbell.com/wired/BHM/AfroAm.html

This site offers excellent support for teachers studying African American events and issues.

www.tolerance.org/teach/find/find.jsp

Founded in 1991 by the Southern Poverty Law Center, Teaching Tolerance provides educators with free educational materials that promote respect for differences and appreciation of diversity in the classroom and beyond.

REFERENCES

Alba, R., & Nee, V. (2003). *Remaking the American mainstream: Assimilation and contemporary immigration.* Cambridge, MA: Harvard University.

Baugh, J. (2000). *Beyond Ebonics: Linguistic pride and racial prejudice.* Oxford, UK: Oxford University.

Beauchamp, T. L. (1998). In defense of affirmative action. *Journal of Ethics, 2*(2), 143–158.

Dovidio, J. F., Mann, J., & Gaertner, S. L. (1989). Resistance to affirmative action: The implication of aversive racism. In F. A. Blanchard & F. J. Crosby (Eds.), *Affirmative action in perspective.* New York: Springer-Verlog.

DuBois, W. E. B. (1965). The souls of Black folk. In J. H. Franklin (Ed.), *Three Negro classics* (pp. 207–389). New York: Avon.

DuBois, W. E. B. (1969). The domination of women. In *Darkwater: Voices from within the veil.* New York: Schocken.

Fordham, S. (1982, December). *Cultural inversion and black children's school performance.* Paper presented at the annual meeting of the American Anthropological Association, Washington, DC.

Fordham, S. (1993). Those loud black girls: Black women, silence, and gender "passing" in the academy. *Anthropology and Education Quarterly, 24,* 3–32.

Giddings, P. (2001). *When and where I enter. The impact of Black women on race and sex in America.* New York: Perennial.

Gorham, Des Jardins, Page, Pettis, & Scherber. (1976).

Green, L. (2002). *African American English: A linguistic introduction.* Cambridge, UK: Cambridge University.

Hayre, R. W., & Moore, A. (1997). *Tell them we are rising: A memoir of faith in education.* New York: John Wiley & Sons.

Hollingsworth, L. A., Didelot, M. J., & Smith, J. O. (2003). REACH beyond tolerance: A framework for teaching children empathy and responsibility. *Journal of Humanistic Counseling, Education & Development, 42*(2), 139–152.

Katz, D., & Baraly, K. (1933). Racial stereotypes of one hundred college students. *Journal of Abnormal and Social Psychology, 28,* 280–290.

Kolchin, P. (1993). *American slavery, 1619–1877.* New York: Hill & Wang.

Labov, W. (1973). *Language in the inner city: Studies in Black English vernacular.* Philadelphia: University of Pennsylvania.

Leach, B. W. (2004). Race as mission critical: The occupational need rationale in military affirmative action and beyond. *Yale Law Review, 113*(3), 1093–1143.

McGill, A. (2000). *In the hollow of your hand: Slave lullabies.* Boston: Houghton Mifflin.

Ogbu, J. U. (1990). Minority education in comparative perspective. *Journal of Negro Education, 59,* 45–55.

Ogbu, J. U. (1991). Minority coping responses and school experience. *The Journal of Psychohistory, 18,* 433–456.

Ogbu, J. U. (1992). Understanding cultural diversity and learning. *Educational Researcher, 21,* 5–24.

Orfield, G., & Kurlaender, M. (Eds.). (2001). *Diversity challenged: Evidence on the impact of affirmative action.* Cambridge, MA: Harvard Education.

Patton, J. M. (1991). The Black male's struggle for education. In L. E. Gary (Ed.), *Black men* (pp. 199–214).

Perdue, C. L., Barden, T. E., & Phillips, R. K. (Eds.). (1976). *Weevils in the wheat: Interviews with Virginia ex-slaves.* Charlottesville: University of Virginia.

Raspberry, W. (1990). The myth that is crippling Black America. *Reader's Digest,* 96–98.

Rickford, J. R., & Rickford, R. J. (2000). *Spoken soul: The story of Black English.* New York: Wiley & Sons.

Rumbaut, R. G., & Portes, A. (2001). *Ethnicities: Children of immigrants in America.* Berkeley: University of California.

Spradlin, L. K. (1999). Taking black girls seriously: Addressing discrimination's double bind. In L. Alvine & L. Cullum (Eds.), *Breaking the cycle: Gender, literacy, and learning, 7–12.* Peterborough, NH: Heineman Boynton-Cook.

Sudarkasa, N. (1991). Absent! Black men on campus. *Essence, 22*(7), 140.

Tatum, B. D. (1997). *"Why are all the black kids sitting together in the cafeteria?" and other conversations about race. A psychologist explains the development of racial identity.* New York: Basic Books.

U.S. Bureau of the Census. (2003). *Statistical abstracts of the United States: 2003* (123rd ed.). Washington, DC: U.S. Government Printing Office.

Wade, M. E. (2001). Women and salary negotiation: The costs of self-advocacy. *Psychology of Women Quarterly, 25,* 65–76.

Washington, B. T. (1965). Up from Slavery. In J. H. Franklin (Ed.), *Three Negro classics.* New York: Doubleday/Random House.

White, D. G. (1999). *Too heavy a load: Black women in defense of themselves, 1894–1994.* New York: Norton & Company.

Wolfram, W., & Thomar, E. R. (2002). *The development of African American English*. Malden, MA: Blackwell.

Young, C. (1986). Afro-American family: Contemporary issues and implications for social policy. In D. Pilgrim (Ed.), *On being Black: An in-group analysis*. Bristol, IN: Wyndham Hall.

Ysseldyke, J. E., Algozzine, B., & Thurlow, M. L. (2000). *Critical issues in special education* (3rd ed.). Boston: Houghton Mifflin.

Actually, the foreman don't run the place, the men run the place. See, I mean if the foreman tries to give you a job, you keep moving around the place and you make it hard for him to tell it to you and pin it down. The other men help and swap around with you and don't help the foreman make sense of what needs to be done. Now, you can't argue with him. If the foreman gives you the job, you do it—but, you take your time and work on it on your own. The foreman may try to get the job done for a week that could have been done by a five year old in a day. That's all run by the men. The foreman don't know it. He knows he can't do the work and he tries to get it done to answer to the boss. But, the men decide when the work will really get done and how.

from an interview with a 39-year-old White factory worker

9 CHAPTER | Learning from Working-Class Stories

The experiences, values, and coping strategies suggested in this brief narrative may also creep their way into U.S. high schools as teachers impose work requirements and standards of behavior that may appear pointless to some (especially male) working-class and poor students. Such conditions may lead to passive resistance and avoidance as forms of opposition to negative school experiences (Willis, 1981; Eckert, 1989).

This chapter explores poor and working-class cultures and how day-to-day struggles and associated value systems often clash with middle-class ideals and standards commonly endorsed in U.S. schools—a clash that is detrimental for poor and working-class student achievement and, ultimately, for all members of society (Collins & Veskel, 2004).

CHAPTER OBJECTIVES

1. Describe common values and worldviews of working-class citizens in the United States.
2. Identify ways the people profiled in this chapter experienced and addressed the six cultural factors explored in this text.

154

3. Explain academic and intercultural interaction implications related to the six cultural factors for members of the working class.
4. Describe coping strategies utilized by members of this group.
5. Identify classroom strategies for cultivating positive relationships with students from poor and working-class families to facilitate their full participation and academic achievement in school.

CULTURAL FACTOR 1: HISTORICAL AND CURRENT TREATMENT IN THE UNITED STATES

Historical Background

From the country's very beginnings, dominant-culture citizens in the United States have coerced subordinates to do their labor. "By the early 18th century slavery, legal in all of British America, was the dominant labor system of the Southern colonies. During the century and a half between the arrival of 20 Blacks in Jamestown in 1619 and the outbreak of the American Revolution in 1776, slavery—nonexistent in England itself—spread through all the English colonies that would soon become the United States" (Kolchin, 1993, pp. 3–4).

Because the colonists came from a hierarchical society, they apparently saw nothing particularly problematic about some people working, even in bondage, for the well-being of others. **Indentured servitude** was a booming institution in the colonies. White individuals who were either kidnapped, sentenced, or simply too poor to afford passage to North America were sold or sold themselves into temporary slavery. Most adults ended up serving four or five years of servitude. Children, however, often served seven years or more. But even when the original terms of their bondage were met, many adults and children found their servitude extended for so-called criminal behavior (including disobedience, attempted escape, and childbearing).

> During their indenture, servants were essentially slaves, under the complete authority of their masters. Masters could (and readily did) apply corporal punishment to servants, forbid them to marry, and sell them (for the duration of their terms) to others. In short, indentured servitude provided the emerging colonial gentry with relatively cheap labor, more land and wealth, and the honor to pose authority over other humans. (Kolchin, 1993, p. 9)

Current Conditions

While slavery is no longer legal and formal indenture is no longer allowed, the structure and practices found within U.S. sociopolitical institutions, including schools, continue to support class stratification and differential treatment and opportunity (Collins & Veskel, 2004; Rose, 2000). With such unequal beginnings, it is clear how the United States has maintained a society comprised of those who have and those who have not.

While the United States is largely viewed as a **class*less*** society, the truth is there are enormous differences in the economic status and conditions of life as a function of one's position in the socioeconomic strata of the United States. The United States is actually a highly stratified society in which social-class distinctions operate in every aspect of life, determining the nature of one's work, the quality of schooling, and the health and safety of one's family. Currently, over 40 million Americans are poor. According to the U.S. Bureau of the Census (2003a), a family of four with an income at or below $8,018 a year lives in **poverty.** In the United States, one out of every four children is born into poverty while families holding the top 1 percent of the country's wealth doubled their share of wealth in the last 30 years. During that same period, the percentage of children living in poverty in the United States also doubled. Since 1980, the percentage of children living in families with medium income has fallen from 41 percent to 34 percent, while the percentage of children living in families in extreme poverty has risen from 17 percent to 24 percent. (U.S. Bureau of the Census, 2003a).

Consider, for example, the decrease in minimum-wage earnings over the past 40 years. In 1955, the average minimum wage was $0.75 an hour; with adjustment taking into account the value of the dollar today, it was $4.39 an hour. In 1965, the minimum wage was $1.25 ($6.23 with adjustment for the value of a dollar). In 1975, the minimum wage in the United States was $2.10 (with adjustment: $6.12). In 1985, the minimum wage was $3.35 (with adjustment: $4.88). In 1995, minimum wage was set at $4.25 (with adjustment: $4.38). And in 2004, the minimum wage in the United States was $5.15 (with adjustment: $4.42) per hour. It is clear from these statistics that the country's economic policies and institutionalized practices have kept the lowest wage earners in their working-class and poor positions in society. These structural barriers to advancement have nothing to do with the amount of motivation and hard work—so-called "boot-strap pulling"—workers demonstrate.

The human side of these statistics is that children in low-income families fare more poorly than children in more affluent families in the areas of economic security, health, and education. Children living in poor families are more likely than children living in other families to have difficulty in school, to become parents, and, as adults, to earn less and be unemployed more (Federal Interagency Forum on Child and Family Statistics, 1998). Further, because public school budgets are based on property taxes, allowing higher-income school districts to spend more than poorer ones, the country's school system is rigged in favor of the already privileged, with lower-class students often tracked into economically deficient classrooms, thus continuing the cycle of oppression (Sklar, 1998; Kozol, 1991).

CULTURAL FACTOR 2: INITIAL TERMS OF INCORPORATION INTO U.S. SOCIETY

The colonists' institution of indentured servitude that began in the 1600s in colonial America created the structures that define the current **social classes** in the United States. Social-class differences have a profound impact on the way people live. Class differences affect how much time it takes to accomplish daily tasks in life (that is, doing laundry, shopping for food and clothing, travel, treatment for illness, and child care, to name only a few). Class differences determine where one lives, how one is educated, who one's friends are, what one does for a living, and even what one expects out of life. There have always been huge differences between the haves and have nots in the United States (Manstios, 1998). However, the United States is perceived by most to be a meritocracy in which all people have equal opportunities to be successful—to live the "American dream." It is widely believed that all it takes is for people to "pull themselves up by their bootstraps" in order to succeed. After all, it is often argued, "poor and working-class people find themselves in their positions because they made bad choices."

With such sentiments as the cultural backdrop, those who are poor often find themselves blamed for the social problems that oppress them. However, people do not choose to be poor or **working class.** Rather, social systems and institutions exist that maintain the **cycle of poverty.** Consider, for example, the impact and process of inheritance. Wachtel (1984) likened inheritance to "a series of Monopoly games in which the winner of the first game refuses to relinquish his or her cash and commercial property for the second game. With such an arrangement, it is not difficult to predict the outcome of subsequent games" (pp. 161–162). Those who are unable to play or those who attempt to play but are hampered by their lack of capital find that they are limited, even prohibited from upward social mobility—limited not by their desire, choices made, merit, or effort but by the reality of the fact that they were born into working-class or poor families.

The image of the "American family" or the lived experience of the "average" American lifestyle that is depicted in televisions shows such as *Friends, The Cosby Show, Laguna Beach, Beverly Hills 90210,* and the like, present lives of comfort in which individuals are free to make a variety of choices about how to spend their days and enjoy all aspects of life. These shows depict lives filled with abundant choices. (See Case Illustration 9-1 for insight into reality for many families living in poverty.)

The problems of the poor are often hidden from mainstream America's view, or when presented, they are greatly distorted. For example, the poor are portrayed as undeserving; having only themselves to blame; and lacking motivation, intelligence, and skills to address their struggles. They are frequently portrayed as people who are temporarily down on their luck, in which case a simple holiday gift basket or a couple of trips to a soup kitchen are all they need to rebound and turn their lives around. At other times, the poor are presented as an inconvenience and an irritation, as in the case of those living in homeless shelters or surviving as panhandlers. Dominant culture in the United States has blamed the poor and working class for their struggles rather than the government polices and institutionalized practices that serve to disadvantage the poor and working class while advantaging the middle and capitalist classes (Manstios, 1998). Exercise 9-1 will help you examine your personal biases regarding the poor and working class in the United States.

Case Illustration 9-1 | That's Not My Life

At first I was thrilled. We were in our apartment, no longer going shelter to shelter; we actually had a place to call our own. I can remember the minister; he was so kind. He was able to give us some old furniture, two carpets, even linens. He also gave us a used television set.

It was still a struggle. Working two jobs and taking care of my two daughters was not always easy, but I was trying. Actually, I was feeling really good about myself and the fact that as a single mom I was feeding and clothing us. We were wearing thrift-shop hand-me-downs, but I was raising my family. One night last month, my five-year-old asked a question—one that I couldn't answer.

We were watching a movie about a regular family—I can't remember the name of it. But the kids in the family were playing with their cute dog in the yard, and then they went into dinner waiting on the table, and then they took their baths. You get the picture. We have sat as a family doing what we love to do many times. Sitting on the couch... comfortable... talking and stuff. It is cool. This time was different though. This time Michelle, my youngest, cried. I asked her what was wrong, and she said, "Why can't we be like them [the families on television]? Why can't I have new dresses and my own room?" And I had no answer for her other than, "We are not like (and most likely never will be like) the families on television." When she asked why (as five-year-olds do), I had no answer.

Source: An interview with Lenora, a 36-year-old single mother.

Exercise 9-1 | Point of Reflection: And the Answer Is?

Directions: This task is simple.

1. Interview five of your friends and record their responses to the following:

   Linda is a mother of four young children and is a high school drop out currently living in a shelter on welfare. What is the most likely explanation for her current state of life and what is one thing you feel needs to be done to change her situation?

2. Share your findings with your colleagues, classmates, or teacher in small-group discussion. Do you find any common themes present among the responses? Is blame assigned? If so where? Are the suggested interventions reasonable given what you know about poverty in the United States?

CULTURAL FACTORS 3 AND 4: SHARED VALUES, TRADITIONS, AND SPIRITUALITY

Living lives filled with day-to-day struggles and often having experienced generations of economic deprivation provide the poor and working class with a perspective that is often different from those in the middle and capitalist classes. Some early research (for example, Kahl, 1968; Lengermann, 1982; Nisan, 1973) suggested that the poor typically share a preference for (1) present-time orientation, (2) action versus reflection, (3) linear social relations, and

Table 9-1 | Comparison of Working-Class and Middle-Class Values

Working Class	Middle Class
Believe one must make as much money as one can to pay for as good a life as one can afford.	Possess "cultural capital" and engage in networking. Use cultural information and contacts to advance. Identify with brand-name clothing, cars, and so on.
Believe in a "whatever it takes" work ethic. Speak in a forthright manner—open and honest. Are proud of cultural customs. Employ the use of nonverbal communication skills.	Have a sense of belonging among members of dominant culture. Speak the language of dominant-culture authorities with fluency.
Have respect for parents and close contact with extended family members. Exhibit a sense of loyalty and solidarity with family and community members. Experience limited choices in school.	Receive privileged education. Expect extra and special treatment from authorities. Emphasize individuality. Children have a say in what they do. Seek intellectual challenges and choices in school.
Confront limited images in the media that portray cultural group members in a positive light. Mistrust "eggheads." Prefer logic that encompasses common sense and intuition.	Relate to predominant images in popular culture. Prefer analytical and logical approaches to problem solving.
Are emotionally expressive. Tend to be tough and loud.	Exercise emotional restraint. Emphasize surface appearances and getting along with dominant-culture authorities.
Seek work that pays well.	Seek work that is fulfilling and pays well.
Respect parents' accomplishments and efforts.	Feel pressured to achieve more than their parents.
Acquiesce to authority when needed, yet refuse to be dominated on one's own turf.	Protest, question, and challenge authority.
Believe "I am what I am."	Believe "I must be someone important."
Experience overt prejudice and oppression.	Largely unaware of social-class oppression.
Expect to be a worker.	Expect to be a manager.

Source: Adapted from Lubrano, A. (2004). *Limbo, blue collar roots, white collar dreams.* Hoboken, NJ: John Wiley & Sons.

(4) subjugation to or at least harmony with nature. Others (for example, Lockwood, 1966) found that the working class and poor value tightly knit family life and conventionality. They were said to embrace nonpolitical solidarity and to share ambitious attitudes toward education, While these values may be shared by members of the working class and poor in the United States, it is difficult to identify clear aspects that characterize members of this cultural group because there is abundant fluidity in the social consciousness among poor and working-class persons (Özüm, 1995). An interesting comparison of working-class versus middle-class values was outlined by Lubrano (2004) (see Table 9-1).

In school, working-class and poor students may demonstrate resistance to dominant-culture values that underlie school practices. It is not uncommon to find working-class and poor (particularly male) students who are less willing

| Case Illustration 9-2 | **"Bus is Exact Change"** |

In the movie, *Stand and Deliver* (Warner Brothers, 1988), the actor who portrays Jamie Escalante walks into class the first day of school and announces to a rather boisterous and distracted group of high school students, "This is Math 1A." The response he received reflected both a lack of interest as well as a practical approach to life.

"We don't need math . . . bus is exact change, no big deal," stated one student, and another recited the fact that one can get a calculator with the purchase of a dozen donuts. And later within the movie, as the teacher discussed Algebra and the use of X's and Y's, a student proclaimed that it didn't make any sense unless he could see it in the real world.

These are examples of students who want to succeed but need to see the practicality of what it is they are learning and doing. Watch *Stand and Deliver* and determine how the teacher provided relevance and meaning to meet the needs of his working-class and poor students.

to follow dominant-culture timetables, routines, and expected forms and degrees of participation or who take informal control of classrooms by limiting work production or finding forms of expression that may disrupt teachers' agendas.

Valuing the Practical

Working-class males, in particular, may reject school due to their knowledge that for them (due to their severely limited and curtailed opportunities), practical skills may prove to be more useful than the obtainment of degrees and a knowledge of theory. For them, "an ounce of keenness is worth a whole library of certificates" (Willis, 1981, p. 254). Case Illustration 9-2 provides awareness of the often-practical focus of many who live as members of the working class.

One approach that facilitates learning for students who prefer a practical orientation and increases the relevance of classroom instruction is the fund-of-knowledge model (Gonzales, Andrade, Civil, & Moll, 2001). These researchers used the fund-of-knowledge concept, which views low-income and minority student households as repositories of diverse knowledge bases and applied this perspective to facilitate the transformation of mathematical knowledge to explain and improve household practices. In their applications, they helped students understand the mathematical potential of their households as they "mathematized" household practices. Their work is an example of relevant and authentic instructional strategies in math that involve cooking, construction, and repair-work school assignments.

Gender Roles

While working-class females are less likely than working-class males to be held responsible for upholding the integrity of the working class, they tend to be staunch supporters of their male counterparts in the home and in schools, even if they are often treated as subordinates by them. It is commonly understood that because the men are forced to fend off the harsh realities of social-class domination in the workplace—laboring in unpleasant conditions, so they can provide for their families—it is the women's place to create a warm and supportive home environment; take most, if not all, responsibility for child care and family obligations; and in all ways help the men in their lives achieve and produce.

Chauvinism frequently reigns in working-class culture, and women are positioned in roles that do not provide them with high status. The roles of homemaker and helper, while strongly needed and called upon by working-class men, are not often compensated with outward displays of respect and value. A lack of respect that becomes outright stigmatization and maligning is experienced by women, as is often seen in the stereotypical portrayal of single mothers. It is not unusual to find public officials describing working-class and poor mothers in derogatory ways, referring to them as "welfare queens" and the like (Zucchino, 1997). The moral behavior of these women is regularly questioned, with the knowledge of their pregnancies creating suspicions that they made their decisions to become mothers in order to exploit the system. Having children is viewed as their ploy or tactic to benefit from the system by remaining on welfare (Roberts, 1999; Solinger, 1999). Recent legislation has even taken away poor single mothers' choice to stay at home to care for their children. Under the Personal Responsibility and Work Opportunity Reconciliation Act (PL 104–193), signed into legislation in 1996, the federal entitlement to public assistance was eliminated and replaced by a system of state block grants, Temporary Aid to Needy Families (TANF), which in fact forces poor women whose incomes are supplemented by welfare to work, even when they have young children to parent (Mourad, 2003; Mink 1998).

While it is not widely covered in the media, however, the vast majority of working-class and poor single mothers have always worked extremely hard to provide for their families. Damning views of these citizens who contribute greatly to society must be challenged and replaced by more realistic depictions of them and their families. In addition, both working-class and poor families must extend enormous and continual effort to maintain their survival. All family members, including children, may be called upon to work to contribute to the family's finances and development.

CULTURAL FACTOR 5: ACCULTURATION AND EXPERIENCE WITH EXCLUSION AND ALIENATION

Working-class and poor students and their parents are excluded in numerous ways by dominant culture. The media routinely depicts the "normal" lifestyles of the middle class in which people are portrayed as living in affluent residences while working in white-collar jobs, and having plenty of discretionary time to pursue their hobbies and interests (Manstios, 1998). Working-class and poor citizens are excluded by such portrayals of "normal lifestyles" that do not reflect their life circumstances and realities. This type of exclusion also exists in U.S. schools—schools established and designed to perpetuate social-class stratification through the preparation of young people for their roles in those social classes (Carnoy, 1974). In fact, school performance (grades and test scores) and educational attainment (level of schooling completed) correlate strongly with socioeconomic class status.

> Through the inequality of resources and practices in schools serving communities of different regions, ethnic groups, and socioeconomic levels, and through the unequal treatment of children of varying backgrounds within the same schools, schooling teaches children both their place in society and how to behave in that place. The gradual accumulation of differential experience in the early years of schooling leads mainstream children to believe that education will ultimately bring rewards and success, while nonmainstream children frequently come to view education as a humiliating and fruitless pursuit. (Eckert, 1989, p. 7)

As with racial stratification influences, Brookover and Erickson (1975) maintained that social-class stratification creates role expectations that define student behavior expectations; that is, role expectations specify how a student should behave in school based on his or her social-class status. Similarly, Eckert's (1989) research on social-class relations among White high school students identified two distinct social-class categories of students: (1) burnouts—coming from the working class and enrolled primarily in general and vocational courses; and (2) jocks—coming from the middle class, moving along a college–bound educational track, playing or participating in school sports and activities, and receiving respectable grades. Eckert found that burnouts had an adversarial relationship with the school, while jocks had a cooperative relationship.

According to Eckert (1989), adolescent social structure characterizes the opposition that integrates the forces of family, neighborhood, and society. The structure and norms of school and peer social interaction, according to Eckert, explain polar social-class orientations to school achievement. Eckert concluded that jocks and burnouts are embodiments of the middle and working classes, respectively; the two separate cultures are in many ways social-class cultures, and opposition and conflict between them define social-class relations and differences that exist in society.

Schools both formally and informally encourage and maintain social-class distinctions. For example, researchers have found that teachers' classroom expectations for working-class and poor students are often lower and that they tend to underencourage these students and underevaluate their work. It is also a common practice of school officials to steer children of the working class into general education and vocational programs, thus limiting their future options (Becker, 1952; Cicourel & Kitsuse, 1963; Eckert, 1989; Rist, 1970).

A rigid form of exclusion often encountered by working-class and poor students in U.S. schools involves the process of tracking. **Tracking** or grouping students in schools based on their so-called "ability" contributes to differential school outcomes and unfairly sorts students for subsequent social and economic roles (Oakes & Lipton, 1990). In fact, numerous research studies have found that tracking and rigid ability grouping are generally ineffective and, for many children, are harmful (Goodlad & Marshall, 1984; National Commission on Excellence in Education, 1983; Noland, 1985).

Tracking is predicated on a belief that prospects for school performance are readily identifiable and, for all practical purposes, unchangeable. This assumption is false (Oakes & Lipton, 1990). The fault of this assumption and

Exercise 9-2	Field Experience: Setting the Direction Early

Directions: Your task is to interview three school principals.

1. Ask the principals if tracking is employed in their schools. If so, ask how students are assigned to tracks and how change in their tracks occurs when students' achievement improves.
2. Conduct research to identify statistics on the demographic profiles of the students placed in

lower tracks (that is, identify socioeconomic status, gender, race, and ethnicity) of low, average, and high tracks in schools.

3. Share your findings with your teacher, colleagues, or classmates in small-group discussion. Are there any apparent connections between track placement and SES? Gender? Race? Ethnicity? Discuss implications for student outcomes and opportunities.

the damage it can create are especially noticeable when tracking is employed in the early grades. Employing this line of thinking and the practice of tracking in the early grades in reading and math groups may severely restrict the educational options available to those placed in low and average tracks. Just as children are being presented for the first time with academic material, they are also being judged severely by their primary-grade schoolteachers in order to be placed into tracks that will most likely endure for their entire lives. Students placed in the highest reading groups will be expected to achieve and will be attended to as achievers in ways that will ensure the best of all educational experiences. Not so for those placed in the lowest reading groups. For many of these students, their educational experience will be one characterized by the teaching and learning of rote skills rather than critical-thinking or decision-making skills. Even though without tracking, so-called "gifted," "average," and "low"-achieving students can fare as well or even better academically, the practice of tracking continues because it benefits those who favor it (occupants of the higher tracks)—mostly middle-class students and their parents (Oakes & Lipton, 1990). Exercise 9-2 invites you to look at the issue of tracking as a mechanism through which class distinctions within U.S. schools are maintained.

CULTURAL FACTOR 6: LANGUAGE DIFFERENCES, STRENGTHS, AND CHALLENGES

While it is certainly an archetype from a different time, the story of Eliza Doolittle and Henry Higgins in the classic film *My Fair Lady* highlights the power of class distinction and language utilization. While the same kinds of speech differences between the cockney dialect and the dialect employed by British aristocracy may not be evident in a comparison of working-class and middle-class individuals in the United States, alternative patterns of speech reflecting social-class distinctions are evident. For example, speech variation has been found in more subtle forms among members of the U.S. working class. Labov and Robins (1969), in studying social class in casual conversation, found a correlation between "g"-dropping (for example, *drinking* to *drinkin'*) and social class. In their study, 80 percent of those in the lower class exhibited g-dropping, whereas only 5 percent in the upper middle class exhibited this behavior.

Others (for example, Bernstein, 1962) have suggested that members of the working class employ restricted codes in their language use. For example, tag clauses, such as "you see" or "you know," are phrases more often employed by the working class that tend to reinforce the social relationship between the speaker and listener rather than to simply convey information (Cook & Gurr, 1981). In addition, research has demonstrated that middle-class parents talk more, have longer utterances, label more, and provide more information about objects than do working-class parents (Hart & Risley, 1992; Lawrence & Shipley, 1996). Many theorists believe this distinction of parent-speak results in middle-class students having communication patterns that more closely match those of middle-class teachers (for example, see Goldfield, 1987, 1993). As such, teachers should be aware of language differences among their students and develop effective ways to help students encounter meaningful and relevant language in a variety of contexts in efforts to increase their linguistic fluency (for example, Brown, Palinscar, & Purcell, 1986; Snow, 1991).

POTENTIAL BARRIERS IN LEARNING–TEACHING RELATIONSHIPS WITH DOMINANT-CULTURE TEACHERS AND SCHOOLS

When working-class and poor parents receive inferior educations and/or drop out of school for reasons that include ostracism in schools, pressures from home, and the economic realities for their families, they end up with less education. This in turn restricts them to lower-paying jobs. Such conditions may negatively affect their ability to provide the best possible opportunities to advance academic goals for their children. Consider the reflection in Case Illustration 9-3 of a White working-class mother, Rita, who wants more for her son in life than she has.

On average, the achievement of students from low-income families is below the achievement of students from middle-class families. And while some students from low-income families beat the odds and are successful in schools, this does not negate the existence of barriers that curtail their achievement. As such, both school improvement and social and economic reform are needed (Rothstein, 2004).

Young children of highly educated parents are read to consistently and are encouraged to participate with schools in ways that increase their academic achievement (Eckert, 1989). These students are more likely to pass an age-appropriate reading test in kindergarten, and so the achievement gap begins. Middle-class parents have been found to ask more questions that require their children to think when they read to them than do working-class and poor parents. There are other stark differences in the ways dominant-culture and working-class parents converse with their children. Children of dominant-culture parents develop a sense of entitlement from an early age that may stem

Case Illustration 9-3	Rita

Every time the phone rings, I'm afraid a bill collector is calling. By 7 a.m. each day, I am behind the wheel of a school bus with my 3-year-old daughter in tow in the front seat. She'll ride with me to pick up and drop off schoolchildren for five hours in the morning and three hours in the afternoon. I also work as a cleaning lady at a nursing home at night. My husband is a construction worker. He does pretty well except in the winter. He also does fix-it jobs to make extra money when he can. We don't see him too much. He's a hard worker. He cleans floors and does landscape maintenance when he can. My oldest son in high school wants to drop out and start working. He sees no reason to learn what they teach in school. I must admit, it didn't help me any. I know there is no place for him in that school. They keep proving to him that he doesn't belong. He's been expelled twice for smoking cigarettes and hanging out in the halls during class. But I'm trying to hold him off and keep him in. We don't want him to end up with this life. It's too hard and long. We have no health benefits, no savings, no car, and no reason to think that things will change.

Source: An interview with Rita, a White, working-class wife, mother, and worker.

from a knowledge of the authority and responsibility their parents enjoy in their occupations. The understanding that one can control her or his own environment is passed down to their children and becomes an important variable in achievement. In addition, children from dominant-culture families gain increased self-assurance when they participate in afterschool activities that require transportation and sometimes fees that children from low-income families may not be able to provide. The confidence that comes from participating in organized sports and extracurricular opportunities, coupled with the other advantages such as numerous and varied educational resources, leads to increased self-confidence for dominant-culture students. Students with greater self-confidence in these areas face unfamiliar school challenges with less fear and anxiety. In addition, homework exacerbates achievement differences between dominant-culture and working-class students. Middle-class parents are more likely to have the time, knowledge, and resources to help their children with their homework.

Not surprisingly, middle-class professional parents tend to associate with and be friends with similarly educated professionals. Such acquaintances provide their children with academic and occupational role models that motivate them to achieve. In addition, these connections serve as resources for their children as academic and professional network systems are formed. Working-class students come from families that generally have fewer professional friends. Working-class and poor students, therefore, often must struggle harder to motivate themselves to obtain high-paying jobs than students who assume, on the basis of their parents' social circle, that they will someday be doctors, lawyers, managers, and business executives.

Overall, lower-income children are in poorer health. They have poorer vision, poorer nutrition, poorer oral hygiene, and higher instances of asthma, which partly stems from living in substandard housing containing high-sulfur

Exercise 9-3	Field Experience: Hidden Alienation

Directions:

1. Contact a school in your area and speak with a counselor or administrator. Identify the various programs, services, activities, and so on that the school employs in an attempt to inform and engage parents in the process of their children's education (for example, back-to-school nights, open houses, PTA meetings, booster club events, newsletters, advisory groups). Be sure to get the description of what these forms of communication entail, when they meet, what is expected of and from parents, and so on.

2. With your classmates, colleagues, and/or instructor, review the data, looking for explicit or hidden barriers working-class and poor parents face in their attempts to partner with schools.

3. Generate recommendations for removing these barriers and engaging all parents across socioeconomic levels in schools.

heating systems or in neighborhoods with heightened air pollution. Each of these health issues contributes to weakened abilities to perform in school, energy deficits, and absenteeism. In addition, transient living conditions and difficulties in finding adequate affordable housing among low-income families contribute to the underachievement of poor and homeless students. Students whose families have difficulty finding stable affordable housing are more likely to be mobile, and student mobility is a significant cause of underachievement.

In addition, parental involvement is correlated with student success. As such, schools have high expectations for parental (particularly for mothers') involvement in their children's education. Parents are expected to attend parent–teacher conferences, respond to the many requests sent home by schools, chaperone field trips, volunteer in classrooms, provide treats for birthday parties, and organize or contribute to fund-raisers. Parents are expected to make sure their children are developmentally prepared for school, to provide supervision and help with homework and school projects, and to read to their children on a daily basis. Certainly all of these activities should prove helpful in the education of students. However, a question remains: To what degree can poor and working-class parents engage in these activities? What seem to be reasonable expectations for families who have ample economic resources may be unrealistic expectations for families who do not (see Exercise 9-3).

Schools must understand the economic hardships encountered by working-class and poor families who are struggling to make ends meet and take steps to facilitate these students' and their families' involvement in school activities and curriculum development.

FROM CONCEPTS TO LIVED EXPERIENCE

The following is a portion of a story provided by Jay Shaft (2003), entitled "Living on the Edge of Disaster: Being a Poor Working Mother in America" that offers a glimpse into the life of Daria. As you read of Daria's work struggles, consider the impact of her circumstances on her daughter's relationships and academic achievement. Think about the readiness with which her daughter is able to approach each new day of learning. Imagine the many mandates her daughter encounters in school that seem realistic for children who come from families with access to many resources yet seem unrealistic for her given her life conditions. Think about the disenfranchisement and restricted resources both she and her mother may experience as a result of their poverty.

DARIA'S STORY

Daria is a 36-year-old white mother of one who has lost five jobs in the last 10 months. She moved from up north to Florida on word of mouth about all the jobs available. Little did she know before moving that the jobs she heard about were vanishing into thin air. The factory jobs and manufacturing jobs that were so prevalent just two years ago have been eliminated or moved to other cities or sectors.

All that seems to be available are low-income service industry jobs or temporary fill-in jobs. What little jobs that become available are sought by hundreds of unemployed workers desperate for any position.

She has struggled to be hired, only to be eliminated due to economic cutbacks within weeks of getting into the job and setting herself up for some sort of job security. After getting the prospect of financial security and the hope of catching up with her bills, she sees the job disappear and has to start her employment search all over again.

"It's an exercise in tenacity at best" she sighs. "Thank you George Bush, we're really seeing our bright future and prosperity!" As she puts on a dim and vague smile she describes her worries and fears. You can see her desperation and fear for tomorrow etched in the worried lines of her face.

She has rarely found reason to smile in the last year and the laughs are few and far between. The ability to relax and have a truly enjoyable time has been yanked out from under her and her good times have dried up.

"I have never had to live like this in my life. This never seemed possible to me before I moved down here. I had to live in a motel for two months and in various shelters before I got a permanent apartment." She now lives in a two-room studio that is barely big enough for her and her daughter.

"This is no way for my kid to live. No kid should have to go through this. I mean I feel so bad sometimes that I can't give her more security and the things she really needs. I tried to file bankruptcy after being forced to live on my credit cards rather than be homeless and have my kid out on the street. I am so broke I can't even afford to pay the lawyer the filing fee for the bankruptcy so the bills keep coming in.

"My neighbors watch out for me and it embarrasses me, like I can't take care of my kid. I never had it where my neighbors have to help me, but I'm not going to turn it down. Everybody has to take help sometimes and it helps me get by with a little extra food to feed my kid."

SUMMARY

Cultural Factor 1: Historical and Current Treatment in the United States While the United States is largely viewed as classless, the truth is that there are enormous differences in the economic status and conditions of life as a function of one's position in the socioeconomic strata of the United States. The human side of these statistics is that children in low-income families fare more poorly than children in more affluent families in the areas of economic security, health, and education.

Because public-school budgets are based on property taxes, allowing higher-income school districts to spend more than poorer ones, the country's school system is rigged in favor of the already privileged, with lower-class students tracked into deficient classrooms, thus continuing the cycle of oppression.

Cultural Factor 2: Initial Terms of Incorporation into U.S. Society The colonists' institution of indentured servitude created conditions for the establishment of social-class stratification in the United States. Social-class differences affect how much time it takes to accomplish daily tasks in life. They determine where one lives, how one is educated, who one's friends are, what one does for a living, and even what one expects out of life. People do not choose to be poor or working class. Rather, social systems and institutions exist that maintain this cycle of poverty.

Cultural Factors 3 and 4: Shared Values, Traditions, and Spirituality The poor typically share a preference for (1) present-time orientation, (2) action versus reflection, (3) linear social relations, and (4) subjugation to or at least harmony with nature. Members of the working class tend to value tightly knit family life and conventionality. They also may embrace nonpolitical solidarity and share ambitious attitudes toward education.

Cultural Factor 5: Acculturation and Experience with Exclusion and Alienation School performance (grades and test scores) and educational attainment (level of schooling completed) correlate strongly with economic class. The gradual accumulation of differential experience in the early years of schooling leads mainstream children to believe that education will ultimately bring rewards and success, while nonmainstream children frequently come to view education as a humiliating and fruitless pursuit. Tracking or grouping students in schools based on their so-called "ability" contributes to differential school outcomes and unfairly sorts students for their subsequent social and economic roles.

Cultural Factor 6: Language Differences, Strengths, and Challenges Members of the working class may employ restricted codes of spoken English that feature tag clauses that reinforce the relationship between the speaker and the listener rather than simply convey information. Middle-class parent–child communication patterns more closely match communication patterns and expectations found in U.S. schools.

Potential Barriers in Learning–Teaching Relationships with Dominant-Culture Teachers and Schools When working-class and poor parents receive inferior educations and/or drop out of school for reasons that include ostracism in schools, pressures of home, and the lack of opportunity for their families, they end up with less education. On average, the achievement of students from low-income families is below the achievement of students from middle-class families. The structure and scheduling of school meetings, outings, and parent associations may preclude the involvement of working-class and poor parents.

Important Terms

chauvinism	cycle of poverty	poverty	tracking
classless society	indentured servitude	social class	working class

Enrichment

Eckert, P. (1989). *Jock and burnouts: Social categories and identity in high school.* New York: Teachers College.

Handel, G. (2000). *Making life in Yorkville: Experience and meaning in the life course narrative of an urban working class man.* Westport, CT: Greenwood.

hook, b. (2000). *Where we stand: Class matters.* New York: Routledge.

Kozol, J. (1991). *Savage inequalities: Children in America's schools.* New York: Crown.

Rogers, J., & Teixeira, R. (2000). *America's forgotten majority: Why the White working class still matters.* New York: Basic Books.

Sanders, M. G. (2000). *Schooling students placed at risk: Research, policy and practice in education of poor and minority adolescents.* Mahwah, NJ: Lawrence Erlbaum.

Shipler, D. K. (2004). *The working poor: Invisible America.* New York: Alfred A. Knopf.

Connections on the Web

http://www.londonmet.ac.uk/research-units/ipse/themes/social-class-and-education.cfm

> The Institute for Policy studies in education is an excellent resource for information on addressing the needs of the poor and working class in and through education.

http://www.ctl.sas.upenn.edu/WC_ped.html

> The website for the Center for Teaching and Learning of the University of Pennsylvania is a

good resource for information on continuing education programs.

http://members.tripod.com/~sadashivan_nair/quotpovertyquotasubject/id24.html

> This excellent site offers links to information about poverty, its extent, its impact, and what teachers can do.

REFERENCES

Bartlett, D. L., & Steele, J. B. (1992). *America: What went wrong.* Kansas City, MO: Andrews & McNeel.

Becker, H. S. (1952). Social class variation in teacher–pupil relationship. *Journal of Educational Sociology, 25,* 451–465.

Bernstein, B. (1962). Social class, linguistic codes and grammatical elements. *Language and Speech, 5,* 221–240.

Bloom, L. R. (2001). "I'm poor, I'm single, I'm a mom and I deserve respect": Advocating in schools and with mothers in poverty. *Educational studies, 32*(3), 300–316.

Brookover, W. B., & Erickson, E. L. (1975). *Sociology of education.* Homewood, IL: Dorsey.

Brown, A., Palinscar, A., & Purcell, L. (1986). Poor readers: Teach, don't label. In U. Neisser (Ed.), *The school achievement of minority children* (pp. 105–143). Hillsdale, NJ: Erlbaum.

Carnoy, M. (1974). *Education as cultural imperialism.* New York: McKay.

Cicourel, A. V., & Kitsuse, J. I. (1963). *The education decision-makers.* New York: Bobbs Merrill.

Collins, C., & Veskel, F. (2004). Economic apartheid in America. In M. L. Andersen & P. H. Collins (Eds.), *Race, class, and gender: An anthology* (5th ed., pp. 127–139). Belmont, CA: Wadsworth/Thomson.

Cook, M., & Gurr, P. J. (1981). Social class and ritualized speech. *Language & Speech, 24*(4), 373–376.

Eckert, P. (1989). *Jock and burnouts: Social categories and identity in high school.* New York: Teachers College.

Federal Interagency Forum on Child and Family Statistics. (1998). America's Children. Retrieved from http://www.childstats.gov

Finkelstein, B., Reem M., & Elyssa, D. (1998). Where have all the children gone? The transformation of children into dollars in Public Law 104–193. In S. Book (Ed.), *Invisible children in the society and its schools* (pp. 169–182). Mahwah, NJ: Lawrence Erlbaum.

Goldfield, B. (1987). The contributions of child and caregiver to referential and expressive language. *Applied Psycholinguistics, 8,* 267–280.

Goldfield, B. (1993). Noun bias in maternal speech to one year olds. *Journal of Child Language, 20,* 85–99.

Gonzalez, N., Andrade, R., Civil, M., & Moll, L. (2001). Bridging funds of distributed knowledge: Creating zones of practices in mathematics. *Journal of Education for Students Placed at Risk, 6*(1, 2), 115–132.

Goodlad, T. L., & Marshall, S. (1984). Do students learn more in heterogeneous or homogeneous groups? In P. P. Peterson, I. C. Wilkinson & M. T. Hallman (Eds.), *The social context of instruction* (pp. 13–28). New York: Academic.

Harrington, M. (1962). *The other America.* New York: MacMillan.

Hart, B., & Risley, T. (1992). American parenting of language-learning children: Persisting differences in family-child interactions observed in natural home environments. *Developmental Psychology, 28,* 1096–1105.

Heath, S. B. (1983). *Ways with words.* New York: Cambridge University.

Kahl, J. A. (1968). *The measurement of modernism: A study of values in Brazil and Mexico.* Austin: University of Texas.

Katz, M. B. (1989). *The undeserving poor: From the war on poverty to the war on welfare.* New York: Pantheon.

Kolchin, P. (1993). *American slavery: 1619–1877.* New York: Whill & Wang.

Kozol, J. (1991). *Savage inequalities: Children in America's schools.* New York: Crown.

Labov, W., & Robins, C. (1969). A note on the relation of reading failure to peer-group status in urban ghettos. *Record, 70*(5), 395–405.

Lawrence, V. W., & Shipley, E. F. (1996). Parental speech to middle- and working-class children from two racial groups in three settings. *Applied Psycholinguistics, 17,* 233–255.

Lengermann, P. M. (1982). The debate on the structure and content of West Indian values: Some relevant data from Trinidad and Tobago. *British Journal of Sociology, 23,* 298–311.

Lockwood, B. (1966). *Four contemporary British working-class novelists: A thematic and critical approach to the fiction of Raymond Williams, John Braine, David Storey, and Alan Sillitoe.* Unpublished dissertation, University of Wisconsin.

Lubrano, A. (2004). *Limbo, blue collar roots, white collar dreams.* Hoboken, NJ: John Wiley & Sons.

Manstios, G. (1998). Class in America: Myths and realities. In P. S. Rothenberg (Ed.), *Race, class, and gender in the United States: An integrated study* (4th ed., pp. 202–214). New York: St. Martin's.

Mink, G. (1998). *Welfare's end.* Ithaca, NY: Cornell University.

Mishel, L., & Bernstein, J. (2004). Education and the economy revisited: How schools matter. *Peabody Journal of Education, 79*(1), 36–63.

Mourad, R. (2003). After Foucault. *Philosophy & Social Criticism, 29*(4), 451–481.

National Commission on Excellence in Education. (1983). *A nation at risk.* Washington, DC: U.S. Government Printing Office.

Nisan, M. (1973). Perceptions of time in lower-class Black students. *International Journal of Psychology, 8*(2), 109–116.

Noland, T. K. (1985). *The effects of ability grouping: A meta-analysis of research findings.* Unpublished dissertation, University of Colorado, Boulder.

Oakes, J., & Lipton, M. (1990). Tracking and ability grouping: A structural barrier to access and achievement. In J. I. Goodlad & P. Keating (Eds.), *Access to knowledge: An agenda for our nation's schools* (pp. 187–202). New York: College Entrance Examination Board.

Özüm, A. (1995). The representation of the working class and masculinity and Alan Sillitoe's *Saturday Night and Sunday Morning. Journal of English Languages and Literature, 3,* 39–50.

Persell, C. J. (1977). *Education and inequality: The roots and results of stratification in America's schools.* New York: Free Press.

Personal Responsibility and Work Opportunity Reconciliation Act of 1996, U.S. Public Law 104–193.

Rist, R. C. (1970). Student social class and teacher expectations. *Harvard Educational Review, 40,* 411–451.

Roberts, D. (1999). Welfare's ban on poor motherhood. In G. Mink (Ed.), *Whose welfare?* (pp. 152–167). Ithaca, NY: Cornell University.

Rose, S. J. (2000). *Social stratification in the United States.* New York: New Press.

Rothstein, R. (2004). *Class and schools: Using social, economic, and educational reform to close the Black–White achievement gap.* New York: Teachers College.

Sennet, R., & Cobb, J. (1973). *The hidden injuries of class.* New York: Vintage.

Shaft, J. (2003). *Living on the Edge of Disaster: Being a Poor Working Mother in America.* Retrieved from http://www.scoop.co.nz/stories/HL0310/S00074.htm

Sklar, H. (1998). Imagine a country. In P. S. Rothenberg (Ed.), *Race, class, and gender in the United States: An integrated study* (4th ed., pp. 192–201). New York: St. Martin's.

Snow, C. E. (1991). The theoretical basis of the home-school study of language and literacy development. In C. E. Snow (Chair), *The social prerequisites of literacy development: Home and school experiences of preschool-aged children from low-income families.* Symposium presented at the meeting of the American Educational Research Association, Chicago.

Solinger, R. (1999). Dependency and choice: The two faces of Eve. In G. Mink (Ed.), *Whose welfare?* (pp. 7–36). Ithaca, NY: Cornell University.

U.S. Bureau of the Census. (2003a). *Money income in the United States.* Retrieved from http://www.census.gov

U.S. Bureau of the Census. (2003b). *Employment characteristics of families in 2003.* Retrieved September 15, 2004, from http://www.bls.gov/news.release/famee.rro.htm

U.S. Department of Education, National Center for Educational Statistics. (2004, February). *Women in the labor force: A data book.* Washington, DC: Author.

U.S. Department of Labor Bureau of Labor Statistics. (1995). *Annual average tables of employment and earnings.*

Wachtel, H. (1984). *Labor and the economy.* Orlando, FL: Academic.

Willis, P. (1977). *Learning to labour.* Westmead, Farnborough, Hants, UK: Saxon House.

Willis, P. (1981). *Learning to labor: How working class kids get working class jobs.* New York: Columbia University.

Zucchino, D. (1997). *The myth of the welfare queen.* New York: Scribner.

Only 100 years ago, women were denied entry to education, politics, and the professions. This is one reason that women's history is so fascinating: so much change, so quickly, and so positive. We tend to take for granted the extraordinary personal, political and professional achievements of women throughout the 20th century.

Dale Spender, author and editor of over 30 books on feminism (1995, p. 260)
"Women as Revolutionary Agents of Change"

10 CHAPTER | Learning from Women's Stories

Dale Spender noted that much positive change has occurred. She also noted that it is all too easy to take for granted the extraordinary personal, political, and professional achievements women have made. But even with this awareness of the many significant achievements made, we must not lose touch with the fact that, as is the case for all minorities, women continue to fight for their voices to be heard in dominant culture.

What are current challenges, opportunities, and conflicting demands for women in the United States? Who serves as role models for success? Who support women's achievements? If educators are to foster and support the development of women, they must have a thorough understanding of the impact of gender socialization and bias on learning, teaching, and classroom dynamics.

CHAPTER OBJECTIVES

1. Describe values and worldviews commonly shared by women in the United States.
2. Identify ways the women profiled in the case narratives experienced and addressed the six cultural factors explored in this text.
3. Explain academic and intercultural interaction implications for women related to the six cultural factors.
4. Describe coping strategies utilized by women as they confront discrimination and pressures of dominant culture.
5. Identify classroom strategies for integrating feminist perspectives and values within your curricula.

CULTURAL FACTOR 1: HISTORICAL AND CURRENT TREATMENT IN THE UNITED STATES

In the United States, **sexism** rests on the assumed inferiority of women. Its history is long, and though its specific manifestations have changed over time, outcomes from this ideology remain today.

In Ancient Greece, Aristotle is said to have regarded women as defective men. In his writings, he classed women and children together, concluding that neither had fully developed rationality. Similarly, during medieval times, Christian doctrine was a strong source of support for views of the inferiority of women; beliefs that positioned the man as the *head* and the women as the *heart* of families were used to support beliefs in male superiority. Women of the time who attempted to move out of subordinate roles were often labeled evil and rebellious and were even burned as witches for their acts of resistance (Adkinson & Hackett, 1995).

One key to understanding women's status in a society is their degree of participation in the economy of their society as well as their control over the products they produce. Every society employs some type of **sexual division of labor,** but the nature of the division of labor by sex affects the relative status of men and women and influences their relationships in society. For example, the plow changed agriculture from a female to a male occupation in many societies. Before the invention of heavy farming machinery, females tended to crops while males hunted or worked in other ways to provide for their families. This division of labor often resulted in a more or less equal contribution to the family's and (society's) economy. Eventually surpluses of food produced wealth that became the property of men. This wealth was passed down from father to son. As wealth and property became the birthright of males, women came to be viewed as possessions (Adkinson & Hackett, 1995).

Historically, **innate qualities** have been used as the basis for differential valuing and treatment of men and women. And while many continue to assume there are widespread intellectual, personality, and behavioral differences between males and females, very few sex differences have been identified (Ferree, 1990; Williams, 2000). In fact, there are many more similarities than differences between boys and girls and between men and women (Matlin, 1987). Further, those differences identified are now generally believed to be socially based rather than innate (Richardson, 1981). Society's **gender-based norms** and expectations account for assumptions of male intellectual and leadership superiority and female nurturance and interpersonal superiority (Albee & Perry, 1998; Coltrane, 1996). However, these social constructions are not based on biological evidence.

Gender role expectations for women and men continue to prohibit all members of society from routinely questioning stereotypical gender expectations, specifically those that disadvantage women. What is defined as "normal" and therefore as right and correct for women and men often goes unchallenged. **Gender stereotyping** functions to support the status quo that maintains the marginalization of women (see Exercise 10-1).

Exercise 10-1

Point of Reflection: Stereotyping: Maintaining the Status Quo

Directions: In the text we have noted how gender-role expectations for women and men prohibit all members of society from questioning stereotypical expectations. What is defined as normal, and therefore as right and correct, goes unchallenged. In this exercise, we invite you to question the "rightness," the "correctness," of several statements.

1. Review each of the following statements.
    *   Women make better parents.
    *   The female is the fairer sex.
    *   Women seek love and romance; men seek sex and physical stimulation.

*   Women are better at the arts and communication (vs. math and science).
*   Women tend to be overly emotional at times.
*   Men are analytical; women more intuitive.
*   Men are not emotional.
*   Women are more nurturing than men.
*   Men know more about cars than women do.

2. Discuss the accuracy of each statement along with the possible societal implications of believing such a statement with your classmates, colleagues, and/or your instructor.

Males are socialized in culturally defined masculine ways that preserve the dominance of men as a group, and women are socialized to think and behave in ways that preserve their inferior status in society. This process of placing differential value and status on the various characteristics associated with each gender results in social and economic inequality (Kobrynowicz & Biernat, 1997). The women's movement began by challenging assumptions that asserted the inferiority of women.

The First Wave of the Women's Movement

The movement from the treatment of White women as possessions and property to treating them as individuals with rights is said to have begun when Elizabeth Cady Stanton questioned the rights White women were permitted in the 1800s. Stanton's questioning is believed to have initiated the women's rights movement in the United States on July 13, 1848, when Stanton and three of her friends met for tea. The women discussed their discontent with the limitations placed on women in the new democracy following the American Revolution. Stanton reasoned that because women had endured equally treacherous dangers in the New World as White men, they should experience the same freedoms gained. With her friends' agreement, days later Stanton organized a convention to discuss the social, civil, and religious conditions and rights of women at the Wesleyan Chapel in Seneca Falls on July 19–20, 1848. The **Seneca Falls Convention** is now seen as the starting point for the women's equal rights movement (Eisenberg & Ruthsdotter, 1998).

Stanton later used the Declaration of Independence as the framework for writing what she titled a **"Declaration of Sentiments"** in which she stated: "The history of mankind is a history of repeated injuries and usurpations on the part of and toward women, having in direct object the establishment of an absolute tyranny over her. To prove this let facts be submitted to a candid world. The evidence she provided included the following:

- Women had no legal rights and were not allowed to vote.
- Women had to submit to laws that they had no voice in forming.
- Women had no property rights.
- Husbands had the power to imprison and beat wives as well as holding all legal power over and responsibility for women.
- Women had no rights to the custody of their own children.
- Women were not allowed to enter the professions of law or medicine.
- Colleges and universities were not open to women. (Eisenberg & Ruthsdotter, 1998, pp. 2–3)

Government laws and politics acted to keep women in their subordinate positions in families and broader society. With the help of Frederick Douglass, African American abolitionist and orator, Stanton and others convened the first Women's Rights Convention at which the delegates unanimously endorsed her Declaration of Sentiments. Afterwards, women's rights conventions were held regularly from 1850 until the start of the Civil War to discuss women's issues. Women like Susan B. Anthony, Lucy Stone, Ida B. Wells-Barnett, and Sojourner Truth traveled the country lecturing and organizing for the next 40 years. Amid great opposition and ridicule from dominant culture, the women's suffrage movement of the 19th century persevered, and 72 years after those initial meetings in Seneca Falls, women won the right to vote in 1920 (Eisenberg & Ruthsdotter, 1998). Case Illustration 10-1 highlights the conflicted experienced of a person trying to be "the person she is" while fighting the pressure to be the person that society demands.

In 1919, as the suffrage movement ended, the **National American Woman Suffrage Association** reconfigured itself into the **League of Women Voters,** and in 1920, the Women's Bureau of the Department of Labor was established to advocate for changes in the workplace. A few years later in 1923, Alice Paul, the leader of the National Woman's Party, drafted the **Equal Rights Amendment (ERA)** for the United States Constitution. At about the same time, the birth-control movement initiated by public health nurse Margaret Sanger sought women's rights to control their own bodies, sexuality, and reproduction, thus adding a new dimension to women's emancipation. In 1936, the Supreme Court eventually declassified birth-control information as obscene. But it was not until 1965 that married couples in all states could legally obtain contraceptives (Eisenberg & Ruthsdotter, 1998).

The Second Wave

The 1960s ushered in what is now known as the second wave of the **women's rights movement.** During that time, President Kennedy convened a Commission on the Status of Women, naming Eleanor Roosevelt as its chair. The commission issued a report in 1963 that documented widespread discrimination against

Case Illustration 10-1　|　An Open Letter

[J]ust got off the phone with a recruiter and I'm still reeling about the things he said to me. Being laid off without notice more than once in my life, I ALWAYS keep my resume up to date and posted somewhere. I got a call yesterday for a WONDERFUL opportunity paying $15,000 MORE than I'm making now. Fortune 500, great employer, great benefits, etc. I decided that the timing wasn't right, told him thanks but no thanks.

Here's what he said that has brought tears to my eyes. He said that since I've become single, I'm now a good catch. He said he was telling me this NOT to offend me but to help me market myself. He said that in my line of work that "women" typically are the secondary earners and most employers don't take us seriously for the "good jobs" as they are afraid we will follow our husbands. I assured him that throughout my marriage . . . I was most often the primary earner and my income was never "secondary." He said that he didn't disagree but the general consensus among employers is STILL that. He told me that I was a hot commodity with my experience now that I'm single.

You know . . . I'd have to say he's right. Before this, I'd had about a dozen or so hits to my resume in the past two years. Since I changed it to reflect my new status . . . I've had TWICE the number of hits in only a few months.

It makes me want to cry. I turned down opportunity after opportunity because of my marriage and my X because I wanted him to be happy. I changed my name. Wore a ring and allowed myself to be addressed as Mrs. I did the neighborhood parties and went with him to his functions as "the good wife." I did my BEST to be both the Enjoli woman AND Martha Frickin' Stewart! I worked a full-time job WITH travel. Did 95 percent of the housework and laundry. Planted flowers EVERYWHERE his little heart desired. Baked for every family member and neighbor every Christmas. Bought all the gifts, sent all the cards. . . . I sacrificed 17 years of MY life for HIM and for what?

The recruiter said I shouldn't worry and there are more offers where this one came from. If my divorce wasn't still in such a state of chaos . . . I might be interested in the job. I NEVER blamed him or accused him of holding me back. I thought WE made these decisions. Yeah . . . WE made HIS decision.

The X used to push my buttons with the "I am woman, hear me roar" comment any time I had an opinion or stood up for myself. He frequently picked on my job/career. However, without MY salary we would NEVER have made it on his alone. When we had the "big discussion," as he put it, where I told him I wanted the divorce, he made it sound as if I was ALL about MY career and he just couldn't support me in the way he needed to. (When in fact the divorce was all about HIS infidelity). He was ALL FOR me being there for him financially and was MORE than willing to stick it out until he "could get a few more bills paid."

He had said in therapy that he was at a point in his life that he needed a stay-at-home wife. I and the therapist asked him if at any point I had ever given him the impression I was that type of person. He very quickly replied, "No, . . . that's just what I'd like." The therapist followed up with, "You don't have kids so what would your wife do all day?" To this he replied, "She could take care of everything around the house, repairs, contractors, etc." She asked him if I did that, then what would he do? He said it would give him time to "pursue his interests." She followed with, "Do you think that will make HER happy or be a satisfying life for her?" He said, "No, that's just what I'd like right now."

Now I'm almost 43 and I'm stunned thinking about how much farther I could be in my life if I'd not married him. He's the one who's pissed and moaned for YEARS about NOT being where he thought he'd be. I stood by him. Supported one job change after another both emotionally AND financially. He NEVER wanted to go back to school but yet ALWAYS wanted to criticize me for having finished college. He picked on my job time after time. I turned down offer after offer. SO . . . is it time for MY mid-life crisis? I'm just SO hurt right now I just can't speak

Source: An open letter from MKRASH (http://forums.about.com/abdivorcespprt/messages/?msg=5841.1)

women in virtually every area of U.S. life. To begin to address identified injustices, Title VII of the 1964 **Civil Rights Act** was passed, which prohibited employment discrimination on the basis of race, sex, religion, and national origin. With its passage, the Equal Employment Opportunity Commission (EEOC) was established to investigate complaints of work discrimination. By 1966, the **National Organization for Women (NOW)** was organized to address the specific needs and treatment of women in society. And with the inclusion of **Title IX** in the education codes of 1972, equal access to higher education and professional schools became the law. The Equal Rights Amendment (ERA) also became law in 1972. It stated: "Equality of rights under the law shall not be denied or abridged by the United States or by any state on account of sex" (Eisenberg & Ruthsdotter, 1998; Whalen & Whalen, 1985).

Current Conditions

Some now believe that women have achieved equality and that sexism no longer exists. Despite the real gains made by women on numerous fronts, compelling evidence exists that demonstrates that inequality and sexism continue to thrive in the United States (Hallock, 1994; Kirchmeyer, 1998; Schneer & Reitman, 1995).

After significant and far-reaching legal and social advances in the '60s and '70s, many conservative political groups in the '80s and '90s used considerable force to stall and reverse women's rights. Some opposed affirmative action programs and other programs established to reduce discrimination against women and other minority groups. Women of today are still employed primarily in jobs that are not equally valued by society (Agars & Kottke, 2004; Heilman, 1983). Women face hiring discrimination, **glass ceilings,** and **maternal walls.** Affordable quality child care is not available for many working mothers, and women receive lower wages for the same work performed by men. In addition. "mommy tracking" is a widespread practice that reflects women's lost career opportunities and advancement when they have children. According to the U.S. Bureau of the Census (2001), the median annual earnings of women working full time is $29,215 per year. For every $1 their male counterparts earn, females earn 76 cents. In addition, women continue to face widespread sexual abuse and sexual harassment on the job. Research suggests that between 35 percent and 50 percent of women in the workforce will be sexually harassed at some point in their careers (Gutek, 2001). The increasing awareness of pay differentials and the ongoing experience of sexual harassment have led to the implementation of antidiscrimination and sexual harassment policies for virtually all employers in the United States. However, not even these changes have resulted in full equality in the workplace.

The gap between men and women in obtaining college degrees has not closed completely, but the percentage is closer: 25 percent of women versus 29 percent of men age 25 and older hold a bachelor's degree or higher. In fact, since 1979, 56 percent of all college students are women. A record 65 women were elected to the U.S. House of Representatives in the November 2004 election, including 57 incumbents and 8 newcomers. In the Senate, all female incumbents held onto their seats, keeping the number of women steady at 14 (Mitchel, 2005).

However, many women remain trapped in traditionally feminine jobs that pay less and are less prestigious and less influential than traditionally male professions (Agars & Kottke, 2004). In the 1970s, 1980s, and 1990s women who were married and/or mothers of young children flooded into the labor market (Bianchi & Casper, 2001). What was thought to be a glass ceiling for all women has turned out to be, in large part, a problem that might more accurately be termed "the maternal wall" for women with children (Williams, 2000). Increasingly, the gender gap in compensation has become an issue of "mother" versus "other," causing some analysts to describe motherhood as the worst economic decision a woman could make (Crittenden, 2001). While the wages of women without children approach those of men, mothers' wages lag far behind. Mothers earn 60 percent of the wages of fathers (Waldfogel, 1998).

Working part time is often seen as viable choice for women with children. However, part-time workers are rarely provided with healthcare benefits, competitive wages, and advancement opportunities. In 2001, 65.6 percent of the part-time work force in the United States was made up of women, and of all employed women, 27 percent worked part time, compared to 12.6 percent of employed men. Two out of three mothers aged 25–44 work less than 40 hours per week year round (U.S. Bureau of the Census, 2002). Most women who work part time do so for family reasons (Institute for Women's Policy Research, 2001). Further, in desirable professions where full time often means overtime, mothers have trouble competing for positions (Williams, 200). Employers of high-status jobs continue to seek a traditionally defined ideal worker who starts work in early adulthood and works full time and full force for 40 years straight, taking no time off for childbearing and childrearing (Crosby, 2004; Mintz, 2000).

The Third Wave

Today, many women's rights advocates think of themselves as members of the "third wave" of the women's rights movement. Those active in this third wave address issues such as women's admissions and treatment in military academies; women's reproductive rights (still contested 25 years after the Supreme Court ruling in *Roe v. Wade* affirmed women's choice during the first two trimesters of pregnancy); women's leadership in religious worship; affirmative action; mommy tracking; sexual harassment; violence against women; the maternal wall; glass ceilings; and other forms of institutional discrimination against women in the United States.

CULTURAL FACTOR 2: INITIAL TERMS OF INCORPORATION INTO U.S. SOCIETY

The early treatment of women in the United States resembled treatment of children. Prior to the industrial era of the 19th and 20th centuries, women were denied the rights and privileges now considered part of adulthood. Prior to this time, women were not allowed to have ownership of any kind and were not even considered the legal guardians and custodians of their own children. Originally, many women came to the United States as indentured servants or slaves. Married women failed to legally exist apart from their husbands.

According to Adkinson and Hackett (1995), at least four major themes have characterized dominant culture's historical treatment and incorporation of women in the United States: (1) neglect—women's health and social issues were ignored; (2) blatant sexism—including searches for the presumed mental and psychological mechanisms of women's inferiority; (3) pathologizing women's concerns—including diagnoses of hysteria and depression assigned to women whom male doctors believed were "overreacting" to their life conditions; and (4) circumstances in which women's needs and issues are more a part of dominant culture awareness.

CULTURAL FACTOR 3: SHARED VALUES AND TRADITIONS

Gender stereotypes greatly sway male and female behavior. While males are expected to be boldly active in pursuing their convictions and rights, task-oriented, and self-assertive, females in the United States are socialized to be passive, dependent, demure, relationship-oriented, and selfless (Eagly, 1987). This permissive attitude regarding men's assertiveness and the more constraining expectation that women act selflessly is a major factor in gender disparity outcomes. If women must be selfless to be approved, when they emerge as social leaders, they are sanctioned (Eagly & Karau, 1991, 2002). Bem (1974) identified masculinity as being independent, assertive, forceful, dominant, and aggressive. Individuals known or assumed to possess this gender-role orientation are perceived to be strong and effective leaders (Wiley & Crittenden, 1992). Women, on the other hand, are socialized to be feminine. Femininity is defined as being dependent, submissive, quiet, and unassuming. Feminine women have been found to reach lower levels of career advancement when compared with masculine men and women and feminine men (Kirchmeyer, 1998).

External social forces have created precise value systems for women in dominant culture. By a young age, females voice a preference for toys and traits that are consistent with society's definition of femininity. It is not clear where females' real values along the aggressive/submissive continuum lie because they cannot be measured outside the social context within which they reside. Females learn early on that they must choose between enhancing their professional or gender identities (Gilligan, 1982). Acting in non-normative ways is linked to decreased likeability; decreased likeability is related to decreased influence; and decreased influence leads to weakened achievement and career success and advancement (Carli, 1990; Rudman & Glick, 1999).

Female Student Identity Development

Belenky, Clinchy, Goldberger, and Tarule (1986) have described five positions that females adopt in their approach to knowledge acquisition. Yet these researchers caution that although these positions reflect female development, they are not necessarily experienced by all female students in linear or hierarchical progression. Girls in the first position of silence do not perceive themselves as competent learners. They lack confidence in themselves and doubt their abilities. Girls in the second position experience received knowledge by listening to authorities. They emphasize external learning and seek gratification by attempting to measure up to the truths they have been given. At the third position, subjective knowledge, the uncertainty of external authority is acknowledged. They engage in a quest for self-understanding and personal knowledge. At the fourth position, procedural knowledge is emphasized. Females use objective thought and reason to learn procedures that give them the power to apply knowledge using reason alone. They also seek opportunities for personal sharing of information in climates of empathy and understanding. Finally, at the fifth position, females begin to integrate intuitive, subjective knowledge with objective, external reason. In this way, they are active constructors of their own knowledge. They are accomplished in their abilities to critically analyze and challenge what is presented to them by others as knowledge. However, Belenky and her colleagues (1986) noted that not all females progress through all five stages of development. As a result of the negative influences of **gender socialization** in U.S. society, many may remain in the earlier positions of silence and acquiescence.

Behaviors, values, and characteristics associated with females and males are neither universal nor timeless; they are socially constructed, reflecting the society and time in which they appear. For example, women during WWII were seen as strong, capable, and independent when they were needed to replace men in the factories as the men went to war. However, with the return of the men from the war back into the labor force, the image of women and the "values" they manifested dramatically changed. They were again expected to be weak and submissive to suit dominant-culture wishes of the time.

Today, the following gender attitudes are prescribed for members of U.S. society:

- **Men (or masculinity):** Includes being strong, aggressive, ambitious, competitive, rational, independent, intelligent, emotionally detached, and tough
- **Women (or femininity):** Involves the opposite of what it means to be male; thus, women are expected to be weak, passive, unambitious, cooperative, relationship oriented, dependent, uninterested and involved in intellectual endeavors, emotional, gentle, and caring

While it is clear that assimilating such values can serve the individual and the society well, they also serve as a hindrance to personal development. For example, women attempting to emerge as social leaders find themselves sanctioned by a society that expects them to be selfless (Eagly & Karau, 1991, 2002) or simply ignored because they are perceived to lack those traits typically associated with masculinity (that is, assertive, forceful, dominant, and aggressive) (Bem, 1974) and leadership (Wiley & Crittenden, 1992).

Teachers and other school officials respond negatively to overly assertive girls who display behaviors that would seem acceptable if they were presented by male students. As such, female students lose opportunities if they act in stereotypically female ways (passive, dependent, and so on) and are looked down upon and disciplined for acting in stereotypically male ways. In either case, female students are disadvantaged (Jones, 1997; Heilman, 1983).

Intercultural Communication Strategies for Teachers 10-1

Classroom Applications: Gender in the Classroom

As noted, women in the United States are viewed as feminine when they act in ways considered by gender definitions to be appropriate for women in U.S. culture. This is also true for female students. Often, what it is to be "feminine" can interfere with female students' active participation in the classroom. To counter this, teachers should do the following:

- Consciously and intentionally call on boys and girls equally. Research suggests that in whole-class teaching, where the teacher decides who should contribute, boys make more contributions than girls do, and their contributions are usually more elaborate. It has been suggested that this happens partly through activities within discussions, for example, hand-raising, and partly because boys' reputations for misbehavior lead to greater monitoring of them by teachers. Therefore, be mindful of calling on children of each gender equally. Use index cards or Popsicle sticks with your students' names on them to keep track of whom you actually call on during class discussions.

- Be sure to monitor the degree to which students interrupt others who may be attempting to contribute. Research shows that boys tend to interrupt and dominate in class discussion.

- Be sure to call on girls for assistance in class, as research shows that teachers more typically call on boys for help.

- Girls both seek and give help more frequently than boys; therefore, provide them the opportunity to use their helping skills to demonstrate competence.

- When working in small groups, encourage students to take turns being recorders and reporters, because some research on mixed-sex groups suggests that girls tend to direct their input through boys.

- While noting the valuable contributions of those offering ideas, answers, and recommendations, be mindful of the value of those (typically girls) who contribute to groups through supportive behavior such as empathic repetition or building upon another's idea. Use effective questioning methods to help female students further develop their positions.

- At least twice per year, set up a video camera in your classroom to observe the gender dynamics and discover the reason for silences and the lack of involvement for some members of your class. If students are quiet but engaged, an encouraging gesture may be all that is needed to include them. If students are being intimidated or interrupted by others in the class, an intervention may be called for in a way that gives them strength. This will provide you with an opportunity to observe your own teaching behaviors as well, so you can analyze the effectiveness of your nonsexist teaching strategies.

Hopefully, the day will come when both women and men will be supported for having nurturing and achieving capacities and ambitions and a knowledge will prevail that neither gender has unique abilities that are suitable only for one particular life arena (Coltrane, 1996; Gilbert & Rader, 2001).

CULTURAL FACTOR 4: VIEW OF SPIRITUALITY AND HUMANS' RELATION TO NATURE

Historically, within the Judeo-Christian tradition and others in which a "higher power" is identified in different ways, God or the higher power has been and continues to be portrayed using masculine form in both iconographic presentations and in literary description. Typically, the higher power is presented as Father, King, Judge, Master. And the masculine image of the higher power has been advanced through creations such as Michelangelo's *The Creation of Adam* (in the Sistine Chapel) or William Blake's *God Creating the Universe,* which depicts God as an old, white-haired, bearded man and serves as a potent source of information about the image of God for millions of people worldwide.

Feminists criticize such patriarchal depictions of God, calling them idolatrous and noting that such practices continue in spite of the theoretical recognition that the higher power transcends gender and that there is nothing normative about patriarchy and god worship. Further, the practices and languages that emanate from such patriarchal perspectives have often isolated women from their own spirituality. Fiorenza (1979) gave voice to this sense of isolation when she wrote:

> We are all used to hearing: God the Father loves you, and if you join the brotherhood and fellowship of all Christians, you will become sons of God and brothers of Christ who died for all men. Such exclusive language has communicated to women for centuries that they are nonentities, subspecies of men, subordinated and inferior to them not only on a cultural, but also on a religious plane. Feminists hold that the combination of male language for God with the stress on the sovereignty and absolute authority of the patriarchal God has sanctioned men's drive for power and domination in the Church as well as in society. (p. 139)

Most feminist thinkers postulate images of God that encompass the full humanity of men and women (Johnson, 1989). In this light, feminist spirituality is not restricted to a female point of view but rather refers to a perspective, an approach to life, that can be claimed by women and men alike.

While variations within the specifics of feminist theology exist, most often there is emphasis on the belief in holism, an emphasis on the connectedness and interdependence of everything on the planet or indeed in the cosmos, much like that found within the Native American, Asian, Latino, and other nature-based spiritual traditions that believe in a sacred, animated universe. Another characteristic of female spirituality is that it goes beyond the traditional

| Exercise 10-2 | Field Experience: The Our Mother |

Directions: The following exercise requires you to interview a person who is affiliated with some form of religious organization, faith, or form of spirituality.

1. Ask the individual the following questions:
   - How would you describe God or your higher power?
   - When you get an image of your higher power, what is the image you perceive?
   - If you have a formal or structured prayer (for example, the Our Father [Lord's Prayer] in Christian religions) that you feel is central to your faith, would you recite it for me?

2. If the description, image, or prayer appears to be particularly male referent, ask the individual if he or she would be willing to do the following:
   - Describe the feminine qualities of your higher power.
   - Envision or image your higher power with feminine characteristics.
   - Say the prayer, replacing male referents with female referents.

3. Share your observations with your classmates, colleagues, and your instructor in small-group discussion.

rigorous asceticism of male spirituality to include acceptance of one's deepest feelings, affectivity, creativity, and mysticism (Kolbenschlag, 1982).

According to Irigaray (1986), "[T]o become a woman, to accomplish her feminine subjectivity, woman needs a God that figures the perfection of her subjectivity" (p. 6). And as Madonna Kolbenschlag (1982) points out in her "Feminist, the Frog Princess and the New Frontiers of Spirituality,"

> Women have discovered the great lie about spirituality. It is not something objective. One cannot study the "Great Masters" and possess it. One cannot probe the past tradition and understand it. One cannot rely on the testimony of others or the authority of experts in order to cultivate it. Women today are discovering that spirituality is authentic when it is intrinsically subjective, when it is brought forth painfully, from the womb of their own experience. They are creating a new "wisdom literature" out of the alchemy of their own lives. (p. 160)

CULTURAL FACTOR 5: ACCULTURATION AND EXPERIENCE WITH EXCLUSION AND ALIENATION

Women have been acculturated in dominant culture in the United States to meet needs, most particularly dominant-culture (male) needs, in society. From colonial times to the present, females have been socialized to serve husbands and children in self-sacrificing ways, to the detriment of their own personal and professional development. Simultaneously, women have been hindered in the obtainment of and alienated from the highest realms of social status and positions of power (for example, president of the United States) in society. As was discussed earlier in this chapter, women have been segregated into low-paying, traditionally "female" professions and alienated in various ways that have resulted in their subordination in society (Chodorow, 1974: Kossoudi &

Case Illustration 10-2 | **Kate**

". . . I have certain sets of maybe principles that I have never really sat and defined. They aren't—morals frequently have religious connotations and things like that . . . I don't have morals that are just for the sake of morals: Someone says this is how it is. I have principles of my own that shift as I get older. But I am always, you know, I live according to [principles] . . . But they are flexible. I would weigh any given situation and . . . it is never a black-and-white, right-and-wrong situation. . . . It [her moral decision-making] is never something I think of as a moral. Because in my mind I think of morals as being structured, binding kind of—and the principles I have for myself aren't that way, so I never really call them morals. . . . So, it's hard to know where and what they [her moral principles] are just because they are such an integral part of my actions and my everything." (p. 95)

Source: Brown, L. (1990). When is a moral problem not a moral problem? In *Making Connections: The Relational Worlds of Adolescent Girls at Emma Willard School*. Gilligan, C.; Lyons, N.P.; and Hanmer, T.J. Eds. pps. 88–109. Cambridge, Massachusetts: Harvard University Press.

Dresser, 1992). But the experience of exclusion and alienation is not limited to their roles in society and lost opportunities presented. For some women, the experience of oppression in a male-dominated society has resulted in alienation from their very selves, as they may lose their voices (that is, connection and attention to their own ideas and knowledge about the world) beginning during their entry into adolescence (Gilligan, 1982) (see Case illustration 10-2). In this case illustration, the description of morality, quoted in Brown (1990), is that of Kate, an adolescent who was interviewed by Brown in her investigation of adolescent female morality. Brown's research found that girls exhibit a kind of political resistance up until the age of about 11 or 12 in which they stand up for what they believe and insist on being heard. Those actions are replaced by psychological resistance that occurs around age 13–14 in which girls may silence themselves in an effort to meet the gender expectations prescribed by dominant culture.

CULTURAL FACTOR 6: LANGUAGE DIFFERENCES, STRENGTHS, AND CHALLENGES

For this marginalized group, it is the language of dominant culture, and not group members themselves, that presents a challenge. Linguistic theory notes that the language one speaks not only reflects one's view of the world but also determines one's power in it (Bolinger, 1968). "Whatever a particular culture considers to be the 'real world' is really constructed, unconsciously for the most part, by the language spoken in that culture. Language then both inculcates and reflects cultural beliefs about, among other things, women and men" (Barnouw, 1963, p. 1). Consider the connotations for the following terms: *tenderness, weakness, vulnerability,* and *timidity.* Each brings to mind femininity and womanliness. These qualities are actually harmful to women when viewed in contrast to the following qualities associated with masculinity: *determination, strength, decisiveness,* and *bravery* (Miller & Swift, 1988). Additionally, the use of pronouns (for example, he, she, him, her) in instances when gender specificity is not essential has led many authors to refer to unspecified or hypothetical persons or things using male pronouns, assuming *he*

Intercultural Communication Strategies for Teachers 10-2

Classroom Applications: Sexist Language in the Classroom

When we think of sexist language, our attention may be drawn to the overuse of the pronouns *him* and *he* as generic terms for any person of any gender or perhaps to the sexist nature of more informal greetings, such as "How are you guys all doing?" (when referring to a mixed-gender classroom). Think about it. You would probably never dream of addressing a mixed-sex group of students by asking, "How are you gals doing?"—right?

The teacher who wishes to create a nonsexist classroom needs to go beyond monitoring such verbal references. You should review all materials—including verbal examples you use within your classroom—for sexist language that may occur in one of the following forms.

- **Omission:** Review all materials: readings, case illustrations, examples, and word problems. Are males and females equally represented?

- **Firstness:** In referring to both females and males, as might be the case when providing an example of Tom and Joan, is the male typically or exclusively first? Is that necessary for the meaning of the illustration?

- **Activities and Occupations:** When mentioning various activities and occupations or using such as illustration, are some occupations more often assigned to a male or a female? For example, when making reference to nurses, secretaries even teachers, is the tendency to employ a female's name? How about when the reference is to a doctor, police officer, or even an athlete?

or *him* implies a generalization for both genders. Such an assumption is akin to the use of *man* as the equivalent for *human being*. Failure to recognize the impact of intentional and inadvertent sexism in language furthers the pervasive absence of females in written and oral discourse (Wilcoxin, 1989).

Sexist language also excludes and objectifies females in U.S. society in the following ways: (1) labeling the supposed exception to the rule (for example, woman doctor, male nurse); (2) trivializing female gender forms (for example, poetess, suffragette); (3) using terminology that refers to women as children (for example, baby, doll); and (4) using terminology that refers to women as food (for example, tomato, sugar, cupcake). These terms single women out as different from and unequal to men. Further, where there is an understood and clear demarcation between the words *boy* and *man*, there is no such distinction (linguistically) between *girl* and *woman* (Unger, 1979). Not only do teachers need to examine their own language use, but they must also thoroughly search for gender bias in print and other media materials they use in the classroom.

POTENTIAL BARRIERS IN LEARNING–TEACHING RELATIONSHIPS WITH DOMINANT-CULTURE TEACHERS

Many teachers believe that teaching should be neutral and gender blind. However, when teachers adopt a neutral stance, the result is often inadvertent sexism. Teachers must be aware of and continually review their own values and biases toward females in order to be advocates for equality and equal opportunities for women and girls (see Exercise 10-3).

Intercultural Communication Strategies for Teachers 10-3

Classroom Applications: A Nonsexist Learning Environment

Children, when they come to school, may well be armed with gender-differentiated patterns of social interaction. These gender-differentiated patterns can be encouraged, practiced, and consolidated within the classroom. For the teacher interested in expanding social interaction patterns to reflect the uniqueness of individuals and not gender differentiated roles, the following should be considered.

- For students who are quiet, allow them to journal or provide input in written form, and refer to their comments in an affirming way.
- Allow for variation in pace. Some question-and-answer exchanges can occur in rapid-fire order, whereas at other times, require a few moments of reflection prior to calling on students for their participation.
- While it is often pleasing to respond to the most animated student, resist always calling on the most aggressive; rather, look for subtle indications that a more quiet student is interested in contributing.
- Break up gendered monopolies by calling on those who have yet to respond.

- Affirm through the conception and implementation of your instructional activities that the value of engaged listening and supportive reflection are as valuable to a classroom exchange as the initiation of a response.
- With the goal of equality, be sure not to overreact by calling exclusively on girls in a class. Seek a balance.
- Eliminate gender-typed activities and assignments (for example, boys will help move the desks, girls can collect the papers).
- Be mindful and monitor all examples and illustrations employed in class. Do they speak to the specific experiences of all children, boys and girls?
- Be careful with gendered forms of address. For example, refer to great writers, scientists, and astronauts as "he or she," as is now more commonly done with teachers, lawyers, and so on.
- Arrange activities so that both girls and boys have opportunities for leadership.

Exercise 10-3   Field Experience: Perspectives on Gender

Directions:

1. Observe an instructor teaching a lesson in her or his classroom. Make note of gender-biased language or references (illustrations, examples, anecdotes, and so on).
2. Following the observation, ask the teacher the following questions, recording his/her response.
   - In your years of teaching, have you noted any *consistent* differences between your male and female students? Please explain.

   - In developing your lesson plans, what steps, if any, do you take to ensure the use of male and female representation? Can you provide references and illustrations?
   - Have you taken any specific steps in designing your classroom environment, your specific lessons, lesson activities, or the ways you interact with your students to insure a nonsexist learning environment?
3. Share your observations with your classmates, colleagues, or your instructor in small-group discussion.

Teaching, for the most part, operates to conceal the existence of social conflict and to preserve the status quo. Thus, female students in the classroom (who often constitute the numerical majority of students) are consumers of practices that work against their best interests. For example, dogmatic authoritarian teaching styles work against female students' interests as much as stereotypic views of masculinity and femininity. Thus, teachers cannot be gender blind or neutral; they must be feminist in the broadest sense of that word.

Feminists (both male and female) are advocates for equality between the sexes. Anyone who seeks equal opportunities for males and females is a feminist. Teachers must be actively feminist in their work with their students. Their teaching strategies must be informed by a comprehensive knowledge of gender socialization and its effect on human development and learning.

Ethical teachers should be knowledgeable about social issues (including violence against women, eating disorders, role changes, stress, and so on) that have particular impact on girls and women. For example, teachers, in their work with female students, must be keenly aware of the place in which women find themselves in society—needing to be perceived as beautiful and sexy in order to be accepted (even for girls as young as 7 or 8) yet also needing to remain chaste lest they be considered promiscuous and therefore undesirable. These and other social issues create great confusion and unrest for female students and affect their interactions in classrooms, which also contain these same expectations and related pressures. Socialized from birth in a society that devalues females and severely limits their choices and opportunities, no female is untouched by sexism.

Ethical teachers are aware of all forms of sexism and oppression and how they affect female student academic performance. The effects of sexism place female students at a great disadvantage that is not merited (Allport, 1954). Teachers need to be aware of the ways that gender attitudes and school practices restrict the lives of female students. They must encourage and support non-traditional gender roles in order to counteract the harmful impact of sexism, and they need to be willing to examine their own gender attitudes and preferences.

Ethical teachers need to be aware of their power and its use in the classroom and how male and female students experience power differently. The act of teaching implies an unequal power relationship between the teacher and the student, although the degree of this power differential varies depending on the theoretical orientation of the teacher (that is, behavioral, cognitive, neo-behavioral, or constructivist). For female students, experience with a commanding teacher in the classroom is one more instance of an unequal relationship in society and one more opportunity to be rewarded for expressing distress and to be helped by being expertly dominated. When submission in the classroom is required, it affects females' sense of adequacy and immobilizes them. While it is difficult, and many would say undesirable, to eliminate all power differentials in the classroom, teachers can and should ensure that they use power in educationally nurturing ways that benefit their students and do not maintain stereotypic dependency behaviors in female students. Teachers who make their students aware of choices, encourage autonomy, and teach critical thinking and decision making exhibit skill in this area.

FROM CONCEPTS TO LIVED EXPERIENCE

The following excerpt from "A Celebration of My Life" (1972) tells how a female employee of the Chicago Liberated Women's Union moved from a dominant-culture perspective of herself to a feminist perspective.

A CELEBRATION OF MY LIFE

I guess you'd have to understand where I've been to appreciate fully where I am now, because in many ways the New Me is not remarkable at all. My new head, new skills, my new hairstyle are all fairly common place, indeed. Certainly not the kind of success story glossy magazine will carry on the cover, not even *MS*.

But for me, the growth and discoveries and achievement have been enormous, and I'd like to share some of this joyous new thing of becoming a person. All the more so, in fact, because I'm not an extraordinary person. I'm not rich or gifted or beautiful or blonde. I don't have a college degree, and I'm a lousy cook. What is extraordinary is that there's more of me than there has ever been in my entire life. And that's exciting!

But let's begin at the beginning.

"Elbows off the Table!"   I spent my oldest-of-seven white Anglo-Saxon Protestant childhood trying to be to be invisible, to hide my ugliness and unworthiness, and to avoid distressing people with my presence, for I was convinced that I was responsible for every bad thing that happened in my household

Although my grossest weight at any time was 140 lbs, at 5' 5", I can't recall a time in my life when I did not think of myself as fat. In fact, I thought about little else. I did not think about what I wanted to be when I grew up. I thought about my body. My sole aspiration in life was to be long and lithe, with a flat tummy and beautiful breasts—like the cover girls on *Seventeen* and *Cosmopolitan,* and the very real girls that occupied so much of my husband's attention. But more of that later.

My parents were decent, well-meaning people, but if they ever had any great expectations of me—aside from standing up straight and keeping my elbows off the table—I can't think what they might have been.

My father always had to sign his approval to my high school curriculum choices, a quarterly source of grief for both of us. I elected groovy things like Latin, Greek and Ancient History, but my father urged me to be practical and to prepare myself for a job before marriage with typing and shorthand. Although he yielded to me, my own judgment was continually undermined in the process.

I was always in awe of "smart" people and I grew up believing in a kind of preordination for book learning. Alas, I was not one of the elect! As soon as I was old enough, I began working after school and weekends to avoid failure in competition for dates, social clubs, cheerleading—whatever girls are supposed to compete for. If you don't try, you can't lose.

Although my job was supposed to be an escape, it was public and, in many ways, rewarding. I was a "nice girl" with a friendly smile. Over the counter I met young men, who became dates as I "fell in love" with each one, and I met older men, who became benefactors. The latter were members of an alumni association that granted me a year's scholarship, for 1956–1957, to Boston University.

I also had a Christian commitment. So, in 1957, my little New England church paid my way to Chicago and the Baptist Missionary Training School. I endured two years of convent-type living, then quit and took a clerical job and a girls' club room, with no plans whatever for my future.

My Crowning Achievement of Failure What came, of course, was marriage, 1959 and children, 1962, 1964, and 1967. If I had "failed" as a daughter and "failed" as a student, my crowning achievement of failure was as a wife and mother. Although I worked faithfully and without complaint while my husband completed his education; although I bent over backwards to keep his socks picked up and his castle neat and clean and welcoming; although I dieted constantly, learned to use makeup and tried desperately to like cooking; although I typed, even wrote, his term papers, shared his interests and enthusiastically supported his ambitions—he strayed continually and ruthlessly.

In typical fashion, I accepted defeat as my lot. I just buried my hurt and more than ever became a nonperson. Motherhood, finally, I felt, was something I could do. Giving birth must mean something, doesn't it? I mean, I couldn't be a total failure . . .

And yet, try as I might to be a good mother, my babies cried and fussed, their ears were always dirty, and they wouldn't pick up their toys. My head ached all the time. I yelled and got cross when Dr. Spock said I shouldn't. I couldn't manage daily baths and walks in the park and peaceful bedtimes. The house got messier, my husband strayed more than ever, and far from feeling fulfilled, I felt more than ever my utter inadequacy as a person. I lived doubled over with knots in my guts and knots in my throat. I clenched my teeth and spoke very little, and sometimes I burst into tears when reading aloud to the children. I kept struggling and hoping, but couldn't see any hope. I hurt and I wanted to die.

Politics Was Fun In the meantime, however, the world changed a little bit, and I suddenly found myself in the midst of the civil rights movement, marching and picketing with babies on my back and a whole new sense of purpose. Something to live for—giving other folks a chance to be as free as me.

Then came the peace movement, and my head began to swim with the realization of the violence perpetuated against mankind. And during the course of these struggles my moral outrage began to be informed by politics, and I soon discovered I'd become a radical.

I Run for Office This was a period of great growth for me. I was doing important work outside the home, and I had a social milieu that challenged my world and everything I stood for. I was forced, for the first time in my life, to deal with the hard fact of being really different—not inferior or inadequate but of being radically set apart from the familiar mainstream.

My windows boasted posters demanding "Let the People Decide." And I was always in the streets, gathering signatures for independent candidates, marching against the war, and exercising free speech on Morse Avenue, while my friends were fighting it out with cops during the Democratic Convention. I developed a lot of strength living in the midst of neighborhood hostility as my lifestyle and politics became more public.

I began to feel better about myself; I was helping to make a revolution. At first my part was small, mostly organizing the office and maintaining the files. But I moved quickly into organizing people, newspaper writing and making speeches. In 1968, I became a candidate for state representative.

During all this time, however, I was still a follower. Decision making in our group was democratic. What happened in practice was that the men debated the issues and we women voted.

The "Woman Question" Arises   About that same time, the world shifted again, and "the Woman Question" came into vogue. Some of my women friends—single women without responsibilities and without husbands to account to—began talking a whole lot about the Woman Question and agitating for respect and equality in our organization. They criticized the men for male chauvinist attitudes at meetings and for relegating to women the least significant work. They criticized the husbands and urged us wives to overthrow our masters.

That was going too far. I had finally found my place in the world. My husband and I were a team, making the revolution side by side for the sake of the children and our children's children. But my women friends persisted and in no time at all I found myself in a rap group.

Dragged Kicking to a Rap Group   Becoming liberated is like being in labor, long and arduous, building in intensity till you think you can't stand it any longer. Even the outcome is uncertain and you panic in fear of a stillbirth or deformity. But there's no reversing the process once it's begun; you can only persevere and hope for successful delivery.

The rap group was a mind blower. Though I was dragged in kicking and screaming, and suffered reprisals from my much-threatened husband, it quickly became the most important place in my life.

I discovered, first, that every one of us suffered feelings of inadequacy and had spent our lives preoccupied with the size and shape of our bodies, comparing ourselves to the glamorous models of the media. Secondly, I learned how all of us had suffered from stunted intellectual growth, how we were taught to be dependent, not independent. I learned too, about how even the single women in their relationships with men and how mobility and sexual freedom were no guarantee of respect. Nor was education any guarantee for them of meaningful, gainful employment.

What "Teams" We Had!   From the rest of my sisters, I learned about marriage, that great "team" my husband and I had developed. None of us women had help with the children. If we couldn't find or afford babysitters, we missed our meetings or carried the kids along and spent our meeting times dealing with bottles, diapers, and crankiness. None of us had help with the housework.

We discovered together how we had been molded and shaped according to models of women that bore little relation to the potential each of us had as a person. The men in our lives, far from rejoicing in our newfound freedom, had no intention of relinquishing the power they held in maintaining us in those molds. Most important, though, we realized we could change. I was basically OK. With the loving and sympathetic support of my sisters, I could start from scratch and make a new life for myself, in my own image, according to my own needs and abilities.

In 1969, over 30 and a mother of three, I continued to work in earnest for the liberation of women. I participated in the founding convention, that year, of the CWLU, and have been actively involved ever since.

I Struggle to Possess My Soul   The first victory in the power struggle for possession of my body, mind, and soul was mine. I had my tubes tied, got my own bed, and said "No" when No was what I was feeling. No more sex because it was expected of me, and certainly no more sex as a way of resolving conflicts.

I took to arranging my own schedule of activities and involving myself in the political pursuits of my choice. Not without grief, mind you, for I was constantly being ridiculed for my decisions. Nor was I getting any assistance with the housework and child care; I just did less of each. As the women's movement grew up around me, more and more women rallied to my support, sharing the lessons of our common struggles and the care of the children.

I Fix the Mimeograph Machine   A whole new sense of confidence in myself and my abilities grew. I began to read and get excited about ideas. Though licensed to drive many years before, a nervous driver, I had let my license expire. Now I renewed it, and for the first time felt secure as a good driver at the wheel. I was learning to take control of my life, my decisions, even machines. Formerly intimidated by them, now I tackled them. I dismantled a malfunctioning mimeograph machine, diagnosed its problem, repaired the faulty parts, and reassembled them. It worked and I was high for days from sheer joy. Tomorrow I will tackle the typewriter.

Meanwhile I have also become economically independent. I have served the Chicago Women's Liberation Union as paid staff person for the past 10 months, sharing administrative responsibility for the entire organization with another woman. The work and decision making are harder in many ways than anything I've ever done, but all the more rewarding for that very reason.

The struggle for my soul is the hardest part of all, because there is nothing to show me what I'm struggling for. When I free myself from all those things in life that oppress me, what will be left?

Guilt keeps impinging. My mother role keeps trying to keep me at home; my wife role keeps demanding another chance. Anxiety about my children and uncertainty about the future interfere a whole lot with the excitement of forging a new life for myself.

Yet the rewards are too great to ignore. The pains of the past are too fresh in my memory; I can no longer pretend it was better before. It wasn't. For all its newness, for all its uncertainty, being the decision maker for my own life is its own best reward, and I am like a brand new person discovering the world.

SUMMARY

Cultural Factor 1: Historical and Current Treatment in the United States   One key to understanding women's status in a society is their degree of participation in the economy of the society as well as their control over the product they produce. Every society employs some type of sexual division of labor. The movement from White women being treated as possessions and property to being treated as individuals with rights has occurred in three waves, starting with Elizabeth Cady Stanton's writing of the "Declaration of Sentiments" and the subsequent rise of the National American Woman Suffrage Association. The second wave of the European American women's rights movement included the passage of Title VII of the 1964 Civil Rights Act, which prohibited employment discrimination on the basis of race, sex, religion, and national origin.

Today, the third wave of the women's rights movement operates with a focus on issues such as women's admission and treatment in military academies; women's reproductive rights (still contested 25 years after the Supreme Court ruling in *Roe v. Wade* affirmed women's choice during the first two trimesters of pregnancy); women's leadership in religious worship; affirmative action; mommy tracking; sexual harassment; violence against women; the maternal wall; glass ceilings; and other forms of institutional discrimination against women in the United States.

Cultural Factor 2: Initial Terms of Incorporation into U.S. Society   At least four major themes have characterized dominant culture's historical treatment and incorporation of women in the United States: (1) neglect—women's health and social issues were ignored; (2) blatant sexism—including searches for the presumed mental and psychological mechanisms of women's inferiority; (3) pathologizing women's concerns; and (4) current circumstances in which women's needs and issues are coming into dominant-culture consciousness.

Cultural Factor 3: Shared Values and Traditions   Behaviors, values, and characteristics associated with females and males are neither universal nor timeless; they are socially constructed, reflecting the society and time in which they operate. While women are presented as passive and submissive, it is not clear where females' real values along the aggressive/submissive continuum lie because they cannot be measured outside the social context within which they reside. Within the existing social context, females are socialized to be passive, dependent, relationship oriented, and selfless.

Cultural Factor 4: View of Spirituality and Humans' Relation to Nature   The practices and language that emanate from the presentation of God and other expressions of higher power in masculine form have resulted in patriarchal perspectives that have often isolated women from their own spirituality. Most feminist thinkers postulate images of God that encompass the full humanity of men and women; thus, feminist spirituality is not restricted to a female point of view but rather refers to a perspective, an approach to life, which can be claimed by women and men alike.

Cultural Factor 5: Acculturation and Experience with Exclusion and Alienation   Women have been acculturated in dominant culture in the United States to meet needs, most particularly dominant-culture (male) needs, in society. From colonial times to the present, females have been socialized to serve husbands and children in self-sacrificing ways, to the detriment of their own personal and professional development.

Cultural Factor 6: Language Differences, Strengths, and Challenges   Failure to recognize the impact of intentional and inadvertent sexism in language furthers the pervasive absence of females in written and oral discourse. Sexist language excludes, objectifies, and sets apart females in U.S. society in the following ways: (1) labeling the supposed exception to the rule (for example, woman doctor, male nurse); (2) trivializing female gender forms (for example, poetess, suffragette); (3) using terminology that refers to women as children (for example, baby, doll); and (4) using terminology that refers to women as food (for example, tomato, sugar, cupcake).

Potential Barriers in Learning–Teaching Relationships with Dominant-Culture Teachers   Teachers must be aware of and continually review their own values and biases toward females in order to be advocates for equality and equal opportunities for women and girls. Teachers must be actively feminist in their work with their students, where *feminist* refers to all (both male and female) who advocate for equality between the sexes.

Important Terms

Civil Rights Act

Declaration of
Sentiments

Equal Rights
Amendment
(ERA)

feminist

gender-based norms

gender socialization

gender stereotyping

glass ceiling

innate qualities

League of Women Voters

maternal wall

National American
Woman
Suffrage Association

National Organization
for Women
(NOW)

Seneca Falls Convention

sexism

sexual division of labor

Title IX

women's rights
movement

Enrichment

Crittenden, A. (2001). *The price of motherhood: Why the most important job in the world is still the least valued.* New York: Metropolitan.

Gay, G. (2000). *Culturally responsive teaching: Theory, research and practice.* New York: Teachers College.

Gilligan, C. (1982). *In a different voice.* Cambridge, MA: Harvard University.

Haag, P. (2002). Single-sex education in grades K–12: What does the research tell us? In *The Jossey-Bass reader on gender education* (pp. 647–676). San Francisco: Jossey Bass.

Richardson, L. W. (1981). *The dynamics of sex and gender: A socialized perspective* (2nd. ed.). Boston: Houghton Mifflin.

Ward, J. (2002). School rules. In *The Jossey-Bass reader on gender in education* (pp. 510–542). San Francisco: Jossey Bass.

Connections on the Web

www.now.org

This site of the National Organization for Women is a good general resource for information on women's issues.

www.distinguishedwomen.com

This website provides biographies of women who have contributed to U.S. culture.

www.cln.org/themes/women.html

A good source of materials for teachers looking to provide gender education, this site contains suggestions for "girl-friendly" sites, lesson-plan ideas, and information on minimizing gender bias.

REFERENCES

A celebration of my life. (1972, October). *Womankind.* Retrieved from http://www.cwluherstory.com/CWLUMemoir/betsy.html

Adkinson, D. R., & Hackett, G. (1995). *Counseling diverse populations.* Madison, WI: Brown & Benchmark.

Agars, M. D., & Kottke, J. L.(2004). Models and practice of diversity management: A historical review and presentation of new integration theory. In M. Stockdale & F. J. Crosby (Eds.), *The psychology and management of workplace diversity* (pp. 55–77). Malden, MA: Blackwell.

Albee, G. W., & Perry, M. (1998). Economic and social causes of sexism and the exploitation of women. *Journal of Community and Applied Social Psychology, 8,* 145–160.

Allport, G. W. (1954). *The nature of prejudice.* Cambridge, MA: Addison Wesley.

Barnouw, V. (1963). *Culture and personality.* Homewood, IL: Dorsey.

Belenky, M. F., Clinchy, B. M., Goldberger, N. R., & Tarule, J. M. (1986). *Women's ways of knowing.* New York: Basic Books.

Bem, S. L. (1974). The measurement of psychological androgyny. *Journal of Consulting and Clinical Psychology, 42,* 155–162.

Bianchi, S. M., & Casper, L. M. (2001). American families. *Population Bulletin, 55,* 2–43.

Bolinger, D. (1968). *Aspects of language.* New York: Harcourt Brace Jovanovich.

Carli, L. L. (1990). Gender language and influence. *Journal of Personality and Social Psychology, 59,* 941–951.

Chodorow, N. (1974). *The reproduction of mothering: Psychoanalysis and the sociology of gender.* New York: Columbia University.

Coltrane, S. (1996). *Family man: Fatherhood, housework, and gender equity.* New York: Oxford University.

Crittenden, A. (2001). *The price of motherhood: Why the most important job in the world is still the least valued.* New York: Metropolitan.

Crosby, F. J. (2004). *Affirmative action is dead: Long live affirmative action.* New Haven, CT: Yale University.

Eagly, A. H. (1987). *Sex difference in social behavior: A social role interpretation.* Hillsdale, NJ: Erlbaum.

Eagly, A. H., & Karau, S. J. (1991). Gender and the emergence of leaders: A meta-analysis. *Journal of Personality & Social Psychology, 60(5),* 685–710.

Eagly, A. H., & Karau, S. J. (2002). Role congruity theory of prejudice toward female leaders. *Psychological Review, 109(3),* 573–597.

Eisenberg, B., & Ruthsdotter, M. (1998). Living the legacy: The women's rights movement 1848–1998. *The National Women's History Project.* Retrieved February 6, 2005, from http://www.legacy98.org/move-hist.html

Ferree, M. M. (1990). Beyond separate spheres: Feminism and family research. *Journal of marriage and the family, 52,* 866–884.

Fiorenza, E. S. (1979). Feminist spirituality, Christian identity, and Catholic vision. In C. P. Christ & J. Plaskow (Eds.), *Women spirit rising* (p. 139). San Francisco: Harper & Row.

Gilbert, L. A., & Rader, J. (2001). Current perspectives in women's adult roles: Work, family, and life. In R. K. Unger (Ed.), *Handbook of the psychology of women and gender* (pp. 156–169). New York: John Wiley & Sons.

Gilligan, C. (1982). *In a different voice.* Cambridge, MA: Harvard University.

Gutek, B. A. (2001). Women and paid work. *Psychology of Women Quarterly, 25(4),* 379–394.

Hallock, P. (1994). Promoting diversity on campus: Thoughts to action. *Thought and Action, 10,* 65–78.

Heilman, M. E. (1983). Sex bias in work settings: The lack of fit model. In L. L. Cummings & B. M. Staw (Eds.), *Research in organized behavior* (Vol. 5, pp. 269–298). Greenwich, CT: JAI.

Institute for Women's Policy Research. (2001, May). *Today's women workers: Shut out of yesterday's employment insurance system* (Pub. No. A127). Washington, DC: Author.

Irigaray, L. (1986). *Occasional Paper 8.* Sydney, Australia: Local Consumption.

Johnson, E. A. (1989). Mary and the female face of God., *Theological Studies, 50,* 500–520.

Jones, J. M. (1997). *Prejudice and racism* (2nd ed.). New York: McGraw Hill.

Kirchmeyer, C. (1998). Determinism and managerial career success: Evidence and explanation of male/female differences. *Journal of Management, 24,* 673–692.

Kobrynowicz, D., & Biernat, N. (1997). Decoding subjective evaluations: How stereotypes provide shifting standards. *Journal of Experimental Social Psychology, 33,* 579–601.

Kolbenschlag, M. (1982, July–August). Feminist, the frog Princess and the New Frontiers of Spirituality. *New Catholic World,* 160.

Kossoudi, S. A., & Dresser, L. J. (1992). Working class rosies: Women industrial workers during World War II. *The Journal of Economic History, 52,* 431–447.

Marcus, E. (2002). *Making gay history: The half-century fight for lesbian and gay equal rights.* New York: Perennial.

Matlin, M. W. (1987). *The psychology of women.* New York: C & S College Publishing.

Miller, C., & Swift, K. (1988). *The handbook of nonsexist writing* (2nd ed.). New York: Harper & Row.

Mintz, S. (2000). From patriarchy to androgyny and other myths: Placing men's family roles in historical perspective. In A. Booth & A. C. Crouter (Eds.), *Men in families: When do they* get involved? What difference does it make? (pp. 3–30). Mahwah, NJ: Lawrence Erlbaum Associates.

Mitchel, P. (2005). Feminism fits busy schedules. *Herizons*, 6.

Richardson, L. W. (1981). *The dynamics of sex and gender: A socialized perspective* (2nd ed.) Boston: Houghton Mifflin.

Rudman, L. A., & Glick, P. (1999). Feminized management and backlash towards agentic women: The hidden costs of a kinder, gentler image of middle management. *Journal of Personality and Social Psychology*, 77, 1004–1010.

Schneer, J. A., & Reitman, F. (1995). The import of gender as managerial courses unfold. *Journal of Vocational Behavior*, 47, 290–315.

Spender, D. (1993). An alternative to Madonna. *Ms.*, 4(1), 44–46.

Spender, D. (1995). Women as revolutionary agents of change. *Women & Therapy*, 17(1/2), 260–261.

Unger, R. K. (1979). *Female and male: Psychological perspectives*. New York: Harper & Row.

U.S. Bureau of the Census. (2001). *Women by the numbers*. Retrieved January 24, 2005, from http://www.infoplease.com/spot/womencensus1.html

U.S. Bureau of the Census. (2002). *Historical income tables—People Table. Work experience of workers by median earnings and sex: 1967–2001*. Washington, DC: U.S. Government Printing Office.

Waldfogel, J. (1998). Understanding the "family gap" in pay for women and children. *Journal of Economic Perspectives*, 12, 137–156.

Whalen, C., & Whalen, B. (1985). *The longest debate: A legislative history of the 1964 civil rights act*. Washington, DC: Seven Lockes.

Wilcoxin, S. A. (1989). He/she/they/it?: Implied sexism in speech and print. *Journal of Counseling & Development*, 68, 114–116.

Wiley, M. G., & Crittenden, K. S. (1992). By your attributions you shall be known. *Sex Roles*, 27, 259–276.

Williams, J. (2000). *Unbending gender: Why work and family conflict and what to do about it*. New York: Oxford University.

Sixth grade at Central: the Irish toughs led by Vinnie O'Connor, a bully's bully, huge hulking with a blood-lust sneer that made even Kite look like a choirboy. It happened in the basement corridor, just outside the boys' lavatory, where the sixth grade had its lockers. Vinnie and a group of three or four others had somebody pinned in a corner. Vinnie was snarling and shoving. "Yeah, you're a homo, ain't ya? Little fairy homo. Ain't that right?" Then he shot out a fist and slammed his victim's head against the wall. A bustle of students streamed past to their lockers, eyes front and pretending not to see.

Paul Monette (1992)
Becoming a Man: Half a Life Story

11 CHAPTER | Learning from Gay and Lesbian Students' Stories

There is much to celebrate in acknowledging lesbian, gay, bisexual, transgendered, and questioning students' (LGBTQ) identities. At the same time, violence against members of this cultural group occurs every day in the United States. Unfortunately, the violence reflected in Monette's story persists in U.S. schools. This chapter explores the lives and perspectives of gay and lesbian students. As is true for all cultural groups presented within this text, a caution to remember is that there is wide variance between the experiences of each member in this group. While the chapter highlights the struggles of gay and lesbian individuals within a society that marginalizes their status, it is important to remember that all such discussion is presented with the knowledge that LGBTQ individuals perceive and address heterosexism differently. As such, oppression that marginalizes the status of LGBTQ people may cause some members of the group to feel conquered, limited, and depressed while others may react by resisting, which may lead to liberation and be experienced with pride and joy. The spectrum of reaction to oppression is wide. Therefore, it is important not to assume that all gay and lesbian students are victims, but rather to understand that as with all other oppressed groups, most lead full, satisfying, and successful lives despite the oppression they face. Even so, it is important to explore the challenges and barriers confronted by members of this group in an effort to reveal institutionalized discrimination as well as group-member resilience and advocacy that exist. Such factors affect opportunity structures, inequities, and effective strategies that, if acknowledged, will help to work toward social justice for members of this group.

The following chapter will explore oppression, resistance, struggles, and successes of gay and lesbian individuals in the United States.

CHAPTER OBJECTIVES

1. Define *sexual identity*.
2. Describe common values and worldviews of gay and lesbian people in U.S. society.
3. Identify ways the people profiled in the case narratives experienced and addressed the six cultural factors explored in this text.
4. Explain academic and intercultural interaction implications related to working with gay and lesbian students and their families.
5. Describe some coping strategies utilized by members of this cultural group.
6. Identify classroom strategies for cultivating the resources provided when gay and lesbian worldviews are integrated in your curricula.

SEXUAL IDENTITY

Human sexuality is complex. **Sexual identity** is the degree to which we identify with the social and biological aspects of being a man or a woman. Some perceive sexual orientation and sexual identity to be simple, straightforward products of biology. Such a position, often termed "an **Essentialist** position," argues that sexual orientation is a part of an individual's' core being. This stance often leads to the conclusion that heterosexuality is the "right and correct" form of sexuality and thus **homosexuality** is "improper." However, Katz (1997) noted, "[B]iology does not settle our erotic fates. The common notion that biology determines the object of sexual desire or that physiology and society together cause sexual orientation, are determinisms that deny the break existing between our bodies and situations and our desiring[, j]ust as the biology of our hearing organs will never tell us why we take pleasure in Bach or delight in Dixieland ..." (p. 64). In fact, not all people who exhibit gender nonconformity are gay or lesbian, and people of various sexual orientations engage in a vast range of sexual behaviors.

Sexual orientation is an integral part of sexual identity and is defined by who we are emotionally and/or to whom we are physically attracted. One's sexual orientation may be **lesbian, gay,** bisexual, transgender, **heterosexual,** or questioning. *Questioning* is included in the list because people may question their sexual orientations at any point in their lives. Each sexual orientation is considered to be normal by all prominent mental health organizations, such as the American Psychiatric Association and the American Psychological Association.

Lesbian, gay, bisexual, transgender, and questioning people are people in all age, gender, social-class, ability, and racial/ethnic groups. A conservative estimate identifies LGBTQ individuals as representing at least 10 percent of the total population in the United States. The way LGBTQ persons experience life and their identities is influenced by cultural and social variables, including social class, race, religion, family, and other forces. As such, all generalizations about members of the lesbian and gay communities must be viewed within context.

CULTURAL FACTOR 1: HISTORICAL AND CURRENT TREATMENT IN THE UNITED STATES

Gay and lesbian people are often described as having an invisible history. Historical records that chronicle perceptions and treatment of gays and lesbians are sketchy at best, and what we do know is most often derived from religious and legal actions exercised to eradicate homosexual behavior (Bullough, 1976, 1979). Yet the history of gay and lesbian individuals is ultimately one of movement toward acceptance and liberation.

Bullough (1979) identified societal reactions to gay people throughout history as having ranged from tolerance to societal and religious condemnation of homosexual behavior as sinful, criminal, and even medically pathological; to widespread societal discrimination; and finally to a more contemporary treatment that recognizes varying degrees of acceptance of gay and lesbian culture. Adkinson and Hackett (1995) described this historical treatment.

Acceptance and Tolerance

In early Melanesian cultures, homosexual activity between young and adult males was a part of youths' passage into manhood (Bohan, 1996). Similarly, Native American culture revered the *berdache* (two-spirited individual), a highly regarded figure who had same-sex partners and assumed male and female gender roles and identity (Williams, 1986). During Greek times, homosexuality was described by some as the only form of pure and lasting eroticism. Plato's view was that only love between persons of the same gender (that is, Platonic love) could transcend sex. Even still, women in Ancient Greece were not encouraged, as men were, to have homoerotic attachments; women of all classes led severely restricted lives. A 6th-century poet, Sappho from the Greek island of Lesbos who headed a girls' school, wrote poetry that celebrated love between women. However, Sappho was married to a man, and there is not much information left about her sexuality following the purposeful destruction of most of her poetry during the Christian era (Bullough, 1979).

Homosexuality Viewed as Religious Sin and Crime

Christian religious tradition has been one of the most forceful opponents of gay and lesbian lifestyles. Attempts to categorize homosexuality as a sin continue today. Much of the evidence for such claims comes from selective reading and interpretation of biblical scriptures in which homosexuality is depicted as a crime against nature. Those taking this position were often less concerned with women who engaged in so-called "unnatural" sexual behavior; historically, great emphasis was placed on the condemnation of men who were wasting their semen (that is, "spilling their seed"), which was perceived to be vital for procreation—the "true" reason for sex. Bullough (1979) identified a 390 AD Roman law that prescribed the death penalty for anal intercourse. The law was intended to halt male prostitution and "later became the foundation for the laws of the Christian Church canon as well as European and English civil law" (Adkinson & Hackett, 1995, p. 61).

Homosexuality Viewed as Sickness

Even in the "enlightened" arena of medicine, homosexual behavior was defined as deviant. While Freud believed homosexuality was "assuredly no advantage," he stated that it was not wrong. Freud's followers, however, interpreted homosexuality as a flight from incest in the absence of a father or in the presence of a weak one. It was believed that the boy suppressed his desire for all women and sought to be like his mother in accepting the father in other roles (Bullough, 1979). For years, professionals in the field of psychology focused on "curing" gays rather than on understanding gay men's and lesbian women's counseling issues (Adkinson & Hackett, 1995).

Harassment, Discrimination, and Exclusion

As noted earlier in this chapter, most of what is known pertaining to the history of this cultural group is scantily reported, and many of the historical events are contested by some on the grounds that they may not truly reflect incidences particular to **LGBTQ** individuals. The following is a list of historical events adapted from an excerpt in *The Reader's Companion to American History* (1991) that involved harassment, discrimination, and exclusion of gay and lesbian individuals in the United States:

1920s–1950s

- Urban gay subculture became visible in the United States as early as the 1920s and 1930s.
- The Chicago Society for Human Rights became the country's earliest known gay rights organization, and many cities had public gay bars during the 1940s.
- Alfred Kinsey published *Sexual Behavior in the Human Male* in 1948, which found that homosexual behavior was far more common among U.S. men than was previously believed. These findings provoked widespread discrimination against gays.
- Consistent with the sentiments of the time, President Eisenhower issued an Executive Order in 1953 that barred gays and lesbians from being hired by the federal government. This federal mandate encouraged state and local

governments to harass gay citizens through surveillance programs and regular police raids on gay bars.

- In 1950, Harry Hay, Charles Rowland, and others formed what would be called the **Mattachine Society,** which was created to address discrimination against gays in the United States.
- Five years later, the Daughters of Bilitus, a lesbian organization founded by Del Martin and Phyllis Lyon, joined the Mattachine Society to work to advance the rights and liberties of gay and lesbian people. Chapters of both organizations were established in several cities in the United States, and journals were published to provide resources and organization for gay and lesbian political action.

1960s–1990s

- The LGBT rights movement, fueled by the Civil Rights movement in the 1960s, led to activists such as Franklin Kameny and Barbara Gittings protesting discriminatory government employment policies.
- Illinois in 1962 became the first state in the United States to decriminalize homosexual acts between consenting adults in private.
- In 1969, the New York City police raided a Greenwich Village gay bar, the now-famous Stonewall Inn. Several days of rioting following this incident ignited a large–scale, mostly grassroots, gay liberation movement.
- The American Psychiatric Association removed homosexuality from its official list of psychiatric disorders, and there were at least 750 registered gay and lesbian organizations in the United States by 1973.
- In 1977, a popular singer at the time, Anita Bryant, led a campaign to repeal a gay rights ordinance in Dade County, Florida. Her actions spurred a Christian-led discrimination movement in the United States in the 1980s against gays and lesbians.
- Civil rights actions from the gay rights movement that followed resulted in federal and state governments not only decriminalizing homosexual behavior but also outlawing discrimination based on sexual orientation.
- In 1982, Wisconsin became the first state in the United States to outlaw discrimination based on sexual orientation.
- When **HIV/AIDS** took center stage in the 1980s, the prevalence of the disease among gays was used to strengthen antigay sentiments. HIV/AIDS was perceived by many in dominant culture to be a "gay disease" and was used as justification for discrimination against gay and lesbian people. The epidemic and ensuing propaganda linking HIV/AIDS to the so-called evils of homosexuality motivated many gay and dominant-culture advocates to join the gay rights movement.
- In 1987, more than 600,000 LGBT people and their allies marched in Washington, demanding equality and social justice.
- By 1990, the number of registered gay and lesbian organizations increased to several thousand.
- A critical moment in the history of gay rights that also helped dominant-culture Americans understand the violence against gay and lesbian people

was the murder of Matthew Shepherd in 1998. Shepherd, a gay college student at the University of Wyoming, was kidnapped, beaten, and left tied to a fence for 18 hours. Because the circumstances of his death received extensive media coverage and even took the form of a play and movie, *The Laramie Project*, U.S. citizens were provided with evidence of the existence of acts of violence that target gays and lesbians and were persuaded to consider the morality of the treatment of gays and lesbians in the United States (Brewer, 2003).

Current Conditions

In 2000, Vermont became the first state to legally recognize civil unions between gay and lesbian couples. The law provides gay and lesbian couples with entitlement to many rights, privileges, and responsibilities previously granted only to married couples. In 2004, same-sex marriages became legal for residents of Massachusetts. However, Massachusetts has an old miscegenation law on the books passed to prevent interracial couples from coming to the state and marrying that now prevents out-of-state same-sex couples from marrying in Massachusetts. Two states—Connecticut and Vermont—currently recognize civil unions; four states—California, Hawaii, Maine, and New Jersey—and the District of Columbia offer domestic partnership rights; and five states—Massachusetts, New Jersey, New Mexico, New York, and Rhode Island—and the District of Columbia have laws that do not explicitly invalidate same-sex marriages performed elsewhere. At the same time, 37 states enacted defense-of-marriage acts (DOMAs) that ban same-sex marriage: Six states limit marriage to one man and one woman, and 19 states have constitutional amendments that limit marriage to one man and one woman. These legal outcomes provide evidence that the gay rights movement is gaining strength, resulting in a growing sense of pride and liberation of LGBTQ individuals along with evidence of mounting dominant-culture acts to curtail the movement and continue discriminatory policies and practices against gay and lesbian citizens.

It is important to note that there is as much variation in lifestyle among members of LGBTQ culture as there is within the identified heterosexual population. The vast majority of gay and lesbian people live much the same as their heterosexual counterparts, seeking long-term relationships and raising families. However, on the macro level, violence against gays (included among criminal acts termed *hate crimes*) and the prohibitions of gays and lesbians to marry create a common cause and related value system for members of this cultural group (Button, Rienzo, & Wald, 2000; Haider-Markel, 2000).

Public attitudes about homosexuality changed dramatically during the 1990s, and a decrease in publicized hostility toward homosexuality has been observed (Wilcox & Norrander, 2002). Yet, in U.S. politics, gay rights support has typically been divided along party lines, with support for gays and lesbians associated with liberalism and the Democratic Party, whereas opposition to gay rights has typically been associated with conservatism and the Republican

Party (Haeberle, 1999; Wilcox & Norrander, 2002). LGBTQ movement gains also have been reflected in the media. In 1997, the title character of the television show *Ellen* (played by an openly lesbian actor, Ellen Degeneres), along with other television shows like *Will and Grace,* provided a positive view of lesbian and gay life for the U.S. public, thus paving the way for other prime-time gay and lesbian protagonist characters (Brewer, 2003).

Yet, to this day, LGBTQ citizens continue to struggle for the protection of federal, state, and local statutes to prohibit discrimination in employment, housing, child custody, adoption, coupling, and health insurance. Gay and lesbian people continue to face violence, job discrimination, and negative stereotyping.

Discrimination occurs at the macro level (for example, health insurance and partner-benefit laws) as well as at the micro level (involving daily personal interactions). Gays and lesbians face economic discrimination as a result of heterosexism in hiring, promotion, and firing practices. The movie *Philadelphia* provided an excellent illustration of the overt and covert discrimination gay and lesbian people may encounter in the workplace and the struggles gays and lesbians may confront when they attempt to secure their rights as citizens through legal action. In addition, gay and lesbian students are all too often harmed by teachers, students, and other members of dominant culture who trivialize their gay identity. Members of this cultural group continue to be disadvantaged by having their problems attributed to their sexual orientation, being assumed to be heterosexual, suffering gross insensitivity with regard to the importance of their close relationships, being alienated or absent in children's literature and academic curricula, experiencing physical assaults, and in other ways having their status marginalized in dominant culture. (See Case illustration 11-1.)

Dominant-culture male attitudes toward homosexuality are more unfavorable than female attitudes towards gay citizens, and attitudes toward gay men are often less favorable than attitudes toward lesbians (Herek, 1994; Kite & Whitley, 1996; Steffens & Wagner, 2004). Particular disdain held for gay men by members of dominant culture was found even among professionals (Berkman & Zimberg, 1997).

Further, with regard to economics, it is accurate to say that lesbian wages are closer to heterosexual women's wages compared to openly gay men's wages in relationship to the wages of heterosexual men. Berg and Lien (2002) found, for example, using a model that controlled for factors such as level of education, years of experience, and place of residence, that lesbians earned some 30 percent more than heterosexual women, while gay men earned around 22 percent less than their heterosexual male counterparts.

CULTURAL FACTOR 2: INITIAL TERMS OF INCORPORATION INTO U.S. SOCIETY

The concept of homosexual identity began to take shape toward the end of the 19th century when a biomedical view of homosexuality was presented (Miller, 1995). The **Kinsey Heterosexual–Homosexual Scale (KHHS)** was the first of the

| Case Illustration 11-1 | There Is No Lesbian Barbie |

In heterosexual families, both parents are sanctioned. They are legally the parents of the children, with the myriad of rights and daily sense of entitlement that confers. They don't have to think about it. They adopt or conceive their children together. Both their names are on the adoption documents or birth certificate. Each parent can travel with the child or take her or him to an emergency room for medical treatment. Both have titles that are recognized, carry meaning, and validate their relationship to the child a thousand times a day. They each think that she and he are the real parents. And everyone else thinks so too. Our situations are different. We have to deal with legal, practical, and psychological issues that arise out of the fact that society does not automatically recognize and honor our families, and that in "double-mommy" families we are not both legally sanctioned parents. In many states, the status of lesbian parents as sexual partners and/or parents is illegal or highly vulnerable. In Georgia, a sodomy statute is still on the books. In New Hampshire, the "Live Free or Die" state, a known lesbian cannot adopt a child or become a foster parent. In New York, an "unmarried couple" (and lesbians are still not permitted to marry) cannot adopt jointly. We may have to struggle for the right for both parents to be present when our child is born, and we rarely have the right to have both names on our child's birth certificate. In most cases of domestic adoption, and always in international adoption, we cannot present ourselves both as parents. Once we have our children, lesbians still face the very real threat of losing them. Although progress has been made, a lesbian in a custody dispute with a biological father is still likely to lose in most states, and in some cases may be permitted visitation only outside her lesbian household and not in the presence of her lesbian partner. A lesbian mother can lose custody of her children to biological grandparents or another biological relative who stakes a claim.... Every form we ever fill out for our child, from preschool application to college application, calls our authenticity into question.... At school, we must say that our family requires two Mother's day cards to be made.... We never see our families validated by the culture that inundates our children. Families like ours are not on *Sesame Street* or *Barney*, not in most children's books, not in movies. There are no songs about us on Raffi's albums. There are no marketing campaigns to celebrate or merchandise the wedding of Ariel to Snow White. There is no lesbian Barbie.

Source: Segal-Sklar, S. (1995). Lesbian parenting: Radical or retrograde? In K. Jay (Ed.), *Dyke life: From growing up to growing old, a celebration of the lesbian experience* (pp. 174–175). New York: Basic Books.

sexual-response scales (Kinsey, Pomeroy, Martin, & Gebhard, 1953). Kinsey and his colleagues categorized individuals in a static way based on variable aspects of sexual orientation, such as attraction, behavior, fantasy, lifestyle, emotional preference, social preference, and self-identification. In their study, 50 percent of males were found to be exclusively heterosexual, 4 percent were categorized as exclusively homosexual, and the remaining 46 percent fell somewhere in between. Later, the **Klein Sexual Orientation Grid (KSOG)** (Klein, Sepekoff, & Wolf, 1986) extended the scope of the Kinsey model. This grid configured sexual orientation along seven components: (1) sexual behavior (With whom do you have sex?); (2) emotional preference (Whom do you like or love?); (3) sexual fantasies (Whom do you fantasize about?); (4) sexual attraction (To whom are you attracted?); (5) social preference (With whom do you socialize?); (6) lifestyle, social world, and community (Where do you tend to spend time and with whom?); and (7) self-identification (How do you identify yourself?). Klein and colleagues asked respondents to rate their positions on each component using a scale of 1 (other sex only) to 7 (same sex only). The researchers contended that using this measure for defining sexual orientation reveals that one's sexual orientation is an ever-changing aspect of oneself.

But with all of the investigations and interest in defining sexual orientation, an obvious question is widely overlooked by many: Why is there is a need for a definition for sexual identity at all? The very process of attempting to define sexual identity and orientation amounts to a subtle form of discrimination and oppression (Hubbard, 1997; Katz, 1997).

A dichotomous portrayal of sexual identity was introduced over 40 years ago by Kinsey. Foucault (1978) maintained that homosexuality is a social construct that is little more than 100 years old, stating there was no definition for homo- versus heterosexuality until there was a sociopolitical need to do so. There was no definition for heterosexuality as normative and correct until homosexuality was identified and defined as different and incorrect (Katz, 1995). The ongoing quest to define sexual identity is also an ongoing insidious process that continues to present one form of identity (that is, heterosexual) as that which is right and normal and another (that is, homosexuality) as wrong.

CULTURAL FACTORS 3 AND 4: SHARED VALUES, TRADITIONS, AND SPIRITUALITY

In attempting to define common or generally held cultural values, one must remember that members of the LGBTQ community are also members of a number of communities and cultural groups. When speaking of the gay and lesbian community, especially in terms of shared values and traditions, it is important to highlight that for all gay or lesbian individuals, values they embrace may be more reflective of and aligned with gender, social-class, racial, or ethnic group than with values prevalent among members of gay or lesbian communities.

For example, Boykin (2005) described African American sexuality, including the increasingly exposed "down low" (referring to "straight" men who have sex with men in secret) cultural phenomenon. His book explores the lack of public awareness of the "down low" phenomenon as an example of dominant culture's discomfort and inability to accurately examine diversity pertaining to gay, bisexual, and African American sexuality. Boykin described ways societal sanctions have helped lead to the development of African American gay and bisexual men's compulsion to lead double lives, leaving gender and sexuality dialogues among members of the African American community to result in battles of the sexes that ignore the complexities of living "closeted," denigrate bisexuality, and disempower African American women.

Clearly, LGBTQ individuals who are people of color are affected and shaped by racial, ethnic, gender, age, social-class, regional, religious, and family values, while they share with dominant culture many traditions, values, and views of spirituality. LGBTQ community members tend to value that which is valued by many in society—authenticity, acceptance, safety, freedom, and community. Taking into account the wide-ranging variation among members in this cultural group, it is fair to say that perhaps the most noticeable common values and traditions of this group have been created in response to the discrimination members of this group face and the need for solidarity and unity. *Intentional* families may be formed to replace families created through biology that may be absent or impaired due to homophobia and discrimination. In fact, this cultural group is one of the only groups that cannot necessarily rely on members of their own families to help them understand the oppression they experience. Family members not only are likely to have little to no experience with similar discrimination faced by gay and lesbian individuals but also may engage in discrimination against their own gay and lesbian family members. Therefore, understanding, support, and coping strategies for addressing discrimination may not be provided by gay and lesbian citizens' biological family members.

Similarly, members of this group are aware that, due to heterosexism that pervades society and therefore all aspects of life, they may not have access to their chosen religious practice that they may have enjoyed before **coming out** as gay and lesbian individuals. It is widely known that many organized religions' policies and practices denounce, exclude, and/or otherwise alienate gay and lesbian people. But even with their marginalized status, LGBTQ individuals do not lead impoverished lives. Advocacy, liberalism, sexual freedom, gender diversity, and human rights are principles that tend to be valued among members of this group. Most often, gay and lesbian people lead full lives that celebrate their identities.

CULTURAL FACTOR 5: ACCULTURATION AND EXPERIENCE WITH EXCLUSION AND ALIENATION

The decision and process to be **closeted** (**passing** as heterosexual by hiding one's gay or lesbian identity) may reflect the experience of pressure to acculturate in dominant culture and/or anxiety tied to the projected discriminatory consequences of "coming out." Gay and lesbian people in the United States are shown through violence and other heterosexist acts that "coming out" as gay or lesbian may place them at great risk for disapproval and discrimination from family members and the larger society. President Clinton instituted the "Don't Ask, Don't Tell" policy in the U.S. military in 1993. While at face value one could argue that this was a step toward acceptance because it "permitted" gays and lesbians to serve in the military, others maintain that such a mandate further stigmatizes gays and lesbians by forcing them to hide their gayness and therefore indicating that gay and lesbian lifestyles are unacceptable. In addition, the policy met with such stiff opposition from dominant culture that it eventually led to the discharge of thousands of men and women from the armed forces (Miller, 1995).

As is often true for members of other minority groups, gay and lesbian citizens have, out of necessity, become adept at passing as heterosexual in order to survive and to be accepted by dominant culture. For some, the choice to "come

| Case Illustration 11-2 | Eres Maricon? Por "Eladio" |

They never understood. Never had and never will. How hard it was to grow up *una mujer* in this *cuerpo de hombre* (a woman trapped in this man's body). A deep dark secret kept safely hidden in a place where no light of day could penetrate the wall of sadness that enveloped what I wanted to be. More important, what I was really meant to be. Why is it that they say your family is the one thing that can never let you down? And yet, with family like mine, God knows I would never want for enemies. The many occasions of supposed family togetherness, the men camping outside in the *jardin* (garden), the women in *la cocina* or *el salon* (the kitchen or the living room). Many times I wished that I could join *la familia femininas* (the females of the family) instead of the machismo men that I was expected to be part of. No one would ever comprehend how much I despised watching the males of *mi familia* strut around talking about who had done what with whom, as if extramarital affairs had made them even bigger men in their minds. Watching them attack one another, first with drunken words, then with their fists; such brutality made me sick. My face kept the same blank look on the surface, never revealing the storm of rage and repulsion that course through my veins. Repeating over and over inside, *"Soy hombre, no sot maricone"* (I'm a man, not a faggot). Being a forced participant to this machismo group, I literally found myself on the outside looking in. *Mi primas* (my

cousins) all pretending to be mommies, or combing the long manes of *pelo de Negro, o pelo de Moreno* (shades of black and brown hair color) into the latest fashion craze. How I envied their freedom, their ability to express love, care, compassion, and nurturing amongst themselves. These were emotions of *las mujeres* (the women). I would hear the *tias* (aunts) talking in conspirational [sic] whispers of the ups and downs of their soap opera lives. I cried a million tears of sadness inside, and yet the expression on my face betrayed nothing. Not even me. As I grew older, the same questions would be asked repeatedly. At first the questions were of the *bueno hombre salud* (good ol' boy salute), slapping my back, sly facial expressions, and lewd comments about when and if the BIG EVENT had occurred for me. Who was the lucky *senoritas* (girl or lady)? If you only knew, I thought bleakly inside. Outside, I blustered and laughed their prying comments off. But as quickly as the humor surfaced, with time it was replaced with looks of hatred and disgust, accusations flying against me fast and furious. The questions then changed to, *"Eres Maricon? Mande? Eres Maricon"* (Are you a faggot? Huh, what did you say? Are you a faggot?) Inside I screamed, "Yes, dam it, *soy Maricon!*" but outside was none the wiser. I would hear my voice betray myself, "Hell no—no *soy Maricon.*"

Source: Garret, M. (2001). Eres marcion? Por "Eladio." In K. Kumashiro (Ed.), *Troubling intersections of race and sexuality* (pp. 34–35). New York: Rowman & Littlefield.

out," while ultimately liberating, may be experienced as a fear that is confronted with great effort and courage through careful planning and that frequently and repeatedly requires explaining and defending their gay, bisexual, or transgender identity—some of the most personal and private aspects of oneself—to others (often strangers). Coming out is clearly a conscious decision to become a target of oppression (Parker, 2001). For many, the path of least resistance is to play the role expected in dominant culture (that of a heterosexual) and struggle with the psychological and emotional consequences of not being true to oneself by embracing one's sexual identity (see Case illustration 11-2).

Exercise 11-1	Increasing Awareness

Directions: As noted in the text, members of the gay and lesbian community continue to be alienated and excluded from the dominant culture. Sometimes the process of exclusion and discrimination is apparent, while at other times it goes unrecognized. The goal of this exercise is to increase your awareness of the subtle ways perhaps you or those with whom you work or go to school discount the value and presence of members of the gay and lesbian community.

Your task is to go through a single day as an observer. Observe the various messages you see and hear that involve sexual orientation. Record your observations and share them with your classmates, colleagues, or teacher in small-group discussion. Consider the impact these incidents may have on a person who is gay or lesbian.

Examples of things to observe:

- Heterosexual privilege (for example, heterosexuals exhibiting public displays of affection in television commercials and TV shows, on billboards in movies, and so on)
- Language (for example, the use of derogatory descriptions of gay and lesbian people)
- Assumptions made, such as the assumption that one is dating a member of the opposite sex (for example, when a male says to another that "he should bring her along" without knowing if the partner is male or female)
- Negative reactions (responses to same-sex individuals holding hands, hugging, and so on)

While it is clear that members of the gay and lesbian community have made great strides to stand up and be counted, as a whole, being known as openly gay or lesbian continues to lead to alienation and exclusion in the dominant culture in that openly gay and lesbian people are not represented in children's literature and academic curricula; they are not typically identified as members of fraternities or sororities or acknowledged on sports teams; and they are frequently ostracized by teachers and other public servants. Many openly gay and lesbian persons in the United States experience isolation and treatment as second-class citizens in U.S. society.

The discounting of a gay and lesbian presence comes in many shapes and forms. Consider the impact of a constant barrage of seemingly benign questions posed to gay and lesbian students from their earliest years in school: "Do you have a girlfriend yet?" "Who do you want to marry when you grow up?" "Who are you taking to the prom?" In addition, alternative family constellations continue to be largely ignored in schools. When students have families that include two mothers, two fathers, or any other variation, they experience marginalization and alienation in classrooms and schools that have yet to decide whether or not it is appropriate to be advocates for the equal treatment of gay and lesbian families. These actions illustrate the exclusion and deeply embedded discrimination gay and lesbian citizens face in schools and wider dominant culture.

CULTURAL FACTOR 6: LANGUAGE DIFFERENCES, STRENGTHS, AND CHALLENGES

Language as Tool and Liberation

Language brings both problems and empowerment to many marginalized groups. It is used to discriminate against members of the LGBTQ group. But, like the other oppressed peoples, gay and lesbian people have reclaimed terms that are used to discriminate against them, and have redefined slurs through double entendre with new meanings that lift up rather than tear down members of this group. When gay and lesbian people call themselves "queer" or "dyke," they do it in such a way that not only helps take the sting out of the slurs they hear from dominant culture but provides them with a tool for uniting through various forms of communication while celebrating their identities. It is important to note that such language use is considered appropriate only among members of the group and their trusted allies. When members of the group use these terms aimed at themselves, they understand the particular purpose and opposite meanings they represent. In this way, language that is used against them becomes a weapon and a tool of liberation for members of this group.

In public high schools, 97 percent of students regularly hear homophobic remarks from their peers (Parker, 2001). The use of antigay slurs in U.S. schools is rampant, and each time an antigay slur is uttered, it is likely to be heard by a gay or lesbian student. It is, for the most part, commonplace and accepted by students and teachers alike for students to show disdain for some action by stating: "That's so gay." Yet, consider the reaction to a student who would state, "That's so Asian." Would such a remark be condoned if uttered in public? A student who makes such a statement would surely be labeled a racist. Why, then, are gay jokes and demeaning comments accepted in dominant culture?

Teachers are slow to intervene when derogatory comments about gay and lesbian students are made. In one study, 77 percent of prospective teachers stated they would not encourage a class discussion on homosexuality (Parker, 2001). And among the reasons students use to explain why they do not stand up for gay and lesbian students when they hear slurs is "My friends will assume that I am gay if I do" (Parker, 2001).

Beyond being the recipients of hate crimes and hate language, members of the gay and lesbian community have, according to some, developed a distinct cultural language. The LGBTQ community has developed ways to communicate with one another that are different from the linguistic practices of dominant culture.

Lionel Tiger, Darwin Professor of Anthropology at Rutgers University, explained that **"lavender language"** is a language comprised of distinct and independently developed linguistic constructions with distinct vocabulary that is specific to the LGBTQ community. Lavender language is not slang nor dialect but an actual language that, in fact, some gay and lesbian people struggle to master (Betsch, 2002).

Intercultural Communication Strategies for Teachers 11-1

Language That Helps

- Avoid heterosexist language. Avoid examples or language that reinforces peoples' assumptions that everyone is heterosexual. For example, rather than saying, "If a girl wants to bring her boyfriend to the dance …," we can say, "If a girl brings her partner. …"

- Help students become aware of their own use of heterosexist/homophobic language in their comments in the classroom. This includes eliminating obviously derogatory use of words like "that's gay" or "fag" but also statements that presume the universality of heterosexuality (for example, "Any guy would like to date her!").

- Intercede when others are using hurtful, heterosexist remarks. Students are sometimes fearful of

challenging these comments and need an adult model.

- Use respectful terminology when discussing LGBTQ issues. Your knowledge of appropriate terms conveys intercultural competence and helps you to be perceived as an ally.

- If you identify yourself as heterosexual when introducing yourself to your individuals or a class or if you discuss your family/lifestyle, refer to your significant other as your partner rather than as your wife, husband, or spouse. Such activism shares heterosexual privilege with gay and lesbian individuals who do not have the right to legally marry in most states and serves to signal to your students that you are aware of and have an appreciation for alternative family constellations.

Exercise 11-2 | Lavender Language

Directions: Members of the LGBTQ community may communicate with one another in ways that are different from the linguistic practices of nongay, or non-LGBTQ individuals. Researchers and writers from various disciplines (for example, philosophy, linguistics, anthropology, speech communication) have studied the ways in which gay individuals may use language.

The following is a list of words that may be employed in gay and lesbian discourse. Your task is to identify the meaning of each term and

discover at least one other meaning for each as well. Share your findings with classmates, colleagues, or your instructor in small-group discussion and discuss the implications of the use of such words by members of the gay and lesbian community.

Chichi (shishi)	Top
Drop beads	Lucy law
Fluff	Wreck
Fruitfly	Beard

Sources: Ringer, R. J. (Ed.). (1994). *Queer words, queer images*. New York: New York University; Stanley Penelope, J. (1970). Homosexual slang. *American Speech, 45*, 45–59.

COPING STRATEGIES FOR ADDRESSING OPPRESSION

While LGBTQ individuals may experience joy and empowerment upon "coming out," for others who may enjoy less social support, the experience of embracing their sexual identities may be difficult. And if gay and lesbian people ingest heterosexism and negative stereotyping perpetuated in dominant culture,

Case Illustration 11-3 | Paul

But my locker was just a few feet away; I couldn't help but hear it all if I wanted to get my lunchbox. Besides, I was drawn to it now, as to a wreck on the freeway. "Homo, homo, homo," Vinnie kept repeating, accompanying each taunt with a savage rabbit punch. The victim pleaded, terrified but trying not to cry. It was Austin Singer, a meek, nervous kid who was always working too hard to make friends; the son of a math teacher at Phillips Academy. He vigorously denied the homo charge, choking it out between punches, which only made Vinnie angrier. He growled at two of his henchboys, who pinned poor Austin's face to the wall. Vinnie made a hawking sound and spit a glob of phlegm on the brick beside Austin's face. "Come on, homo—lick that off." Austin whimpered and tried to pull back. Vinnie brought up his knee into Austin's kidney, making him cry out. Where were the teachers? All old maids, two floors away in the teachers' room, eating their own bird lunches. "Lick it, homo," Vinnie hissed. One of the brute lieutenants pushed Austin's face along the brick, scraping it raw. And now Austin, broken, surrendered whatever dignity was left. His tongue lolled out, and he licked up the phlegm while the bullies cheered. "Swallow it!" Vinnie commanded. From where I stood, by my locker, I saw a daze of horror, the self-disgust in Austin's face as he got it down without retching. Vinnie and his boys sprang away, shrieking with laughter. Instantly I busied myself with my lunchbox, terrified they would notice me. As they swaggered away, neither I nor anyone else made a move toward Austin—slumped in the corner as if it would have been easier to die than survive this thing. We all went hurrying away to eat our waxed-paper lunches. I never, never talked to Austin again. But, as I hastened to assure myself, we hadn't been friends anyway. The cold truth I took from the scene of Austin Singer's humiliation was this: At least I could still pass. I never gave a thought to the evil of what Vinnie had done, how sick with confused desire, the carnal thrill of degradation. The only reality lesson in it for me was not to be recognizably Other. At all costs I would discipline myself to appear as regular as Vinnie's boys, lest he suspect me and pin me to the wall.

Source: Monette, P. (1992). *Becoming a man: Half a life story.* New York: HarperCollins.

they internalize hatred directed at themselves in ways that may lead to anxiety and depression (Sayce, 1995). Anxiety, depression, and suicide have been linked to the effects of prejudice and discrimination and internalized negative feelings associated with living as a gay or lesbian person in U.S. society (Health Education Authority, 1998).

While not the experience for all gay and lesbian citizens, more LGBTQ individuals attempt suicide, suffer from depression, and misuse substances (Bridget, 1994). Further statistics on the use of alcohol indicate that alcoholism affects the gay and lesbian community at a rate of 20–33 percent, which far exceeds the general population rate of 10 percent. The most often cited reason for drug and alcohol use in the gay and lesbian community is that it is a means for coping with depression and societal oppression (Herbert, Hunt, & Dell, 1994).

Identifying strategies that address oppression that confronts gay and lesbian people in dominant culture is not monolithic. Coping strategies and styles for addressing oppression vary as much as the individuals who employ them. The following two narratives demonstrate a part of the spectrum of responses and varied coping styles exhibited by gay and lesbian persons as they address discrimination (see Case Illustrations 11-3 and 11-4).

Case Illustration 11-4	**Tales of a Suburban Columnist**

For a year, in Palo Alto, birthplace of Hewlett Packard and Silicon Valley, I had the rare opportunity to write for a straight audience as a lesbian. My vehicle was the *Palo Alto Weekly,* a free newspaper delivered to homeowners in five surrounding towns. When the paper actively solicited people of color to write a column, I proposed that they spice up the attempt to diversify and offered myself as a woman of "some color" who was willing to write from a lesbian perspective. It was a measure of the paper's liberal stance that they took me on.

My first column was entitled "Tales of a Media Slut," an account of my search for role models in the media as a young, biracial, lesbian immigrant. I was thrilled to have a voice in the community I had lived in since I was 10 years old. The local lesbian and gay population wrote me letters of praise, just for being visible, especially since the column included a photograph. Strangers stopped me on the street with friendly hellos. My co-workers were amused to be able to tell their friends they worked with the notorious town queer. My boss, who had participated in the civil rights movement of the 1960s, drew parallels in support of my activism. Homophobes wrote anonymous letters quoting the usual biblical passages and phoned the newspaper demanding that it stop publishing the opinions of a pervert. My parents had mixed feelings. Though I had been out to them for some years, they didn't know whether to be proud of me or apologetic when their friends mentioned having seen my column.

My second column, "Ten Good Reasons to Be a Lesbian," generated a handful of protest letters, mostly from men who were outraged that I had pointed out that lesbians didn't have to take care of men. The paper was delighted at the response. But when I addressed more serious issues of identity versus assimilation, I exceeded the paper's tolerance level. The editor asked me to cut out the personal details of "motorcycles vibrating between our legs" and stick to the issues the public would understand, like Clinton's waffling on gays in the military. When I continued to write about lesbian life rather than political issues, the paper terminated my column. Somehow it was permissible to have strong political opinions, but the line was drawn at descriptions of queer folk living their "radical" lives.

Source: Kovattana, A. (1995). Tables of a suburban columnist. In K. Jay (Ed.), *Dyke life: From growing up to growing old; A celebration of the lesbian experience* (p. 273273). New York: Basic Books.

POTENTIAL BARRIERS IN LEARNING–TEACHING RELATIONSHIPS WITH DOMINANT-CULTURE TEACHERS AND SCHOOLS

As noted throughout this chapter, gay and lesbian students may celebrate their identities and feel accepted in their homes, communities, and school environments. In that case, it is imperative that existing facilitative conditions be broadened and enhanced to provide support for values and perspectives of LGBTQ individuals, including the recognition and inclusion of alternative family structures and participation in advocacy for the rights of LGBTQ students and families. Still, studies have shown that gay and lesbian students are far more likely to experience violence in school (Gay, Lesbian, and Straight Education Network, 2003; Uribe & Harbeck, 1992). Many gay students go through the school day fearing violence and harassment from their peers. For these students, the stress and anxiety encountered inhibit their ability to learn.

Intercultural Communication Strategies for Teachers 11-2

Supporting Your Students

- Make no assumption about sexuality. If a student has not used a pronoun when discussing a relationship, do not assume one.
- Do not assume that all your students are straight. Such an assumption reinforces the invisibility that most gay and lesbian students already suffer.
- Identify yourself as a safe person to speak with. It helps to identify yourself as a safe person to talk with by using a safe-zone sticker, a rainbow ribbon/button, and so on.
- Confidentiality is important. Students need to believe that their privacy will be respected. They should not be encouraged to "come out." This is always an individual's own right to decide.
- Be a role model—exhibiting respect, concern, and advocacy for all students.

- Challenge homophobia and heterosexism among students and colleagues.
- Develop a list of referral resources for students and families needing information.
- Work for the development of antidiscrimination policies that include sexual orientation.
- Monitor curricula and advocate for antiheterosexist materials and texts.
- Do not simply include gay and lesbian issues into the curriculum as a token of your own liberal, culturally sensitive orientation. Instead, involve alternative family issues and examples and the perspectives/voices of members of this cultural group in your curricula in meaningful ways.
- Create safe and effective guidelines for classroom discussions of sexual orientation.

As with members of other minority groups, some gay and lesbian students try to make themselves invisible (passing as dominant-culture others) in schools so their sexual orientation will not be detected, and as a result, the energy required to create such a disguise limits a focus on school work needed for effective learning. Gay and lesbian students, on the whole, tend to have a more difficult journey through adolescence (a time when identity and sexuality are explored) than dominant-culture students because they may feel even more confined by the pressure to conform to societal roles and believe it is highly likely that they will be dismissed, despised, or deleted from school life if they do not meet society's expectations (Khayatt, 1994). Along with these factors potentially interfering with their personal and academic development, gay and lesbian students' social and emotional needs and concerns often go unrecognized and unmet in schools.

Perhaps one of the biggest barriers to a gay or lesbian student's learning and development of a facilitative relationship with a dominant-culture teacher is the teacher's potential lack of awareness and experience with diversity. Either through ignorance or denial, teachers are often unaware of the reality and experiences of gay and lesbian students within their classes. Further, once they are aware, they are often ill prepared to respond in ways that create safe, facilitative learning environments.

The suggestions found within Intercultural Communication Strategies 11-2 are provided as ways to reduce heterosexism in schools and to help students feel safe and accepted in the classroom. Teachers are likely to ignore heterosexist comments, refrain from setting guidelines for respectful discussions, and ask questions that denote their beliefs that all of their students or their students' parents are heterosexual (for example, "When you get married, you'll probably ..." or "Ask your mom and dad for help with this assignment."). These types of student–teacher interactions leave a lasting impression communicating that teachers believe the only correct sexual orientation is heterosexual. Whether intentional or not, this is a form of oppression and exclusion that serves to alienate gay and lesbian students from their teachers, their classes, and their schools. When no one speaks up when teachers make such seemingly harmless remarks, gay and lesbian students may believe everybody in the room shares the same heterosexist viewpoints. These students often feel isolated and sometimes paralyzed by fear of what might happen if anyone in the room knew that they are gay or lesbian.

FROM CONCEPTS TO LIVED EXPERIENCE

In this narrative, Deborah Perkins describes her resolve when confronting heterosexism during the process of coming out to her mother.

WHAT I SHOULD HAVE SAID

"I'm gay. I'm sorry. Please don't hate me." "I think you're very sick," Mom replied. Then she turned and walked away. I sat there on her mountain of rejection, calling out, "I'm still your daughter and I love you," and hearing only the echo of my own voice. My heart broke like a pane of glass. If only I could do it over again, I wouldn't search day after day, trying to find just the right words to ward off her anger and quell her disgust.

"You don't know," I would tell her, "how it feels to discover you're not who you think you are. You don't know what it's like to learn at the age of 32 that you've fallen in love with a woman, and nothing in your fundamentalist, heterosexual background has prepared you for that. You don't know how it feels to realize after all those years that you're a lesbian.

"You don't know what it's like to sit in a classroom or an office with people who are supposed to be your friends and listen to their sneering comments about 'dykes and faggots.' You don't know what it's like not daring to speak the truth about yourself. You don't know what it's like to have to learn how to lie and how to hide.

"You don't know the fear of being backed into a corner by a man bigger and stronger than you, who is trying to convince you that he can turn you back into a 'real' woman.

"You don't know what it's like to be judged for who you love instead of for who you are. You can't imagine the never-ending ache of wanting to tell your parents the one thing you know will hurt them most of all. And you can't begin to know the depth of that pain when you see the disappointment in their eyes."

If I could go back and do it again, I wouldn't try to find the words that are the easiest to say and the easiest to hear. This time, I would just tell the truth. (quoted in Jay, 1995, p. 45)

SUMMARY

Cultural Factor 1: Historical and Current Treatment in the United States Gay people have a largely invisible history due in large part to the purposeful destruction of their writings and the fact that most of what we know about gay and lesbian people historically comes from legal actions that were leveled against LGBTQ individuals. Urban gay subculture existed in the United States as early as the 1920s and 1930s. The Society for Human Rights in Chicago was the country's earliest known gay rights organization. In 1950, a small group of men led by Harry Hay and Charles Rowland met to form what would be called the Mattachine Society, created to address the perilous conditions of gay men in the United States. In 1955, the Daughters of Bilitus, a lesbian organization founded by Del Martin and Phyllis Lyon, joined the Mattachine Society to work to advance the rights and liberties of gay and lesbian people. When HIV/AIDS took center stage in the 1980s, antigay sentiments strengthened. HIV/AIDS was perceived by many in dominant culture to be a "gay disease" and was used as justification for discrimination against gay and lesbian people. By 1990, the number of registered gay and lesbian organizations increased to several thousand. In 2000, Vermont became the first state to legally recognize civil unions between gay and lesbian couples. The law provides that gay and lesbian couples are entitled to about 400 rights, privileges, and responsibilities that had been previously granted only to married couples. And in 2004, same-sex marriages became legal for residents of Massachusetts. However, 37 states enacted defense-of-marriage acts (DOMAs) that ban same-sex marriage.

Cultural Factor 2: Initial Terms of Incorporation into U.S. Society The dichotomous portrayal of sexual identity was introduced over 40 years ago, by Kinsey's (1948) *Sexual Behavior in the Human Male,* which revealed to the U.S. public that homosexuality was far more widespread than previously believed. Prior to the widespread stigma associated with having an "alternative" lifestyle or sexual identity, the definition for homo- versus heterosexuality was not significant.

Cultural Factors 3 and 4: Shared Values, Traditions, and Spirituality In attempting to define common or generally held cultural values, one must remember that members of the LGBTQ community are also members of a number of communities and cultural groups. It is important to highlight that for all gay or lesbian individuals, values they embrace may be more reflective of and aligned with gender, social-class, racial, or ethnic group than with values prevalent among members of gay or lesbian communities. Taking into account the wide-ranging variation among members in this cultural group, it is fair to say that perhaps the most noticeable common values and traditions of this group have been created in response to the discrimination members of this group face and the need for solidarity and unity. But even with their marginalized status, LGBTQ individuals do not lead impoverished lives. Advocacy, liberalism, sexual freedom, gender play, and human rights are principles that tend to be valued among members of this group. Most often, gay and lesbian people lead full lives that celebrate their identities.

Cultural Factor 5: Acculturation and Experience with Exclusion and Alienation The decision to be closeted (hiding one's gay or lesbian identity) is a product of the pressures of acculturation. Gay and lesbian people in the United States know that "coming out" places them at great risk for disapproval and discrimination from family and the larger society and as such have become adept at "passing." Members of the gay and lesbian community continue to be alienated and excluded from the dominant culture. Issues regarding unique health and psychological needs, legal rights, and social support networks remain unaddressed.

Cultural Factor 6: Language Differences, Strengths, and Challenges Beyond being the recipients of hate language, members of the gay community have, at least according to some, developed their own language. "Lavender language" is described as a form of lesbian/gay discourse that is comprised of distinct and independently developed linguistic constructions.

Coping Strategies for Addressing Oppression Coping both with the discrimination and oppression of the dominant culture, as well as with internalized homophobia, can be highly detrimental to LGBTQ mental health. There appears to be no single or universal pattern of coping that members of the gay and lesbian community have employed as they address the oppressive power of the dominant culture. Coping strategies and coping styles vary, as do the individuals employing them.

Potential Barriers in Learning–Teaching Relationships with Dominant-Culture Teachers and Schools Many gay and lesbian students go through the day fearing violence and harassment from their peers, and this constant anxiety inhibits their ability to learn. Either through ignorance or denial, teachers are often unaware of the reality and existence of gay and lesbian students within their classes. Further, once they are aware, they are often ill-prepared to respond in ways that create a safe, facilitative learning environment.

Important Terms

closeted	HIV/AIDS	Klein Sexual Orientation Grid (KSOG)	Mattachine Society
coming out	homosexuality	lavender language	passing
Essentialist	Kinsey Heterosexual–Homosexual Scale (KHHS)	lesbian	sexual identity
gay		LGBTQ	social constructivists
heterosexual			

Enrichment

Badgett, M. V. (1999). Assigning care: Gender norms and economic outcomes. *International Labour Review*, *138* (3), 311.

Blackburn, M. V. (2005). *Sexual identities and schooling*. New York: Lawrence Erlbaum Associates.

Due, L. (1995). *Joining the tribe: Growing up gay & lesbian in the 90s*. New York: Doubleday.

Epstein, D., & Johnson, R. (1998). *Schooling sexualities*. Buckingham, UK: Open University.

Foucault, M. (1978). *History of sexuality, Vol. I: An introduction*. New York: Pantheon.

Fradenburg, L., & Freccero, C. (1996). *Premodern sexualities*. New York: Routledge.

Gay, Lesbian, and Straight Education Network. (2003). *The 2003 national school climate survey: The school related experiences of our nation's lesbian, gay, bisexual and transgender youth*. New York: Author.

Jay, K. (Ed.). (1995). *Dyke life: From growing up to growing old. A celebration of the lesbian experience*. New York: Basic Books.

Katz, J. N. (1995). *The invention of heterosexuality*. New York: Dutton.

Kumashiro, K. (2001). *Troubling intersections of race and sexuality: Queer students of color and anti-oppression education*. Lanham, MD: Rowman & Littlefield.

Monette, P. (1992). *Becoming a man: Half a life story*. New York: HarperCollins.

Roscoe, W. (1988). *Living the spirit: A gay American Indian anthology*. New York: St. Martin's.

Savin-Williams, R. (1998). *And then I became gay: Young men's stories*. New York: Routledge.

Sonnie, A. (2000). *Revolutionary voices: A multicultural queer youth anthology*. Los Angeles: Alyson.

Connections on the Web

http://www.outproud.org/brochure_be_yourself.html/

Parents, Families and Friends of Lesbians and Gays promotes the health and well-being of gay, lesbian, and bisexual persons, their families, and friends through support to cope with an adverse society, education to enlighten an ill-informed public, and advocacy to end discrimination and to secure equal civil rights.

http://www.glsen.org/

The Gay, Lesbian, and Straight Education Network (GLSEN) is a national organization that brings together teachers, parents, students, and concerned citizens to work together to end homophobia in our schools.

http://www.personproject.org

PERSON is an acronym for Public Education Regarding Sexual Orientation Nationally. The group's focus is on providing proactive strategies to improve the treatment of LGBTQ persons in K–12 schools and ensuring that fair, accurate, and unbiased information regarding LGBTQ people and the nature and diversity of sexual orientation is presented to U.S. youth as part of public school education.

http://www.safeschoolscoalition.org/

The Safe School Coalition: A Public–Private Partnership in Support of Gay, Lesbian, Bisexual and Transgender Youth provides information about how to make schools safe places where every family can belong, where every educator can teach, and where every child can learn, regardless of gender identity or sexual orientation.

http://www.uc.edu/ucwc/lgbtq.html

The UC Womens Center website offers links related to religion, people of color, women, men, bisexuality, health/fitness, activism, allies, and so on.

REFERENCES

Adkinson, D. R., & Hackett, G. (1995). *Counseling diverse populations*. Madison, WI: Brown & Benchmark.

American Psychological Association, Committee on Lesbian and Gay Concerns. (1991). Avoiding heterosexual bias in language. *American Psychologist, 46*(9), 973–974.

Berkman, C. S., & Zimberg, G. (1997). Homophobia and heterosexism in social workers. *Social Work, 42*, 319–332.

Berg, N., & Lien, D. (2002). Measuring the effect of sexual orientation on income: Evidence of discrimination? *Contemporary Economic Policy, 20*(4), 394–414.

Betsch, M. L. (2003). *University conference focuses on "gay language."* Retrieved from http://www.conservativenews.org/ViewCulture.asp?Page=/Culture/archive/200302/CUL20030206c.html

Bohan, J. S. (1996). *Psychological and sexual orientation: Coming to terms*. New York: Routledge.

Boykin, K. (2005). *Beyond the down low: Sex, lies, and denial in Black America*. New York: Carroll & Graf.

Brewer, P. R. (2003). The shifty foundation of public opinion and gay rights. *The Journal of Politics, 65*(4), 1208–1220.

Bridget, J. (1994). *Treatment of lesbians with alcohol problems in alcohol services in Northwest England*. Lesbian Information Service.

Bullough, V. L. (1976). *Sexual variance in society and history*. New York: Wiley & Sons.

Bullough, V. L. (1979). *Homosexuality: A history*. New York: New American Library.

Button, J. W., Rienzo, B. A., & Wald, K. D. (2000). The politics of gay rights at the state and local level. In G. A. Rimmerman, K. D. Wald, & C. Wilcox (Eds.), *The politics of gay rights* (pp. 347–376). Chicago: University of Chicago.

Editorial. (2005). Survey says . . . *Gay & Lesbian Review Worldwide, 12*(1), 17–21.

Garret, M. (2001). Eres marcion? Por "Eladio." In K. Kumashiro (Ed.), *Troubling intersections of race and sexuality* (pp. 34–35). New York: Rowman & Littlefield.

Gay, Lesbian, and Straight Education Network. (2003). *The 2003 national school climate survey: The school related experiences of our nation's lesbian, gay, bisexual and transgender youth*. New York: Author.

Haeberle, S. H. (1999). Gay and lesbian rights: Emerging trends in public opinion and voting behavior. In E. D. B. Riggle & B. L. Tadlock (Eds.), *Gays and lesbians in the democratic process* (pp. 146–169). New York: Columbia University.

Haider-Markel, D. P. (2000). Lesbian and gay politics in the states: Interest groups, electoral politics, and policy. In G. A. Rimmerman, K. D. Wald, & C. Wilcox (Eds.), *The politics of gay rights* (pp. 347–376). Chicago: University of Chicago.

Health Education Authority. (1998). *Sexual identity.* World Mental Health Day.

Herbert, J. T., & Hunt, B. (1994). Counseling gay men and lesbians with alcohol problems. *Journal of Rehabilitation, 60*(2), 52–57.

Herek, G. M. (1994). Assessing heterosexuals' attitudes toward lesbians and gay men: A review of empirical research with the ATLG scale. In B. Greene & G. M. Herek (Eds.), *Lesbian and gay psychology: Theory, research, and clinical applications. Psychological perspectives on lesbian and gay issues* (Vol. 1, pp. 206–228). Thousand Oaks, CA: Sage.

Hubbard, R. (1997). The social construction of sexuality. In P. S. Rothenberg (Ed.), *Race, class, and gender in the United States: An integrated study* (4th edition, pp. 52–55). New York: St. Martin's.

Jay, K. (Ed.). (1995). *Dyke life: From growing up to growing old; A celebration of the lesbian experience.* New York: Basic Books.

Katz, J. N. (1997). The invention of heterosexuality. In P. S. Rothenberg (Ed.), *Race, class, and gender in the United States: An integrated study* (4th edition, pp. 52–55). New York: St. Martin's.

Khayatt, D. (1994). Surviving school as a lesbian. *Gender and Education 6*(1), 47–61.

Kinsey, A. C., Pomeroy, W. B., Martin, C. E., & Gebhard, P. H. (1953). *Sexual behavior in the human female.* Philadelphia: Saunders.

Kite, M. E., & Whitley, B. E., Jr. (1996). Sex differences in attitudes toward homosexual persons, behaviors, and civil rights: A meta-analysis. *Personality and Social Psychology Bulletin, 22,* 336–353.

Klein, F., Sepekoff, B., & Wolf, T. J. (1986). Sexual orientation: A multivariate dynamic process. *Journal of Homosexuality, 11,* 35–49.

Kovattana, A. (1995). Tables of a suburban columnist. In K. Jay (Ed.), *Dyke life: From growing up to growing old; A celebration of the lesbian experience* (p. 273). New York: Basic Books.

Leap, W. (Ed.). (1995). *Beyond the lavender lexicon: Authenticity, imagination, and appropriation in lesbian and gay languages.* Luxembourg: Gordon & Breach.

Miller, N. (1995). *Out of the past: Gay and lesbian history from 1869 to the present.* New York: Vintage.

Monette, P. (1992). *Becoming a man: Half a life story.* New York: HarperCollins.

Parker, J. (2001). Language: A pernicious and powerful tool. *English Journal,* 74–78.

Reader's companion to American history [Electronic version]. (1991). New York: Houghton Mifflin. Retrieved from http://print.infoplease.com/ipa/A0194028.html

Sayce, L. (1995). *Breaking the link between homosexuality and mental illness: An unfinished history.* MIND Discussion Document.

Schachet, C. (n.d.) Talking politics with Barbara Smith. An interview. *The Resist Newsletter.*

Segal-Sklar, S. (1995). Lesbian parenting: Radical or retrograde? In K. Jay (Ed.), *Dyke life: From growing up to growing old, a celebration of the lesbian experience* (pp. 174–175). New York: Basic Books.

Steffens, M. C., & Wagner, C. (2004). Attitudes toward lesbians, gay men, bisexual women, and bisexual men in Germany. *Journal of Sex Research, 41*(2), 137–149.

Uribe, V., & Harbeck, K. M. (1992). Project 10 addresses needs of gay and lesbian youth. *Education Digest, 58*(2), 50–54.

Wilcox, C., & Norrander, B. (2002). Of moods and morals: The dynamics of opinions on abortion and gay rights. In B. Norrander & C. Wilcox (Eds.), *Understanding public opinion* (2nd edition, pp. 121–148). Washington, DC: Congressional Quarterly.

Williams, N. L. (1986). *The spirit and the flesh: Sexual diversity in American Indian Culture.* Boston, MA: Beacon.

Wolfson, E. (1991). Civil rights, human rights, gay rights: Minorities and the humanity of the different. *Harvard Journal of Law & Public Policy, 14*(1), 21–40.

It wasn't my body that was responsible for all my difficulties, it was external factors, the barriers constructed by the society in which I live. I was being dis-abled—my capabilities and opportunities were being restricted—by prejudice, discrimination, inaccessible environments and inadequate support. Even more important, if all the problems had been created by society, then surely society could un-create them. . . . As individuals, most of us simply cannot pretend with any conviction that our impairments are irrelevant because they influence so much of our lives. External barriers create social and economic disadvantage and our subjective experience of our bodies is also an integral part of our everyday reality.

Liz Crow (1996)
"Including All of Our Lives: Renewing the Social Model of Disability"

12 CHAPTER | Learning from the Stories of People with Disabilities

Impairment and disability touch us all. At some point, every human being will experience either physical or mental impairments or both. Those who currently designate themselves as nondisabled must come to understand that such a designation is surely temporary. This chapter explores the lives of persons with disabilities, their history of oppression, their strengths, their resilience, and their cultural identities. In this chapter, you will encounter the voices of people with disabilities who are differently abled. A closer look at the shared experiences, unique challenges, and strengths found among members of this group will increase your ability to make your school an effective learning community in which students with disabilities experience full inclusion and achieve well.

CHAPTER OBJECTIVES

1. Define *disability, impairment, handicap, exceptionality*, and *giftedness*.
2. Describe cultural characteristics shared by persons with disabilities.

3. Discuss significant sociopolitical changes that have occurred in the process of incorporating persons with disabilities in dominant culture.

4. Identify ways the people profiled in case narratives in this chapter experienced and addressed the six cultural factors explored in this text.

5. Explain academic and intercultural interaction implications related to the six cultural factors addressed by members of this group.

6. Describe coping strategies utilized by members of this group.

7. Identify classroom strategies for cultivating resources provided when the needs and strengths of students with disabilities are integrated into your curricula.

DEFINITIONS

Exceptionality

Exceptionalities are created by differences among students. Exceptional students are defined as students who require supplemental services to effectively facilitate their academic development. Students with disabilities and gifted students are two groups of exceptional students.

Disability

The Education for All Handicapped Act of 1975 defined disabilities as involving mental retardation or hearing, visual, speech, learning, emotional, orthopedic, or other health impairment (Fagan & Wallace, 1979). Amendments to this act in 2004 expanded the list of recognized **impairments** to include students who have physical or mental impairments that substantially limit one or more major life activities, students who have a record of impairment, and/or students who are regarded as having impairment(s). Physical or mental impairments were defined as any physiological disorder or condition, cosmetic disfigurement, or anatomical loss affecting one or more of the following body systems: neurological; musculoskeletal; special sense organs; respiratory, including speech organs; cardiovascular; reproductive; digestive; genitor-urinary; hemic and lymphatic; skin; and endocrine; or any psychological disorder, such as mental retardation, organic brain syndrome, emotional or mental illness, and specific **learning disabilities**.

Nevertheless, defining *disability* continues to be a matter of social debate and construction as it is contrasted with *impairment* and *handicap*. **Disability** has been defined as an observable, measurable characteristic of an individual that interferes with the individual's functioning—a functional limitation within the individual caused by physical, mental, or sensory impairment. Recently, *disability* has come to refer to a restriction or lack of ability to perform an activity in the manner or within the range considered "normal" for humans, while *impairment* is defined as the loss or abnormality of psychological, physiological, or anatomical structure or function. **Handicaps,** on the other hand, involve the loss or limitation of opportunities to take part in the "normal" life of the community on an equal level with others due to physical or social barriers. Handicaps may be considered barriers, demands, and environmental pressures placed on people by various aspects of their environments, including other people.

The medical model of disability focuses on individuals' functional limitations (impairments) and identifies impairments as the cause of disadvantages experienced by **persons with disabilities**. The social model, in contrast, shifts the focus from impairment to disability. In this case, *disability* refers to the disabling social, environmental, and attitudinal barriers rather than on individuals' "lack of ability." Thus, the only way to rectify conditions using the medical model is through treatments and cures, while social change and the removal of disabling barriers are solutions for those who support the social model.

Giftedness

There was a time when gifted students were included with students with disabilities as a group of students who required special education services. At that time, the category that included both groups of students was called "Students with Exceptionalities." With the passage of the No Child Left Behind Act of 2001, Congress reauthorized the Elementary and Secondary Education Act (ESEA)—a principal federal law that affects school-aged children. No Child Left Behind was created to increase accountability, flexibility, and federal support for education. Rather than including gifted students as students with exceptionalities, this legislation currently defines gifted students as students who provide evidence of high achievement capability in artistic, intellectual, creative, or leadership capacities, or in specific academic fields who require services or activities not ordinarily provided by the school in order to fully develop their capabilities. If this definition sounds to you like it might include all students, you are not alone in your thinking.

Most researchers in the field today believe that **giftedness** is multidimensional, with high aptitude being only one factor (Renzulli & Reis, 1997). These researchers have identified multiple intelligences within individuals that help us to recognize talents present in all students (Gardner, 1993). So, how are gifted students identified and then singled out for special services? Grades and test scores should not be the only identifiers of gifted students. When schools limit their identification efforts to test scores and grades, they contribute to one of the most pernicious problems that schools face: the underrepresentation of minority students in gifted programs (National Center for Educational Services, 1994; Brown, 1997). Schools should use multiple sources of data to effectively identify gifted students that include a variety of other forms of assessment to provide more accurate demonstrations of students' strengths and abilities, such as teacher observations, interviews with students, information from parents, and portfolios of student work (Hunsaker, Finley, & Frank, 1997). It is also important for teachers to realize that gifted students may not fit common stereotypes of high-ability students. For example creativity (a form of intelligence that is characterized by divergent thinking and the production of original ideas) and task commitment also may be significant aspects of giftedness. These definitions of giftedness are clearly more inclusive than previous ones. In fact, gifted students may have disabilities that accompany their talents as well as exhibit high ability in some academic areas but not in others (Nielsen, Higgins, & Hammond, 1993).

Common myths about gifted students include beliefs that these students do not need help, have fewer problems than other students due to their intellect, are self-directed, have the same social and emotional development experiences of other same-age students, are social isolates, have families who prize their abilities, and are naturally creative. Gifted students share some common characteristics, including performing at high academic levels, thinking abstractly and connecting ideas easily, demonstrating effective problem-solving skills, persevering in academic pursuits, tending to equate achievement with self-worth, struggling with heightened sensitivity with regard to their performance, and experiencing academic problems that result from curricula that do not meet their needs (Freeman, 1994; Roberts & Lovett, 1994). While these are some common qualities, gifted students are members of a highly diverse group. Teachers must develop methods for continually assessing all students in attempting to identify their strengths rather than weaknesses. It is imperative that teachers advocate for and provide opportunities that meet the needs of their students. Most schools employ an **enrichment** (the addition of topics and skill development activities to traditional curricula) and/or an **acceleration** (moving students through curricula or years of schooling in a shortened time period) approach to address the needs of gifted students. Tracking ("ability" grouping) is another popular approach in which schools offer advanced placement and honors courses to address the needs of gifted students (Kulick & Kulick, 1997). However, such strategies are highly criticized because research consistently confirms evidence that gifted students perform equally well in heterogeneous learning groups while so-called "average" students are disadvantaged by such practices (Sapon-Shevin, 1996; McDaniel, 1993; Oakes & Lipton, 1990). Teachers must take responsibility for creating environments in which students at all levels achieve. To accomplish this goal, they must become expert and collaborative curriculum designers who know all of their students well; value and build on students' strengths; and provide strategies, tools, and opportunities that will enhance all students' academic development, while simultaneously monitoring the effectiveness of their methods.

CULTURAL FACTOR 1: HISTORICAL AND CURRENT TREATMENT IN THE UNITED STATES

The *Rig-Veda*, an ancient sacred poem of India (3500 BC) is identified as the first written record that contains the existence and use of a prosthesis. Such documentation as the beginning of the history of disabled persons illustrates depersonalization and a focus on forcing persons with disabilities to become as close to "normal" or "able" as possible—a phenomenon that is often experienced by persons with disabilities. For persons with disabilities, confronting a history that begins with a focus on impairment rather than on lived experiences is no small obstacle.

Historical Background

Hohenshil and Humes (1979) found that throughout history, persons with disabilities have been ignored, exiled, exploited, tortured, and even destroyed. Adkinson and Hackett (1995) outlined these views of persons with disabilities throughout history. Many nomadic societies saw persons with disabilities as problems—actual barriers to the group's productivity—because people with disabilities were unable to contribute to the physical work of their communities. During the agricultural era, persons with disabilities received some acceptance in mainstream society (Bowe, 1978). However, physical differences were often seen as deformities that were explained as resulting from evil or sin dwelling within the individual or individual's family. As Western civilization progressed and Christianity spread, persons with disabilities continued to be seen as unproductive in terms of what was believed they could contribute to their society. Adults and children with disabilities were commonly placed in institutions and mental asylums, whether or not their individual differences and needs could be positively affected by such treatment. In effect, they were "warehoused"—kept out of the way and out of the sight of dominant culture, their needs largely disregarded and unmet. Persons with disabilities were seen as people who deserved the pity and charity of society (Bowe, 1978). Later, persons with disabilities were labeled *handicapped*—a term that implies dependence—as they continued to be seen by many as needy and deficient.

Beginning in the 1960s, rehabilitative counseling was developed to try to help persons with disabilities "fit" into society (Bowe, 1980). This often meant that persons with disabilities had to find a way to meet the demands of the environments they were seeking to enter rather than changing the environments to incorporate them and their differences. Melanie's story (see Case Illustration 12-1) illustrates how attempts to assimilate in an inaccessible rigid structure can be severely thwarted—a consequence that can affect one's entire life.

Civil rights actions helped pave the way for the assimilation of persons with disabilities, and currently, access and equality battles continue to be fought by members of this group.

Current Conditions

In the United States, claims addressed by the American Disabilities Act were debated and deliberated throughout the 1980's. Forty-three million Americans were reported to have one or more **physical** or **mental disability**. More recent census data would revise this figure upwards to an estimated 53 million. According to the Census Bureau's March 1996 Current Population Survey, 12 percent of Americans aged 25 to 64 had some type of disability, and 64 percent of that group had a disability serious enough to require assistance with daily activities. These numbers grow each year as the population continues to age and life span is increased through improved medical care and technology. Also, advances in medical practice, such as the development of prenatal specialization, trauma care centers, and the treatment of life-threatening diseases, tend to increase rather than

| Case Illustration 12-1 | Melanie |

I'm 45 years old and I have cerebral palsy. I've had it all my life. My parents have always been able to afford my care and address my "special" physical needs. I've always had wonderful doctors and equipment. They even had a swimming pool built in our backyard from the time I was an infant to provide me with the needed exercise for my legs and arms. They were and are a terrific support system. I was quite successful all throughout school—always really well dressed and everybody treated me with kindness. I always thought that was mostly because we were considered pretty rich, even among my rich friends. It was clear to the world and the school that I came from a family who cared about and took good care of me. Did teachers think I was dumb because of the way I walked and moved my arms? I'd have to say, "Yes." But, I made them see that I was smart— that having trouble walking and moving did not make me stupid. I worked really hard and they got it. I was in student government and on the yearbook staff. I was considered smart all throughout school. I was also pretty popular. But, it was always a struggle. I never used a wheelchair or walked with crutches. Instead, I learned to balance myself so I could move along slowly yet effectively. This meant I left each class early so I wouldn't get literally knocked down in the halls with all the bustle and confusion at class change. It also meant that I couldn't buy a school lunch like my friends did. I couldn't carry a lunch tray. You can imagine that I was often excluded—people who bought their lunches usually sat in a different place in the cafeteria than people who brought their lunches. This meant I couldn't choose who I sat with unless students sought me out to sit with me. I never called attention to this though all through school. One thing that really bothered me was not being able to attend a football game in high school. The football game was the place in my high school where one was seen. It was the place to be. Kids dressed up and went out—not to watch the game—but to "hook up." The game was where you could accidentally bump into someone you wanted to meet. You could play it cool at the game. You could have your friends back you up and give you courage to talk to someone you were afraid to speak to in school. I'm really smart. But, I could never figure out how to get to the game; how to get myself down that sloping decline to the bleachers that outlined the field; how to "fit in" with the "cool" kids at the game; how to join in with my friends who were trying to show no weaknesses in their attempts to gain the attention of the objects of their affection. Even though I had lots of money—more than almost everybody else who I went to school with, I couldn't make it happen. I never figured it out. The school was "accessible" but the football games weren't. I took this to mean that I didn't belong there. No guy was going to see me at the game anyway and ask for my number. Why was I sweating it? But it was more than not being able to date. I deserved to have a social life. But, I couldn't have one—not like I wanted—not really.

Source: Personal communication, April 20, 2005.

decrease incidence of disability. However, policymakers and professionals tend to use advanced medical technology to reinforce negative stereotypes about the lives of persons with disabilities as tragic. Prenatal screening and other such "preventative" measures actually exist to avoid or escape disability. Because of the assumptions of the poor quality of life for persons with disabilities, prenatal screenings were developed to identify when abortion is indicated. Screening is rarely offered to help parents make plans for children with disabilities (Crow, 1996). Additional data on disabled adults and children are available on the Census Bureau's website: www.census.gov/hhes/www/disable.html.

Case Illustration 12-2　Paul

In second grade, I was in a Catholic school with 40 or 50 kids in my class. We were supposed to learn to read prayers and match letter blocks to the letters in the prayers. By April or May, I still didn't know the alphabet and couldn't read. I memorized the prayers so the nun thought I was reading. Finally, she figured out that I didn't even know my alphabet, and I can remember her expression of total shock that I had gotten all the way through second grade without her knowing this.

My parents offered my brother and sister $50 to teach me the alphabet but that didn't work. So I flunked second grade. I had the same nun again, and she was mean. She paddled me for two years, but I still didn't learn the alphabet or how to read.

After that, my mother had me tested everywhere, at this college, that clinic. For two years they thought I couldn't read because I had bad muscles in my eyes. I went to an eye doctor to do eye exercises. Then I went to a speech teacher who thought I had a lazy tongue because I switched my R's and W's.

Every summer I went to summer school, and during the school year I was in every little special group. I was in the speech group, the corrective posture group, the purple reading group, the green reading group. In third grade, the only word I could read was "the." I used to keep track of where the class was reading by following from one "the" to the next.

Finally my mother found a famous remedial reading teacher who knew I needed to learn phonetics and who understood my dyslexia. By seventh and eighth grade, I still had barely learned how to read. I wasn't too worried about it then because I somehow knew I'd have my own business one day, and I figured I'd hire someone to read to me.

By the time I was 15 or 16, I could get by in class with reading. But I could never spell. I was a workshop major in high school, and my typical report card was two C's, three D's, and an F. I just got used to it.

When I graduated from high school, I had a 1.2 grade-point average. I was eighth from the bottom of my class of 1,500 students. To be honest, I don't even know how seven people got below me.

Everyone in my family and all my parents' friends had their own businesses. So, for me, college was just for fun because I knew I was going to own my own business. In college, I majored in business and "loopholes." I knew who all the easy teachers were. Once, I had to take a literature class in which we had to read 13 books. That's like a lifetime of reading for me! So, to get by, I read *Cliff Notes* and watched great plays on TV.

In my investment strategies class, my teacher almost failed me because I made so many spelling errors on his tests. When he found out I had a learning disability, he announced to the class that I was "on the brink of brilliancy" because he looked at my ideas instead of the spelling. The students were impressed after that, and they thought I saw the world a little differently.

While I was in college, I rented a little garage for $100 a month on the main road of campus, which was the perfect location for my business. I sold notebooks, pens, pencils, and had a small copying machine. I made $1,000 some days.

Though reading is still difficult for me, I do like readers. I like the written language because I like photocopying. I believe in double-spacing, since it helps my business.

When I talk to college students about all this, I tell them to work with their strengths, not their weaknesses. Go where you're strong.

Source: Paul Orfalea, founder and chairperson of Kinkos, Inc. Retrieved from http://www.ldonline.org/first_person/orfalea.html

Even if the definition of *disability* was restricted to those having health problems or disabilities that prevent them from working or that limit the kind or amount of work they can do, in 2004 there would still have been an estimated 7.9 percent (plus or minus 0.2 percentage points) of civilian, noninstitutionalized men and women aged 18–64 in the United States categorized as disabled with regard to work limitations. This would amount to 14,152,000 of 179,133,000 Americans, or about 1 in 13 (Houtenville, 2005).

Despite the advances in medicine, education, and laws attempting to remove barriers that exclude persons with difficulties, individuals with disabilities continually encounter discrimination ranging from outright intentional exclusion to limited access to services, programs, activities, benefits, jobs, or other opportunities. Paul's story (see Case Illustration 12-2) highlights his lifelong battle against the discrimination experienced by most people with disabilities.

Women with disabilities are additionally disadvantaged. The work of Esther Boylan (1991) illustrates the greater degree of discrimination faced by women with disabilities in the workforce. She found that women with disabilities have higher levels of unemployment and were paid significantly lower wages than men with disabilities.

CULTURAL FACTOR 2: INITIAL TERMS OF INCORPORATION INTO U.S. SOCIETY

Prior to 1975, little if any public or governmental attention concerned the education of students with disabilities (Thomas & Russo, '1995) (see Table 12-1). Students who were identified as having special needs were regularly excluded from public education. Education for these students was either nonexistent or was the responsibility of students' families or caretakers. Examples include early court cases like an 1893 ruling by the Massachusetts Supreme court that upheld the exclusion of a mentally retarded student from the public school system (*Watson v. City of Cambridge, 32 N.E. 864,864 [Mass. 1993]*) and a 1919 Wisconsin Supreme Court ruling that determined that a student can be excluded from public education when the presence of that child is harmful to the best interest of the school (*State ex rel Beattie v. Board of Education, 1972, N.W. 153 [Wis. 1919]*). The 1919 case cited that the physically paralyzed student was excluded because his frequent drooling was deemed to interfere with other students' education. Such exclusion was continued late into the 1960s, with many states having laws that excluded children who were categorized as deaf, blind, emotionally disturbed, physically disabled, and/or mentally retarded (Yell, 1998).

It has been suggested (Wodatch, 1990) that the modern disability rights movement began more than 40 years ago during the 1960s, at which time people with disabilities around the world successfully challenged dominant social stereotypes. In the United States, Ed Roberts, a postpolio quadriplegic who used a ventilator to assist his breathing, broke educational barriers when he became the first person with such a significant disability to attend college.

Table 12-1 | Persons with Disabilities: Educational History

Before 1800	• Children with disabilities are kept at home and few, if any, receive a formal education.
1800 to 1850	• In 1817, William Gallaudet creates the first formal special education program in the United States.
	• Education programs for children with disabilities are created, primarily as residential institutions. While [these programs] claim to "educate," most of these children are simply removed from society's view and contribute to a growing segregation in the educational system.
1850 to 1950	• Special schools for children with visual, hearing and cognitive disabilities are created, including many residential "schools" or institutions for children with disabilities. Unfortunately, most children with disabilities are still uneducated.
	• By 1918, all individual states mandate state-financed education for [their] citizens, creating a nationwide public school system that guarantees a free education for all citizens.
	• Minorities and children with disabilities are almost always excluded from this emerging public school system.
	• As more children attend public schools, teachers notice more pupils who are "slow" or "backward." Teachers begin to call for special classes and persons with special training to take care of these students.
	• Some parents pool their resources to start a school or program for children with developmental disabilities. While sporadic, these attempts prove that children with disabilities can be educated in the community.
	• Rhode Island opens the first public special education class in the United States in 1896.
	• By 1923, almost 34,000 students are in special education classes.
	• By the mid-1920s, professional views of persons with disabilities are changing. Superintendents begin to see the positive results of education and community interaction for people with disabilities.
	• Special education classes are offered primarily in large cities. Many families send their children to institutions because they believe that is the only place the children will receive training.
1950 to 1975	• In 1954, the landmark *Brown v. Board of Education* decision rocks the educational system. The U.S. Supreme Court decides that schools cannot discriminate on the basis of race, establishing that a "separate" education is not an equal education.
	• During the 1960s and 1970s, the parents' movement works to improve conditions in state institutions; create community services, educational and employment opportunities; initiate legislation; and challenge the conventional wisdom that persons with disabilities cannot be helped.
	• Only one in five students with disabilities in the United States is educated. More than 1 million students are excluded from public schools and another 3.5 million do not receive appropriate services. Many laws specifically exclude students with certain disabilities.
	• In 1973, Congress enacted Section 504 of PL 93-112 as part of the Rehabilitation Act. This legislation and the amendments of 1986 and 1992 guarantee the rights of individuals with disabilities in employment and in educational institutions that receive federal funding.

1975 to mid-1980s	• In 1975, the Education for All Handicapped Children Act, PL 94-142, was passed. This is the first major legislation to require all school districts to develop and provide a free, appropriate public education (FAPE) for all children and youth[s] with disabilities.
	• An important provision of the legislation requires that the education of children with disabilities be provided in the least restrictive environment (LRE) for each child, opening the door for children to be educated in general education classrooms in their neighborhood schools.
	• The legislation challenges educators to reassess the way they view children with disabilities and their potential to learn.
Mid-1980s to 1999	• *The Timothy v. Rochester School District* ruling establishes that "all means all." The U.S. Court of Appeals decision requires all school districts to assume responsibility for educating every child, including those with disabilities—no exceptions.
	• Inclusive education begins to take root in neighborhood schools across the nation. However, system-wide endorsement of inclusion is years away.
	• In 1990, the Individuals with Disabilities Education Act (IDEA) and PL 101-336, the Americans with Disabilities Act (ADA), are passed, expanding services to include individuals aged 3–21 and ensuring that school-aged children with disabilities also are protected outside of school—including employment and access to a range of public and private services.
	• For school districts that have embraced the idea of inclusion, children with physical limitations now have physical access to neighborhood schools for the first time.
	• In 1993, an unequal education is still the rule for children with developmental disabilities. Fewer than 7 percent of school-aged children with disabilities are educated in general education classrooms.
	• In 1997, the Reauthorization of IDEA passes. This law ensures that children with disabilities have the right to more than access to education—they have the right to a quality education and quality outcomes.
2000 to present	• Significant progress has been made but there's still room for improvement. During the 2000–2001 school year, 6.3 million children aged 3 to 21 receive[d] some form of special education, according to the U.S. Department of Education. That's over 10 percent of the total student population!
	• Among students with disabilities aged 14 and over, the high school graduation rate is more than 56 percent.
	• The idea of full inclusion is beginning to take hold and students with disabilities can now be found in an increasing number of regular classrooms on at least a part-time basis.
	• In the 1999–2000 school year, 96 percent of students with disabilities [were] served in regular school buildings and nearly half spen[t] 80 percent of their day in a regular classroom.
	• In 2004, IDEA was reauthorized, [with] changes including modified definitions, policies and procedures for implementing services for students with disabilities with the newest regulations distributed in July 2006.

Source: Partners in Education. (n.d.). Retrieved from http://www.partnersinpolicymaking.com/education/history_overview.html

Roberts entered the University of California at Berkeley in 1962. During a lifetime of fighting for equality for people with disabilities, he became an international representative of human rights to overthrow discrimination. And yet even though the 1960s were a time of heightened political action, when the United States saw the passage of the Civil Rights Act of 1964, it must be noted that this legislation did not include protections for persons with disabilities. While the act prohibited discrimination on the basis of race, religion, and national origin, it did not include disabilities, and they would not be included or addressed in legislation until almost a decade later with the passage of **PL 93-112**, Section 504 of the Rehabilitation Act in 1973, which provided the link between disability and antidiscrimination laws (Wodatch, 1990). Of course, legislation is only the beginning of the struggle for equality. Overt and subtle forms of discrimination continue to exist in schooling, employment, hiring, access, and political representation.

Unlike the Civil Rights Act of 1964, Section 504 of PL 93-112, part of the Vocational Rehabilitation Act, did not mandate compliance or public accommodations by employers in the private sector or for those programs that did not receive federal financial assistance. The mandates found within Section 504 applied only to federal and federally funded programs. In 1975, **Public Law 94-142**, the Education for All Handicapped Children Act, mandated a free and appropriate education for all children, including the right to the following:

- Learning in the least restrictive environment (**LRE**)
- Learning with the aid of an individualized education program (**IEP**) designed to meet the student's unique needs
- A plan to screen and identify students with disabilities
- Full-service schooling at no cost to their families
- **Due process**
- A nondiscriminatory evaluation
- Confidentiality
- Services performed by personnel who receive ongoing training

In 1990, the Individuals with Disabilities Education Act (**IDEA**) and subsequent revisions of its regulations amended PL 94-142, including replacement of the word *handicapped* with the word *disabilities* and expanding services to include individuals aged 3–21 (Yell, 1998).

Passage of PL 94-142 was highly significant for students with disabilities and their families in that it required a free, appropriate public education for all students with disabilities with specific criteria to define the process. Changes implicit in the law included efforts to improve how children with disabilities were identified, evaluated, and educated. This mandate resulted in dramatic changes in public school systems (Sarason & Doris, 1979). Even still, students of color are disproportionately placed in special education classes. Students enrolled in classes for mildly retarded students and severe emotional disturbance are disproportionately male, African American, and working class or poor. Most referrals are made by elementary school teachers

| **Exercise 12-1** | **Field Experience: Identifying Disabilities Commonly Found in Schools** |

Directions: You may want to consult Heward (2003) and/or other sources to research and define the disabilities listed here to improve your knowledge of disabilities that teachers often encounter in schools. After listing functional definitions for each term, write an academic strength that you imagine would exist among persons who have these disabilities.

Physical and Sensory Challenges

Epilepsy

Cerebral palsy

Hearing impairment

Visual impairment

Communication Disorders

Articulation disorders

Stuttering

Voicing problems

Language disorders

Other Learning Challenges

ADD

ADHD

Autism

Cancer

Diabetes

Dyslexia

HIV/AIDS

who are mostly White, middle-class females whose definitions for acceptable behaviors and cultural values are frequently incongruent with those of minority students, representing a kind of soft bigotry of low expectations and educational constraint that results from this type of racial discrimination (Losen & Orfield, 2002). Such placements occur even when these minority students do not actually have disabilities, resulting in unjust stigmatization and severely limited opportunities for academic success (Artiles & Harry, 2004).

In the more than 30 years since the passage of Public Law 94-142, significant progress has been made toward meeting national goals for developing and implementing effective programs and services for early intervention, special education, and related services. But the passage of IDEA signaled more than change in the U.S. educational system; it also prompted change in the national perspective and treatment of persons with disabilities. IDEA forced a reevaluation of the role of persons with disabilities in U.S. society for decades to follow. As such, stronger and broader-based political support for persons with disabilities came into existence in the late 1980s (Wodatch, 1990).

A significant focus that took center stage in the 1980s was developing services and resources necessary to support independent living for people with disabilities—an independence that would allow for more options for participating fully in society. Such actions have resulted in the formation of a national network of centers for independent living, which combine self-help services and advocacy; the elimination of custodial institutions; the development of adaptive equipment; and the passage of the Air Carriers Act (1986), which provides persons with disabilities with the right to use air transportation (see Table 12-2).

Table 12-2 | Legislated Support for Independent Living

- The Fair Housing Amendments Act (1988) was passed, bringing people with disabilities under the protection of the Fair Housing Act of 1968. This act prohibited discrimination toward people with disabilities in the sale or rental of properties.

- The U.S. Department of Housing and Urban Affairs (HUD) issued regulations covering federally funded public housing and other recipients of HUD funds, including Community Development Block Grant Programs. These policies required design standards that opened entrances and passageways to persons with disabilities and provided access to facilities.

Table 12-3 | ADA: Addressing Potential Barriers

State and Local Government	The ADA expanded the accommodations requirement for public programs that were not recipients of federal financial assistance to include all public programs.
Public Accommodations	The ADA requires that a wide range of "public accommodations" in the private sector eliminate physical, communications, and procedural barriers to access.
Employment	The ADA prohibits discrimination against qualified individuals with disabilities in public and private sector employment. This includes a requirement that employers make reasonable accommodations for the known physical or mental limitations of qualified applicants and employees, unless providing such accommodations would impose an undue hardship on employers.
Telecommunications	The ADA requires that all common telecommunications carriers provide nationwide telecommunications relay services, which provide operator systems that relay conversations between people who use TDDs (Telecommunication Devices for the Deaf) or nonvoice terminal devices and those who use the general voice telephone network.
Transportation	The ADA seeks to ensure that individuals with disabilities have access to a full range of public and private transportation.

While PL 101-336, the Americans with Disabilities Act (**ADA**), opened many doors that served as barriers to inclusion and full participation in U.S. society for persons with disabilities (see Table 12-3), there is much yet to be achieved to accomplish its goals (Wodatch, 1990). Movement from reinforcing the dependency of persons with disabilities to facilitating their independence and from forcing persons with disabilities to adapt to inadequate environments to adapting environments to meet the needs of persons with disabilities has been substantial; however, dominant-culture attitudes and beliefs about persons with disabilities have been slow to change. Exercise 12-2 will help you generate ideas for teaching in a nondiscriminatory classroom.

Exercise 12-2	**Field Experience:**

Directions: Make arrangements to visit a local public, private, or charter school. Use the following guidelines to prepare for and implement this field-work.

1. Arrive early, visit the school office upon arrival, and dress professionally.
2. While you are in the school, conduct yourself with poise and professionalism.
3. Be respectful and courteous to all students, faculty, staff, and others you encounter during your school visit.
4. Try to obtain a copy (it may be available online) of the school's philosophy of teaching and learning or mission and demographic information about the school (for example, faculty-to-student ratio; ethnic composition of faculty, staff, and students; socioeconomic status attributes [number of free-lunch recipients]; and gender composition of faculty, staff, and students).
5. Note the grade level, subject taught, and age range of the students in classrooms in which you observe.
6. If possible, meet briefly with the teacher you are scheduled to observe to identify and/or obtain number of years of teaching experience, any information about included students, and the day's lesson objectives and plan.
7. Sit in the back or side of the classroom and *do not* participate in the learning activities. (If the teacher asks for your help to work with individual students, you may, but do not teach the entire group any content that you are not prepared to teach. And reserve some time [at least an hour] during your visit to observe.)
8. Take notice of the class composition. List the number of male and female students; identify the ethnic diversity present and students with exceptionalities (when possible). Later, ask the teacher(s) you observed to identify which students were students who had identified disabilities.
9. Write down several of the questions the teacher asks the students. Later, determine whether they are mostly convergent or divergent questions.
10. Take note of the existence of ability grouping in the school and classroom. Later, identify characteristics and effects of tracking on students' behavior and achievement.
11. Observe ways the teacher utilizes a variety of strategies to address students' individual needs and learning styles.
12. Note whether the teacher calls on students equitably or calls on more dominant-culture students, as the literature has suggested. Observe the quality of student–teacher interactions in order to compare them in exploring the possibility of gender bias.
13. Notice what kinds of feedback (verbal and nonverbal) the teacher provides to students after their responses.
14. Note how the teacher helps students remember the material taught.
15. Observe strategies the teacher uses to motivate the students.
16. Observe classroom management strategies utilized (both preventative and reactive).
17. Identify the climate (comfort, decoration, and feel) of the classroom and the school visited. You may want to draw the classroom to help you remember the physical set-up. Examine the impact of the school and classroom climate on instruction and educational outcomes.
18. Meet with the special education teacher, school psychologist, and school counselor to discuss assessment procedures and services provided for students with disabilities.
19. After observing in the school, reflect on the treatment of students with disabilities within the school, and write a report of your observations summarizing your findings. Discuss your findings with your classmates, colleagues, or instructor in small-group discussion. Don't forget to send a thank-you note to school personnel who helped you carry out this assignment.

CULTURAL FACTORS 3 AND 4: SHARED VALUES, TRADITIONS, AND SPIRITUALITY

Print media may provide the clearest indications that a **disability culture** exists. Hundreds of books have been written that feature disability culture; political newsletters and organizations that promote independence for persons with disabilities are produced in huge numbers and have given form to shared values and experiences that constitute culture for members of this group (McKee, 2003).

Persons with disabilities have indeed forged a group identity. As with other minority groups, those with disabilities have identifiability and differential power, experience differential and pejorative treatment, and seek group awareness (Dworkin & Dworkin, 1976). Members of this group share a common history of oppression and a common bond of resilience yet vary greatly in terms of their views of themselves and discrimination they confront. In his work *Investigating a Culture of Disability: Final Report* (1994), Brown surveyed a number of disability activists at the forefront of an emerging movement and reported references to the legacy of customs and values that represent the common experiences of disabled people and the reality of their different ways of coping, relating, and expressing themselves to support the notion of disability culture.

The Deaf community is widely known for the establishment of Deaf culture. Deaf culture refers to values and beliefs upheld by members of the Deaf community. Members of the Deaf community describe themselves as being proud to be Deaf and feeling that Deafness is a vital part of their identity, cherished as much as ethnicity, gender, and religious background. Members in this community most often attend or have attended residential schools for the Deaf, use American Sign Language (ASL), and view Deafness as a difference rather than a disability. Deaf people often feel a cultural bond based on their shared common language and experience with oppression and may or may not use speech to communicate. A "pathological" or "clinical-pathological/medical model" view of Deaf people accepts values of hearing people as "standard" or "normal" and then focuses on how Deaf people deviate from that "norm." Through such a lens, Deaf people are seen as a group whose hearing loss interferes with their communication, learning, mental health, and adjustment. This approach results in paternalistic oppression of Deaf people. Recently, this view has been called *audism* to emphasize the fact that it shares much in common with racism, sexism, classism, ageism, and heterosexism—the other *isms* of oppression. The "pathological" view is sharply contrasted with the cultural view shared by most linguists and sociologists. The cultural view recognizes a complex set of factors that are important to the Deaf community. Those who hold a cultural view see members of the Deaf community as a group who share a common means of communication that provides a basis for group cohesion and identity and whose primary means of relating to the world is visual (Frasu, 2004). This view supports principles of social justice by focusing on the abilities and strengths that diverse members of the human community contribute to society.

Persons with disabilities have also created a body of art, music, literature, and traditions embodying other expressions of their lives that form the "matter" of their culture built around experience with disability. Most importantly, as noted in Brown (1994), persons with disabilities are proud of themselves, claiming disabilities with pride as part of their identity.

Having encountered negative stereotypes depicting those with disabilities as deficient, deformed, weak, and incompetent, many persons with disabilities have been motivated to create awareness centering around their positive attributes and abilities. As with other cultural groups, disability culture tends to be most visible in artistic expressions and other work produced by and about members of the group. In 1995, a youth dance ensemble composed of teens with and without physical disabilities formed Restless Dance Company and created a dance theatre performance called *Talking Down* that reflected cultures of disability. It explored the idea that Down syndrome not only existed but was long overdue for exposition and celebration. Other artists, including performance artists (for example, Cheryl Marie Wade, Wry Crips Women's Theatre), dancers (for example, the Axis Dance Troupe), playwrights (for example, Neil Marcus), and musicians (for example, Jeff Moyer, Jane Field), illuminate disability culture. Their work celebrates their uniqueness and challenges along with their talents and skills as persons with disabilities. More in-depth analysis and descriptions of the disability culture movement may be found in Brown (1994) and at http://www.dimenet.com/disculture.

CULTURAL FACTOR 5: ACCULTURATION AND EXPERIENCE WITH EXCLUSION AND ALIENATION

Acculturation in Schools

Inclusion in schooling involves integrating students with disabilities in regular classrooms whenever possible *with* the supports necessary for them to succeed. It is mandated as a byproduct of PL 94-142 (Turnbull, Turnbull, Shank, & Smith, 2004). This often-debated educational policy differs greatly from mainstreaming. Supporters of inclusion criticize mainstreaming for the following reasons:

1. A disproportionate number of students currently placed in special education are from oppressed groups in the United States.
2. Curriculum pull-out programs are often poorly integrated with the curricula of general education classes.
3. Special education students who are pulled out generally do not feel and are not treated as though they are a part of the school.
4. Entrance criteria into special education are often vague and inconsistently applied.
5. Special education has become a dumping ground for students who do not actually have learning, physical, or **mental disabilities**, and it is often used to "warehouse" students whose first language is not English or who do not have academic skills and knowledge comparable to their same-age counterparts due to educational failures.

It is common for school officials and dominant-culture families to oppose inclusion in schooling, fearing that "regular" students' education will be harmed when teachers must place "special" attention on students with disabilities when they are enrolled in "regular" classrooms. Research has repeatedly found that such claims are inaccurate and ignore the fundamental rights of persons with disabilities to experience full participation in schooling and society (Smith, 2004). Inclusion initiatives provide supports for students to enable them to achieve in "regular classrooms" to meet needs created by their disabilities, be they in the form of modified instruction, adaptations, or aides who may accompany them to "regular" classrooms to work with classroom teachers to meet their needs. Inclusion is a reality that is long overdue for students with disabilities (Turnbull, Turnbull, Shank, & Smith, 2004). However, if teachers and other school officials hold negative views of students with disabilities and oppose inclusion initiatives, educating students with disabilities in "regular" classrooms may result in underachievement and tacit abuse of these students. Teachers and school officials must be held responsible for embracing the mission of their school by working as and with diversity advocates to help students with disabilities actualize their academic potentials in "regular" classrooms. Explore your beliefs about inclusion and the rights of students with disabilities by completing the assignment in Exercise 12-3.

In 1986, Assistant Secretary of Special Education and Rehabilitative Services Madeline Will suggested a delivery approach (targeting mostly students with mild disabilities) to correct the perceived deficiencies of the special education system. Special education services were criticized from their inception as ineffective, excessively costly, segregating, and stigmatizing (Hocutt, Martin, & McKinney, 1990). This approach evolved into the most extreme form advocacy for students with disabilities in schooling, known as the Regular Education Initiative (REI), which argues for a major reorganization of educational services that would emphasize the regular classroom and restructure the relationship between regular, special, remedial, and compensatory education programs and eliminate segregated schooling for special education students (Salend, 1994; Fuchs & Fuchs, 1994). Proponents of this approach believe that all special education support should be provided in the context of the general education classroom and in other integrated environments. Many people mistakenly believe that inclusion advocates are proponents of the REI. The current thrust for the delivery of education for persons with disabilities emphasizes **full inclusion**—the commitment to educate each student in the school and classroom he or she would otherwise attend to the maximum extent appropriate (Rogers, 1993).

Experience with Exclusion and Alienation

As evidenced by the historical treatment of persons with disabilities, dominant culture has ignored, ridiculed, and excluded members of this group, defining their differences as deficiencies to be feared. Fear may be one of the greatest

| Exercise 12-3 | **Point of Reflection: Inclusion Values Clarification** |

Part I

Directions: You have 10 minutes to work alone to rank (not rate) the items listed from 1 to 10 (1 = least appropriate and therefore most problematic for you to condone). After finishing your individual ranking, work together with your classmates or colleagues in a small group to come to agreement in reranking the top-three items, using the same ranking system (that is, identify the three most problematic and inappropriate statements for the group). You have 15 minutes to complete the group-consensus ranking.

Individual Ranking	Group Ranking	Items
_____	_____	A. Having a regular student's education impaired because you have included students with disabilities (SWD)
_____	_____	B. Limiting a student who has the ability to succeed in "regular" classes by enrolling her/him in a special education classroom
_____	_____	C. Requiring teachers to work twice as hard in order to provide quality education for SWD and all other students
_____	_____	D. Requiring taxpayers to pay for expensive in-service training for teachers to learn to work effectively with SWD
_____	_____	E. Exposing an included SWD to potential ridicule in the "regular" classroom
_____	_____	F. Using funding to finance programs for included SWD
_____	_____	G. Creating the potential for included students to feel frustrated when included in "regular" classrooms because they can't do the same work as "regular" students
_____	_____	H. Exposing SWD to ridicule in school hallways and cafeterias because they are excluded and taught in special education classrooms and other students do not have a chance to get to know them
_____	_____	I. Requiring parents to pay for learning opportunities not provided for their SWD who are attending separate segregated "special" schools
_____	_____	J. Causing teachers to feel frustrated because they have to learn new ways to teach SWD that they never wanted to teach when they chose the teaching profession

Part II

Directions: When your group has finished ranking the items, review the ranked list and identify those assumptions, principles, or criteria that the group used to determine rankings. In other words, why was letter X ranked number 10? Do this for 4–5 of the assumptions. You have approximately 10 minutes to complete this task.

barriers that members of this group face in their interactions with dominant culture. One reason they may be alienated is the vulnerability and mortality members of dominant culture may associate with disability (Funk, 1987). Because humans tend to choose to associate with what they perceive to be strength as opposed to weakness, persons with disabilities often have trouble being accepted because members of dominant culture may be reminded that they, too, someday will be vulnerable and face disability. The fear of having a disability and of being treated with neglect, condescension, and disrespect all contribute to dominant-culture group members' tendencies to alienate and exclude persons with disabilities.

CULTURAL FACTOR 6: LANGUAGE DIFFERENCES, STRENGTHS, AND CHALLENGES

Language not only reflects attitudes but can give shape to attitudes and actions. Many of the terms employed to describe persons with disabilities serve to exclude and unfairly characterize them. Words like *retard, spaz,* and *crippled* are characterizations of persons with disabilities that are widely used among members of dominant culture. Attitudes demonstrated in the use of these terms also exist in subtle, more pervasive characterizations of persons with disabilities. For example, when a term like *blind* is used as a synonym for *ignorant, unaware,* or *unknowing* (for example, "They robbed him blind"), one may conjure up images of a pitiful, naïve, incompetent person who has been duped (Hayes, 2001).

In addition, some forms of body language that are equally disrespectful include touching someone's assistive device (for example, walker, wheelchair, or prosthetic) without permission (Hayes, 2001), speaking loudly to a person with visual impairment, and communicating with a caretaker who accompanies a person with a disability or interpreter for a Deaf person rather than communicating with the person to whom the interaction is directed. Such actions send the message that persons with disabilities do not have rights, capabilities, thoughts, and feelings of their own.

It is important to the more than 53 million Americans with disabilities that they be portrayed realistically and spoken to respectfully. For example, the word *disabled* ignores the fact that persons with disabilities are people with abilities. Focusing on disability through the use of the labels like *disabled* and *handicapped* reflects a stereotype of persons who once had no other means of support than taking off their hats (caps) and begging for help from dominant-culture individuals in order to survive—"cap in hand" became "handicapped." Such terminology does not represent the reality of persons with disabilities.

With regard to people who have disabilities, preferred identifications are those that reference persons first. An emphasis on characteristics of a person rather than on a person as a human being is not only disrespectful but it is also inaccurate. Thus, describing someone as a "person with a disability" is more accurate than referring to her or him as a "disabled person." Saying that someone "uses" a wheelchair or other assistive device avoids the assumptions embedded in phrases like "confined to a wheelchair" or "wheelchair-bound," which imply that persons and their wheelchairs are inseparable (Hayes 2001). In addition, emotionally neutral terms are preferable to those with negative connotations (Maki & Riggar, 1997). The term *visually impaired* is more accurate than *blind* because the latter term does not recognize the range of impairments that people with disabilities have. In addition, many persons with hearing impairment do not consider themselves to have a disability at all. It is widely believed among members of this group that it is the hearing world's ignorance of their language that creates disability (Olkin, 1999).

COPING STRATEGIES FOR ADDRESSING OPPRESSION

Throughout this text, we have noted how various minority groups have addressed oppression and responded to their exclusion in dominant culture. In addition to facing isolation, **persons with disabilities** may also find themselves treated like children or treated with disdain. When they are assumed to be incompetent or totally dependent, when they are pitied or not taken seriously, when they are ridiculed and avoided, they are greatly challenged by oppression. Imagine the student with a physical disability who comes to understand that if he wants to attend college, he must be able to conquer any barriers in the physical environment of the school that would prohibit his attendance. And think about the student with a learning disability who is constantly told to try harder as she tries to make sense of language presented to her that she sees through the lenses of a person with dyslexia—a perceptual learning disability that causes letters and numbers to appear scrambled. The emphasis has changed in many ways from "helping" persons with disabilities exist in a world that denigrates their differences and prohibits their inclusion to one that creates accessibility and acceptance. Ramps and other physical support devices are widely manufactured and installed, and schools are required to provide instruction to address the distinct needs of students with learning disabilities. Simultaneously, to address the challenges of their oppression, persons with disabilities have united and formed supportive communities that provide information, resources, and advocacy similar to that of other minority groups. Such alliances not only shed the light of awareness on the needs and issues of the group but also facilitate changes in society that affect the welfare of members of the group. With increased visibility and advocacy come acceptance and inclusion.

Many persons with disabilities have coped with oppression by calling attention to their abilities and making themselves visible as people who exist beyond their disabilities. Rather than trying to fit into a world that often rejects them, many persons with disabilities have created standards and values that are different from those embraced by dominant culture. Some believe that true integration is achieved only on the basis of a full recognition of difference and the ability to make the free choice to identify as a social group (Finkelstein, 1987). Tables must turn to recognize that persons with disabilities should be accepted as they are and not made to feel inadequate because they do not move, perceive, learn, and communicate in the same ways members of dominant culture do. Standards must be reshaped to include values and skills embodied by persons with disabilities that are often overlooked and undervalued. Standards for optimum physical movement, expression, learning style, and existence must be re-envisioned to include the physical movements of persons with physical disabilities, the communication strategies of persons with vision and hearing impairment, the learning styles of students with learning disabilities, and the lives of a myriad of people who lead lives that function differently from others in dominant culture. U.S. society must perceive and applaud the beauty of sign language and skillful wheelchair locomotion. They must marvel at the strength and creativity of students who put meanings together in ways that defy customary logic. Until such changes occur, persons with disabilities will continue to be marginalized.

POTENTIAL BARRIERS IN LEARNING–TEACHING RELATIONSHIPS WITH DOMINANT-CULTURE TEACHERS AND SCHOOLS

The history of exclusion and oppression of persons with disabilities is long. And while significant steps have been taken to remove barriers to inclusion, work must continue. Initially, the Individuals with Disabilities in Education Act emphasized the process of **mainstreaming** students with disabilities with those who did not have identified disabilities. The process of "mainstreaming" entailed placing students with disabilities in "regular" classes to the "maximum extent appropriate." Typically, "mainstreaming" was implemented by having students with disabilities participate in the so-called "nonacademic" portions of the general education program, such as art, music, and physical education. It was believed that special education students could participate in these classes without having demonstrated "abilities" in these subjects because these subjects were not perceived to be as rigorous and important as the academic subjects that lead directly to academic, and therefore economic, opportunity. It was also believed that enrolling students in these types of classes would not interfere with the education of "regular" students in the "more important" academic subjects. Most students with disabilities were, however, still enrolled in self-contained special education classes; they "visited" general education classes for a relatively small portion of the school day. These initial attempts to include students with disabilities were ill-conceived and ineffective and served to squelch efforts to improve academic opportunities and conditions for students with disabilities because it appeared that their needs were being met. Despite the proliferation of

Table 12-4 | Mental Retardation

According to the American Association on Mental Deficiency (**AAMD**), mental retardation (**MR**) refers to substantial limitations in intellectual functioning as measured by an IQ test with a score between 70 to 75 *and* significantly subaverage functioning in two or more adaptive skill areas (that is, communication, self-care, social skills, self-direction, health and safety, leisure, functional academics, and work). It manifests by age 18. About 1 to 2 percent of the U.S. population fit this description. Those classified as MR are placed into one of four categories:

1. **Intermittent:** Requires support on an as-needed basis
2. **Limited:** Requires time-limited treatment, few staff members, employment training, and transitioning from school to adult world
3. **Extensive:** Requires regular involvement (daily) in some treatment environments
4. **Pervasive:** Requires highly intensive care provided across environments, potentially life-sustaining treatment, and many staff members

Source: Drew, C. J., & Hardman, M. L. (2004). *Mental retardation: A life cycle approach* (8th ed.). Upper Saddle River, NJ: Prentice Hall.

research that dispels the myth that nondisabled students are disadvantaged by the inclusion of students with disabilities, some educators continue to resist inclusion mandates. Not only do such actions ignore the fundamental rights of persons with disabilities, but they also ignore the enormous benefits gained by nondisabled students in full-inclusion classrooms and, therefore, the potential to provide a more effective education for all students (Friend & Cook, 1993; Lipsky & Gartner, 1997: Salend, 1994).

But for full inclusion to occur, more than bricks and mortar need to be adjusted. Inclusion is first and foremost a matter of mindset and perspective. Stereotypes, misconceptions, bias, ignorance, and anxiety can serve as a basis for resisting inclusion. Teachers, parents, staff, and all others involved must understand the concept of inclusion as a fundamental right. Current attitudes, policies, practices, and services all need to be assessed to ensure that those necessary to facilitate full inclusion are in place. An example of policy changes that have developed to reduce bias experienced by students with disabilities is the current criteria for defining mental retardation (see Table 12-4). Whereas in the past, persons were labeled mildly, severely, and profoundly mentally retarded, current definitions are based on services utilized by individuals, which helps to keep a focus on individuals' capabilities rather than their disabilities (Drew & Hardman, 2004).

Funding for coordinated services and individual support mechanisms for ensuring adequate transportation and access not only serve to facilitate inclusion but also create an environment in which equality is possible. Finally, and most importantly, the programs and curricula offered to all students must be tailored to each student's special needs and unique talents.

Intercultural Communication Strategies for Teachers 12-1

Strategies for Facilitating the Academic Achievement of Students with Disabilities

Utilize the following strategies to adapt your instruction to help students with disabilities achieve in your classroom:

1. Collaborate with special education teachers to help screen and identify students with disabilities and then identify appropriate strategies and curriculum revision to meet the needs of students with disabilities.
2. Participate actively in the Individualized Education Program Planning Committee at your school.
3. Provide a structured written overview before each lesson.
4. Use visual aids, demonstrations, simulations, and manipulatives frequently to ensure that students understand concepts presented.
5. Use transparencies and an overhead projector to outline course concepts and keep each transparency for later review by students who need it.
6. Color-code outlines with chalk or pens to add emphasis.
7. Provide a copy of teacher or peer notes for students to allow students to focus on listening during instruction.
8. Provide "turn and talks" or other interactive activities to assist students' abilities to understand and refine their understandings of concepts before learning new material.
9. Enable students to tape-record material presented orally, if needed.
10. Use computer-assisted instruction when appropriate.
11. Include a variety of activities integrating students' multiple intelligences to help students understand and apply content learned in each lesson.
12. Break assignments into smaller parts and provide feedback as each part is completed.
13. Provide additional time to complete assignments or tests when needed.
14. Provide checklists, outlines, and advanced organizers to assist comprehension.
15. Supply reading materials at various reading levels.
16. Enable students to demonstrate understanding using a variety of media, including oral presentations, creative projects, audio- or video-taped assignments, bulletin board displays, dramatizations, written assignments, and demonstrations.

FROM CONCEPTS TO LIVED EXPERIENCE

In the following story, Liz Bogod (2006) describes her struggles in coming to terms with her disability.

FINDING MY LD PRIDE

This is the story of how I came to accept that my learning disability [LD] is nothing to be ashamed of. Through a long, painful journey to arrive at this acceptance, I have come to know my many strengths and to find skills that I did not know I possessed. I offer my story to other LD children, youth, and adults, in the sure knowledge that, if they can come to the realization of their own true abilities and talents, like me, they can shed the sense of shame which all too often leaves LD people feeling dumb, stupid and altogether incapable.

I was 6 years old. It was September and the long, hot summer had come to an end. When I got to school, I knew something was not quite right. I was returning to the same classroom and the same teacher but there were none of the same students. I was in Kindergarten again. My parents told me that my birth date was in the wrong

17. Allow students to word-process rather than hand-write assignments, if needed.
18. Give frequent, shorter quizzes rather than longer tests that require a great deal of memorization.
19. Give tests and exams orally or on audio tape when needed.
20. Assist students in setting short-term goals and provide opportunities for self-evaluation of progress towards those goals.
21. Teach students to organize and keep track of materials.
22. Set up a regular communication system to provide consistent structure and support between parents and teachers.
23. Provide instruction and practice in using study skills.
24. Provide instruction and practice in using self-monitoring strategies.
25. Identify students' strengths, skills, and interests.
26. Establish effective and efficient routines in the classroom.
27. Establish positive rapport with students and model respectful behavior.
28. Provide opportunities for student selection of learning materials and assignments.
29. Minimize classroom clutter and distractions.
30. Work individually with students frequently.
31. Do not view lack of student participation as lack of motivation or student resistance.
32. Re-examine the notion of what is fair. Fair does not mean that every child gets the same treatment but that every child gets what he or she needs.
33. Research information, state and federal laws, and school policies pertaining to working with students with diabetes, HIV/AIDS, epilepsy, autism, cancer, and so on (see Exercise 12-1 for topics). Summarize information and related educational strategies and place it in a handy file for quick reference. Follow suggestions you identify in your research (for example, keeping orange juice on hand for diabetic students, and so on).

Links

http://www.allabilities.com/society.html

www.dpi.org

month, which meant I could not go into first grade and would have to repeat Kindergarten. At that time, I accepted the explanation.

It was not until the following year in grade 1 that I had an inclination that the excuse my parents used for my repeating Kindergarten was a lie. I did not know that the real reason was because I could only count to 10 while my classmates were counting to 100; I could not tie my shoes while classmates were tying them and I could not write my name.

I have vivid memories of my parents meeting my grade-1 teacher to discuss my school difficulties. After being sent out of the room fully aware of the topic of conversation, I was mad! How dare you, I thought, have a conversation about me without including me! My attempts to eavesdrop failed, but I did not need to hear what they were saying. I knew exactly what they were talking about—me and my unfinished math book! I had tried to hide the fact that I could not cope with math and had hidden the math book in my desk.

Soon I was faced with one of the most traumatic experiences of my childhood. I found myself with my mother in an interview with a scary doctor who seemed to have no rapport with children. I was commanded to answer her questions. She frightened me and I instantly took a dislike to her. I shut up like a clam and was totally uncooperative. I remember my mother arguing with her, so evidently things did not go well. Many years later, I discovered this scary dictator was a very eminent child psychiatrist at a major children's hospital.

The next thing that happened to me was that I was moved into a special education class. I wondered what was so special about me? I was just a normal kid who wanted to fit in, do well in school, and make my parents proud of me, but somehow my inability to do math and other learning disabilities seemed to make me "special." So, the "special" kid went into "special" class with seven other "special" kids with other "special" problems. I felt different and abnormal.

I remained in the special education class for two years. During this time, I was slowly reintegrated back into the mainstream class. My academic reintegration went fairly smoothly, but my social reintegration was a disaster. On my first day, I went to class wanting to make friends, but I really did not know how. My poor social skills made it difficult for me to relate to people. I had trouble understanding humor, keeping up with conversations, and using and understanding body language. As a result, children did not want to play with me.

The memories I have of my early school years are isolation, loneliness and the many recesses when I sat alone on the school steps. When I set out to find a friend the kids ran away from me. One well-meaning, but misguided, teacher took pity on me sitting by myself and decided to assign me a "friend." News of this assigned friend got around and I was told, "You are such a loser, you had to be assigned a friend." Throughout my elementary school years, I experienced this kind of social rejection over and over again. This was the part of my learning disability nobody understood.

In high school, to help with my learning disabilities in math, science, and French, I would spend one period a day in the school learning center, often referred to as the Romper Room! Math and French were compulsory in grade 9 and I had a lot of difficulty with these credits, but coping socially weighed much more heavily on my mind. I dreaded group work because I was always the last one to be picked to join a group. I was very unhappy—totally isolated and soon became depressed. I was labeled mentally ill and passed from one psychiatrist to the next. Many interpretations were made to explain my problem. I was told that I had a depressive mental illness and was put on medication. I was told I was too dependent on my parents, which I have since learned is very common among children with learning disabilities.

With hindsight, I know all my pain could have been prevented if I had known that I had a learning disability and learned how to cope with it. As an adult, I filled out a learning disabilities checklist; I was amazed to find out how much on the list applied to me. I realized that I had a reason for being as I am. I was not mentally ill, retarded or stupid. As I continued to explore the subject and found out how many famous people have learning disabilities, . . . I was able to speak to others about the topic. I've learned that though it takes us longer and is more difficult, those of us with learning disabilities get there in the end and can be successful, productive members of society.

SUMMARY

Definitions Exceptionalities are created by differences among students. Exceptional students are students who require supplemental services to facilitate their academic development. Students with disabilities and gifted students are two groups of exceptional students.

A *disability* is a restriction or lack of ability to perform an activity in the manner or within the range considered "normal" for humans, while *impairment* is defined as the loss or abnormality of psychological, physiological, or anatomical structure or function. Handicaps involve the loss or limitation of opportunities to take part in the "normal" life of the community on an equal level with others due to physical or social barriers.

Cultural Factor 1: Historical and Current Treatment in the United States Throughout history, persons with disabilities have been ignored, exiled, exploited, tortured, and even destroyed. The focus has been on the disability rather than on persons' lived experiences. Through the 1960s, the provision of rehabilitative counseling simply extended the view that the disabled needed to adjust—to fit in—rather than have society adjust to incorporate them. According to the Census Bureau's March 1996 Current Population Survey, 12 percent of Americans aged 25 to 64 had some type of disability, and 64 percent of that group had a disability that was serious enough to require assistance with daily activities. These numbers are expected to grow.

Cultural Factor 2: Initial Terms of Incorporation into U.S. Society Prior to 1975, little, if any, public or governmental concern and attention concerned the education of students with disabilities. While the Civil Rights Act of 1964 prohibited discrimination on the basis of race, religion, and national origin, it did not include disabilities, and they would not be included or addressed in legislation until almost a decade later, with the passage of Section 504 of PL 93-112, the Rehabilitation Act, in 1973. In 1975, Public Law 94-142, the Education for All Handicapped Children Act, mandated a free and appropriate education for all children. A significant focus that took center stage in the 1980s was on developing services and resources necessary to support independent living for people with disabilities—an independence that would allow for more options for participating fully in society.

Cultural Factors 3 & 4: Shared Values, Traditions and Spirituality Print media may provide the clearest indications that a disability culture exists. The expression of customs and values that represent the common experiences of disabled people and the reality of their different ways of coping, relating, and expressing themselves sup-

ports the notion of disability culture. Persons with disabilities have created a body of art, music, literature, and other expressions of their lives that form the "matter" of a culture built around experience with disability.

Cultural Factor 5: Acculturation and Experience with Exclusion and Alienation Inclusion in schooling is mandated as a byproduct of PL 94-142. The most extreme advocacy for students with disabilities in schooling comes in the form of the Regular Education Initiative (REI), which argues for the elimination of segregated special education classes altogether. The fear of having a disability and of being treated with neglect, condescension, and disrespect all contribute to dominant-culture group members' tendencies to alienate and exclude persons with disabilities.

Cultural Factor 6: Language Differences, Strengths, and Challenges The word *disabled* ignores the fact that persons with disabilities are people with abilities. Focusing on disability through the use of the labels like "disabled" and "handicapped" reflects a stereotype of persons who in the past had no other means of support than taking off their hats (caps) and begging for help from dominant-culture individuals in order to survive—"cap in hand" became "handicapped." Preferred identifications are those that reference a person first. Thus, describing someone as "a person with a disability" is more accurate than referring to her or him as a "disabled person"; saying someone "uses" a wheelchair or other assistive device avoids the assumptions embedded in terms like "confined to" or "wheelchair-bound."

Coping Strategies for Addressing Oppression The emphasis has changed in many ways from "helping" persons with disabilities exist in a world that denigrates their differences to creating accessibility and acceptance. To address challenges of their oppression, persons with disabilities have united and formed communities for information, resources, support, and advocacy similar to those of other minority groups. Many persons with disabilities have coped with oppression by calling attention to their abilities and making themselves visible as people who exist beyond their disabilities.

Potential Barriers in Learning/Teaching Relationships with Dominant-Culture Teachers and Schools   The Individuals with Disabilities in Education Act emphasized the process of mainstreaming students with disabilities with those who did not have identified disabilities. For full inclusion to occur, more than bricks and mortar need to be adjusted. Inclusion is first and foremost a matter of mindset and perspective. Most importantly, the programs and curricula offered to all students must be tailored to students' special needs and unique talents.

Important Terms

ADA	exceptionality	impairment	persons with
acceleration	full inclusion	inclusion	disabilities
disability	giftedness	learning disabilities	physical disabilities
disability culture	handicap	LRE	PL 93-112
due process	IDEA	mainstreaming	PL 94-142
enrichment	IEP	mental disabilities	

Connections on the Web

www.dpi.org

Disabled Peoples' International is a network of national organizations or assemblies of disabled people, established to promote human rights of disabled people through full participation, equalization of opportunity, and development. The goals of DPI are to promote the human rights of disabled persons, promote economic and social integration of disabled persons and develop and support organizations of disabled persons.

http://ericec.org/digests/prodfly.html

The CEC information center on disabilities provides links to ERIC digests. The digests are short reports (1500 to 2000 words) that provide a basic overview, plus pertinent references, on topics of interest to the broad educational community.

http://ericec.org/faq/incluson.html

This website is a good resource for developing effective methods for accommodating students with disabilities in inclusive settings.

http://teaching.berkeley.edu/bgd/disabilities.html

This site provides academic accommodations for students with disabilities from the hard copy book *Tools for Teaching* by Barbara Gross Davis (1993).

REFERENCES

Artiles, A. J., & Harry, B. (2004). *Addressing culturally and linguistically diverse student overrepresentation in special education: Guidelines for parents.* Denver: National Center for Culturally Responsive Education Systems.

Bogod, L. (2006). First person: Finding my LD pride. *LD Online.* Retrieved from http://ldonline.org/first_person/bogod.html

Bowe, F. (1978). *Handicapping America: Barriers to disabled people.* New York: Harper Row.

Bowe, F. (1980). *Rehabilitating America*. New York: Harper Row.

Boylan, E. (1991). *Women and disability*. London: Zed Press.

Brown, C. N. (1997). Legal issues and gifted education: Gifted identification as a constitutional issue. *Roeper Review, 19,* 157–160.

Brown, S. E. (1994). *Investigating a culture of disability: Final report*. Las Cruces, NM: Institute on Disability Culture.

Charlton, J. I. (1998). *Nothing about us without us, disability, oppression and empowerment*. Berkeley: University of California.

Crow, L. (1996). Including all of our lives: Renewing the social model of disability. In J. Morris (Ed.), *Encounters with strangers: Feminism and disability* (pp. 55–72). London: The Women's Press.

Demographics and Statistics (StatsRRTC). (2005, April 4). Retrieved November 16, 2005, from http://www.disabilitystatistics.org

Drew, C. J., & Hardman, M. L. (2004). *Mental retardation: A life cycle approach* (8th edition). Upper Saddle River, NJ: Merrill.

Dworkin, A. G., & Dworkin, R. J. (1976). *The minority report*. New York: Praeger.

Fagan, T., & Wallace, A. (1979). Who are the handicapped? *Personnel and Guidance Journal, 58,* 215–220.

Finkelstein, V. (1987). *Disabled people and our culture development*. Retrieved from http://www.independentliving.org/docs3/finkelstein87a.html

Frasu, A. (2004). Which is correct: Deaf, deaf, hard of hearing, or hearing impaired? *Deaf Linx*. Retrieved May 8, 2006, from http://www.deaflinx.com/label.html

Freeman, J. (1994). Some emotional aspects of being gifted. *Journal for the Education of the Gifted, 17,* 180–197.

Friend, M., & Cook, L. (1993). Inclusion. *Instructor, 103,* 52–56.

Fuchs, D., & Fuchs, L. S. (1994). Inclusive schools movement and the radicalization of special education reform. *Exceptional Children, 60,* 294–309.

Funk, R. (1987). Disability rights: From caste to class in the context of civil rights. In A. Gartner & T. Joe (Eds.), *Images of the disabled, disabling images* (pp. 7–30). New York: Praeger.

Gardner, H. (1993). *Multiple intelligences: The theory in practice*. New York: Basic Books.

Hayes, P. A. (2001). *Addressing cultural complexities in practice: A framework for clinicians and counselors*. Washington, DC: American Psychological Association.

Heward, W. L. (2003). *Exceptional children* (7th ed.). Upper Saddle River, NJ: Merrill/Prentice Hall.

Hocutt, A. M., Martin, E. W., & McKinney, J. D. (1990). Historical and legal context of mainstreaming (Inclusion). In J. W. Loyd, N. N. Singh, & A. C. Repp (Eds.), *The regular education initiative: Alternative perspectives on concepts, issues & models* (pp. 17–28). Sycamore, IL: Sycamore Publishing.

Hohenshil, T. H., & Humes, C. W. (1979). Roles in counseling in ensuring the rights of the handicapped. *Personnel and Guidance Journal, 58,* 221–227.

Houtenville, A. J. (2005). *Disability statistics in the United States*. Ithaca, NY: Cornell University Rehabilitation Research and Training Center on Disability.

Hunsaker, S. L., Finley, V. S., & Frank, E. L. (1997). An analysis of teacher nominations and student performance in gifted programs. *Gifted Child Quarterly, 41,* 19–24.

Kitano, M. K. (1997). Gifted Asian American women. *Journal for the Education of the Gifted, 21,* 3–37.

Kulick, J. A., & Kulick, C. L. C. (1997). Ability grouping. In N. Colangelo & G. A. Davis (Eds.), *Handbook of gifted education* (2nd edition, pp. 230–242). Boston: Allyn & Bacon.

Lipsky, D. K., & Gartner, A. (1997). *Inclusion and school reform: Transforming America's classrooms*. Baltimore: Paul H. Brooks.

Losen, D. J., & Orfield, G. (2002). *Racial inequality in special education*. Cambridge, MA: Harvard Education.

Lupart, J. L., & Pyryt, M. C. (1996). "Hidden gifted" students: Underachiever prevalence and profile. *Journal for the Education of the Gifted, 20,* 36–53.

Maki, D. R., & Riggar, T. F. (1997). Rehabilitation counseling: Concepts and paradigms. In D. R. Maki & T. F. Riggar (Eds.), *Rehabilitation counseling* (pp 3–31). New York: Springer.

McDaniel, T. R. (1993). Education of the gifted and the excellence–equity debate: Lessons from history. In C. J. Maker (Ed.), *Critical issues in gifted education: Programs for the gifted in regular classrooms* (pp. 6–18). Austin, TX: Pro-Ed.

McKee, B. J. (2003). *Disability culture.* Retrieved from http://www.chairgrrl.com/DisabilityTimeline/disability_culture.htm

Murdick, N., Gartin, B., & Crabtree, T. (2002). *Special education law.* Upper Saddle River, NJ: Prentice Hall.

National Center for Education Statistics. (1994). *Digest of education statistics.* Washington, DC: U.S. Government Printing Office.

Nielsen, M. E., Higgins, L. D., & Hammond, A. E. (1993). The twice-exceptional child project: Identifying and serving gifted/handicapped learners. In C. M. Callahan, D. A. Tomilson, & P. M. Pizzat (Eds.), *Contexts for promise: Noteworthy practices and innovations in the identification of gifted students* (pp. 145–196). Charlottesville, VA: National Research Center on the Gifted and Talented.

Oakes, J., & Lipton, M. (1990). Tracking and ability grouping: A structural barrier to access and achievement. In J. I. Goodlad & P. Keating (Eds.), *Access to knowledge: An agenda for our nation's schools* (pp. 187–202). New York: College Entrance Examination Board.

Olkin, R. (1999). *What psychotherapists should know about disability.* New York: Guildford.

Renzulli, J. S., & Reis, S. M. (1997). The schoolwide enrichment model: New directions for developing high-end learning. In N. Colangelo & G. A. Davis (Eds.), *Handbook of gifted education* (2nd ed., pp. 136–154). Boston: Allyn & Bacon.

Roberts, S. M., & Lovett, S. B. (1994). Examining the "F" in gifted: Academically gifted adolescents' psychological and affective responses to scholastic failure. *Journal for the Education of the Gifted, 17,* 241–259.

Rogers, J. (1993). The inclusion revolution. *Phi-Delta-Kappa-Research Bulletin, 11,* 1–6.

Sailor, W. (Ed.). (2002). *Whole-school success and inclusive education: Building partnerships for learning, achievement, and accountability.* New York: Teachers' College.

Salend, S. J. (1994). *Effective mainstreaming: Creating inclusive classrooms.* New York: Macmillan.

Sapon-Shevin, M. (1996). Beyond gifted education: Building a shared agenda for school reform. *Journal for the Education of the Gifted, 19,* 192–214.

Sarason, S. B., & Doris, J. (1979). *Educational handicap, public policy and social history: A broadened perspective on mental retardation.* New York: Free Press

Smith, D. (2004). *Introduction to special education: Teaching in an age of opportunity* (5th ed.). Needham Heights, MA: Allyn & Bacon.

Thomas, S., & Russo, C. (1995). *Special education law: Issues and implications for the '90s.* Topeka, KS: NOLPE.

Turnbull, R., Turnbull, A., Shank, M., & Smith, S. (2004). *Exceptional lives: Special education in today's schools.* Upper Saddle River, NJ: Prentice Hall.

Wodatch, J. (1990). The ADA: What it says. *Worklife, 3,* 3.

Yell, M. L. (1998). *The law and special education.* Upper Saddle River, NJ: Prentice Hall.

Promoting Change and Achievement

I knew I wasn't gonna have a chance. The whole thing is rigged. It's fake. You think I was gonna stick around and get punked—by these punks?

Manny, age 17

13 CHAPTER

Understanding the Achievement Gap between Minority and Dominant Culture Students

Stratification Effects

Schools continue to reproduce a sorting system based on caste that prevails in society. Whether it is through structural barriers like tracking (so-called "ability" grouping) or through more informal social interactions that separate people based on race (for example, placing minority students in special education classrooms based on their race), gender (for example, segregation in academic subjects like industrial arts and consumer economics), social class (for example, sorting students into early-childhood reading groups based on how well students read when they enter kindergarten), sexual orientation (for example, school proms that permit only self-identified heterosexual couples to attend), or "**ability**" (for example, pull-out programs that educate students with identified learning disabilities separately), sorting kids out for rewards or discrimination occurs every day in U.S. schools. Students are often treated differently in schools based on race, gender, sexual orientation, ability, and socioeconomic status. The differential treatment of those who systematically encounter discrimination has resulted in stratified educational resources, opportunities, and outcomes.

Race and social-class achievement gaps have been widely researched, discussed, and well documented in the literature (Coleman et al., 1966; Irvine & Irvine, 1995; Jenson, 1969; Kozol, 1991; Oakes, 1985; Persell, 1977; Pollard, 1989). In spite of the improvements made in the United States in civil rights and race relations since 1960, minority students generally continue to exhibit lower levels of achievement than dominant-culture students in U.S. schools

(Fordham, 1982; Fordham & Ogbu, 1986; Irvine & Irvine, 1995; Ogbu, 1992b, 1994).

Various theories and models have been presented to explain achievement differences between minority and dominant culture students. This chapter presents three theories—cultural deprivation, cultural difference, and oppositional cultures—and discusses the forms and processes of differential treatment and stratification of students within U.S. schools.

CHAPTER OBJECTIVES

1. Describe cultural deprivation and cultural differences theory explanations for minority student underachievement.
2. Describe Ogbu's oppositional cultures theory.
3. Explain the difference between voluntary and involuntary minorities and the impact of these different orientations on academic achievement.
4. Discuss the effects of gender and socioeconomic stratification on academic achievement.
5. Discuss the effects of heterosexism and ableism on academic achievement.
6. Describe what is meant by the term *opportunity structures* and the role they play in the reduction of stratification effects on minority students.

CULTURAL DEPRIVATION THEORY

Cultural deprivation theory blames minority student underachievement on cognitive or linguistic deficiencies that supposedly exist within impoverished minority student community environments. This theory assumes that the fundamental educational practices and skills that White middle-class children learn are not represented and taught in minority student homes and thus disadvantage children from these communities in schools (Ausubel, 1964; Bloom, Davis, & Hess, 1965; Coleman et al., 1966). Interventions stemming from the cultural deprivation model seek to supplement existing school curricula with remedial education programming. These approaches have not been consistently successful in closing the achievement gap between minority and dominant-culture students.

Reasons for the failure of such programs are many, including the fact that in general, these programs are not designed to maintain academic achievement once it has been boosted by temporary singular programs. In addition, remediation programs often teach students basic academic skills that, if learned, will not prepare students to function in classes that require critical thinking and problem-solving skills. The failure of such programs, especially in relation to African American student education, has resulted in the strengthening and further endorsement of an old myth that achievement gaps are reflections of the inadequacy of minority students' genetic backgrounds (Jenson, 1969).

While this line of reasoning enjoyed a surge in popularity (Murray & Herrnstein, 1994), the claims posited by genetic theorists are unsubstantiated to the extent that they are discredited by most educators and researchers (Hirsch, 1987; Hudley & Graham, 1995; Valentine & Lloyd, 1989). We now know that genetic explanations are baseless. For example, they do not explain why some African American students succeed in U.S. schools and why racially mixed students do not necessarily perform better academically than students who are classified as African American (Ogbu, 1974).

CULTURAL DIFFERENCE THEORY AND SOCIAL STRATIFICATION: AN UNJUST CYCLE OF BLAME

Cultural difference (Moll & Diaz, 1987; Trueba, 1987) and **multicultural education** (Banks, 1987; Banks & Banks, 1989) theories have also been used to explain and guide attempts to improve minority student achievement. These perspectives move from blaming minority students for their underachievement in U.S. schools to blaming the schools for their general lack of sensitivity to the different learner needs of culturally diverse student populations. However, interventions developed and implemented as an outgrowth of these approaches have come up short. Various school reform strategies employed by schools, in efforts to address recommendations emphasized by cultural difference and multicultural approaches, have not resulted in the closing of racial achievement gaps (Ogbu, 1992a).

> [M]ulticultural approaches to curriculum reform really do not offer a viable explanation for or 'solutions' to the problem of racial inequality in schooling. Proponents of multiculturalism fail to take into account the differential structure of opportunities that help to define minority relations to dominant white groups and social institutions in the United States. (McCarthy, 1990, p. 56)

It is understandable that schools continue to be blamed for the consistently unsatisfactory academic performance of minority students. Americans have historically placed emphasis on the role of the school in preparing the nation's students for their jobs in society (Anyon, 1981; Apple, 1989; Bowles & Gintis, 1976; Goodlad, 1984; Spring, 1989; Wise, 1979). Most Americans agree that desirable jobs are acquired by those who are successful in school and are, therefore, more qualified to attain the highest-paying positions in the economy. "Americans of all classes send their children to school to prepare them to get jobs and high wages, as well as to achieve fine lifestyles and to be able to live in better neighborhoods when they grow up ... [They] do not send their children to school because they want them to become intellectuals" (Ogbu, 1974, p. 5). However, the logic of confidence (see Meyer & Rowan, 1977) at work in this line of reasoning assumes that students have equal and fair opportunities to succeed in schools. A review of the functional **social stratification** that exists in our schools demonstrates that this is not the case.

Because the same **opportunity structures** present in society are replicated in schools, societal stratification that assigns status and rewards to individuals not only places and maintains minority students in subordinate positions in society but also justifies their stratified placement in those positions in school. Rothenberg (1995) noted:

[O]ur society is organized in such a way as to make hierarchy or class itself appear natural and inevitable. We grade and rank children from their earliest ages and claim to be sorting them according to something called natural ability. The tracking that permeates our system of education both reflects and creates the expectation that there are A people, B people, C people, and so forth. Well before high school, children have come to define themselves and others in just this way and to accept this kind of classification as natural. (pp. 11–12)

So, if we buy this way of thinking, A people will be placed in rich learning environments that provide the best possible resources, and C people will be located in skeletal learning environments that stress the basics in order to "help them catch up." But will students who are placed in remedial programs ever catch up while they are enrolled in remedial programs? Probably not, if they are never presented with the same content and instruction that fuel college-preparation programs of study. When remedial programs do not work to reduce the academic achievement gap between minority and dominant-culture students, school success, once again, is equated with individual student ability, effort, and responsibility. So, in effect, **cultural difference theory** (like cultural deprivation theory) removes the responsibility for minority student under-achievement from schools, school systems, and society at large and again places it squarely on the shoulders of minority students. Minority students thus become more intensely blamed each time another school reform plan fails to result in overall minority student success.

OGBU'S OPPOSITIONAL CULTURES THEORY AND RACIAL STRATIFICATION

According to Ogbu (1974), race alone does not explain minority student variability in school achievement. Ogbu developed a structural model of racial stratification to explain why subjugated minority groups achieve poorly in school. His model begins with an articulation of minority student "type" as an outgrowth of the form of their initial terms of incorporation into U.S. society.

Types of Minority Students

Two types of minority students were identified by Ogbu (1974) as determined by their initial terms of incorporation into U.S. society: (1) immigrant or voluntary minorities and (2) caste-like subordinate or involuntary minorities. While we have previously introduced the concepts of voluntary and involuntary incorporation, they are worth reviewing to help illuminate the ways racial stratification affects minority student achievement.

Voluntary minority students are defined as persons whose ancestors came into this country by choice, probably because they believed the change would lead to better opportunities for success. Meanwhile, involuntary or subordinate minority students' ancestors were initially brought into U.S. society against their will, through slavery or conquest.

This model suggests that now—even generations later—the descendents of voluntary minority students probably see the discrimination they receive from members of the dominant culture in the United States as an obstacle that can be overcome through hard work and compliance with rules established by dominant culture. Precisely because voluntary minorities' families have chosen to take part in U.S. society, voluntary minority students are more willing to play by dominant-culture rules. In contrast, subordinate or involuntary minorities' families have historically received inferior education in the United States and may have been forced by the effects of racial stratification to terminate their educations early. In addition, subordinate minorities continue to be offered jobs and wages below those extended to members of dominant culture. Therefore, having experienced an entire history of discrimination and injustice from dominant culture in the United States (including dominant-culture schools), subordinate minorities often display distrust of traditional paths (schooling) to success.

To Achieve Is to Be White

Under these conditions, subordinate minority students may believe they must in some ways change their attitudes and behaviors to, in fact, surrender their identities in order to succeed in the United States and in U.S. schools. They may feel they must publicly abandon characteristics that they generally equate with their racial identity so that they may be more readily accepted and rewarded for their efforts within dominant-culture schools.

One way this may appear is in the imitation of the behavior of dominant culture. The imitation can take various forms: Some may try to treat other members of their minority group as destructively as dominant-culture members treat them. A few may develop enough of the qualities valued by dominant culture to be partially accepted. Usually they are not wholly accepted, and even if they are, it is only if they are willing to forsake their own identification with other members of their cultural group. Consider women in a profession that does not accept and view them as successful; it is not unusual to hear them praised with phrases like "She thinks like a man" (Miller, 1995).

Whereby voluntary minority students often view education in the United States as one of their main means for achieving opportunities for success, **involuntary minority** students often see U.S. education as being partially responsible for the loss of their racial and cultural identities. Involuntary minority students, having experienced generations of discrimination and prejudice in the United States, may have determined that they cannot succeed by following the traditional educational routes to economic success. They may be convinced that they must choose between taking one of two major paths on their educational journeys. One involves assimilation and, in turn, estrangement from other involuntary minority students and results in academic achievement. The other involves resistance toward dominant culture, public expression of self and racial identity, alignment with other involuntary minority students, and resultant academic underachievement. In reality, there are more than two ways

Table 13-1
A Continuum
of Adaptive
Strategies

Ogbu (1992b) described the following strategies as those often employed by African Americans in order to promote school success:

1. **Emulation of Whites or cultural passing:** Adopting "White" academic attitudes and behaviors or trying to behave like middle-class White students.

2. **Accommodation without assimilation:** An alternation model, a characteristic strategy among voluntary minorities. A student adopting this strategy behaves according to school norms but at home in the community behaves according to African American norms.

3. **Camouflage:** Disguising true academic attitudes and behaviors, using a variety of techniques. One technique is to become a jester or class clown. Since peer group members are not particularly interested in how well a student is doing academically, the student claims to lack interest in school and that schoolwork/homework or getting good grades is not important. The camouflaging student studies in secret. The good grades of camouflaging students are attributed to their "natural smartness." Another way of camouflaging is to become involved in "African American activities." For example, if an African American athlete gets A's, there is no harm done.

4. **Involvement in church activities:** Promotes school success.

5. **Attending private schools:** For some, a successful way to get away from peer groups.

6. **Mentors:** Another success-enhancing strategy.

7. **Protection:** A few students secure the protection of bullies from peer pressures in return for helping the bullies with their homework.

8. **Remedial and intervention programs:** Help some students succeed.

9. **Encapsulation:** May become encapsulated in peer group logic and activities. These African American students do not want to do the "White man's thing" and as a result, often fail.

---

involuntary-minority students can respond, but often the choice is one that ultimately costs them in terms of their own academic achievement and/or social adjustment. Ogbu (1992b), for example, has indicated that a rather complex continuum stretches between the two extremes noted (see Table 13-1). The variety of strategies that subordinate minority students may use to reject dominant-culture expectations for educational standards of behavior or to put forth academic achievement efforts are often the means by which these students survive within racially stratified school environments.

The strategies appear to be those employed by involuntary minority students in an attempt to survive the barriers they confront in schools. While such coping responses may be advantageous for addressing psychological survival needs and enhancing one's racial identity, many of these tactics have an unfortunate side effect: The rejection of many or all behaviors and values endorsed by dominant culture also serve to undermine achievement and achievement-striving in school. In addition, the safety that emerges from withdrawal from competition for teachers' praise (see Sennett & Cobb, 1972) precludes assimilation. In this sense, the opposition expressed toward dominant-culture practices, including participation in school activities, greatly hinders involuntary minority student achievement. So, while a rejection of the dominant-culture White frame of reference helps to defend against prejudice and enhances minority student identity, it simultaneously prohibits involuntary minority students from using traditional academic success strategies that have typically been beneficial for White and voluntary minority students.

GENDER STRATIFICATION EFFECTS ON ACHIEVEMENT: TO ACHIEVE IS TO BE MALE

Gender, when used as a class distinction, is also a factor that contributes to a castelike or subordinate minority positioning within schools. It is a position that can negatively affect achievement. Gilligan (1982) and other contemporary researchers (Bowker, 1993; Brown, 1991; Debold, Wilson, & Malave, 1993; Kerr, 1985; Robinson & Ward, 1991) emphasized how the different (often neglectful) treatment of female students in schools affects female student identity and academic development.

Since the early 1970s, researchers have documented the inequitable expectations, insensitive and/or inadequate teacher-approval behaviors, and unfair patterns of teacher–student interaction that sustain gender bias in schools (Keating, 1990). Belenky, Clinchy, Goldberger, and Tarule (1986) maintain:

> [F]emale students more often express the existence of gaps in their learning and doubt their intellectual competence than do male students. For many women, the real and valued lessons learned did not necessarily grow out of their academic work but from their relationships with friends and teachers, life crises, and community involvements. Women may feel alienated in academic settings and experience formal education as either peripheral or irrelevant to their central interests and development. (p. 4)

Belenky and colleagues (1986) contend that education, as traditionally defined and practiced, does not adequately serve the needs of females. "The commonly accepted stereotypes of women's thinking as emotional, intuitive, and personalized ha[ve] contributed to the devaluation of women's minds and contributions, particularly in Western technologically oriented cultures, which value rationalism and objectivity" (p. 6).

In order to achieve, female students may, therefore, engage in **gender passing** by acting more like male students in order to be accepted and promoted (Fordham, 1993). Lever (1976) concluded after studying 181 5th- and 6th-grade White, middle-class student academic behaviors that "if a girl does not want to be left dependent on men, she will have to learn to play like a boy" (cited in Gilligan, 1982, p. 10). Fordham (1993) agreed that female students are compelled to pass as male dominant others. "Gender passing or impersonalization suggests masquerading or presenting a persona or some personae that contradicts the literal image of the marginalized or doubly refracted self" (p. 3). Fordham argued that gender passing is a reality for both African American and White women in finding that the first and only commandment for all women in

| **Case Illustration 13-1** | **Managing AP Calc—I Guess** |

I can remember the feeling I had entering class that first day. Our family had just moved to town because my mom got a new job. I had worked it all out in my mind and figured I could do one year and then it would be off to college. This was my senior year and I was psyched about getting in, getting out, and getting on with it (college and life!). I had a pretty heavy course load my senior year, and I was taking an advanced-placement calc course. I figured since I was going into engineering I needed all the math I could take, plus I liked math.

Anyway I take my seat as the teacher calls the roster. He gets to me and says, "Melissa Hankins" and before I can say, "Here," he says, "...I'm sorry, Melissa, did you know that this is advanced-placement calculus? Are you supposed to be here?" No one made a sound, and I wasn't sure if he was kidding or not. I said yes, I had signed up for

this and AP Physics, and you should have heard the murmurs from the class. It was liked I announced I had some socially transmitted disease. The teacher's response? "Oh, that's nice!" (with a tone that was saying, "Yeah right!")

Throughout the entire first marking period I literally had to fight to get recognized to answer a question or to ask one. It was like I was invisible. Then the kicker was when people starting talking about the senior prom ... guys in the class started assuming I was a lesbian. Why? Because I was kicking their butt in math, I guess.

I let them think what they wanted. I knew I'd never get a prom date, or even a date, for that matter from that bunch but that was not my goal—early college admission was. And, I got it!

I wonder if I'll date in college.

Source: Personal communication with Margaret, February 21, 2005.

the academy is "Thou shalt be taken seriously." For these female students, to achieve is to be male. (See Case Illustration 13-1.)

SOCIAL-CLASS STRATIFICATION EFFECTS OF ACHIEVEMENT: TO ACHIEVE IS TO BE WEAK

U.S. society is stratified not only according to race and gender classifications, but also largely on the basis of social-class distinction. Within U.S. society, each social-class culture is not equally valued. Furthermore, because the societal standard of respectability in the United States is middle class, to be from the working class is to be defined as inferior and subordinate (Gardner, 1993).

Differences between rich and poor people in society are actually socially constructed. These differences are, then, used to rationalize and justify the unequal distribution of wealth and power in U.S. society. Schools are an integral part of the societal social-class stratification system. They operate as social microcosms embodying the prejudice, oppression, and discrimination evident in larger society. According to Greer (1972), schools select individuals for opportunities according to a hierarchical schema that runs closely parallel to existing social-class patterns. The resultant social structure disadvantages working-class students—weakening their academic achievement levels (Gans, 1995; Sennett & Cobb, 1972).

Educational researchers have documented a statistically significant relationship between working-class and poor student status and academic achievement. According to Wolf (1977), a poor child is roughly twice as likely to be a low academic achiever as a child who is not poor. Brookover, Beady, Flood, Schweitzer, and Wisenbaker's (1979) research with preadolescent students identified the presence of heightened academic futility among African American and working-class students. These students, perceiving weakened opportunities for future job attainment and economic success, also exhibited lower academic achievement than White and middle-class students. Brookover and colleagues (1979) found that students who exhibited higher levels of academic futility exhibited lower academic achievement. These researchers noted, "[O]ur data indicate that high-achieving schools are most likely to be characterized by students' feeling that they have control, or mastery of their academic work and that the school system is not stacked against them" (p. 143).

When working-class students experience conflict between their desire to achieve and a sense of futility and anticipation of failure, they may develop coping strategies that negatively affect their academic achievement. One such strategy is simply to manifest a **not-learning** posture. "*Not-learning* is a strategy that makes it possible for them to function on the margins of society instead of falling into madness or total despair. It helps them build a small, safe world in which feelings of being rejected by school and society can be softened. Not-learning plays a positive role and enables them to take control of their lives and get through difficult times" (Kohl, 1991, p. 9). Others researchers (for example, Willis, 1981) have found that working-class students express opposition to oppressive school structures mainly through stylistic means. Willis found that working-class students performed acts of conspiracy almost ritualistically in rejecting the standards and cultural expectations of the dominant group. He also observed working-class male students pressuring other students into reducing their academic work output as a "massive attempt to gain informal control of the work process and output" (p. 53). While perhaps providing a sense of control, such actions also inhibit achievement.

Their limited privilege may lead working-class students who want to achieve in school to believe that imitating middle-class student behavior while leaving social-class ties behind is perhaps their only option. Langston (1993) contended that because the physical conditions of working-class students' lives permit limited access to resources, "working class students seeking privilege and rewards must be willing to become middle-class impersonators" (p. 69). Unfortunately, when male working-class students engage in this form of cultural inversion, they risk being rejected by their peers. Both Eckert (1989) and Willis (1981) found that for working-class male students, compliance with teachers' wishes was registered with social-class peers as weak, acting "girlish," and lacking a backbone. The machismo persona that tends to dominate the working-class male code of conduct provides no tolerance for weakness or so-called "feminine" behavior.

Therefore, for working-class male students who wish to achieve in middle-class institutions, compliance may mean giving up ties to the working-class male community. For these working-class male students, to achieve is to be

| Exercise 13-1 | **Point of Reflection: Active and Passive Oppression** |

Directions:

1. In Column 1, list *active* acts of oppression and persons and groups who oppress (for example, Ku Klux Klan, tracking in school).
   Note: Oppression requires stratification in that some groups are subordinate to a dominant group that has the power to carry out the subjugation of other groups. As in the case of tracking, middle-class students benefit from tracking while the middle class operates, sets standards for, evaluates, and doles out rewards and outcomes in schools.
2. In Column 2, list *active* acts, groups, and people who work against oppression (for example, Civil Rights Act, Dr. Martin Luther King Jr.).
3. In Column 3, list *passive* acts of oppression (for example, not speaking up when you hear a sexist joke, not standing up when your co-workers refuse to hire a qualified candidate because he or she is a member of a minority group).
4. In Column 4, list *passive* acts that work against oppression.

You probably have noticed that there are no *passive* acts of oppression to put in Column 4. The point of this exercise is to help you to realize that one must take action—even small action—to reverse the effects of stratification. Because oppression exists in the United States, in order to be a social-justice advocate, one must be proactive in fighting against it. All advocacy that you do within your spheres of influence makes you an advocate. If you have done anything in your life to *actively* work against oppression, place your name in Column 2. Keep this list and continue to add to your list of acts of advocacy throughout your teaching career.

Active Acts of Oppression and Oppressors	*Active* Anti-Oppression Acts and Persons Who Work against Oppression	*Passive* Acts of Oppression	*Passive* Acts of Anti-Oppression

Source: Adapted from Tatum, B. D. (1992). Talking about race, learning about racism: The application of racial identity development theory in the classroom. *Harvard Educational Review, 62,* 1–24.

weak in the eyes of their male peers. Exercise 13-1 will introduce you to the concepts of active and passive oppression.

HETEROSEXISM EFFECTS ON ACHIEVEMENT: TO ACHIEVE IS TO BE STRAIGHT

While LGBTQ individuals may experience joy and empowerment upon "coming out," the experience of embracing their sexual identities may be difficult for others who may enjoy less social support. And if gay and lesbian people ingest heterosexism and negative stereotyping perpetuated in dominant culture, they may internalize hate in ways that distance them from themselves, society, and schooling (Sayce, 1995). Anxiety, depression, self-harm, suicide, and attempted suicide have all been linked to the combined effects of the experience of prejudice, discrimination, and internalized negative feelings associated with heterosexism (Health Education Authority, 1998).

Addressing oppression that confronts LGBTQ students in schools is not easy. LGBTQ students may utilize a myriad of strategies to cope with their mistreatment. As with members of other minority groups, many gay and lesbian students may try to make themselves invisible (passing as dominant-culture others) in schools so their sexual orientation will not be detected, and as a result, they limit their focus on schoolwork needed for effective learning experiences. Gay and lesbian students, on the whole, tend to have a more difficult journey through adolescence than dominant-culture students because they feel more confined by the pressure to conform to society's sexual identity definitions and believe it is likely that they will be dismissed, despised, or deleted from school life (Khayatt, 1994). Along with these factors potentially interfering with their personal and academic development, gay and lesbian students' social and emotional needs and concerns often go unrecognized and unmet in schools. For LGBTQ students who feel they must pretend to be heterosexual in order to have opportunities to be accepted and an environment in which to succeed in schools, to achieve is to be straight.

ABLEISM EFFECTS ON ACHIEVEMENT: TO ACHIEVE IS TO BE "NORMAL"

Because their disabilities are often emphasized in schools and may be seen as great deterrents to their education, students with disabilities may come to know that they will not be accepted for the strengths they have but rather for the ways in which they are able to overcome their disabilities and conform to expectations and standards for so-called "normal" students. Persons with disabilities often experience a lack of regard for contributions that develop from their differences. Schools instead tend to place a focus on finding ways for students with disabilities to perform in ways that "regular" students perform. They are taught to communicate, move, learn, and behave in ways that are as similar to dominant-culture students as they can manage. The message underlying such strategies is clearly that difference and disability equal deficiency. For students who attempt to meet these standards rather than being valued and respected for their unique contributions and being allowed to build on their different strengths within the school environment, to achieve is to be "normal" in as many ways as possible given their individual circumstances, therefore forsaking disability culture identification and values.

REDUCING THE EFFECTS OF STRATIFICATION ON MINORITY STUDENT ACHIEVEMENT

One might argue that decreasing effects of societal stratification is beyond the mission and purpose of schools. Famed educator Horace Mann would disagree. Mann noted: "Education, then, beyond all other devices of human origin, is a great equalizer of conditions of men—the balance wheel of the social machinery" ("Horace Mann Quotes," 2006). If education is to function as "the balance wheel of the social machinery," it must ensure just and equal educational experiences for every student.

Some contend that access to just and equal educational conditions merely requires that minority students model the behavior and meet expectations of members of dominant culture. This view dismisses minority students' needs to maintain cultural integrity throughout their development. Others place blame on the schools for embodying the values and standards present in larger society while ignoring the values and perspectives of minority group members. Schools have always functioned to translate the values of dominant culture and produce conditions for students to take their parents' places in society.

One cannot blame minority students or schools for minority student underachievement. Instead, both minority students and schools, when permitted opportunities through knowledge and resource appropriation to improve learning conditions, together facilitate the academic achievement of minority students. However, both minority students and school officials lack significant direct power to make substantial structural changes in the larger sociopolitical economy that are essential for solid educational reform. Further minority students and schools exist in adverse conditions in which they find themselves reacting to existing, sometimes conflicting mandates (legal, education reform, accreditation and so on) and therefore utilize often-inefficient coping strategies that serve to distance both parties. Thus, decisions and actions made by minority students and school officials, when developed mainly to endure stressful times and conditions, further serve to divide schools and minority students and therefore hinder academic progress.

The process of allocating blame to one or the other is neither useful nor productive and is not the position taken here. We have already identified a number of strategies in previous chapters to increase inclusion and to share availability of opportunity within the classroom with all students. These strategies will help to begin to reduce school and classroom effects of stratification.

While it may seem that no one person, teacher, or school can change society—topple the stratification monster that steals our honor and punishes U.S. students—the opposite is actually true. We all have people who listen to us—people who look up to and admire us. They may be our own children or our family members, our students, or our friends. These people who like and want to be like us are within our sphere of influence. We suggest that you begin to think of yourself as a powerful person. Your personal power enables you to carefully choose what you do and say as you go about your daily activities. These carefully considered actions that you make (the schools to which you send your children, the friends you choose, the magazines to which you subscribe, the causes you support) are the makings of your social justice advocacy. But activism in larger society must take place as well (Darling-Hammond, French, & Garcia-Lopez, 2002; Gay, 2003).

Exercise 13-2 | Think!

Directions: Ogbu advised that individual students can be helped when school officials and community members begin to think through an ideology that connects achieving with selling out. The goal is helping students realize that achieving in school is not an act of cultural betrayal.

1. Review the information for each cultural group presented in Chapters 5–12. Identify two unique characteristics, orientations, or behavioral styles for each cultural group that might come into play within a school setting and within the educational process and serve as barriers to their academic achievement. For example, lower-income students may exhibit great proficiency in practical knowledge, arts, and skills as compared to theoretical knowledge and skills.

2. Take the list you created and discuss with a classmate, colleague, or instructor in a small group how these factors could be addressed in schools if they were perceived as differences rather than deficiencies. How might the qualities you identify be built upon to enhance school success for these students?

We agree with Ogbu's (1992b) position that opportunity structures in society need to be changed so that subordinate minority students may have fair access to economic success. The opening of opportunity structures through lobbying efforts and legislation for minority students would provide students with incentives for academic achievement. Minority communities must also strengthen their efforts to help minority children learn to disassociate achievement striving with denial of identity. It is essential for teachers and schools to support this notion and help minority students separate the idea of "rule following" from "the selling out" and loss of their identity (see Exercise 13-2). Further, it is essential that we become advocates for all students and the right to a just, free, and equal system of education (see Chapter 14).

FROM CONCEPTS TO LIVED EXPERIENCE

Joshunda Sanders is an African American woman who describes her own personal journey through the U.S. educational system. Her study (n.d.) brings Ogbu's adaptive strategies (see Table 12-1) to life.

JOSHUNDA

When I first began kindergarten, I would sit at home and arrange my box of Crayola crayons so that they were in perfect order for the next school day. My mother tells me that I would actually pout when the weekend came because I wanted to be in school. I could never understand kids who I saw on television who *wanted* to stay home and even feigned sickness just so they wouldn't have to go to school. Later, I would realize that my love for education was the only source of organization and stability in my life, which is why I clung to it for dear life.

The institutions where I have been educated are both numerous and distinct, some small and cozy, others large and impersonal. Wherever I was, whether it was a small suburban public elementary school in Pennsylvania or a large Catholic high school in the South Bronx, I often felt like a burden to the community. As a child, I was ashamed to be poor, because I knew others looked down on you if you were poor. So, I constantly worried about how the people in my school perceived me and I tried to behave as if there was nothing out of the ordinary happening in my life.

There was heat and food at school, normally. Those two factors only added to my enthusiasm about going to school. And while my mother and I lived a rather nomadic life, my enthusiasm for learning got me into schools that my family could never have afforded on our own. But those scholarships also landed me in some sticky circumstances. For instance, I often couldn't afford to buy lunch at the private schools I attended. I usually complained of sickness so that I would be in the nurse's office during lunchtime, not sitting with my peers. It was also rare that the winter coat I had was warm enough for me to bear the frigid temperatures of the winter months.

Despite my eagerness to be "normal," my poverty followed me into the classroom. When I attended a parochial school on the Lower East Side as a 4th grader, I owned one used uniform that I wore every day and I was sure that none of the other kids' parents needed to make use of our parish's pantry to make dinner for the evening.

I was very careful to disguise these setbacks and keep them from my classmates. I learned during my earliest exposure to education in the New York City public school system that being different was something that just was not accepted. It didn't matter that most of my peers were as poor as I was. The important thing was to look as if you were not poor (as if the problems that came with being poor stemmed from looking the part). If you looked poor, you got picked on. If you had on clothes that were too big, too small or (God forbid) out of style, you were ostracized as "the poor kid"—a stigma that usually meant you were also the kid without friends, since no one wanted to be associated with the poor kid.

My attempts at disguise didn't always work. Since I was doomed socially as the "poor girl," I found my salvation in books. I was never an "outcast" as far as literature was concerned. I became a part of whatever world I wanted to be a part of. And I decided that I wanted to be a part of every world I could find. I read everything from Judy Blume's *Are You There God? It's Me, Margaret* to Claude Brown's *Manchild in the Promised Land*. I would apply myself to every assignment I received so I could be done with my work and read whichever book I was consumed with for the day.

Unfortunately, my classmates were not enthused about the attention I received from my teachers. They found ways to tease me and discourage me from doing well, taunting me for being a "bookworm" and reminding me constantly that I wasn't "cool." Even though I loved to learn and I enjoyed reading, as I approached adolescence, I decided that being "cool" might be more exciting than doing my work and having the favor of my teachers. I tried on one occasion to be "cool" by not doing my homework. I was so ashamed by the disappointment on my teacher's face that I decided being "cool" wasn't worth it.

At home, my mother had her own issues to sort out. She had to find a way to pay the rent. She had to think about where we would go when we were locked out of our apartment. She never had time to express her pride in my diligence.

The one thing that she gave to me in abundance was her own love of learning. Although she never stayed at one school long enough to get a degree, she always made the attempt because she loved to learn new things. This may have been why she didn't see my interest in school as anything special.

Because she didn't treat my excellence in school as anything out of the ordinary, I didn't know that everyone wasn't performing the way I was. I didn't know that there was anything special about my love for books. I just knew that I had finally found something I could call my own: knowledge.

By the time I realized how education had transformed my life, I had graduated as valedictorian from 6th grade. I had become used to achieving. I began to understand that I could rise above my environment using my mind.

The most phenomenal part of my educational experience has been the teachers I have been blessed to come in contact with. They helped instill in me a sense of community. Every step of the way, people have given of themselves and their resources to me. In addition to material assistance, the encouragement and enduring confidence of these adults—teachers and others—led me through experiences I could not have overcome otherwise.

The gift of confidence in the ability of a child is one of the most powerful things in the world. Because of the gifts that each one of my teachers and mentors in my life have given me, I made a way for myself out of the ghetto. I attended a prestigious boarding school, which led me to Vassar College, where I am a full-time scholarship student.

Now I know that even when things seem darkest and we feel most alone, we are still a part of a community. That meant the world to me because I went through so much as a child that I could not have survived school were it not for the people who extended their support to me.

Each of us should understand how much power we have individually. Your mere presence in a child's life can make a world of difference. Giving of yourself and your resources is what helps strengthen society. These are the lessons that my short lifetime of education has given me. And I will pass these gifts of knowledge on to others.

SUMMARY

Cultural Deprivation Theory Cultural deprivation theory blames minority student underachievement on minority students' cognitive or linguistic deficiencies, in effect blaming the victim for the discrimination s/he receives. Interventions stemming from a cultural deprivation model seek to supplement existing school curricula with often ineffective remedial education programming.

Cultural Difference Theory and Social Stratification Cultural difference theory explains minority student underachievement as a result of schools' failure to respond to the unique needs of a culturally diverse student population. Curriculum reform efforts based on this position have proven insufficient. Cultural difference and multicultural education approaches to curriculum reform fail to take into account the differential structure of opportunities that help to define

minority relations to dominant-culture White groups and social institutions in the United States.

Society is organized or stratified in hierarchies that disadvantage minority group members. Tracking (so-called "ability" grouping), grading, and ranking systems employed in our schools sort students in hierarchical, stratified ways that negatively affect all students except those enrolled in the highest tracks (honors and gifted programs).

Ogbu's Oppositional Cultures Theory and Racial Stratification Voluntary minority students are defined as persons whose ancestors came into this country by choice probably because they believed that the change would lead to better opportunities for success. Involuntary or subordinate minority students' ancestors were initially brought into U.S. society against their will, through slavery or conquest. Voluntary minority students are more willing to play by rules set by dominant culture in order to achieve. Involuntary minority students, having experienced an entire history of discrimination and injustice from dominant culture in the United States, often display distrust of traditional paths to success.

Gender Stratification Effects on Achievement   Gender is also a factor that contributes to a caste-like or subordinate minority positioning within U.S. schools. Research has documented inequitable expectations, insensitive or inadequate teacher-approval behaviors, and unfair patterns of teacher–student interaction to sustain functional sex-role stereotyping and disadvantage for female students in schools. In order to achieve, female students may, therefore, engage in gender passing by acting more like male students in order to be taken seriously.

Social-Class Stratification Effects on Achievement   U.S. society is stratified not only according to race and gender classifications, but also largely on the basis of social-class distinction. Educational researchers have documented that a statistically significant relationship exists between working-class student status and academic achievement, with poor children being more likely to be low academic achievers.

Heterosexism Effects on Achievement   Anxiety, depression, self-harm, suicide, and attempted suicide have all been linked to the combined effects of the experience of prejudice and discrimination and internalized negative feelings associated with living as a gay or lesbian person in U.S. schools. For these students, the stress and anxiety encountered inhibit their ability to learn. Perhaps one of the biggest barriers to a gay or lesbian student's learning and developing a facilitative relationship with a dominant-culture teacher is the teacher's potential lack of awareness and experience with diversity. Either through ignorance or denial, teachers are often unaware of the reality and experiences of gay and lesbian students within their classes. Further, once they are aware, they are often ill prepared to respond in ways that create safe, facilitative learning environments.

Ableism Effects on Achievement   In addition to facing isolation, persons with disabilities may also find themselves treated like they are incompetent or with disdain. Initial attempts to include students with disabilities (**mainstreaming** in particular) were ill conceived and ineffective and served to squelch efforts to improve conditions for students with disabilities because it appeared that their needs were being met. Despite the proliferation of research that dispels the myth that nondisabled students are disadvantaged by the inclusion of students with disabilities, some educators continue to resist full inclusion mandates.

Reducing the Effects of Stratification on Minority Student Achievement   Teachers and other individuals in society all have spheres of influence that can affect great change in working to reduce racial, gender, sexual orientation, and social-class stratification. Opportunity structures in society need to be changed so that subordinate minority students gain access to economic success. Subordinate minority communities need to strengthen their efforts to help subordinate minority children learn to disassociate achievement striving from denial of cultural identity.

Important Terms

cultural deprivation theory	involuntary minority	not-learning	social stratification
cultural difference theory	mainstreaming	oppositional cultures theory	voluntary minority
gender passing	multicultural education	opportunity structures	

Field Experience Activities

As suggested throughout the chapter, stratification, or the creation of caste-like systems within society and schools, is detrimental to the academic achievement of those placed in the lower strata by definition of gender, sexual orientation, ability, socioeconomic condition, and race. The creation, maintenance, and impact of this stratification may be subtle yet have powerful ramifications.

The following are a series of field experience questions related to the topics covered within this chapter. Use them to guide a classroom observation. Share your experience with your teacher, your colleagues, or your classmates.

1. Interview teachers in a local high school and ask them for their opinions (both pro and con) on the process of tracking. How many cited the differential and detrimental treatment received by those in lower tracks? What criteria for placement is employed? Are these criteria valid?
2. Observe the various extracurricular activities in which the students of an elementary or middle school are engaged. This could include sporting activities, music, art, or even field trips (for example, trips to a museum or ski trips). List these activities and then identify the potential subtle barriers that may restrict the participation of students. For example, are activities segregated based on gender? Is there provision for students who cannot afford to buy the equipment needed or the bus fare required to participate?
3. Visit a school in a suburban area and a school in an inner city or rural setting. What differences, if any, did you find in terms of available classroom resources? Compare age and condition of textbooks, facilities, desks, and even the school building itself. Compare the presence of supplementary materials or instructional aids and technological support for teaching (for example, use of audio-visual aids or blackboard). How might the resource allocation impact curriculum? Instructional strategies? Academic achievement?

Enrichment

Artiles, A. J. (2003). Special education's changing identity: Paradoxes and dilemmas in views of culture and space. *Harvard Educational Review, 73*(2), 164–202.

Beeghely, L. (2005). *The structure of social stratification in the United States* (4th edition). Boston: Allyn & Bacon.

Ferri, B., & Connor, D. J. (2005). Tools of exclusion: Race, disability, and (re)segregated education. *Teachers College Record, 107*(3), 453–474.

Levine, D., Lowe, R., Peterson, R., & Tenorio, R. (Eds.). (1995). *Rethinking schools: An agenda for change.* New York: The New Press.

Lucas, S. R. (1999). *Tracking inequality: Stratification and mobility in American high schools.* New York: Teachers College.

Connections on the Web

http://www.childalert.co.uk/absolutenm/templates/newstemplate.asp?articleid=35&zoneid=1

This interesting site will help you answer the question: Is your school "girl-friendly"?

http://www.freshschools.org/whatisFRESH.htm

This website is dedicated to focusing resources on effective school health (FRESH).

http://www.k12.wa.us/equity/jointpolicy.aspx

Prepared by the Washington State Human Rights Commission and the Washington State Superintendent of Public Instruction, this site offers information and resources for increasing education equity.

REFERENCES

Anyon, J. (1981). Schools as agencies of social legitimation. *International Journal of Political Education, 4,* 195–218.

Apple, M. W. (1989). *Teachers and texts: A political economy of class and gender relations in education.* New York: Routledge.

Ausubel, D. P. (1964). How reversible are cognitive and motivational effects of cultural deprivation? Implications for teaching the culturally deprived. *Urban Education, 1,* 16–39.

Banks, J. A., (1987). *Teaching strategies for ethnic studies* (4th edition). Boston: Allyn & Bacon.

Banks, J. A., & Banks, C. A. (Eds.). (1989). *Multicultural education: Issues & perspectives.* Boston: Allyn & Bacon.

Belenky, M. F., Clinchy, B. M., Goldberger, N. R., & Tarule, J. M. (1986). *Women's ways of knowing.* New York: Basic Books.

Bloom, B. S., Davis, A., & Hess, R. D. (Eds.). (1965). *Compensatory education for cultural deprivation.* New York: Holt, Rinehart & Winston.

Bowker, A. (1993). *Sisters in the blood: The education of women in Native America.* Newton, MA: The Women's Educational Equity Act Publishing Center.

Bowles, S., & Gintis, H. C. (1976). *Schooling in capitalist America: Educational reform and the contradictions of economic life.* New York: Basic Books.

Brookover, W. R., Beady, C., Flood, P., Schweitzer, J., & Wisenbaker, J. (1979). *School social systems and student achievement: Schools can make a difference.* Brooklyn: Praeger.

Brown, L. M. (1991). Telling a girl's life: Self-authorization as a form of resistance. In C. Gilligan, A. G. Rogers, & D. C. Tolman (Eds.), *Women, girls, and psychotherapy: Reframing resistance* (pp. 71–86). New York: Harrington Park.

Coleman, J. S., Campbell, E. Q., Hobson, C. J., McPartland, J., Mood, A. M., Weinfeld, F. D., & York, G. (1966). *Equality of educational opportunity.* Washington, DC: U.S. Office of Health, Education and Welfare.

D'Amato, J. (1987). The belly of the beast: On cultural differences, castelike status, and the politics of school. *Anthropology & Education Quarterly, 18,* 357–382.

Darling-Hammond, L., French, J., & Garcia-Lopez, S. P. (2002). *Learning to teach for social justice.* New York: Teachers College.

Debold, E., Wilson, M., & Malave, I. (1993). *Mother-daughter revolution: From betrayal to power.* New York: Addison Wesley.

Eckert, P. (1989). *Jocks and burnouts: Social categories and identity in the high school.* New York: Teachers College.

Fordham, S. (1982, December). *Cultural inversion and black children's school performance.* Paper presented at the annual meeting of the American Anthropological Association, Washington, DC.

Fordham, S. (1993). "Those loud black girls": (Black) women, silence, and gender "passing" in the academy. *Anthropology and Education Quarterly, 24,* 3–32.

Fordham, S., & Ogbu, J. U. (1986). Black students' success: Coping with the "burden of 'acting white.'" *The Urban Review, 18,* 176–206.

Friend, M., & Cook, L. (1993). Inclusion. *Instructor, 103,* 52–56.

Gans, H. (1995). Deconstructing the underclass. In P. S. Rothenberg (Ed.), *Race, class, and gender in the United States: An integrated study* (pp. 51–56). New York: St. Martin's.

Gardner, S. (1993). What's a nice working-class girl like you doing in a place like this? In M. M. Tokarczyk & E. A. Fay (Eds.), *Working-class women in the academy: Laborers in the knowledge factory* (pp. 49–54). Amherst: University of Massachusetts.

Gay, G. (Ed.). (2003). *Becoming multicultural educators: Personal journey toward professional agency.* San Francisco: Jossey Bass.

Gay, Lesbian, and Straight Education Network. (2003). *The 2003 national school climate survey: The school-related experiences of our nation's lesbian, gay, bisexual and transgender youth.* New York: Author.

Gilligan, C. (1982). *In a different voice: Psychological theory and women's development.* Cambridge, MA: Harvard University.

Goodlad, J. I. (1984). *A place called school: Prospects for future.* New York: McGraw Hill.

Greer, C. (1972). *The great school legend: A revisionist interpretation of American public education.* New York: Basic Books.

Health Education Authority. (1998). *Sexual identity.* World Mental Health Day.

Herrnstein, R. J. (1973). *The I.Q. in the meritocracy.* Boston: Little, Brown.

Hirsch, E. D. (1987). *Cultural literacy: What every American needs to know.* Boston: Houghton Mifflin.

hooks, b. (1989). *Talking black.* Boston: South End.

Horace Mann quotes. (2006). *Brainy Quote.* Retrieved from http://www.brainyquote.com/quotes/authors/h/horace_mann.html

Hudley, C. A., & Graham, S. (1995, April). *Adolescents' perceptions of achievement striving.* Paper presented at the annual meeting of the American Educational Research Association, San Francisco.

Irvine, J. J., & Irvine, R. W. (1995). Black youth in school: Individual achievement and institutional/cultural perspectives. In R. L. Taylor (Ed.), *African-American youth: Their social and economic status in the United States* (pp. 129–142). Westport, CT: Praeger.

Jensen, A. R. (1969). How much can we boost IQ and scholastic achievement? *Harvard Educational Review, 39,* 1–123.

Keating, P. (1990). Striving for sex equity in schools. In J. I. Goodlad & P. Keating (Eds.), *Access to knowledge* (pp. 91–106). New York: College Board Publications.

Kerr, B. A. (1985). *Smart girls, gifted women.* Dayton: Ohio Psychology Press.

Khayatt, D. (1994). Surviving school as a lesbian. *Gender and Education, 6*(1), 47–61.

Kohl, H. (1991). *"I won't learn from you" and other thoughts on creative maladjustment.* New York: The New Press.

Kozol, J. (1991). *Savage inequalities: Children in America's schools.* New York: Harper Perennial.

Langston, D. (1993). Who am I now? The politics of class identity. In M. M. Tokarczyk & E. A. Fay (Eds.). *Working-class women in the academy: Laborers in the knowledge factory* (pp. 60–74). Amherst: University of Massachusetts.

Lever, J. (1976). Sex differences in the games children play. *Social Problems, 23,* 478–487.

Lipsky, D. K., & Gartner, A. (1997). *Inclusion and school reform: Transforming America's classrooms.* Baltimore: Paul H. Brooks.

Mann, H. (1902). The ground of the free school system. From 10th *Annual Report as Secretary of the Massachusetts State Board of Education* (1846). Boston: Director of the Old South Work.

McCarthy, C. (1990). *Race and curriculum: Social inequality and theories and politics of difference*

in contemporary research on schooling. New York: The Falmer Press.

Meyer, J. W., & Rowan, B. (1977). Institutionalized organizations: Formal structure as myth and ceremony. *American Journal of Sociology, 83,* 340–363.

Miller, J. B. (1995). Domination and subordination. In P. S. Rothenberg (Ed.), *Race, class, and gender in the United States: An integrated study* (pp. 57–62). New York: St Martin's.

Moll, L. C., & Diaz, S. (1987). Change as the goal of educational research. *Anthropology & Education Quarterly, 18,* 300–311.

Murray, C., & Herrnstein, R. J. (1994). *The bell curve: Intelligence and class structure in America life.* New York: Free Press.

Oakes, J. (1985). *Keeping track: How schools structure inequality.* New Haven, CT: Yale University.

Ogbu, J. U. (1974). *The next generation: An ethnography of education in an urban neighborhood.* New York: Academic.

Ogbu, J. U. (1992a). Adaptation to minority status and impact on school success. *Theory into Practice, 31,* 287–295.

Ogbu, J. U. (1992b). Understanding cultural diversity and learning. *Educational Researcher, 21,* 5–24.

Ogbu, J. U. (1994). Racial stratification and education in the U.S.: Why inequality persists. *Teachers College Record, 96,* 264–298.

Persell, C. H. (1977). *Education and inequality: The roots and results of stratification in America's schools.* New York: Free Press.

Pollard, D. S. (1989). Against the odds: A profile of academic achievers from the urban underclass. *Journal of Negro Education, 58,* 297–308.

Robinson, T., & Ward, J. V. (1991). "A belief in self far greater than anyone's disbelief": Cultivating resistance among African-American female adolescents. In C. Gilligan, A. G. Rogers, & D. L. Tolman (Eds.), *Women, girls, & psychotherapy* (pp. 87–104). New York: Harrington Park.

Rothenberg, P. S. (1995). *Race, class, and gender in the United States: An integrated study.* New York: St. Martin's.

Salend, S. J. (1994). *Effective mainstreaming: Creating inclusive classrooms.* New York: Macmillan.

Sanders, J. (n.d.). School as salvation and a ticket out of the ghetto. *Horizon Magazine* [Electronic version]. Retrieved from http://www.horizonmag.com/5/adversity.htm

Sayce, L. (1995). *Breaking the link between homosexuality and mental illness: Unfinished history.* Mind discussion document.

Sennett, R., & Cobb, J. (1972). *The hidden injuries of class.* New York: Vintage.

Spring, J. (1989). *The sorting machine revisited: National educational policy since 1945.* New York: Longman.

Tatum, B. D. (1992). Talking about race, learning about racism: The application of racial identity development theory in the classroom. *Harvard Educational Review, 62,* 1–24.

Trueba, H. T. (1987). The ethnography of schooling. In H. T. Trueba (Ed.), *Success or failure? Learning and language minority student* (pp. 1–13). Cambridge, MA: Newburg House.

Uribe V., & Harbeck, K. M. (1992). Project 10 addresses needs of gay and lesbian youth. *Education Digest, 58*(2), 50–54.

Valentine, P., & Lloyd, A. (1989, March). *Living in Franklin Square: An exploration of black culture.* Paper presented at the American Educational Research Association Conference, San Francisco.

Willis, P. (1981). *Learning to labor: How working-class kids get working-class jobs.* New York: Columbia University.

Wise, A. E. (1979). *Legislated learning: The bureaucratization of the American classroom.* Los Angeles: University of California.

Wolf, A. (1977). Poverty and achievement (1991, No. 3). Washington DC: National Institute of Education.

If we would have new knowledge, we must get a whole world of new questions.

Susanne K. Langer (n.d.)

14 CHAPTER | **Transforming Knowledge**

A Primary Form of Teacher Advocacy

Educators are not only in the business of teaching what is known, but they also reinforce and, in fact, teach what they value and what is valued in society. As such, it is important for teachers to question and scrutinize all that they have come to know because they will certainly pass it along to their students as fact.

We live in the information era. Advanced technology permits rapid accumulation of information from various sources around the world. This is a time of growing research, ever-expanding information, and the potential for greater depth of understanding across all disciplines. But it is not simply new information emerging in every content area that should be of interest to educators. It is also the changing versions of "truth" and assumptions on which "truth" is built that require attention. Knowledge growth must be transformative as well as additive. Transformative knowledge growth occurs through teachers' integration of knowledge from marginalized groups who have heretofore been silenced or, at the very least, quieted by their oppression. This chapter explores what curriculum transformation is, why it is needed, and how to adopt this approach as an aspect of **social justice education** and advocacy.

CHAPTER OBJECTIVES

1. Explain what transforming knowledge and curriculum transformation involve.
2. Describe ways in which knowledge in various disciplines is restricted and distorted to support and reflect dominant-culture perspectives.
3. Explain how prevailing modes of thought and standards of judgment serve to maintain curriculum bias.
4. Describe six stages of curriculum transformation.

5. Explain why it is important to challenge not only the content (*what* we know) but also the processes by which members of dominant culture *come* to know information in your field of study.

A NEED FOR CRITICAL ANALYSIS OF SUBJECT CONTENT

In order to truly know, one must commit oneself to a continuous journey of curiosity, investigation, and critical analysis of what is presented as knowledge. Teachers stand before their classes as those who know and as those who wish to share and explore that knowledge with their students. But teachers who are knowledgeable about oppression theory and stratification effects on academic achievement must be more than simple depositories of information that has been gathered, organized, and packaged for their students' consumption. They must be aware that the best ways to actually engage students as scholars is by helping students develop skills that will allow them to construct their own knowledge through assimilation and critical analysis (Apple, 2004). Teachers and students alike must also come to understand that what is presented as "truth" cannot help but be reflective of dominant-culture values and biases of the time. Information embraced and promulgated in each field as worth knowing is always affected by the needs and wishes of the certified producers of knowledge in a given society. Because what has come to considered knowledge is necessarily incomplete and inaccurate due to the absence of minority voices, it must be replaced by knowledge that is informed by the full inclusion of the world's inhabitants. It is incumbent on teachers to reflect upon what they know and teach, allowing their curiosities to lead them to their own critical analysis of what is known in their fields in order to refine and broaden the knowledge they teach.

Clearly, the questioning and challenging of knowledge described here are not part of the typical teacher's education curriculum. Understandably, it may be scary and unsettling for teachers to criticize the very foundation on which their education rests. Content knowledge in one's field of study is knowledge believed to be solid and true. It is undoubtedly disconcerting to come to the realization it may be flawed by omissions, distortions, or inaccuracies. But as the Nigerian proverb reminds us, "Not to know is bad; not to wish to know is worse." Therefore, educators must endeavor to discover how to come to know what has been ignored and devalued in their fields (Darling-Hammond, French, & Garcia-Lopez, 2002)

TRUTHS THAT AREN'T: WHAT HAPPENS WHEN TEACHERS DO NOT QUESTION WHAT THEY KNOW AND TEACH?

When educators critically analyze knowledge in their own disciplines, they are likely to discover knowledge that has been lost or intentionally concealed in order to support dominant-culture perspectives and interests. The desire to support a particular perspective can be blatant and intentional, as in the case of many controversial topics in science and social studies curricula. Evolution, birth control, and various incidents in U.S. history are excluded from curricula in support of a particular set of values stemming from dominant-culture best interests. For instance, the example of African American soldiers in the Civil War is clear. "Even in the 1930s, evidence of their contributions was plain for all to see in the primary sources.... Depression-era textbooks, however, omitted those facts, not because they were unknown but because including important acts by African Americans did not mirror the attitudes of [W]hite society" (Loewen, 1995, p. 286). Hidden "truths" that you will discover in your field are much more likely to result from less obvious and more insidious actions. Consider, the primary manner in which information, and therefore knowledge, is conveyed to students.

"Who controls the present, controls the past" (Orwell, 1949, p. 35). Knowledge in each discipline is legitimized by its presence in textbooks. In many instances, that which is not contained in textbooks is not transmitted as knowledge to students. Apple (1989) noted that curricula in most U.S. schools are not defined by teachers, "courses of study or suggested programs, but by one particular artifact, the standardized, grade-level-specific text" (p. 85).

You might be asking yourself why this would be a problem. It is a problem for at least two reasons. First, when teachers rely heavily on textbooks for instruction, they do not take responsibility for organizing their courses of study to carry out learning theories they endorse and meet the pedagogical needs of their students. Therefore, someone else (the textbook author or editor) decides what and often how they teach subjects. Second, textbooks cannot help but reproduce perspectives that reflect dominant-culture views unless they actively seek (as this text does) to do so by challenging assumptions on which bodies of knowledge are based and in so doing provide worldviews (voices) of marginalized others. Teachers cannot assume that textbooks are written as unbiased, comprehensive compendiums of information. What is included and what is excluded from textbooks often mirrors biases that permeate society. Consider the following process: Textbook companies seek to have their textbooks adopted by school districts, so they can sell large numbers of books to the biggest consumers. Textbooks are selected by school districts based on reviews from state and federal agencies that will pay a substantial amount of the textbook price for school districts that elect to use textbooks they approve. Textbook publishers aim their efforts to meet with the approval of state and federal agencies. The result of these exchanges—one feeding into the next—is the production, distribution, and reception of textbooks that reproduce and inculcate dominant-culture values and views of what constitutes knowledge in every field of study (Apple, 1989). Standardized tests and mandated curricula that stem from texts approved for K–12 instruction provide another arena in which bias is sure to occur; when texts contain knowledge that omits and discredits minorities, standardized curricula and tests stemming from those texts will result in biased outcomes that further exclude and disadvantage minority students. One cannot blame textbook publishers for doing what is necessary to sell their products. They must utilize strategies that will garner the approval of those in power—their dominant-culture consumers.

Controlling the record of society's past is particularly important to **dominant-culture** members in stratified societies. (Stratification that exists in U.S. society is explained in Chapter 13.) In addition to other controls, maintaining a stratified system also requires control over ways that citizens perceive the system. If dominant-culture members are depicted such that their privilege is historically unjustified, for example, they face embarrassment and a potential loss of status. As such, dominant culture has a vested interest in maintaining control of text materials that will contain the record of the times. Clearly, teachers must understand how knowledge presented in textbooks is affected by stratification (Apple, 1982) and take steps to critically analyze textbooks, frequently supplementing them with knowledge from other sources.

WHAT DOES CURRICULUM TRANSFORMATION INVOLVE?

Effective educators are careful not to simply teach preset curricula conceived by someone else; instead, they engage in **curriculum transformation**. To do this, they recognize that what is accepted as knowledge in their disciplines was derived from a system of knowing that is influenced, for the most part, by the dominant-culture perspective. But they do not stop there. Beyond acknowledging the influence of dominant culture on curricula, they critically examine that curricula.

For example, the widespread use of the universal referent is another way in which dominant culture maintains control of knowledge. The universal referent puts the "man" in *mankind*—a term used to describe all the diverse women and men in the world. The problem with this type of false **universality** has worked to perpetuate the widespread exclusion of women and people of color from U.S. curricula because it is the same exclusion that permits humanity (i.e. "man"kind) to be equated with maleness. Such partiality may seem benign, but it serves to endorse forms of thinking and knowledge embraced by the dominant culture while discrediting the contributions, thinking, and perspectives (for example, the Harlem Renaissance, Latino poetry, women's literature) of minority artists, researchers, and scholars. Teachers must begin to identify errors in thinking such as this, errors so familiar as to be virtually invisible. Such awareness will lead to teachers' investigating and recognizing knowledge that has not been uncovered before in their fields but that sheds light on valued and important truths. For this kind of discovery (and ultimate transformation of knowledge) to take place, voices of marginalized groups who historically have been silenced must be heard and included (Minnich, 1990).

> As long as educators and scholars refrain from engaging in critique and correction of faulty assumptions in the thinking within curricula, the framework of meaning behind particular questions of what and how to teach will continue to be inhospitable

to those who have been excluded from knowledge and knowledge-making. Marginalized groups will also systematically be excluded from effective participation in exercising power in dominant culture. These voices will continue to be excluded from curricula and will likely to be forgotten and to continue to be devalued. (Minnich, 1990, pp. 11–12)

CURRICULUM TRANSFORMATION CHALLENGES

To transform curricula, educators must place emphasis not simply on adding to what is currently taught in schools but on changing it from the ground up. To merely add information about marginalized groups (women, minorities, gay and lesbian people) as a subset of or compliment to traditional knowledge is ineffective and inadequate (see Case Illustration 14-1). Such an approach perpetuates a system built on conceptual errors that exclude meanings and content from others who exist outside dominant culture in the margins of society. The practice of simply including a member of a marginalized group

---

Case Illustration 14-1

Understanding Moral Development: An Example of Ways to Expand What Is Known and Valued in the Fields of Education and Psychology

A good example of the impact of the influence of dominant-culture ways of knowing on knowledge is the treatment of the works of Lawrence Kohlberg and Carol Gilligan in the fields of education and psychology. Kohlberg's theory of moral development was, and still is, accepted as a universal theory for understanding all human moral development. When Gilligan (1982) researched and reported female moral development and outlined a model that has become highly respected knowledge about the way female moral decision making develops, it called into question Kohlberg's application of his model for understanding female moral development. Gilligan's theory posits that gender socialization in the United States has shaped the way women in U.S. society are required to think and act, and that gender socialization therefore affects women's moral decision making. Until Gilligan provided this knowledge, compiled using research methods qualitatively different from the traditional scientific methods used by Kohlberg and other dominant-culture researchers, women were disadvantaged by Kohlberg's theory that identified females as less moral than men. Using Kohlberg's theory, women

tended to be classified in Stage Three, at which their moral decisions were said to be based on pleasing others, while men were most commonly classified at Stage Four, at which moral decisions were said to be based on the need to conform to laws established in society for the sake of doing what is considered "right." Gilligan looked beyond traditional ways of thinking and reasoning to modify her research methods such that they met accepted standards of "making sense" in the behavioral sciences field while introducing a different way of knowing, thinking, reasoning, and perceiving that included the voices of adolescent girls and women to provide rich detail and insight into the thoughts and feelings that led to their moral decision making. Gilligan's model is now the standard, the accepted and highly regarded scholarship in the field of moral development. Yet, even today in most education and psychology textbooks, Kohlberg's theory is emphasized, often taking up most of an entire chapter on moral development, while Gilligan's theory is presented secondarily, often as a two-paragraph supplement to the knowledge on moral development that Kohlberg provides.

| Exercise 14-1 | **Point of Reflection: Where Does What We Know Come From?** |

Directions: Think for a minute about the adage, "Children should be seen and not heard." Ask yourself:

a. Who in society does this line of thinking benefit?

b. What might be the repercussions of such a view on children's cognitive and social development or knowledge?

c. How does such thinking cause harm and limit parents' relationships with their children or other relations and understandings?

1. Consider an adage or "truth" that is widely known in your field (for example, in the field of science: "Quantitative research is more credible than qualitative research"; in biology: "Field guide books on birds feature only the pictures of male birds because they are more colorful and therefore easier to identify in nature for study of the species.") Using the same three questions as examples, provide questions relevant to the adage you have identified from your field of study.

2. Discuss your revelations with your classmates, colleagues, or your instructor.

(**tokenism**) in curricula reveals a profound lack of understanding of the nature and depth of the problem of exclusion. While tokenism provides evidence of an awareness of exclusion as a problem, it minimizes the extent and complexity of the problem. To add a few minority contributions to a course of study does not solve the problem. Ultimately, tokenism leaves the systems that produced and maintained exclusion and devaluation of minorities untouched. As Minnich (1990) points out:

> [D]iscoveries indicating the world is round did not merely supplement knowledge shaped by and supportive of the theory that the world was flat. Likewise, work by and about women, persons with disabilities, and people of color is not just missing from the academic canon: it is incompatible with some of the canon's basic founding assumptions. (p. 30)

Transforming curricula is, in fact, a radical political act. It is radical because it requires questioning all that one knows to be true and replacing it with information coming from nontraditional sources that are devalued and silenced in society. When curriculum transformation is accomplished, however, advocacy occurs. In effect, by listening to these voices and integrating their teachings, minority groups are empowered—provided with opportunities to contribute evidence and reasoning that had previously been denied them. Exercise 14-1 will help you begin this process for your particular field of study.

How Established Modes of Thought Perpetuate Curriculum Bias

Major contributors to the problem of curriculum bias are the processes employed to construct knowledge (Apple, 2004). Scholarship that leads to the production of knowledge operates from an orientation in which only objective, rational scientific methods of inquiry are accredited. Because this requirement

Exercise 14-2 | Classroom Applications: Content Analysis

Directions: Go to a library and obtain a current textbook dealing with one of the following content areas: American history, biology, or health sciences. Then complete the following:

1. Focusing on only one chapter of the textbook you chose, answer the following:

   a. How are Native Americans depicted and/or other marginalized groups completely excluded from awareness in the content? Repeat the question for African Americans, Latinos, Asian-Americans, and so on.

   b. In what ways are marginalized groups relevant to the discussion presented in the chapter even though they are not addressed (included) or sufficiently addressed (included)?

2. With your colleagues, classmates, or instructor, discuss who benefits from the knowledge presented in the textbook chapter you critically analyzed and who would benefit if what you identified in 1 was taken into account.

3. Now research Native American fables, African American poetry, and/or other typically excluded sources of knowledge. Write a reflection about what you learned that you would not have known if you had not read it in these works.

exists, it excludes thinkers who have not come to know in those ways. Using such criteria for the production of legitimate knowledge, content in slave diaries, for example, is excluded. When such knowledge is ignored, only a small part of a picture is considered. Loewen's (1995) *Lies My Teacher Told Me: Everything Your American History Textbook Got Wrong* retells U.S. history by replacing myths and misinformation contained in mainstream high school textbooks with a thorough presentation of documented events, enriched by plantation records, speeches, city directories, songs, photographs, newspaper articles, diaries, letters, and secondary works. This book is an excellent example of curriculum transformation and integration. The nontraditional sources featured throughout provide testimony that is not simply added to what was commonly known and called U.S. history. Instead, the previously ignored voices provide countless windows (each with a different vantage point) for peering into the world of U.S. history that were previously closed. The result is a new information, new knowledge, new truths. Exercise 14-2 will teach you how to examine content for bias.

Limited by Standards of Judgment

Sometimes, even well-intentioned educators fall prey to standards reinforced by the status quo when attempting to include minority perspectives in their curricula. Consider, for example, the teacher who, while wishing to integrate minority voices and perspectives in her curricula finds herself frustrated by the fact that she can find no artists or writers who are people of color or persons with disabilities to include. What this teacher fails to realize is that her inability to include minority perspectives is not a result of the absence of talented minorities but rather the result of the assumption and standard used to define "great" artists or writers worthy of inclusion. This teacher is operating with the

Exercise 14-3 | **Field Experience: Investigating Knowledge**

Directions: Research a gender topic (such as gender effects on communication or gender effects on learning). Find at least five research articles on the gender topic of your choice, then complete the following steps.

1. Read each article, identifying where the researchers agree and disagree about what is presented as knowledge on your topic (for example, does gender affect the way students learn? If yes, why and how do the different researchers explain their position?).

2. After summarizing four findings (the major positions with supporting evidence) from your research, think about who in society benefits from the different positions taken by each of the researchers featured in the articles.

3. Discuss with your classmates, colleagues, or your instructor how what you have uncovered and analyzed affects what you know about your topic. Decide, if you were to teach the material you researched, what you would teach as the truth about the topic and why.

assumption that in order for minorities to be considered great, they must meet existing standards for "greatness." Such judgments assume the centrality of White, middle-class, abled men and "tradition" as it has come to be known as a universal (Minnich, 1990), leaving little room for alternative values and standards.

If minorities create art, write, and think in modes that are not accepted as those prescribed and valued as reputable means for coming to know, then their contributions to the construction of knowledge are ignored and excluded. While amazingly off-base, this is a pervasive way of thinking among educators. Here is a case of victim blaming—blaming minorities for not being talented artists, writers, and leaders when they face enormous obstacles in their quests to achieve amid discrimination and oppression in the "mis-education system" (as we have noted in Parts 1 and 2 of the text) In addition, they are not given credit for their accomplishments because the system that judges them, that awards value, is so biased it cannot see or hear their accomplishments. Exercise 14-3 will show you how to recognize such bias and misinformation.

THINKING THROUGH CURRICULUM TRANSFORMATION

Curriculum transformation begins with questioning one's own discipline and assumptions about how knowledge comes to be in that field. Schuster and Van Dyne (1984) identified six stages of the curriculum transformation process:

Stage 1: The absence of the marginalized group is not noticed. There is no knowledge of the need for nor the belief in curriculum transformation.

Stage 2: Teachers begin a search for missing voices in their curricula. Teachers believe their students need diverse role models at this stage and engage in a search of minority figures who are good enough to be included in their programs of study.

Stage 3: Teachers begin to question why they have trouble finding leaders, writers, artists, and so on who are members of marginalized groups to include in their curricula.

Stage 4: Teachers recognize that to document the experiences of the marginalized means documenting everything—for marginalized people have always been a part of human life. Instead of looking at the productions and outcomes of minority group member contributions to knowledge, teachers ask why marginalized groups and their perspectives are devalued and not included in their curricula. The answers to this question lead teachers to uncover biased processes and assumptions in their fields. It is during this stage that teachers may experience student resistance as classrooms heat up when discussions occur about oppression, subordination, and understanding the experiences of marginalized groups.

Stage 5: Teachers ask, "How valid are current definitions of standards of excellence, historical periods, and norms of behaviors within my discipline?" They reshape organizing questions in their disciplines to account for diversity.

> Teachers, at this stage, give up the need for content that had seemed most stable, efficient, and free of personal values, to use gender, race, sexual orientation and social class as primary categories of analysis in order to transform perspectives on current data and concepts. This stage brings the classroom into a realization of the loss of old certainties. The gains at this stage include the recovery of meaningful historical and social context, the discovery of previously invisible dimensions of subjects, and access to tools of analysis that expose students to formerly suppressed material. (p. 425)

Exercise 14-4 | Classroom Applications: Questions to Guide Curriculum Transformation

Directions: The following are questions developed by Fiol-Matta (1994, p. 142) as a litmus test for educators to guide curriculum transformation. Your task is to select a lesson plan you have taught before or will teach at some point in your life. You can find published lesson plans in every field of education that you can use to some extent if you do not have lessons that you have created. Then, critically analyze the plan using the questions.

1. What previously excluded groups have I included, and where in the course outline do they appear?

2. How often do I talk about these groups in class discussion instead of letting them speak for themselves? How much new knowledge by women and people of color have I included?

3. How often have I sought out colleagues who are more knowledgeable about women and people of color to critique concepts and discuss issues or concerns that are contained in the content of my course?

4. What tangible change can I see in my revised lesson/syllabus that reflects my new thinking? The new scholarship?

5. What are the race, gender, and class underpinnings of my course? Where are they manifested?

Note: You can use these same questions to analyze an entire curriculum or syllabus. Please consider doing just that before you begin to teach any body of knowledge.

Stage 6: Process, instead of products, is emphasized. Courses taught at this stage include inquiries about how an awareness of race, gender, social class, ability status and sexual orientation leads teachers and students to other sources of evidence.

A specific set of guiding questions that can help teachers begin the process of transforming curriculum is listed in Exercise 14-4. Clearly, transforming curricula results in fundamental change. It is a process that will result in changing what, how, and in what order one teaches. It will change what is emphasized, what is valued, who is credited, and why one even cares about the content presented to students.

FROM CONCEPTS TO LIVED EXPERIENCE

The following dialogue was an exchange between a 1st-grade teacher and Leigh Hall ("Ask the Literacy Teacher," n.d.). As you read the teacher's letter, see if you can identify how she has been influenced by dominant-culture values and why she is having trouble seeing things from her students' perspectives. Identify the knowledge that the 1st-grade teacher holds to be true about child development, literacy, and learning theory as you read.

Dear Literacy Teacher,

I have taught 1st grade for six years and in my short time of teaching things are getting worse! I teach in Texas where students in grades 3–12 are expected to pass state tests to pass to the next grade. My frustration is in the parents and dealing with beginning readers. What does one do when there is absolutely no reinforcement of reading skills outside of school? I have explained to parents the importance of my students being able to read on a 1st-grade level by May or they will be retained, but still I get no response.

To help these students, I tutor everyday after school for 45 minutes—they attend tutoring during school for 45 minutes—and I work with each child in a small group daily for 25 minutes (one-on-one) and still they make no progress. The body of children I work with is Hispanic, low socioeconomic children whose parents are on welfare and seem uninterested. I'm at my wits end to make these students successful, but I feel I'm getting nowhere. At this point in the year, I have seven children who are so far behind there's little hope for catching up. What can I do????? I've even considered leaving this profession because it's harder and harder every year. I use phonics programs, early literacy, whole language, and write-to-read programs with little results. The stress is baring [sic] down.

Signed,

Help

Dear Help,

As a former Texas teacher I understand what you are talking about! Your letter raises many issues, three of which I would like to deal with here: parent involvement, poverty and success.

The problem that you described around parent involvement is a common one that many teachers feel frustrated about. What solutions are out there? While there are no definitive answers, I do have some suggestions that could get you thinking about parent involvement in a new and different way. Consider these questions:

1. What is your cultural background and what are your expectations? Many teachers are white, female and middle class. They tend to expect families that are not white and/or middle class to respond in the same manner that they would. Determine what your expectations for parents and families are. Try to articulate why you hold these expectations and where they come from. Think about how your own cultural background and experiences with school as a child might play a part in these ideas.

2. What is the background of the families that you serve? You already know that they are Hispanic. Do you know if English is spoken in the home? If the families do not speak English, then it would not be realistic to expect them to work with their children on English-only activities. In thinking about this question further, it would be helpful to know the makeup of the family (how many children in the home ... how many adults ... etc.) and the schedules that they keep. Do they work at night and sleep during the day? Once you have a solid understanding of these families then you can begin to consider strategies for getting them involved in school. This, of course, is only a beginning.

The second issue that you raised deals with poverty. You claim that most of your students come from homes of low socioeconomic background whose parents are on welfare and seem uninterested. First, the term *low socio-economic background* is just that—a term. It is a way to sort and classify people. I encourage you to talk to the families whose children you serve. If you learn about what their lives were like in Mexico, you may find that they are not poor people. Poverty [...] is relative. Usually these families have a great deal more living at what we consider to be below the line of poverty than if they were still living in Mexico. The idea that they "seem uninterested" is just that—an idea. Your attempts to connect with parents may have failed but that does not mean that these parents do not care about their children's education. I urge you to return to the two questions I stated earlier and begin to consider other routes that you can try to get parents involved.

Finally you are worried about students who are not being successful. How do you define success? We tend to live in a society that expects all students to be functioning at the same level in the same place at the same time. Yet I am sure you know that this is just not possible. Kids learn at their own pace. If your students are in the process of learning English, then you know that this only adds to the amount of time it will take them to become proficient in reading and writing. Perhaps then success could be seen by how much they can do at the end of the year as opposed to the beginning or even a month ago. With all the hard work you do tutoring it sounds like they must have made some progress! Keep documentation that shows how they progress and the successes that they have made. Not only will this make you feel better, it can serve as a way to communicate to parents and administrators what your students have accomplished!

The Literacy Teacher

Now that you have read Leigh Hall's response to the first-grade teacher, see if you can identify the curriculum transformation steps she is suggesting. Exercise 14-5 will help you apply what you have learned about curriculum transformation in this chapter.

| Exercise 14-5 | Classroom Applications: Identifying Steps for Transforming Curricula |

Directions: Work with your instructor, your classmates, or your colleagues to identify the knowledge transformation principles (discussed in this chapter) Leigh Hall suggests in her response. Use language from Schuster and Van Dyne's (1984) six stages of curriculum transformation to explain where in the stage theory the 1st-grade teacher is functioning and what steps that she must take to begin to transform her curricula.

SUMMARY

A Need for Critical Analysis of Subject Content Teachers must reflect upon what they know and teach. They must critically analyze and challenge what is known in efforts to refine and broaden knowledge. Teachers must question and challenge principles they have come to know to open themselves to new ways of knowing and different perspectives.

Truths That Aren't: What Happens When Teachers Do Not Question What They Know and Teach Knowledge continues to be lost or intentionally concealed in order to support dominant-culture perspectives and interests. The desire to support a particular perspective can be blatant and intentional, as in school districts that promote a creationist approach—excluding theories of evolution. Truth is more often distorted in less obvious and more insidious ways, such as allowing textbooks (which reflect dominant-culture bias) to dictate instruction.

What Does Curriculum Transformation Involve? The errors of exclusion and universality lead to the loss of knowledge. For example, assuming the issues of one group apply to all (such as equating humanity with maleness—putting the "man" in *mankind*) represents bias so deeply embedded that it is invisible to most educators. Educators who are concerned with **transforming knowledge** need to identify errors in thinking and investigate and recognize perspectives that have not been uncovered in their disciplines.

Curriculum Transformation Challenges To transform curriculum, educators must place emphasis not on adding to what is currently occurring in schools but on changing it. Simply adding knowledge about marginalized groups (women, minorities, gay and lesbian people) as a subset of or compliment to traditional knowledge is ineffective and inadequate because it continues to rest within a system built on conceptual errors that exclude meanings and content from others outside dominant culture. Transforming curriculum is a radical political act. It is radical because it requires questioning all that we have known to be the whole truth and replacing it with information coming from sources that have for centuries been devalued and silenced.

Thinking through Curriculum Transformation In Stage 1 of Schuster and Van Dyne's (1984) six stages of curriculum transformation, there is no knowledge of the need for nor the belief in curriculum transformation; during Stage 2, teachers begin a search for missing voices in their curricula; in Stage 3, teachers begin to have trouble finding members of minority groups who are leaders, writers and artists that they can include in their curricula; when they reach Stage 4, teachers ask why marginalized groups and their perspectives are devalued in their curricula; at Stage 5, teachers give up the need for content that had seemed most stable, efficient, and free of personal values to use gender, race, sexual orientation, and social class as primary categories of analysis in order to transform perspectives on current data and concepts; and finally in Stage 6, process, instead of products, is emphasized. Courses taught at this stage include inquiries about how an awareness of race, gender, social class, and sexual orientation suggest other sources of evidence.

Important Terms

curriculum transformation

dominant culture

established modes of thought

social justice education

standards of judgment

tokenism

transforming knowledge

universality

Field Experience Activities

Observe a teacher in action and assess the degree to which he/she integrates curriculum transformation strategies. Use the following questions as your observation guide. When finished, discuss your observations with your classmates, colleagues, or instructor. For all those items to which the answer is "no," brainstorm ways you could create a more generative learning environment

1. In the classroom you observed, did students
   a. Have a chance to use examples and experiences that draw on their own interests?
   b. Have exposure to problems and illustrations grounded in real-life situations?

2. Did the teacher
   a. Use language that was inclusive of different students' backgrounds?
   b. Provide activities for students to develop ideas that conflicted with what he or she presented as knowledge?
   c. Allow adequate wait time (3–5 seconds) for students to answer questions?
   d. Encourage students to question what she or he taught?
   e. Provide learning activities to help students gain critical analysis skills?

Enrichment

Adams, M., Bell, L. A., & Griffin, P. (Eds.). (1997). *Teaching for diversity and social justice: A sourcebook for teachers and trainers.* New York: Routledge.

Chenoweth, T. G., & Everhart, R. B. (2002). *Navigating comprehensive school change: A guide for the perplexed.* Larchmont, NY: Eye on Education.

Loewen, J. (1995). *Lies my teacher told me: Everything your American history textbook got wrong.* New York: The New Press.

Mayberry, J. J. (1996). *Teaching what you're not. Identity politics in higher education.* New York: New York University.

Sparks, L. D., & Phillips, C. B. (1997). *Teaching/learning anti-racism: A developmental approach.* New York: Teachers College.

Connections on the Web

http://www.concernamerica.org/CANews.html

This quarterly newsletter entitled *With Eyes to See* helps teachers connect their curriculum with peace and justice issues. Each newsletter focuses on a peace and justice concept, providing information, stories, classroom activities, and lists of resources relating to the concepts.

http://www.diversityweb.org/Digest/W97/advice.html

This website for Diversity Digest provides information and advice to guide curriculum transformation.

http://www.edchange.org/multicultural/sites/curriculum.html

EdChange Multicultural Pavilion is a website with links to supportive information on curriculum transformation and cultural diversity.

www.tolerance.org

This site provides news and information for teachers, parents, teens, and children interested in fighting hatred and promoting the teaching of tolerance.

REFERENCES

Adams, M. (1995). Pedagogical frameworks for social justice education. In M. Adams, L. A. Bell, & P. Griffin (Eds.), *Teaching for diversity and social justice: A sourcebook* (pp. 30–43). New York: Routledge.

Ahlquist, R. (1991). Manifestations of inequality: Overcoming resistance in a multicultural foundations course. In C. Grant (Ed.), *Research and multicultural education* (pp. 89–105). London: Falmer.

Apple, M. W. (1982). *Education and power.* Boston: Routledge & Kegan Paul.

Apple, M. W. (1989). *Teachers and texts: A political economy of class and gender relations in education.* New York: Routledge.

Apple, M. W. (2004). *Ideology and curriculum* (3rd edition). New York: Routledge Falmer.

Ask the literacy teacher. (n.d.). Retrieved from http://teachers.net/gazette/MAR02/hall.html

Darling-Hammond, L., French, J., & Garcia-Lopez, S. P. (2002). *Learning to teach for social justice.* New York: Teachers College.

Dee, J. R., & Henkin, A. B. (2002). Assessing dispositions toward cultural diversity among pre-service teachers. *Urban Education, 37,* 22–40.

Fiol-Matta, L. (1994). Litmus tests for curriculum transformation. In L. Fiol-Matta & M. Chamberlain (Eds.), *Women of color and the multicultural curriculum.* New York: New York Press.

Gay, G. (1986). Multicultural teacher education. In J. Banks & L. Lynch (Eds.), *Multicultural education in western societies* (pp. 154–177). New York: Praeger.

Gilligan, C. (1977). In a different voice: Women's conception of self and morality. *Harvard Educational review, 47,* 481–517.

Gilligan, C. (1982). *In a different voice.* Cambridge, MA: Harvard University.

Golembiewski, R. T., & Blumberg, A. (1977). *Sensitivity training and the laboratory approach: Readings about concepts and applications.* Itasca, IL: F. E. Peacock.

Kaplan, L., & Edelfelt, R. (Eds.). (1996). *Teachers for the new millennium.* Thousand Oaks, CA: Corwin.

Kohlberg, L. (1963). The development of children's orientation toward moral order: Sequence in the development of human thought. *Vita Humana, 6,* 670–677.

Kohlberg, L. (1984). *Essays on moral development: Vol. 2. The psychology of moral development.* New York: Harper.

Knapp, M., Shields, P., & Turnbull, M. (1995). Academic challenge in high-poverty classrooms. *Phi Delta Kappan, 76,* 770–776.

Kushner, K., & Brislin, R. (1985). Bridging gaps: Cross-cultural training in teacher education. *Journal of Teacher Education, 37,* 51–54.

Susanne K. Langer quotes. (2006). *ThinkExist.com quotations.* Retrieved September 4, 2006, from http://einstein/quotes/susanne_k._langer/

Loewen, J. (1995). *Lies my teacher told me: Everything your American history textbook got wrong.* New York: The New Press.

Melnick, S., & Zeichner, K. (1995). *Teacher education for cultural diversity.* East Lansing, MI: National Center for Research on Teacher Learning.

Minnich, E. (1990). *Transforming knowledge.* Philadelphia: Temple University.

National Center for Education Statistics. (1999). *Teacher quality: A report on the preparation and qualifications of public school teachers.* NCES No. 1999080. Washington, DC: U.S. Department of Education.

Orwell, G. (1949). *1984.* New York: Harcourt Brace.

Sarason, S. (1990). *The predictable failure of educational reform: Can we change course before it's too late?* San Francisco: Jossey Bass.

Schuster, M., & Van Dyne, S. (1984). Placing women in the liberal arts: Stages of curriculum transformation. *Harvard Educational Review, 54*(4), 413–419.

Swartz, E. (2003). Teaching White preservice teachers: Pedagogy for change. *Urban Education, 38*(3), 255–278.

Zeichner, K. (1993). *Educating teachers for cultural diversity: NCRTL Special Report.* East Lansing: Michigan State University, National Center for Research on Teacher Learning.

Transformative pedagogy turns the lens on social realities. These are, in turn, critically analyzed by students through a process of collaborative dialogue. Using the cultural capital of the students, classrooms become a forum in which students are able to voice opinions which have been silenced within practices of traditional pedagogy. This process can be both validating and empowering as students come to learn that their actions can enable change.

Ena Lee and Caterina Reitano (n.d.)
"A Critical Pedagogy Approach: Incorporating Technology to De/Reconstruct Culture in the Language Classroom"

Moving from Me to We

CHAPTER **15**

Advocacy for Educators

Throughout the text, we have demonstrated that the composition of classrooms, schools, and society is wonderfully diverse. In fact, minority students are projected to make up more than 46 percent of the nation's student population by 2020 (Pallas, Natriello, & McDill, 1989). Is it enough for school officials to be aware of diversity, or should they also be charged to enrich the lives of all of students by integrating diversity into their curricula? Is it teachers' primary goal to teach content matter? Or are they to be dedicated to teaching the whole student—helping to make significant academic and social changes in the lives of students? Are teachers to become teacher advocates who employ **transformative pedagogy** while validating and empowering their students to learn in an equitable environment? Is it true that schools' actions can actually affect social change that results in social justice?

If it is school officials' charge to influence and change lives, they must become student advocates. Most educators are keenly aware of the existence and impact of prejudice, discrimination, and oppression. However, their strategies for addressing these issues have often been limited to the addition of information about diverse peoples in their lessons. Teaching students about different cultural groups is not a bad thing; by itself, it is simply inadequate. It is necessary but not sufficient. Prejudice, discrimination, and oppression thrive on ignorance and inaction. To work to decrease the isms in society requires action—proactive steps taken to advocate for all students and especially for those whose voices have been silenced. Educators must act, and act with a precision that is informed by a thorough understanding of diversity. It is essential that they take steps to increase educational opportunities and equity for all students in order to serve the missions they promise to fulfill when they become educators. To do so, they must become advocates who know and effectively integrate diversity.

The current chapter examines the qualities of educators as advocates—advocates for educational equity for all students, advocates for reversing overt and covert forces of oppression within classrooms, within schools, and within communities.

CHAPTER OBJECTIVES

1. Describe the need for educators to become advocates for integrating diversity.
2. Identify reasons for system resistance to change.
3. Describe principles to be followed when working as agents of change.
4. List forms of advocacy in classrooms.
5. List forms of advocacy in schools.
6. Create a personal **activism plan** for helping members of marginalized groups.

WHY ADVOCATE?

It certainly appears that it would be easier to ignore oppression created by the *isms* that exist in society and schools. However, to do so would not have a benign outcome. Failure to **advocate** for equality within classrooms and schools not only negatively affects those oppressed by the *isms* but also disadvantages all students, humankind, and the production of scholarship worldwide as it diminishes the significance and therefore supports the continuance of suppression of knowledge in society. Educators cannot simply take a passive stance. They must do more than merely have an awareness of the issues concerning minority students in schools; they must actively confront the oppressive forces that interfere with their students' academic achievement.

Many educators, while recognizing the need to be proactive, exhibit real anxiety about that possibility. Often, this anxiety is rooted in their perceptions about what it means to be an advocate (see Exercise 15-1). For many, the thought of acting as an advocate conjures images of conflict, hostility, of an "us vs. them" encounter. This need not be the case. Social justice educators are advocates for equality. They seek to fulfill schools' missions to effectively educate all students within equitable learning environments (see Exercise 15-2). And while the fulfillment of school missions might seem to be something all school officials routinely pursue, that is not always the case. So, if social justice advocacy is good for all and not meant to be adversarial, why does it divide groups of people?

Advocacy, by definition, necessitates change. Schools, like all organizational systems, are known for their tendencies to resist any change, particularly

| Exercise 15-1 | Point of Reflection: Extreme Challenge |

Directions: Consider this list of statements that educator allies and advocates have made in the past as they began their journeys to become effective social justice advocates. Mark those that fit with the way you currently feel about becoming or continuing as an educator advocate.

1. I'm afraid that if I become a social justice advocate:

   _____People will think I'm so radical that they will be afraid to associate with me.

   _____My family and/or friends will not like me as much—they'll think I'm judging them for not being activists.

   _____My students will think I'm pushing my own personal social agenda on them during class time. Why should I expect them to have the same passions and causes I have chosen?

   _____I don't really know enough about diversity to do a good job of implementing social justice education in my classroom/school—I don't know all the facts, statistics, and theories.

   _____My students might ask me questions about diversity that I can't answer. I'll feel uncomfortable talking about racism and the other *isms*, and my students might even start experiencing conflict with each other if I bring these topics up in class/school.

   _____I haven't experienced enough diversity in my life and been exposed to enough difference to be a good advocate. I might insult marginalized groups when I try to interact with them, and I'll be seen as someone who doesn't "walk the talk"— I'll be found out as a fraud who doesn't really know what he/she is talking about in terms of diversity.

   _____I'm not sure if I really believe in social justice. I kind of think everyone should just be treated equally and we shouldn't call attention to differences among students.

2. After you have indicated which statements you agree with, discuss your feelings with your instructor, your classmates, or your colleagues in small-group discussion.

3. Write a reflection that explains what would make becoming or continuing as a social justice advocate difficult for you, then list actions you believe you need to take to move you one step closer to becoming a better social justice advocate.

---

significant change, in the ways they operate (Argyris, 1970; Bennis, 1969; Blake & Mouton, 1976; de Jager, 2001; Wickstrom & Witt, 1993). Change is viewed as a threat not just to the organization's stability but to its very identity—its very existence. Any force, person, or idea that would indicate the existing system should be changed, be it as small as expanding or modifying a job definition or as large and complicated as decentralizing the form of management or changing curriculum, runs contrary to the system's self-maintenance goal (stability of the system) and evokes **system self-preservation resistance** (Napierkowski & Parsons, 1995). Moving to the new and different also requires an expenditure of great energy. If change is to occur, schools must redefine their processes, structures, and ways of doing things. Such actions are time consuming and threatening because they result in imbalance and

Exercise 15-2	Classroom Applications: Advocacy and School Mission

Directions: Using the tenets listed by the San Francisco Unified School District's (1982) mission, identify what an individual educator could do (consistent with the state's mission) to advocate for minority students (as they have been defined and explored in this text).

- All individuals are treated with respect and dignity.
- All individuals are given the opportunity to learn in many different ways and at varying rates.
- All individuals are given recognition for their achievements.
- All individuals are recognized as both potential learners and potential teachers.
- The learning process includes cognitive, creative and affective dimensions.

- The learning environment is characterized by interdependence and cultural diversity.
- Instruction is focused and subdivided into a number of specific, concrete competencies.
- All teachers must accept responsibility for student failure and take appropriate instructional and other supportive actions.
- Parents want their children to attain their fullest potential as learners and to succeed academically.

1. After you compile a list of at least 10 potential acts of advocacy, put a check mark next to those that you (if you were that educator) would be willing and able to do.
2. Reflect on the items you checked and evaluate your current strengths and weaknesses as a potential advocate.

Case Illustration 15-1	Why Do We Have to Know This?

In their paper on Multicultural teaching in a monocultural school, Sandra Lawrence and Heather Krause (1996), share their frustrations with attempting to introduce multicultural perspectives into the curriculum.

The biggest roadblock that I have faced ... is that unfortunately, in this community, there's a lot of parents that are really prejudiced and there's almost a stereotype of (this community) as white upper middle class. Parents, at times, will balk if you try to share different things with their children, and it's like, "Well, we don't have a lot of black kids, we don't have a high proportion of Latinos in this community ... Why do we have to teach the kids about it?" (p. 33)

For Reflection

1. Identify the source and nature of the fears experienced by the various school constituents referenced in the quote.
2. Describe the nature of power redistribution that is suggested in the suggested curricular change.
3. With the help of your teacher, colleagues, or classmates, identify two strategies you could employ to reduce the fears and resistance and facilitate the curriculum adjustment desired.
4. Answer the following questions: What makes the suggested changes unsettling to some? What is the reason, as you see it, for their resistance?

uncertainty and increased work for members of the school community. Social justice advocacy is geared to elevate and include minority groups that are devalued and excluded. This elevation and inclusion denotes a change in the way power in the system is distributed. Whenever power is at stake, resistance is inevitable. Case Illustration 15-1 shows this in action.

BECOMING AN ADVOCATE AND AGENT FOR CHANGE

School Advocacy

Change within schools often comes at the hands of major sociopolitical initiatives. Consider the changes that influenced the U.S. educational system following the launching of Sputnik and the resulting National Defense Education Act of 1958, or the ongoing changes experienced as a response to PL 94-142.

Aligning with School Mission   Rogers and Shoemaker (1971) have suggested a number of principles, which serve as useful directives for educators who want to become advocates for change. These principles suggest that educators seeking to introduce a change in curricula, procedures, structures, and even composition of schools should plan change with an eye toward tying the change to the fundamental mission of the school. Thus, they need to articulate and amplify the mission of the school and demonstrate how the changes they suggest will bring the school more closely in line with the fulfillment of that mission.

Taking Small Steps   Because change involves imbalance and requires expenditures of great energy and resources, it will most probably meet with resistance, especially when the anticipated positive effects of such change have yet to be proven and experienced. It is prudent that innovation be presented in ways that help members of the system take ownership in the proposed changes. Weick (1984), for example, found that a sequence of well-articulated small wins (that is, measurable outcomes of moderate importance) set a pattern that can "attract allies, deter opponents and lower resistance" (p. 43) to system change.

Linking Advocacy to Need   Systems, like people, resist change if it appears that the current way is working. Privilege among those in power in schools and school districts works to disguise the enormous and widespread problems that result from institutionalized discrimination. The "if it ain't broke, don't fix it" approach to life is alive and prevalent in all institutions, including schools. Given this reality, it is helpful for educators attempting to initiate change, be it in classrooms or in their school, to tie that change to a need—a pain—experienced by others in the system. Initiating rules within the classroom or school as a way of helping the organization more effectively meet its goals can create the best paths to successful change. Similarly, administrators who feel pressure from federal, state, and community forces tend to be more receptive to suggested change geared to relieve these pressures. Consider the speed and willingness to incorporate safety measures (including expensive and inconveniencing security systems) within U.S. schools following the recent dramatic incidents of school violence. When a need is perceived to be greater than the cost of the innovation, change is more likely to be embraced. Exercise 15-3 will help you find ways to suggest change that fall in line with the school's needs.

| Exercise 15-3 | Field Experience: Assessing the Need for Advocacy |

Directions: While it may be easy for us to detect the stereotyped images presented in text materials or the clear void of information supporting the contributions and values of minority group members, the subtle ways schools convey devaluing of others are, by definition, harder to detect.

1. Spend a day in a school observing and talking to teachers, students, and administrators. Use the following questions as your guide to assess the degree to which subtle biased attitudes and beliefs may exist within the school you visit. An alternative may be to conduct the observation at your own or the local university or college.

    a. How do teachers, administrators, and staff verbally and nonverbally interact with students from different racial/ethnic groups?

    b. How do teachers, administrators, and staff respond to languages and dialects of students from different ethnic and racial groups?

    c. Which groups are represented among administrators, teachers, cooks, bus drivers, and maintenance workers? Is there any clear distinction in group membership and power positions?

    d. What is the primary learning style (for example, field independent, dependent) and/or motivational system (for example, competitive, cooperative) promoted within the school? Does this favor or disadvantage any one group of students?

    e. Are students grouped based on ability? What is the criteria for grouping them? Are students essentially in the same groups that the previous teacher put them in? Are marginalized students mostly in lower "ability" groups?

    f. Ask teachers to identify five students they feel most comfortable with in the school. Are these students similar to the teacher in terms of race, social class, gender, ability, sexual orientation, and so on?

    g. Do teachers have trouble relating to certain students? Are these students dissimilar to the teacher in terms of race, social class, gender, ability, sexual orientation, and so on?

    h. Is more instructional time spent with high achievers?

    i. Have the teachers and/or the administration evaluated test materials for bias? Do they feel they have a sufficient background in tests and measurement to do so?

    j. Do marginalized students tend to perform more poorly on tests than do dominant-culture students?

    k. Do teachers assume some responsibility for students' failures as well as successes?

    l. Are comparisons of students' performance on display?

    m. Do instructional materials treat different groups honestly, realistically, and sensitively?

    n. Does the curriculum help students learn to function effectively in different cultures?

    o. Does the curriculum include positive and negative aspects of minority-group experience?

    p. Has the faculty and administration evaluated textbooks and other curriculum materials for bias?

    q. Does the faculty make an effort to get to know the students and their families? Do they know about their cultural backgrounds, values, and ways of thinking? Do they use this information to improve their teaching methods?

    r. Do teachers provide students with many opportunities to contribute to the focus and emphasis of instruction?

    s. Do teachers deal sufficiently with the concepts of oppression and discrimination in their curricula?

    t. Do teachers spend time helping students become critical thinkers so that they can learn to question, challenge, and critically analyze what they have been taught?

2. Share your observations with your teacher, colleagues, or classmates in small-group discussion and talk about ways that you might combat such bias. For example, are there specific workshops or training experiences that would be helpful? Would curriculum and instructional materials be needed? Perhaps more parental involvement and collaboration are needed? These are examples of strategies that could be implemented to advocate for all students.

Classroom Advocacy

Studies starting as early as 1952 (Johnson, 1966; Litcher & Johnson, 1969; Trager & Yarrow, 1952) have suggested that children's racial attitudes can be modified by school experiences (materials, curricula, and pedagogy) specifically designed for that purpose. **Incidental teaching**, however, is not effective. Clearly defined objectives and strategies targeting reduction of prejudice, discrimination, and oppression are needed. School administrators need to review not only their curricula but also all formal and informal structures and processes that work to maintain the status quo. Within individual classrooms, teachers need to examine their learning environments, content, and instructional strategies to be sure that each reflects a valuing of diversity and the promotion of educational equity.

Classroom Atmosphere   While it is important to decorate the walls and provide visual reminders of varying cultures, family compositions, and gender models of achievement, the equitable classroom is also one in which teachers overtly exhibit the value of and respect for diversity. Teacher advocates create a social organization in which the teacher and students know one another, trust one another, and are encouraged to express opinions and feelings. To do this, teachers must have a thorough understanding of the perspectives, values, interests, and concerns of their students, as well as their preferred learning styles. Teachers must demonstrate flexibility and creativity in organizing their classrooms and designing their instructional activities to meet the diverse needs of students. Teacher advocates' classrooms are organized in ways that invite student expression and participation and result in students' positive feelings about their contributions and worth within that classroom.

Seating Arrangements   In studying classroom organization, Lloyd and Duveen (1991) found that some teachers used gender to organize classroom activities. For example, teachers often formed lines of boys and girls or even had seating arrangements based on gender. And while it could be argued that the teachers were not necessarily discriminating based on gender, the practice of separate organization, or at least subgroup identification, might continue to reinforce gender distinction in the minds of the students and increase the chances that their own gender biases might operate more strongly in interacting with classmates (Eder, Evans, & Parker, 1995). Research indicates that a simple way to encourage gender-fair classrooms, or at a minimum help to reduce gender stereotypes, is to create work and play groups that include both sexes (Pellegrini & Perlmutter, 1989). These groups can be formal, as in organizing mixed-gender and cultural groups for cooperative learning activities, or more informal, such as simply encouraging spontaneous interaction as would occur when students mingle and check work against that of others. In either case, the removal of the physical distinction of placement within the classroom is a valuable step toward creating an equitable classroom setting.

Classroom Structures   In U.S. schools, the typical social organization of learners, or the structure that organizes classroom functions, is characterized by mainly whole-group, direct instruction. Students typically are seated in individual seats arranged in rows or in small groups around tables. Children listen to a teacher explain and demonstrate, engage in some type of independent practice, and then are tested.

Many have suggested this organizational structure is more compatible with educational values of the dominant culture than with that of minority students' cultures (Cushner et al., 1992; Franklin, 1992). Minority students may experience a difficult home–school transition because of the differences in social organization. Tharp (1989), for example, noted that Hawaiian and Navajo children grow up with social organization structures that are characterized by small-group cooperation, collaboration, and assisted performance that may account for their lagging reading achievement and language development promoted by a school organization that emphasizes individual, independent, and competitive learning. Native American, Latino, and African American students and many students with disabilities prefer to work with the support of other students, especially when academic tasks link to their prior personal experiences (Brown & McGraw-Zoubi, 1995; Morales-Jones, 1998). Such preferences would be frustrated in a classroom that promotes mostly individual competitive achievement. A similar dissonance is created for African American students, who experience a mutually supportive, process-oriented environment at home but find themselves in classrooms that encourage academic competition, formality, and task-completion rather than relationships (Clark, 1991). This mismatch between home and school values and organizational structures can lead to students' failure to achieve.

Fostering Positive Social Identities   A strategy that helps students maintain a positive social identity while interacting cooperatively with others students is the use of **jigsaw instruction** (Aronson et al., 1978). Not only does this technique facilitate the development of positive social identities but it provides positive, equitable contact between members of different groups, which in turn can effect positive change in intergroup relationships (Johnson & Johnson, 1992a, 1992b; Stephan & Stephan, 1996). Jigsaw activities involve the teacher dividing materials into as many parts as there are students in the group. Each student then learns his or her own part of the material and presents this piece of the instructional puzzle to the other members of the group. Using this strategy, students in each group are dependent on one another to learn all the material. The groups do not compete with one another, and each student is graded individually on his or her performance. The groups usually work together for four to six weeks and then new groups are formed. Research on this technique suggests that the benefits for students include higher self-esteem, greater liking for school and classmates, and improved performance on tests (see Aronson & Gonzalez, 1988).

INSTRUCTIONAL TASKS AND SOCIAL INTERACTION

Whereas middle-class U.S. culture tends to emphasize task completion (product), other cultures emphasize process—how one works to accomplish a task, including social interaction and communication, critical thinking, and problem-solving skills. It is important to understand that students from different cultures may differ in their attitudes toward what constitutes an appropriate balance between task and social functioning. Students coming from a process-oriented cultural background (social-functioning orientation) may find themselves being disciplined for talking during class work or penalized when the quantity of their product is not equal to those who focused strictly on the assigned task.

STUDENT INTERACTION

Teachers need to be mindful of how and with whom they interact in the classroom. They must be aware of whom they call upon and ask themselves: Do I ask more questions of students from one group or another? Do I tolerate behaviors differentially? Do I use gender-based illustrations and examples? Do I provide more support, affirmation, or approval for achievement to one group of students than to another? Do I listen more intently, teach more directly, and reward more freely one group of students over another? These are questions that teachers must ask if they are to become social justice advocates.

CONTENT AND METHODS

Pick up a textbook from the early 1960s, and what you will find presented is "happy, neat, wealthy, [W]hite people whose intact and loving families live only in clean, grassy suburbs" (Fantini & Weinstein, 1968, p. 133). When culturally different peoples were finally added to textbooks, they were depicted in full stereotype. People of color were presented only in stories about their native lands or as foreigners to U.S. soil. Women were relegated to careers as mothers or nurses or teachers. And issues of disability, religious diversity, or sexual orientation were rarely, if ever, mentioned. Textbooks largely presented a monocultural view of society.

While textbooks today tend to provide a more diverse and broader pictorial view of society, it is important for teachers to critically review the materials they use, noting narrow views when present and offering assignments or supplementary materials that will help students expand their perspectives of their world to integrate the experiences of those whose voices are not heard or accurately presented. Teachers need to evaluate curriculum materials to identify linguistic bias, stereotyping, invisibility, omission, imbalance, inaccuracy, and fragmentation.

Multicultural education is designed to teach students about the characteristics of various ethnic groups, their histories, their current experiences, and the ways they are similar and different to other ethnic groups. The hope is that such knowledge will change students' attitudes and behavior in ways that facilitate their functioning more competently in intercultural interactions (Banks, 1997). But beyond provision of this type of information, teachers need to take steps to actively change negative attitudes and behaviors that permeate society and to provide students with the opportunity to truly experience life (through content and curriculum) from the perspectives of marginalized groups.

CRITICAL PEDAGOGY

While the definition and particulars of what constitutes **critical pedagogy** may differ from theorist to theorist, most agree that they entail a commitment to engage in critical reflection, dialogue, and social activism (Friere, 1996; McLaren & Fischman, 1998; Schor, 2000). Teachers engaging in critical pedagogy implement curricula that encourage students to develop critical consciousness, think critically, pose questions, and become socially and politically active (Edelsky, 1999). At a minimum, teacher advocates expose their students to the processes of oppression and subjugation as they are enacted through texts and other curriculum materials used in the classroom. Instead of focusing on increasing awareness of diversity alone, they also invite students to challenge educational and social inequities within their schools and communities. Ayers (2001) explained that it is important for teachers to be "both dreamers and doers, to hold onto ideals but also to struggle continually to enact those ideas in concrete situations" (p. 126). Thus, teacher advocates are involved in transformative social activism within their own classrooms and schools and extending to their communities at large (Montano et al., 2002). Critical pedagogy helps learners process and reflect on their own experiences and the experiences of oppressed groups, while awakening in them expectations of benefit that energize them to work toward social change.

Teachers must not only infuse their curricula with minority voices and oppression theory, but they must also employ instructional strategies that facilitate social justice education. To do this, they must (1) balance the emotional and cognitive components of the learning process, paying attention to safety, respect, and valuing behaviors; (2) acknowledge and support their students' individual experiences while illuminating the realities of institutional discrimination; (3) create opportunities for meaningful social relationships and group cohesion to form in their classrooms; (4) utilize reflection exercises and other student-centered learning strategies, including problem posing and self-reflection; and (5) value personal growth, awareness, and change for themselves and as outcomes of the learning process while taking into account student interest and readiness (Adams, 1997). Such strategies require cooperative, interactive teaching that engages students as active co-investigators who learn to explore and synthesize multiple perspectives throughout the learning process (Maher, 1985). Through these methods, students will come to know that oppression is not the natural order but rather the result of socially constructed forces that can be changed. The goal of critical pedagogy is to help students experience education as something they *do* instead of as something *done to them* (Freire, 1996). Exercise 15-4 will help you come up with a plan for instituting this in your classroom.

FROM CONCEPTS TO LIVED EXPERIENCE

The first story in this section is of one teacher's "awakening" to the need and opportunity to become an advocate. It is the reflection of Alice G., a White 9th- and 10th-grade social studies teacher who describes her experiences with system resistance to social justice advocacy.

| Exercise 15-4 | Classroom Applications: Creating a Personal Activism Plan |

Directions: Keeping in mind your own spheres of influence (see Chapter 13), create a personal activism plan for your own family, classroom, school, neighborhood, or larger community.

1. The first step requires that you identify a person or a group within your family, classroom, school, or local community who is marginalized. This may be an elderly family member who is discounted because of age or loss of sensory abilities (for example, physically impaired, deaf, or blind), a student who is ostracized because of his or her sexual orientation, or a group that is shunned by the community (for example, a group of Muslims living in your neighborhood or who attend your local YMCA).

2. Identify one way in which this person or group has had their needs frustrated or restricted in terms of the means and degree to which their needs can be satisfied. For example, the student who has been ostracized due to his or her sexual orientation may feel alone and may develop a negative self-concept because of peer isolation.

3. Identify specific actions that could enable the person or group to function better as a more included and valued part of your family, classroom, school, neighborhood, or larger community. For example, perhaps a teacher could have a group sharing activity during which students shared times when they have felt isolated and alone. Such an activity may help your identified student recognize the feelings of the isolation of others and begin to express her or his feelings of isolation. Or perhaps a teacher could place the student in a role, such as small-group project reporter, which would by its nature increase interaction and in turn allow for the development of personal relationships.

4. Decide what you are willing and able to do to be a part of the solution in making the changes stated in #2 happen (for example, learning sign language so you can communicate with a deaf relative or beginning a book group that enrolls a lesbian student so she can interact with her peers and you in the discussion of meaningful topics found in books read).

5. Enact your activism plan.

Congratulations! You are an advocate. You have changed society for the better by taking one step at a time. Celebrate!

The second story describes Kay Toliver's teaching career, spanning 34 years at the elementary and middle school levels. Teaching in East Harlem, she had students with diverse levels of interest, motivation, knowledge, and skill. It was a career also guided by a singular principle: All students can learn at high levels. Her career is celebrated in the film *Good Morning Miss Toliver* (PBS, 1993).

DOMINANT-CULTURE ADVOCACY: AN ADVOCATE'S STORY

It seemed benign. We are sitting at the faculty meeting, one of the last for the year and most everyone was talking, well actually complaining, about this child or that child. Everyone seemed to be looking forward to the end of the school year—and most were hoping to get out of the meeting ASAP and enjoy what had become a beautiful spring day.

Well, the principal started the meeting by announcing that "this should be a brief meeting (to which everyone applauded), but there were a few pieces of information that needed to be discussed." She began by highlighting upcoming events in the school calendar, then passed out a district report on anticipated enrollments for the next year, and finally proceeded to congratulate the baseball team for going to the district championship.

As everyone was talking about the baseball team I began looking at the enrollment sheets. I noticed that, because of redistricting, we are going to have a large number of children from a predominately Latino area of our school district. Prior to this redistricting our student composition was 95 percent Caucasian, 3 percent African American, 2 percent defined as other. If there were one or two Latino children in our school, they were included in the "other" category.

As the faculty chatted about the great baseball season, I raised my hand. When recognized, I asked the simple—or at least what I thought was simple—question. "I see from the redistricting statistics that we will be adding over 80 students from Southside. My assumption is that most of these students are Latino. Are we making any provisions for insuring that our school is welcoming and supportive?" Wow! People chuckled and made comments like "[O]kay bleeding heart Alice!—let's get movin'." Even the principal snickered! I tried to clarify—and said "No, seriously— do we have any bilingual teachers? Or will we receive any in-service training on developing curriculum and teaching strategies to increase my knowledge of Latino culture?" Understanding that I was serious, the principal responded by saying that she "was sure that central office will be addressing these issues"... and then she moved on to the last item: the faculty picnic.

I left that meeting feeling like I had rocked the boat—or in some way said something I shouldn't have. It was not all comfortable, and I really kind of wished I had kept my mouth shut. It concerns me that I was the only one to bring up these issues. I wonder—Am I so right? Or is everyone else in my school so wrong?

MINORITY GROUP MEMBER ADVOCACY: AN ADVOCATE'S STORY

I was born and raised in East Harlem and the South Bronx. I am a proud product of the New York City public school system, graduating from Harriet Beecher Stowe Junior High, Walton High School and Hunter College (AB 1967, MA 1971) with graduate work at the City College of New York in mathematics.

Becoming a teacher was the fulfillment of a childhood dream. My parents always stressed that education was the key to a better life. By becoming a teacher, I hoped to inspire African American and Hispanic youths to realize their own dreams. I wanted to give something back to the communities I grew up in.

For more than 30 years, I taught mathematics and communication arts at P.S. 72 East Harlem Tech in Community School District 4. Prior to instructing 7th- and 8th-grade students, I taught grades 1 through 6 for 15 years.

My educational philosophy is simple: All students can learn. It is a teacher's job to expand minds and take children from the known to unknown.

I have made my classroom a place where students can talk without fear, write, manipulate ideas, and listen. I focus upon integrating math with other curriculum areas, for I want students to begin to see that mathematics goes beyond numbers and computation.

Over the years I have shared my knowledge and skills primarily with students. Over the past few years, I began working with teachers as a staff developer for my school district. I am also acting as a panelist and a speaker at educational conventions, when my school schedule permits.

At East Harlem Tech, with the support of my principal, I established the "Challenger" program. Challengers are students who can face any problem in life.

The program, for grades 4–8, presents the basics of geometry and algebra in an integrated curriculum. This is a program for "gifted" students, but following my belief that all children can learn, I accept students from all ability levels. ("Kay Francis Tolliver," n.d.)

SUMMARY

Why Advocate?   Failure to advocate for equality within the classroom and within the school not only negatively affects those oppressed by *isms* and results in less attention, and thus achievement, within the schools, but it also can be seen as, at a minimum, trivializing such oppressive forces or, worse yet, supporting them. Teachers need to do more than simply understand the issues concerning minority students within the class; they must actively confront the issues, the forces oppressing those students and interfering with their academic achievement. When advocating for our students, we are by definition advocating for change. Schools, like all organizational systems, are known for their ability to resist significant change in the ways they operate.

Becoming an Advocate and Agent for Change   In schools, it is helpful to link advocacy to school mission. Introduce a change in curriculum, procedures, and structures with an eye toward tying the change to the fundamental mission of the school. Introduce change in small steps (shaping). It is important that innovation be presented in ways perceived as tolerable and only minimally disruptive to the status quo. Tie change to felt need. When a need is experienced as greater than the cost of the innovation, change is more likely to be embraced.

In classrooms, teachers must review and address barriers associated with classroom climate, content, and processes that do not value and integrate diversity and the promotion of educational equity. Teachers should organize the environment so that respect for and valuing of students is demonstrated. Such actions will lead to the encouragement of positive student social identities.

Instructional Tasks and Social Interaction   It is important to understand that students from different cultures may differ in their attitudes toward what constitutes an appropriate balance between task completion and social functioning.

Student Interaction   Teachers need to be mindful of how and with whom they interact in the classroom.

Content and Methods   Teachers need to evaluate curriculum materials for bias—linguistic, stereotyping, invisibility, imbalance, inaccuracy, and fragmentation.

Critical Pedagogy   Teachers engaging in critical pedagogy implement curricula that encourage students to become social and politically active by writing letters, participating in demonstrations, or at a minimum exposing their students to the processes of oppression and subjugation as they may be enacted through texts and other curricular materials. We are all challenged to create learning environments that address the pluralist needs of a student body diverse in terms of race, ethnicity, social class, gender, national origin, native language, and physical and mental abilities.

Important Terms

activism plan	incidental teaching	multicultural education	transformative pedagogy
advocate	jigsaw instruction	system self-preservation resistance	
critical pedagogy			

Enrichment

Adams, M., Bell, L. A., & Griffin, P. (Eds.). (1997). *Teaching for diversity and social justice: A sourcebook.* New York: Routledge.

Bartunek, J. M. (2003). *Organizational and educational change: The life and role of a change agent group.* Mahwah, NJ: Lawrence Erlbaum.

Darling-Hammond, L., French, J., & Garcia-Lopez, S. P. (2002). *Learning to teach for social justice.* New York: Teachers College.

Delpit, L. (1995). *Other people's children: Cultural conflict in the classroom.* New York: The New Press.

Fine, M., & Powell, L. (Eds.). (1997). *Offwhite: Critical perspectives on race.* New York: Routledge.

Gay, G. (Ed.). (2003). *Becoming multicultural educators: Personal journey toward professional agency.* San Francisco: Jossey Bass.

Palmer, P. J. (1993). *To know as we are known: Education as a spiritual journey.* New York: Harper & Row.

Connections on the Web

http://www.goenc.com/

The Eisenhower National Clearinghouse has an extensive section on equity that includes articles about classroom issues by leading educators, case stories, articles, and an extensive listing of their publications focused on equity.

http://www.wallacefoundation.org/WF/Knowledge Center/KnowledgeTopics/EducationLeadership/ ?source=wfgawg0201&adgroup=Bm-

This site offers a comprehensive review of and updates on educational change.

www.nwrel.org/scpd/natspec/coldev.html

The School Change Collaborative is a national association providing support for school change.

http://mingo.info-science.uiowa.edu/~stevens/critped/ otherdefs.htm

Critical Pedagogy on the Web is a resource for finding articles, newsletters, and position papers on the issues of transformative curriculum and critical pedagogy.

REFERENCES

Adams, M. (1997). Pedagogical frameworks for social justice education. In. M. Adams, L. A. Bell, & P. Griffin (Eds.), *Teaching for diversity and social justice: A sourcebook.* New York: Routledge.

Argyris, C. (1970). *Intervention theory and method: A behavioral science view.* Reading, MA: Addison Wesley.

Aronson, E., & Gonzalez. A. (1988). Desegregation, jigsaw and the Mexican-American experience. In P. Katz & D. Taylor (Eds.), *Eliminating racism* (pp. 301–304). New York: Plenum.

Aronson, E., Stephan, C., Sikes, J., Blaney, N., & Snapp, M. (1978). *The jigsaw classroom.* Beverly Hills, CA: Sage.

Ayers, W. (2001). *To teach: The journey of a teacher* (2nd edition). New York: Teachers College.

Banks, J. A. (1997). *Educating citizens in a multicultural society.* New York: Teachers College.

Bennis, W. G. (1969). *Organizational development: Its nature, origins and prospects.* Reading, MA: Addison-Wesley.

Blake, R. R., & Mouton, J. S. (1976). *Consultation.* Reading, MA: Addison Wesley.

Brown, G., & McGraw-Zoubi, R. (1995). Successful teaching in culturally diverse classrooms. *The Delta Kappa Gamma Bulleting, 61*(2), 7–12.

Clark, M. L. (1991). Social identity, peer relations and academic competency of African American adolescents. *Education and Urban society, 24,* 41–52.

Cushner, K., McClelland, A., & Safford, P. (1992). *Human diversity in education: An integrative approach.* New York: McGraw Hill.

Davis, L. (1996). Equality of education: An agenda for urban schools. *Equity & Excellence in Education, 29*(1), 61–67.

de Jager, P. (2001). Resistance to change: A new view of an old problem. *Futurist, 35*(3), 24.

Edelsky, C. (1999). On critical whole language practice: Why, what and a bit of how. In C. Edelsky (Ed.), *Making justice our project: Teaching towards critical whole language practice* (pp. 7–36). Urbana, IL: National Council of Teachers of English.

Eder, D., Evans, C., & Parker, S. (1995). *School talk: Gender and adolescent culture.* New Brunswick, NJ: Rutgers University.

Fantini, M. D., & Weinstein, G. (1968) *The disadvantaged: Challenge to education.* New York: Harper & Row.

Franklin, M. E. (1992). Culturally sensitive instructional practices for African-American learners with disabilities. *Exceptional Children, 59,* 115–122.

Freire, P. (1996). *Education for critical consciousness.* New York: Continuum.

Johnson, D. W. (1966). Freedom school effectiveness: Changes in attitudes of Negro children. *The Journal of Applied Behavioral Science, 2,* 325–330.

Johnson, D. W., & Johnson, R. T. (1992a). Positive interdependence: Key to effective cooperation. In R. Hertz-Lazarowitz & N. Miller (Eds.), *Interaction in cooperative groups* (pp. 174–199). New York: Cambridge University.

Johnson, D. W., & Johnson, R. T. (1992b). Social interdependence and cross-ethnic relationships. In J. Lynch, C. Modgil, & S. Modgil (Eds.), *Cultural diversity in the schools* (Vol. II, pp. 179–190). London: Falmer.

Kast, F. Z., & Rosensweig, J. E. (1974). *Organization and management: A systems approach* (2nd edition). New York: McGraw Hill.

"Kay Francis Tolliver." (n.d.). Retrieved from http://www.fasenet.org/store/kay_toliver/about_kay_toliver.htm

Lawrence, S. M., & Krause, H. E. (1996). Multicultural teaching in a monocultural school: One cooperating teacher's personal and political challenges. *Equity & Excellence in Education, 29*(2), 30–36.

Lee, E., & Reitano, C. (n.d.). A critical pedagogy approach: Incorporating technology to de/reconstruct culture in the language classroom. Retrieved from http://mingo.info-science.uiowa.edu/~stevens/critped/otherdefs.htm

Litcher, J. H., & Johnson, D. W. (1969) Changes in attitudes toward Negroes of White elementary school students after use of multiethnic readers. *Journal of Educational Psychology, 60,* 148–152.

Lloyd, B., & Duveen, G. (1991). Expressing social gender identities in the first year of school. *European Journal of Psychology of Education, 6*(4), 437–447.

Maher, F. A. (1985). Pedagogies for the gender-balanced classroom. *Journal of Thought, 20*(3), 48–64.

McLaren, P., & Fischman, G. (1998). Reclaiming hope: Teacher education and social justice in the age of globalization. *Teacher Education Quarterly, 25*(4), 125–133.

Montano, T., Lopez-Torres, L., DeLissovoy, N., Pacheco, M., & Stillman, J. (2002). Teachers as activities: Teacher development and alternate sites of learning. *Equity & Excellence in Education, 35*(3), 265–275.

Morales-Jones, C. (1998). Understanding Hispanic culture: From tolerance to acceptance. *The Delta Kappa Gamma Bulleting, 64*(4), 5–12.

Napierkowski, C., & Parsons, R. (1995). Diffusion of innovation: A model for implementing a change in role and function of counselors within the schools. *The School Counselor, 42,* 364–369.

Pallas, A. M., Natriello, G., & McDill, E. L. (1989). The changing nature of disadvantaged population: Current dimensions and future trends. *Educational Researcher, 18*(5), 16–22.

Palmer, P. J. (Ed.). (2002). *Stories of the courage to teach: Honoring the teacher's heart.* San Francisco: Jossey Bass.

Parsons, R. (1996). *The skilled consultant.* Needham Heights, MA: Allyn & Bacon.

Parsons, R. D., & Kahn, W. J. (2005). *The school counselor as consultant.* Belmont, CA: Brooks/Cole.

Pellegrini, A. D., & Perlmutter, J. C. (1989). Classroom contextual effects on children's play. *Developmental Psychology, 25*(2), 289–296.

Rogers, E. M., & Shoemaker, F. F. (1971). *Communication of innovations.* New York: Free Press.

Shor, I. (2000). (Why) education is politics. In I. Shor & C. Pari (Eds.), *Education is politics: Critical teaching across differences, postsecondary* (pp 1–14). Portsmouth, NH: Heinemann.

Stephan, W. (1999). *Reducing prejudice and stereotyping in schools.* New York: Teachers College.

Stephan, W. G., & Stephan, C. W. (1996). *Intergroup relations*. Boulder, CO: Westview.

Tharp, R. G. (1989). Psychocultural variables and constants: Effects on teaching and learning in schools. *American Psychologist, 44,* 349–359.

Trager, H. G., & Yarrow, M. R. (1952). *They learn what they live*. New York: Harper.

Weick, K. E. (1984). Small wins. *American Psychologist, 39*(1), 40–49.

Wickstrom, K. F., & Witt, J. C. (1993). Resistance within school-based consultation. In J. E. Zins, T. R. Kratochwill, & S. N. Elliot, *Handbook of consultation services for children* (pp. 159–178). San Francisco: Jossey Bass.

Index